Palgrave Studies in Nineteenth-Century Writing and Culture

Series editor
Joseph Bristow
Department of English
University of California, Los Angeles
Los Angeles, CA
USA

Palgrave Studies in Nineteenth-Century Writing and Culture is a new monograph series that aims to represent the most innovative research on literary works that were produced in the English-speaking world from the time of the Napoleonic Wars to the fin de siécle. Attentive to the historical continuities between 'Romantic' and 'Victorian', the series will feature studies that help scholarship to reassess the meaning of these terms during a century marked by diverse cultural, literary, and political movements. The main aim of the series is to look at the increasing influence of types of historicism on our understanding of literary forms and genres. It reflects the shift from critical theory to cultural history that has affected not only the period 1800–1900 but also every field within the discipline of English literature. All titles in the series seek to offer fresh critical perspectives and challenging readings of both canonical and non-canonical writings of this era.

More information about this series at
http://www.springer.com/series/14607

Jason David Hall

Nineteenth-Century Verse and Technology

Machines of Meter

Jason David Hall
Department of English
University of Exeter
Exeter, UK

Palgrave Studies in Nineteenth-Century Writing and Culture
ISBN 978-3-319-53501-2   ISBN 978-3-319-53502-9 (eBook)
DOI 10.1007/978-3-319-53502-9

Library of Congress Control Number: 2017940348

© The Editor(s) (if applicable) and The Author(s) 2017
This work is subject to copyright. All rights are solely and exclusively licensed by the Publisher, whether the whole or part of the material is concerned, specifically the rights of translation, reprinting, reuse of illustrations, recitation, broadcasting, reproduction on microfilms or in any other physical way, and transmission or information storage and retrieval, electronic adaptation, computer software, or by similar or dissimilar methodology now known or hereafter developed.
The use of general descriptive names, registered names, trademarks, service marks, etc. in this publication does not imply, even in the absence of a specific statement, that such names are exempt from the relevant protective laws and regulations and therefore free for general use.
The publisher, the authors and the editors are safe to assume that the advice and information in this book are believed to be true and accurate at the date of publication. Neither the publisher nor the authors or the editors give a warranty, express or implied, with respect to the material contained herein or for any errors or omissions that may have been made. The publisher remains neutral with regard to jurisdictional claims in published maps and institutional affiliations.

Cover credit: Antonio M. Rosario/Getty Images

Printed on acid-free paper

This Palgrave Macmillan imprint is published by Springer Nature
The registered company is Springer International Publishing AG
The registered company address is: Gewerbestrasse 11, 6330 Cham, Switzerland

For
Jeremy Maarten Hall
who loves machines of all varieties and whose innate sense of rhythm
and rhyme already well surpasses his father's.

"All children like verses, even when they do not comprehend them;
it is the rhythm and rhyme that pleases."
Baroness von Marenholtz-Bülow, *The Philosophy and Methods
of the Kindergarten* (English translation of 1872)

Acknowledgements

At the University of Exeter, where the book was conceived and written, many supportive colleagues, across a number of disciplines, made direct and indirect contributions to the project. Indefatigable in her encouragement from the very beginning was Regenia Gagnier. Without her guidance, I might not have taken a leap of faith from Irish to Victorian Studies in the first place; she is a generous evaluator of her colleagues' work, and her comments on early drafts of this book helped to anchor some of its more speculative assertions. Thanks also to Jane Spencer, who, as erstwhile Head of English and my academic mentor at various points, helped me to see where the project was going and how to make sure it got there. Members of Exeter's Centre for Victorian Studies—namely Joe Kember, John Plunkett, Angelique Richardson, Paul Young, and Patricia Zakreski—offered up their expertise in countless ways, never turning me away when I drifted into their offices to pick their brains, let off steam, or simply prattle. It was also a big help that the CVS played host to so many conferences and visiting scholars, giving me more opportunities than I deserved to press the project's various parts on new audiences. In particular, I am grateful to three visitors whose arrival in the early and middle stages of the book's research provided timely prompting. First, the late Simon Dentith, who, after hearing me present my first sketch of the Eureka machine, fixed me with an inscrutable stare and gave me a great fillip when he exclaimed, "Jason, that's just weird!" Second, Dennis Denisoff, whose visit to Exeter opened up new possibilities for research beyond the strictly literary. Third, Chip Tucker, who shared his capacious knowledge of Victorian poetry with me, chatting amiably about Tennysonian hoofbeats and Quakers.

Beyond Exeter's English department and its community of Victorianists, I am grateful to colleagues in the departments of Computer Science, Drama, Engineering, History, Humanities, and Modern Languages. In their respective capacities as Dean of the College of Humanities and Associate Dean for Education, Andrew Thorpe and Sarah Hamilton assisted in finding ways for my research to carry on even while I took over as Head of Department. During that appointment and for years before, my colleagues in Cornwall (some long gone, others still present) were excellent readers and interlocutors, as well as collaborators. I am particularly grateful to Tim Cooper, Marion Gibson, Nick Groom, Kate Hext, Adeline Johns-Putra, Jim Kelly, Alex Murray, Richard Noakes, Chris Stokes, Bea Underwood, Nicola Whyte, and Shelly Windsor. On Exeter's Streatham Campus I owe so much to Richard Everson and Alma Rahat, whose interest in the techniques and technologies of meter and whose expertise on matters of mechanical and computer systems have enhanced my understanding of verse mechanics greatly. It was an absolute pleasure to work with them and other extremely knowledgeable collaborators (in particular Neil Bollen and Richard Jaeschke) on the "Poetry by Numbers" project, which was supported by a Science in Culture Innovation Award from the Arts and Humanities Research Council. That project—a direct offshoot of this book—confirmed my hunch that meter is a truly interdisciplinary subject. Dialogue with interested persons outside of English departments has been one of the most rewarding features of this endeavor.

As has dialogue with the many scholars of prosody, science and technology, and nineteenth-century studies—at home and abroad. The "historical poetics" folks in particular have given me an imagined community that has been equally sustaining and challenging. I'm so glad to have discussed this book and its mechanics with Kirstie Blair, Max Cavitch, Meredith Martin, Yopie Prins, and Jason Rudy, as well as many others at conferences and symposia in the USA and UK. Also extremely encouraging, in person and in print, have been Isobel Armstrong, Derek Attridge, Charlotte Berry, Jim Buzard, Richard Clark, Bland Crowder, Dino Felluga, Nick Freeman, Andy Hamilton, Linda Hughes, Alice Jenkins, Ewan Jones, Catherine Maxwell, David Nowell-Smith, Max Paddison, Ana Parejo-Vadillo, Stephen Regan, Catherine Robson, Lacy Rumsey,

Chris Stray, Ryan Sweet, Keir Waddington, Natalie Watson, Jason Whittaker, Adam Watt, Martin Willis, and Susan Wolfson.

Support to undertake research trips, visit archives, and carve out time to write has been enabled by various institutions. Much of the early research for the book was facilitated by the British Academy, whose generous research and travel grants got the project up and running. Later a Research Fellowship funded by the Leverhulme Trust released me from teaching and administrating responsibilities for 12 months, allowing me to make crucial headway with the drafting of the book. While on study leave and, in some cases, during term, I had the good fortune to work in a number of world-class research libraries and archives—the research conducted there helped to lay bare not only the vastness of the prosody corpus but also the memorable curiosities contained therein. The project benefited immensely from working at the Alfred Gillett Trust Heritage Collections, Street; the British Library, St. Pancras; the Charterhouse School Archive, Godalming; the Harry Ransom Center, University of Texas at Austin; the Library of the Society of Friends, London; and the Lit. & Phil., Newcastle-upon-Tyne. Going places, finding (or not) what one hopes to find, and taking advice from friendly and knowledgeable library staff are, for me, among the greatest joys of being a historical researcher.

A book this long in the making is bound to have leaked out in a few places before its parts are gathered and bound together. Parts of Chapter "Automaton Versifiers" originally appeared as "Popular Prosody: Spectacle and the Politics of Victorian Versification," in the journal *Nineteenth-Century Literature* 62.2 (2007), pp. 222–249, and I would like to thank the University of California Press for granting permission to reproduce extracts of that work, in revised form, here. Sections from Chapter "Instrumental Prosody" originally appeared in two journal articles: West Virginia University Press kindly allowed me to reproduce material from my article "Materializing Meter: Physiology, Psychology, Prosody," from *Victorian Poetry* 49.2 (2001), pp. 179–197; and the Johns Hopkins University Press granted permission to reproduce material from my article "Mechanized Metrics: From Verse Science to Laboratory Prosody, 1880–1918," from *Configurations* 17.3 (2009), pp. 285–308.

For taking a chance on this strange beast, I am extremely grateful to Joseph Bristow, who has watched the project evolve from a speculative article into an expansive monograph. As editor of the Palgrave Studies in Nineteenth-Century Writing and Culture series he made many detailed and helpful comments that have improved the manuscript that I first submitted to the press. I'm also very much indebted to Ben Doyle, Milly Davies, and the rest of the Palgrave Macmillan editorial team for guiding the book toward publication. It's a pleasure to be working, yet again, with you guys.

Finally, a word of thanks to those at home. I can't even begin to imagine what it's like to live with a man who comes home to talk about (or brood silently upon) this book's subject matter. I'm not sure I'd choose to live with a prosodist, but I'm so glad that two longsuffering souls—Vike Martina Plock and Jeremy Maarten Hall—do so choose. From reading and commenting on the work-in-progress to teaching me about rhythmical possibilities I would never have considered on my own, they have given so much of their time—often without even knowing it. It's not a lie when I say that there is probably no aspect of this book they haven't improved in some way or another. Jeremy, I'll do my best to make sure the next book includes pirates and astronauts.

Contents

Introduction	1
Measurement, Temporality, Abstraction	15
Meter Manufactories	61
Automaton Versifiers	111
The Automatic Flow of Verse	165
Instrumental Prosody	207
Afterword	255
Bibliography	259
Index	281

LIST OF FIGURES

Measurement, Temporality, Abstraction

Fig. 1 Plate from Nicholas Wood's *A Practical Treatise on Rail-Roads, and Interior Communication in General. Containing Numerous Experiments on the Powers of the Improved Locomotive Engines and Tables of the Comparative Costs of Conveyance on Canals, Railways, and Turnpike Roads* (London: Longman, Orme, Brown, Green & Longmans, 1838)   21

Fig. 2 Diagram of counterpoint from Gerard Manley Hopkins's *The Journals and Papers of Gerard Manley Hopkins*, ed. Humphry House and Graham Storey (London: Oxford University Press, 1959), 282. By permission of Oxford University Press on behalf of the British Province of The Society of Jesus   22

Meter Manufactories

Fig. 1 Extract from C. D. Yonge's *A Gradus ad Parnassum for the Use of Eton, Westminster, Winchester, Harrow, Charterhouse, and Rugby Schools, King's College London, and Marlborough College* (London: Longmans, Green, and Co., 1868), 1   84

Automaton Versifiers

Fig. 1 Eureka as depicted in the *Illustrated London News* (July 19, 1845), 27   114

Fig. 2 Illustration of the Difference Engine No. 1, frontispiece of Charles Babbage's *Passages from the Life of a Philosopher* (London: Longman, Green, Longman, Roberts, and Green, 1851)   120

Fig. 3   Dactylic hexameter foot patterns, from William Ramsay's
         A Manual of Latin Prosody, 2nd edn (London and Glasgow:
         Richard Griffin and Company, 1859), 162   124
Fig. 4   *Tables for Making Hexameter and Pentameter Latin Verses*
         (London [?], 1878)   133
Fig. 5   Example of word selection from hexameter table   134
Fig. 6   View of gears from Clark's Eureka Latin Hexameter Machine.
         Photograph by author, 2015   135
Fig. 7   Detail of lettered staves from Clark's Eureka Latin
         Hexameter Machine. Photograph by author, 2015   136

The Automatic Flow of Verse
Fig. 1   Illustration from Oliver Wendell Holmes's "The Physiology
         of Walking," from *Pages of an Old Volume of Life:
         A Collection of Essays, 1857–1881* (Boston and New York:
         Houghton, Mifflin, and Company, 1892), 121   186

Instrumental Prosody
Fig. 1   "Mr. Tennyson Reading 'In Memoriam' to His Sovereign,"
         from Max Beerbohm's *Poet's Corner* (London:
         Heinemann, 1904). Hulton Archive. Photo by
         The Print Collector/Print Collector/Getty Images   211
Fig. 2   Endstopped lines from Milton's *Paradise Lost*, as printed in
         Wilkie Collins's novel *Man and Wife*
         (Leipzig: Bernhard Tauchnitz, 1870), 265   217
Fig. 3   "Time and the Sea-Tide—Tennyson" ["Break, Break, Break"
         in prose], from David Charles Bell and Alexander Melville
         Bell's *Bell's Standard Elocutionist* (London: William
         Mullan and Son, 1878), 297   217
Fig. 4   Example of wave scansion from Mark H. Liddell's *An
         Introduction to the Scientific Study of English Poetry:
         Being a Prolegomena to a Science of English Prosody* (London:
         Doubleday, Page & Company, 1902), 244   220
Fig. 5   Musical scansion for Tennyson's "Break, Break, Break," from
         Sidney Lanier's *The Science of English Verse* (New York:
         Scribner, 1880), 138   221
Fig. 6   Drum kymograph according to Ludwig (Trommelkymographion
         nach Ludwig). Petzold, Wilhelm. Preis-Verzeichniss der
         Werkstätte für Präcisions-Mechanik von Wilh. Petzold:
         Abtheilung der Instrumente und Apparate für physiologische
         Experimente und Vivisectionen. Leipzig, 1891. Reproduced
         by permission of the Virtual Laboratory, Max Planck Institute
         for the History of Science, Berlin. http://vlp.mpiwg-berlin.mpg.de/ 224

Fig. 7	Illustration of a "Tuning-fork tracing its Curve," from Hermann von Helmholtz's *On the Sensations of Tone as a Physiological Basis for the Theory of Music*, trans. Alexander J. Ellis (London: Longmans, Green, and Co., 1885), 20	227
Fig. 8	Example of a "Curve traced in Phonautograph," from Hermann von Helmholtz's *On the Sensations of Tone as a Physiological Basis for the Theory of Music*, trans. Alexander J. Ellis (London: Longmans, Green, and Co., 1885), 20	228
Fig. 9	Example of "centroid" scansion, from Edward Wheeler Scripture's *Elements of Experimental Phonetics* (New York: Charles Scribner's Sons, 1902), 554	235
Fig. 10	Example of a "wave-graph" record of a subject "repeat[ing] the sound a continuously in what he felt to be a trochaic rhythm (thus, a' a a' a a' a…), or an iambic (a a' a a' a a'…), or dactylic (a' a a a' a a…), or an amphibraphic one (a a' a a a' a…)." From Edward Wheeler Scripture's *Elements of Experimental Phonetics* (New York: Charles Scribner's Sons, 1902), 509	238
Fig. 11	"Specimens of the Records [of Verses]." From Warner Brown's *Time in English Verse Rhythm: An Empirical Study of Typical Verses by the Graphic Method* (New York: Science Press, 1908)	239
Fig. 12	Plate showing graphic record of Tennyson's "Break, Break, Break," from Ada Snell's *Pause: A Study of Its Nature and Its Rhythmical Function in Verse, Especially Blank Verse* (Ann Arbor: University of Michigan, 1918)	240

Introduction

> The earth moves slowly, if it move at all,
> And by the general, not the single force.
> Of the link'd members of the vast machine.
> In all these crowded rooms of industry,
> No individual soul has loftier leave.
> Than fiddling with a piston or a valve.
> —Arthur Hugh Clough, *Dipsychus* (written 1850)

In these fairly regular, pneumatic pentameters—mechanically smooth for a poet adept at mixing feet and adding an irregular conversational variety to his experimental English hexameter poems—Clough imagines not only individuals' working lives but even the Earth's diurnal course as modulated to the movement of a "vast machine." He was not alone. Thomas Carlyle, in his 1829 essay "Signs of the Times," was more declamatory, memorably characterizing the early decades of the century as the "Mechanical Age," when technologies of manufacture and related forms of "calculated contrivance" asserted a mechanical imperative that extended beyond the obvious workspaces of industrialism and into the realms of culture more generally.[1] Industrial technologies disrupted, recalibrated, and ushered in new working practices, and the "machinery question," which focused on the proliferation of and working conditions in Britain's factory system, at once "defined the lines of division between [the] classes" and "stimulated analysis in political economy."[2]

Even beyond the 1830s–1860s, when debates about manufactories were at their height, emblematic mechanical innovations—notably "machine ensembles" such as the railway, telegraph, and scientific laboratory—continued to exert a seemingly inexorable force, their buzzing and humming and whirring and clanking signifying "progress" to some and "doom" to others.[3] Across the nineteenth century, machines transformed social relationships, facilitated new cultural networks, mediated people's everyday experiences of modernity, and unsettled contemporary understandings of humanistic endeavor, as well as the concept of the human itself. It is no exaggeration to say that machines took—and set—the measure of the nineteenth century.

The measures of nineteenth-century verse had their own distinctive mechanics, and this book examines the ways in which machine culture impacted on fundamental conceptions of what poetic meter was and how it worked. Even while the "industrialization of publishing" was effectively diminishing poetry's market share,[4] meter and versification were more than ever subjects of discussion. Not only did printed accounts of prosody proliferate in the age of steam printing and stereotyping technologies, enjoying new forms of production and consumption,[5] but also machinery increasingly provided the means for metrical analysis and defined the terms on which that analysis could be undertaken. In short, meter was not a narrowly philological pursuit, much less a "mere pedantry" whose cultural niche was ever shrinking with the ascendency of scientific and industrial agendas. Quite the contrary: meter participated fully in the machine culture of the nineteenth century, consequently extending its discursive purchase beyond the more traditional locus of humanistic inquiry. One key implication of this imbrication of meter and machines is that, between the 1810s and 1910s (roughly the period covered by this book), meter became a subject expounded upon not only by poets and prosodists but also—and significantly—by scientists, engineers, inventors, and a host of other commentators on the period's proliferating technologies. The contributions made to the study of versification by Oliver Wendell Holmes, a physician and poet, James Yearsley, an expert in orthophonics, Alexander Melville Bell, a proponent of vocal physiology, or Edward Wheeler Scripture, an experimental psychologist, to name but a few, form part of the period's diversifying metrical discourse that is no less relevant or revelatory than the poetic innovations or prosodic positions of figures such as Elizabeth Barrett Browning, Alice Meynell, Coventry Patmore, and Alfred Tennyson.

Along with this extension of meter's discourse community goes an expansion of meter's meaning. It is worth saying at the outset that *meter* as understood here denotes considerably more than a pattern of stress or accent in a given line of poetry. Readers expecting primarily close readings of poems by major Victorian poets may well be disappointed to find a dearth of line-by-line analysis in the pages below. Undoubtedly, there is much to be gained from what Caroline Levine has termed "reflective" readings of meter. She cites Herbert Tucker's careful attention to how the "stop-and-start versification" of Elizabeth Barrett Browning's "Cry of the Children" (1843) "mimics the strain and clatter of steam-driven machinery."[6] But taking a more inclusive view of meter's engagement with the nineteenth century's systems of mechanization and attendant technologies, precisely what the present study sets out to provide, necessitates looking beyond any single poem's reflection of mechanical rhythms; often, it involves looking beyond the period's poetic corpus altogether. As Yopie Prins and other scholars have demonstrated in recent years, the nineteenth-century "metrical imaginary" was by no means confined to writing *in verse*[7]: indeed, some of its most significant expressions recede from view considerably if we restrict our attention to "meter" as simply a verse product—an intrinsic feature of a poem that can be isolated for description or analysis—rather than exploding our view of meter to imagine it as a set of *processes*, including meter as idea or abstraction, as a mental or physiological predisposition or experience, or as a practice or habit of reading or pedagogical instruction—each of these being characterizations of meter and metrics that Victorians would have recognized. Taking its cue from recent work in the field of "historical prosody," not least Prins's exemplary analyses of meter's participation in aspects of "technologically mediated nineteenth-century modernity,"[8] *Nineteenth-Century Verse and Technology* places not poems but metrical processes and specific *systems* of meter at the center of its examination, demonstrating how they take shape alongside the nineteenth century's new technologies and regimes of mechanically oriented measurement. Thus, *meter* dilates to include familiar definitions of poetic periodicity—"recurring units of rhythm" or the "measure of sound patterning in verse"[9]—as well as methodologies and apparatuses that facilitate the manufacture, circulation, and assessment of metrical information. For this reason, the primary "metrical" sources consulted comprise not only poems, prosodical treatises, grammars, and primers—the usual suspects of metrical analytics—but also manuals of elocution and vocal physiology, contributions to scientific and medical publications, records of laboratory experiment, expositions of industrial technology and manufacture, and numerous ephemeral pieces from widely circulating periodicals. Because the technologies of nineteenth-century metrics were not confined to a particular discipline or genre of writing, an interdisciplinary approach to meter—one that is prepared to follow meter's promiscuous feet wherever they might lead—is best adapted to the task of taking their measure.

That this book does not privilege the discrete metrical features of poems is not to say that it neglects scansion—a critique of historical prosody that some scholars have registered.[10] In fact, scanning is absolutely central to my examination of metrical mechanics: in the form of institutional exercises founded upon the "mechanical" disarticulation of syllables, stylized and often monotonous mouthings of verse deriving from such exercises, cerebral or somatic impulses that resulted in a robotic, scansion-like segmentation of speech, and metrical training methods advocated as remedies for deficiencies of the vocal mechanism. The "stop-and-start versification" that Tucker notices in Barrett Browning's poem is, as we will see in the chapters below, but one example of a widespread pattern of mechanical repetition and spacing, of decomposition and assembly that characterizes Victorian prosodic practice. Indeed, scanning in these broader senses—the deliberate or, in some cases, unconscious disarticulation of language into discrete syllabic, metrical or related rhythmic units, whether in writing or speech—is, I argue, among the more visible manifestations of meter's interface with the logic of machines. That said, *Nineteenth-Century Verse and Technology* nevertheless holds a particular conception of scansion—that is, an attempt through close reading or linguistic analysis to establish a "correct" diagram of a poem's metrical pattern—at arm's length, not least because there was no single, unified, or universally accepted method for measuring meter available during the period covered by this book. Recent scholarship—such as Meredith Martin's *The Rise and Fall of Meter* (2012) and Joseph Phelan's *The Music of Verse* (2012)—has begun to chart the various systems of scansion that proliferated—the more and the less familiar (to us now) names and notations for describing and representing the functions of pitch, period, cadence, and stress (not to mention several other elements) that obtain to the subjects of meter, versification, and prosody, as well as a broadly cognate subject such as rhythm. Across the nineteenth century, opinions differed significantly about whether models of quantitative scansion inherited from ancient Greek and Latin poetry remained valid—as classroom tools for conducing exercises in classical versification or as a means of measuring poetry in modern languages such as English. For many the received forms of scansion—whether primarily temporal and accentual—were at once too subjective and too imprecise. Attending to the "sciences" of versification that asserted themselves across the nineteenth century and into the early decades of the twentieth involves an admission of the provisional nature of both well-known nomenclature (accent, syllable, quantity, foot) and other, in some cases less well-known, units of measurement (musical periods, rhythm-waves, centroids, graphic records). This profusion of prosodic systems was itself complexly related to the mechanical imperatives of the period: not least attempts to extend systematic knowledge—often based on the structural logic and measurement sophistication of machines themselves—to assess both abstractions (such as time) and materialities (such as modulations of the voice). Given the various competing modes of scansion in circulation, perhaps, as some asserted, a machine could provide the most trustworthy and "objective" representation of a poem's metrical character.

Many of the methods and systems of metrical measurement found correlates in the period's technologies: for example, in the increasing systematization of spatio-temporal knowledge represented by the railway; new epistemologies for conceiving of beats, periods, and rhythmical modulations found expression in the emerging information networks and agricultural implements, as well as in understandings of metrical marking; apparatuses for assessing, representing, and reproducing sonic data transformed contemporary understandings of voiced verse; cutting-edge scientific research, frequently as conducted in laboratories with specially designed machines, advanced "scansions" that promised for some the dawning of a new age of mechanically verifiable metrical fact. And like the various meters and modes of scansion, these machines and others examined in this book take a number of forms. On the one hand, *machine* denotes a material fabrication or other apparatus: an engine, tool, or instrument that "perform[s] some special duty."[11] Machines in this sense include telegraphs, steam-threshers, kymographs, and poetry "processors," to mention just a few. One the other hand, *machine* describes a technology in the sense of a systematic form of knowledge—what Friedrich Kittler termed a "discourse network"—that facilitates and determines forms of data management. "Every culture," notes Kittler, "has different techniques and standards to govern the concrete manipulation of language."[12] *Nineteenth-Century Verse and Technology* focuses on how particular nineteenth-century "technologies"—namely, education, manufacture, and experimental science—effected the "manipulation" of language in the forms of prosody, versification, and rhythm through concrete practices and techniques such as speech instruction and acoustical analysis—in a few cases by means of an actual machine in the sense described above. From the "decomposition and composition" models that figured significantly in the assembly systems of Victorian metrical education to the preference for measuring the "real" and unsegmented flow of verse facilitated by the new technological media of experimental physiologists and psychologists at the *fin de siècle*, the technologies of meter comprised a rich but by no means uniform or necessarily complementary array of texts, pedagogies, procedures, and methodologies.

The story this book tells about meter and machines is the result of attention to the materials it showcases—not from any *a priori* assumptions about nineteenth-century metrics. The book did not begin as an idea about "meter" and "machines" and how the two concepts might be related. Rather, it came about in a wholly unexpected, yet fittingly metrical, way: one unit at a time, the first finding some form of modulation with the next, until a pattern began to assert itself. Initially, I had envisaged writing a much more expansive cultural history of Victorian meter, in which machines were only one component among many others. That story, which I do not think will ever be written (not by me, at least), kept turning up material that pointed in one direction: toward objects, mainly objects of one mechanical variety or another. When I uncovered—in *Punch*, at first—a reference to John Clark's Latin Hexameter Machine, I thought it was a joke. When I later found other references to it, and later still arranged to visit it in the Alfred Gillett Trust's archive in Somerset, my curiosity was excited about meter as a "thing" that I could experience in real life, very much off the page—not unlike other objects that I could touch and hear, such as a piano or a lawnmower. I next came across I. A. Richards, in *Practical Criticism* (1929), contemplating whether something called a kymograph, an object unfamiliar to me at the time, could be of any benefit to the student of versification. Here, then, were two *machines*—gadgets that had a metrical story to tell—and there might be others. In the process of searching for similar material manifestations of nineteenth-century metrics, I uncovered other, not as obviously thing-like, machines that I began to understand as belonging to a continuous narrative—one of metrical discovery and experiment, of rhythmical authority and skepticism, of measurement fidelity and fallacy—that was peculiar to the nineteenth century. Many of the signal theories, instantiations, and institutions of meter in a 100-year period of intense prosodical activity had, I began to see, machines at their heart or were so shot through with traces of contemporary technologies that they asserted a mechanics of their own, moving in syncopation with the gears and cogs and engines of the age.

Each of the five chapters in this book tells the story of one such meshing. More thematic than strictly chronological in sequence, these chapters isolate a particular machine of meter—typically as expounded in a crucial theorization or process, sometimes in a single device or a set of related practices or inquiries: (1) mid-century theories of prosodical abstraction and technologies of smoothness and even spacing; (2) a deeply influential, though rarely credited, system of metrical manufacture; (3) verse produced by machine; (4) the mechanics of the human body and mind and the meters that issued from them; (5) the promise of machines to resolve metrical dilemmas once and for all.

The book begins not with the earliest interface between meter and machines but with one that occurs at "a turning point for Victorian metrical theory."[13] With the publication in 1857 of his review essay "English Metrical Critics" (subsequently gaining influence under the title "Essay on English Metrical Law"), Coventry Patmore inaugurated the so-called New Prosody, which asserted meter in English poetry as an abstract system of spacing marked by an immaterial yet mentally perceived beat. Patmore's theory considerably reoriented English-language metrical theory in the nineteenth century, and its implications were still being assessed when twentieth-century proponents of the New Criticism began articulating their own theories of metrical abstraction.[14] "Measurement, Temporality, Abstraction" reads the New Prosody's emphasis on abstraction and proportionate spacing (namely its promotion of meter as a series of "isochronous intervals") as correlates of the standardizing impulses of two iconic Victorian machines: the railway and the telegraph. Their assertion of standard measurement, regularly recurring marks or beats, and forms of symbolic abstraction exerted, I argue, a pervasive machine logic that echoes the presiding features of Patmore's temporal metrics. Not only did these machine conglomerations provide a set of almost unavoidable material experiences with which an emerging metrical theory might achieve a powerful resonance, but that theory, as it gathered momentum over the course of the century, so conditioned poets' rhythmic perception as to produce metrical consternation when confronted by other distinctive beat signatures offered by contemporary devices—in particular ones with an apparently irregular or imperceptibly fast engine cadence. While some machines beat in time with the metrics of the New Prosody, others seemed to have no discernible "metrical" organization at all.

"Meter Manufactories" does not isolate a specific metrical theory; instead, it assesses one of the most powerful and pervasive technologies of meter in the nineteenth century: the manufacture of classical (i.e., Latin and Greek) meters by schoolboys as a mainstay of nineteenth-century liberal education. This machine of meter—the institution known to many by the name "scholastic prosody"—constituted not only a pedagogical apparatus that fundamentally structured the Victorian metrical imaginary—fostering many of the period's poets and prosodists—but also purveyed a set of processes and assembly techniques that were, in some cases, effectively imported from the factory system itself, where, from the early decades of the century, educational innovators such as Andrew Bell and Joseph Lancaster were promoting models of learning and curricula that facilitated instruction on a large scale for working-class pupils. Demonstrating how the Bell-Lancaster scheme of mass education, grounded in forms of syllabic reading, was adapted for use in classical schools, where its emphasis on serial assembly of linguistic elements was modified to underpin the prosodic curriculum, this chapter identifies continuities of practice between group exercises in syllabic reading and another central feature of Victorian classical education—namely, schoolboys' solitary work with encyclopedias of classical quantity such as the *Gradus ad Parnassum*. Whether in groups or not, metrical learning was both metaphorically and often materially a technology for alienating pupils from the verse products they spent so much of their time manufacturing: the labor central to their exercises was founded upon a segmentation of linguistic and prosodic units that divorced them from the complete line of verse and any sense of unified metrical or semantic meaning it might convey. Making a foot—and avoiding a so-called false quantity—became an end in itself, and a boy might spend many an hour toiling with a tome such as the Gradus trying to compose Latin hexameters that made a modicum of metrical sense, though perhaps little else. Further, the piecemeal nature of their verse assembly frequently resulted, through widely adopted (though by no means uniform) modes of recitation, in a monotonous, quasi-robotic manner of speaking classical verse, a sing-song delivery the mechanics of which signified, in other scenarios, not a fluent mastery of versification but a vocal—or, worse still, cerebral—pathology.

The step-by-step metrical assembly promoted in classical schools found a fitting machine corollary in a contraption exhibited at London's Egyptian Hall in the summer of 1845. John Clark—cousin of James and Cyrus Clark, founders of the well-known Clarks shoe company of Somerset—was no stranger to mechanical contrivance, and his decision to use his knowledge of machines to design and construct a device for "composing" Latin hexameters gave material, automatic form to the piecemeal manufacture of meters by schoolboys. Chapter "Automaton Versifiers" examines Clark's Eureka, which was much more than a showplace diversion; rather, it was at once the uncanny technological embodiment and a parodic indictment of the Victorian science of prosody and an interactive discursive site where debates about the function of prosody as part of a pedagogical model in the universities and, more specifically, the public schools became immediately visible and accessible to a popular and reform-minded audience. As the Latin hexameters that it was capable of "grinding out" were transcribed, explicated, and judged in the improving pages of popular print media, the Eureka figured briefly as the material signifier of an education reform agenda that was, by and large, hostile to the centrality of prosody in Victorian pedagogy. Exploiting the "mixed" measures of the dactylic hexameter, but reducing their expression to a repeatable pattern, the hexameter machine seemed to some an absurdity: the opposite of the mechanical utility that inspired a contemporary such as Charles Babbage to design a calculating or "thinking" machine. While many saw Clark's "automaton versifier" as a mere curiosity—not unlike the diverting automata of Vaucanson or Kempelen—there was, in the Eureka's ability to produce a vast number of verses, each one different from the next, a notable intimation of machine intelligence.

Debates about whether meter was the result of intelligent cognition or a merely mechanical exercise were not confined to the Eureka and schoolboys' verse composition exercises. In both conscious and unconscious ways, the human body and mind turned out to be among the most curious machines of meter the period had to offer. "The Automatic Flow of Verse" assesses meter in relation to contemporary thinking about the "man-machine." In particular, it shows how meter, primarily in English verse, became a topic of interest to phrenologists, physiologists, physicians, and surgeons, who assessed metrical ability and deficiency from the perspective of their specialist fields. Their pronouncements about meter—often grounded in the materiality of the body or the embodied mind—advanced a new vocabulary and disciplinary frameworks for engaging with question about prosodic agency and volition, as well as organic metrical determinism. Not only was versification considered by some a "mechanical" practice that might have little to do with genius or a predisposition to rhythmical composition; further, it might be the consequence of "mechanistic" or "automatic" somatic and cognitive processes. While some saw meter as a measure of a person's ability to impose his or her will over the unruly forces of the body—for example, exercises in spoken scansion might effectively enable one to govern the tongue and other elements of the "speech mechanism"—others, in particular advocates of an increasingly materialist agenda, suggested that meter, along with other human linguistic capacities, might in some cases be a manifestation of the body's or brain's mechanics. An individual's respiratory rhythms, as Oliver Wendell Holmes asserted, or cerebral health, as postulated by Frederic Bateman and other physicians, might have more to do with his or her versified speech than any conscious thought process or formal training in metrics.

The book's final chapter closes the circuit opened by the first, demonstrating how models of meter predicated on abstraction, proportionate spacing, and the artificial segmenting of rhythmical flow were scrutinized by a newly mechanized verse science. By the turn of the century, metrical verse was being subjected to a rigorous measurement regime, underwritten by a robust materialism in physiology and psychology, in coordination with burgeoning technologies of sound. In 1857, the year Coventry Patmore published the first version of his influential "Essay on English Metrical Law," the German scientist Hermann von Helmholtz, a pioneer of experimental physiology, delivered in Bonn a lecture entitled "The Physiological Causes of Harmony in Music." Also that year, the French printer and inventor Edouard Léon Scott patented his phonautograph, which recorded sound waves as visible impressions on a blackened cylinder. As Chapter "Instrumental Prosody" argues, experimentalists such as Helmholtz and technology pioneers who designed and augmented devices such as Scott's assisted in the development of what Jason Rudy has termed a "physiological poetics," which placed considerable emphasis on the voice and body as the true subject of rhythmical evaluation: the actual movement of verse was to be found in the modulations of the voice, rather than in the arbitrary systems for describing and representing metrical movement. Machines—in this case, specially designed laboratory measurement apparatus such as the kymograph—were capable not only of recording the rhythmic frequencies of the voice as it uttered lines of metered poetry—such as Tennyson's "Break, Break, Break"—but also of inscribing their own, ostensibly more accurate and trustworthy, "record" of a poem's rhythm. This experimental phase of prosodic enquiry, which prized material acoustic rhythms over metrical abstractions, offered a counterpoint to the theories and practices of meter associated not only with the New Prosody but also with scholastic prosody and other forms of monotonous delivery, where the immaterial or purely textual presence of meter asserts itself in spoken verse. By looking to the laboratory, where empirical procedures were underwriting developments in phonetics and speech physiology, this chapter charts a significant moment in the contest between idealist and materialist understandings of meter. The possibilities afforded by the "new languages of recording instruments," I argue, enabled a reconceptualization of not only the discrete properties of metrical verse but also the practice of scansion.

While some of these chapters reach backwards or forwards into the eighteenth or twentieth centuries, they all pivot on metrical and mechanical developments that are distinctively shaped or pitched during the nineteenth century. Thus, the machines of meter examined here are ones whose story belongs to a particular time and set of cultural circumstances. Like Clark's hexameter machine, which started me on this journey, they are unique. Nevertheless, they will probably have, for most metrically sensitive readers, implications for the study of versification in our own time. Indeed, it may not be a coincidence that several new-media technologies of metrics—for example, Meredith Martin's Princeton Prosody Archive or Herbert Tucker's "For Better, For Verse" scansion tutorial—have behind them scholars so well versed in nineteenth-century poetry and poetics.[15] Though I have not attempted to offer a comprehensive or rigorously joined up metrical genealogy, connecting the current technologies of meter with the historical ones assessed here, I do hope that the cogs and gears I set in motion will relay a useful impulse to others working on the mechanics of modern meter.

Notes

1. Thomas Carlyle, "Signs of the Times" (1829), *A Carlyle Reader: Selections from the Writings of Thomas Carlyle*, ed, G. B. Tennyson (Cambridge: Cambridge University Press, 1984), 34.
2. Maxine Berg, *The Machinery Question and the Making of Political Economy, 1815–1848* (Cambridge: Cambridge University Press, 1980), 2, 9.
3. See Robert Gray, *The Factory Question and Industrial England, 1830–1860* (Cambridge: Cambridge University Press, 1996); Wolfgang Schivelbusch, *The Railway Journey: The Industrialization of Time and Space in the Nineteenth Century* (Berkeley and Los Angeles: University of California Press, 1986); Matthew Beaumont and Michael Freeman, eds, *The Railway and Modernity: Time, Space, and the Machine Ensemble* (Bern: Peter Lang, 2007); and Laura Otis, *Networking: Communicating with Bodies and Machines in the Nineteenth Century* (Ann Arbor: University of Michigan Press, 2001).
4. See LeeErickson, "The Market," in *A Companion to Victorian Poetry*, ed. Richard Cronin et al. (Malden, MA: Blackwell, 2002), 345–360; and Samantha Matthews, "Marketplaces," *The Oxford Handbook of Victorian Poetry*, ed. Matthew Bevis (Oxford: Oxford University Press, 2013), 655–672.
5. See Meredith Martin, *The Rise and Fall of Meter: Poetry and English National Culture, 1860–1930* (Princeton: Princeton University Press, 2012).
6. Caroline Levine, "Rhythms, Poetic and Political: The Case of Elizabeth Barrett Browning," *Victorian Poetry*, 49, 2 (2011), 235. Levine has in mind Tucker's article "Of Moments and Monuments: Spacetime in Nineteenth-Century Poetry," in *Modern Language Quarterly*, 58, 3 (1997), 269–297.
7. See, for example, Yopie Prins, "Metrical Translation: Nineteenth-Century Homers and the Hexameter Mania," *Nation, Language, and the Ethics of Translation*, ed. Sandra Bermann and Michael Wood (Princeton: Princeton University Press, 2005), 229–256.
8. Yopie Prins, "Robert Browning, Transported by Meter," *The Traffic in Poems: Nineteenth-Century Poetry and Transatlantic Exchange*, ed. Meredith L. McGill (New Brunswick and London: Rutgers University Press, 2008), 206.
9. See the *Oxford English Dictionary* and *The Princeton Encyclopedia of Poetry and Poetics*.
10. See, for example, BenGlaser's "Scanners, Darkly," review of *Meter Matters: Verse Cultures of the Long Nineteenth Century*, ed. Jason David

Hall (Athens, OH: Ohio University Press, 2011), in *Papers on Language and Literature*, 49, 3 (2013), 327–333.
11. See S. Edward Warren on the "classification of machines," *Elements of Machine Construction and Drawing* (New York: John Wiley and Son, 1872), 13.
12. Friedrich A. Kittler, *Discourse Networks 1800/1900*, trans. Michael Metteer (Stanford: Stanford University Press, 1990), 42.
13. Yopie Prins, "Victorian Meters," *The Cambridge Companion to Victorian Poetry*, ed. Joseph Bristow (Cambridge: Cambridge University Press, 2000), 107.
14. See, for example, W. K. Wimsatt and Monroe C. Beardsley, "The Concept of Meter: An Exercise in Abstraction," *PMLA*, 74, 5 (1959), 585–598.
15. See http://prosody.princeton.edu/ and http://prosody.lib.virginia.edu/.

Measurement, Temporality, Abstraction

> Come nearer, and you may hear the clangor and the whirl still going on, and note the steady beat of the huge engine, that, like the heart of a giant, puts all in motion....
> —William Harrison Ainsworth, *Mervyn Clitheroe* (1858)

> Musical rhythm is the recurrence of an accent or beat at successive regular intervals.... But even without music there may be rhythm: as in the ding-dong of a bell, the plash of a water-wheel, the pulsation of a heart, or the uniform march of machinery. A railway train often runs with a rhythm to which you can easily adapt a tune, of which the engine will mark the time.
> —"Phenomena of Music," *All the Year Round* (1868)

Below are two documents about meter. Both are from 1857, and both appeared in widely circulating periodicals.

March–May. Not quite 6 years after the industrial "spectacle" of the Great Exhibition had galvanized public fascination with "things" of all kinds, and machinery in particular,[1] a series of short articles entitled "A Chapter or Two on Meters" appeared in a new magazine called the *Friendly Companion and Illustrated Instructor*. These "meters" were not the iambic or dactylic variety that many of us associate with the cognate subjects of prosody and versification, but an alphabetically arranged catalog of measurement apparatuses. The first of three monthly installments contains three entries: actinometer ("for measuring the intensity of solar or terrestrial radiation"), aërometer ("for correctly ascertaining the mean bulk of gases"), and barometer ("for ascertaining the weight of the atmosphere"). The next "chapter" begins with a lengthy entry on the chronometer ("for the correct measuring of time"), before going on to define such strange-sounding instruments as electrometers, eudiometers, galactometers, and gasometers. The concluding number explains goniometers, hydrometers, manometers, pedometers, pluviometers, pyrometers, and saccharometers, before closing with a long entry on the thermometer.[2]

August. In the respectable *North British Review*, Coventry Patmore published his major contribution to nineteenth-century verse theory: a review essay with the title "English Metrical Critics." Partly a response to recent accentual theories, such as the one advanced by Edwin Guest in his 1838 *A History of English Rhythms*, and partly an elaboration of temporal, quasi-musical theories, such as those of Joshua Steele and E. S. Dallas, Patmore's treatise—more often referred to by its later title "Essay on English Metrical Law"—asserts that meter is properly a measurement of "the time occupied in the delivery of a series of words." At the heart of Patmore's synthesizing and supplementing of existing temporal theory is a "law" based on the division of lines into units of equal time or "isochronous intervals," which are marked by an "imaginary" time-keeping beat, the ictus. Patmore's "Essay" underscores the ideal nature of what he terms the "modulus" (the regular pattern of meter) and its difference from, as well as its potential for interaction with, the "real" (i.e., voiced) rhythms of language. This abstracting of meter, in conjunction with Patmore's attempt to set out a systematic temporal metrics based on isochrony, played a significant role in the articulation of English versification not only in the second half of the nineteenth century but also well into the twentieth.[3]

At first glance, these two examples of "meter" might not appear to have very much in common. The meters cataloged by the *Friendly Companion* are quite literally mechanisms, machines with gauges, dials, and moving parts. Patmore's meter, "the mechanism of English verse,"[4] is arguably more *techne* than *technology*—that is, an example of the art, skill, or craft of metrical composition, or the study of that art, as in *ars poetica*. As Carl Mitcham and Timothy Casey have observed, historically *techne* has "include[d] making crafts and art as well as the skills of sport and argument," while *technology* has been used to denote "the study of industrial arts or industrial technics, and in its original restricted meaning indicated only scientific or science-based making."[5] In the middle decades of the nineteenth century, however, these categories were not obviously discrete. A reader who struggled with terms such as those listed in the *Friendly Companion* might well have turned to one of several popular pronouncing dictionaries, where he or she would have found "terms of art [and] science" placed side by side,[6] words obtaining to manufactures and technology mingling with those belonging to the study of grammar, prosody, and poetics. For example, in R. Harrison Black's *The Student's Manual: Being an Etymological and Explanatory Vocabulary of Words Derived from the Greek* (1838), readers would have seen the terms "Aræo-meter," "Baro-meter," "Chrono-meter," and "Eudio-meter" listed under the heading "MĔTRŎN, μέτρον, *a measure.*—MĚTRĚO, μετρέω, *I measure*," along with a definition of *meter* in the sense of versification: "[s]peech confined to a certain number of harmonical syllables . . . [and the study of] time and the order of syllables . . . ."[7]

There is more than just an etymological connection worth pursuing here. Both "A Chapter or Two on Meters" and Patmore's "Essay on English Metrical Law" are framed by and exhibit signs of the standardizing impulses associated generally with the machine age. Specifically, they construe measurement as a systematic process where standardization and uniformity of proportion are not only desirable but essential. Whether the object of study is a physical property (atmospheric pressure, sugar content) or an abstraction (time, the mental spacing of beats), one cannot possess an accurate understanding of it (indeed, one may not even be able to verify its existence) without mechanisms of measurement that establish "proper units and standards" as insurance against what Graeme Gooday calls "material contingency" or "cultural subjectivity." At its most technologically ambitious, what the machine age promised was nothing less than "an objective universal knowledge [obtained] through measurement," where quantities were uniform and "the regular working of machines," which historians of modern technology have read as a defining feature of nineteenth-century industrial modernity, was a prerequisite.[8] As we will see, the "industrial principle of standardization," an offshoot of the "inherent logic of mechanization,"[9] subtended not only the factory system and the railway—two emblematic machine conglomerations of the Victorian period—but also the defining theoretical principles of a metrics that was beginning to establish itself at the mid-century. Alongside the systematic development of the "practical arts" and the concomitant rise and disciplinary consolidation of the natural and physical sciences, where the *Friendly Companion*'s "meters" were transforming working practices and underwriting laboratory experiments, nineteenth-century metrical discourse was asserting a "science" and applying technologically informed methods (and in some cases actual machine technologies) of its own, often working out its calculations in explicit dialogue with the knowledge economies of engineering, industry, and science.

In his 1921 book *English Metrists*, T. S. Omond credits Patmore's "Essay" with "inaugurating" this more scientific, systematic, and decidedly modern approach to English versification—he terms it the "new prosody."[10] It is, therefore, a good place to begin an investigation of the conjunctions between nineteenth-century meters and machines. One thing this book claims is that the "more rational and real methods" that for Omond characterize the New Prosody's approach to the study of English meter and versification[11] did not stand aloof from but were active participants in the "age of machinery," depicted so memorably by Thomas Carlyle in "Signs of the Times" (1829), as well as in a variety of generalist and specialist texts about machines, manufactures, sciences, and industries that I will discuss throughout this book. By examining this "new" phase of metrical enquiry in relation to three iconic technologies of the age—the railway, the telegraph, and the steam thresher—I hope not only to present a case for considering the defining elements of the New Prosody (including the abstraction of meter and the regular, isochronous spacing of the ictus) as belonging to the "complex social and institutional matrix" that Leo Marx has described in relation to modernity's machines[12] but also to provide a framework for the other meshings between meter and machinery (both conceptual and material) that the chapters below scrutinize. These instances of what we might call "tooth contact" will help set *Nineteenth-Century Verse and Technology* in motion.

Networking the New Prosody

"The modern world of the nineteenth century," observes Marita Sturken, "prized synchronization, standardization, efficiency, and the predictability that this produced."[13] These hallmarks of that century's networked world—which, as Laura Otis and Friedrich Kittler, among others, have shown, radically changed the way people thought (of themselves, of others, and of their place on a linked-up globe)—were "facilitated by new modern technologies" that, in turn, became enduring material expressions of what Richard Menke has termed "the world-as-network."[14] Menke has in mind, among other things, aspects of what Wolfgang Schivelbusch called the "machine ensemble," and his attention to the interplay between "imaginative writing" and new communication technologies gives us a good sense of what it meant to write and read prose fiction in a world increasingly defined in interactions with machines—whether they were designed to convey messages or people and freight.[15] The machine-defined standards of linearity and spatio-temporal homogeneity, so frequently associated with the communication revolution effected by the railway and electric telegraphy in particular, had, I argue, a significant exchange with the period's verse and related metrical theorizations as well. If the nineteenth-century novel, with its multiple plot lines, gave literary form to a world increasingly characterized by its networked relations, as Menke observes, then the articulation of the New Prosody, with its abstracting and standardizing of metrical values, constituted another expression of the regulation of information in networked modernity.

To see how a networked world and the standards on which it was predicated intersect with mid-century metrics, let's begin by returning to Patmore's description of the ictus, which he asks us to imagine as "like a post in a chain railing."[16] Yopie Prins—whose work on Patmore and abstraction has set the tone for a reinvigorated examination of his poetic theory—suggests that the "spatial terms" of Patmore's simile are significant. For Prins it is particularly the "spaces between" the marks of the ictus that matter; the "mark itself" effectively stands outside of time and space.[17] After all, it is, as Patmore himself asserts, "imaginary."[18] Yet for Patmore's mid-century readers, the image very likely brought to mind familiar *material* objects: ordinary wooden or iron posts and chain railings, such as those cordoning the entrances of buildings or lining busy pavements, but also the seemingly endless chains of wire-topped telegraph posts that stretched alongside an expanding network of railway lines. According to contemporary accounts, the proliferation of these posts was hard to ignore. Across Britain, Europe, and North America, the "continual rising of [telegraph] poles" was a phenomenon still worth remarking in 1869, when R. W. O'Brien composed his poem "Telegraph Lines."[19] Further, to persons traveling by railway, telegraph poles were not just ubiquitous; they were useful as well. As material markers of "spacetime," they enabled passengers to reckon railway velocity. A short piece entitled "Telegraph Posts as Indicators of Time and Speed," from *The London Anecdotes Reader* (1848), explains what Schivebusch has called the "poetic perception of telegraph poles":

> To calculate the speed at which you are traveling on a telegraphed railway, multiply by two the number of telegraph posts you pass in a minute, by four those you pass in half a minute or by eight those you pass in a quarter of a minute; and the result, in each case, will be the number of miles you are then travelling per hour; the posts being arranged thirty to a mile.[20]

Here we have a veritable exercise in railway "scansion," in which telegraph poles divide the railway's linear movement into equal units of space and time. To "mark" the posts as they appear is to establish the line's "meter" (or, more precisely, the meter of the train that travels on it)—that is, to perform the function of the *speedometer*. Given the widespread awareness of this pastime, it may be more than a coincidence that Patmore, seeking to explain the isochronous spacing of a fundamentally "imaginary" ictus, should offer readers an objective correlative that "[e]very railway traveller knows."[21]

If telegraph posts provided a "metrical" index against which the railway line could be measured, then the line itself, which relied on viaducts and tunnels to impose desired smoothness where nature failed to offer it, became an emblem of perfect measurement: an ideal "ruler" or abstract "grid" superimposed upon the unruliness of topographical inflections. However the land might rise and fall, the railroad would enforce upon it the uniformity of mechanical propulsion, providing what Dionysius Lardner would regard as "the optimal approximation of [the] ideal road." Nicholas Wood's illustration, from *A Practical Treatise on Rail-Roads* (1838), offers a graphic representation of this interplay of line and land (Fig. 1). The two lines—an unflinchingly straight one representing track and a wavy one denoting terrain—demonstrate the subordination of problematic "natural irregularity" to reliable "mechanical regularity." This drive toward a regular, idealized linearity, conceived in remarkably similar spatial terms, also underpinned, as Prins has shown, the New Prosody's thinking about "meter as a formal grid," a perfect, abstract rule against which the poet or prosodist could measure the rise and fall of speech rhythms.[22] Patmore asserted the importance of "a perpetual conflict between the law of the verse and the freedom of the language"—the one a fixed ruler modulating and "giving effect to the other." This

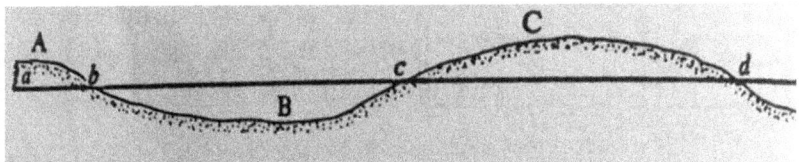

Fig. 1 Plate from Nicholas Wood's *A Practical Treatise on Rail-Roads, and Interior Communication in General. Containing Numerous Experiments on the Powers of the Improved Locomotive Engines and Tables of the Comparative Costs of Conveyance on Canals, Railways, and Turnpike Roads* (London: Longman, Orme, Brown, Green & Longmans, 1838)

metrical axiom, though not exactly new, would gain momentum over the course of the century as proponents of the New Prosody, following Patmore's lead, reinforced the division between the abstraction of meter and the materiality of rhythm. In his theory of counterpoint, for example, Gerard Manley Hopkins (a correspondent with Patmore on the subject of meter) relies on this tension between (regular) meter and (irregular) speech rhythm. In an 1874 essay, he even offers a line drawing to illustrate the contrapuntal movement of the two (Fig. 2). Hazel Hutchison makes a compelling case for reading Hopkins's "mapping" of meter in relation to work on light waves conducted by scientists such as James Clerk Maxwell and Hermann von Helmholtz.[23] The spatial awareness of Hopkins's graph resonates also, I suggest, with Wood's illustration of the contrast between railway line and topography.[24]

While "the prescribed pattern of meter," at least as Hopkins represents it, seems fluid and wavy by comparison with the perfect smoothness of railway linearity, one legacy of the New Prosody was that meter was increasingly construed in abstract, ruler-like terms. Patmore himself, though he shared Hopkins's appreciation of counterpoint, nevertheless imagined meter as an unbending course from which speech inflections deviate. Unmitigated meter, as we will see in more detail below, is analogous to the monotonous ticking of a clock—on its own mechanically "over-smooth" and perfectly isochronous. But a line comes to life when we speak it so as to introduce "departures from the modulus" of meter. Even the dips and bumps of voice, however, remain effectively subordinated to the straight-and-narrow path of the metrical roadbed, which, maintains Patmore, "should continually make its existence recognized."

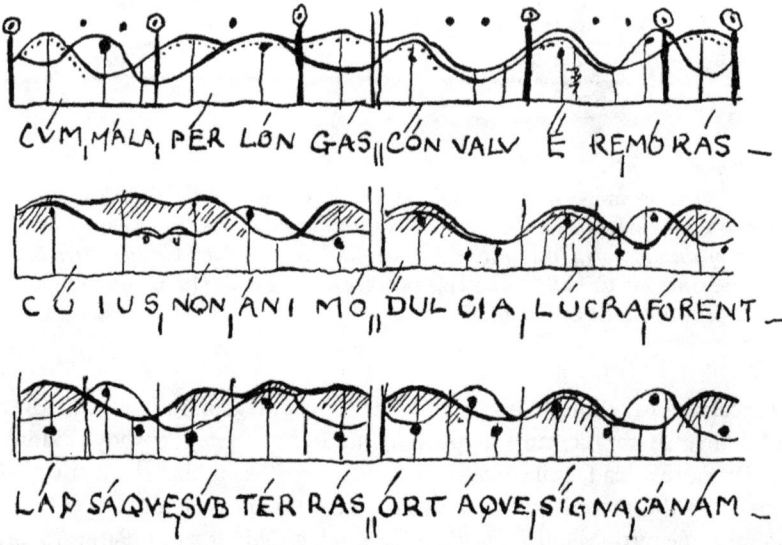

Fig. 2 Diagram of counterpoint from Gerard Manley Hopkins's *The Journals and Papers of Gerard Manley Hopkins*, ed. Humphry House and Graham Storey (London: Oxford University Press, 1959), 282. By permission of Oxford University Press on behalf of the British Province of The Society of Jesus

If we read verses as we ought, then there should be no mistaking the presence of the modulus informing our vocalization, even if word accents do not always keep time with the mental beating of the ictus. This is what Patmore understands as "law" directing "life," meter regulating how we voice verse.[25] As Prins notes, one corollary of Patmore's theory of meter in the mind, and of the nineteenth-century emphasis on metrical abstraction more generally, is that "voice," like recalcitrant landscape, is made to "follow meter," even "reinscrib[e]" it. For Patmore in particular, a dedication to meter as a grid or ruler manifests itself not only in theory but also in practice: his poem *The Angel in the House* (1854–6), as Jason Rudy has shown, is an exaggeration of metrical restraint in which the perfectly even modulus regulates the "free play" of rhythm. The detailed close readings that Rudy offers in *Electric Meters* (2009) exhibit how *The Angel* "privileges metrical structure over rhythmic experience" in ways that he will go on to elaborate theoretically in his 1857 "Essay."[26] The cultural embeddedness of Patmore's metrics, as explicated by Rudy, is further foregrounded by attending to how it maps onto the mechanics of abstraction focused upon the burgeoning British railway network. At this point in his career, then, by which time the railway had been asserting a mechanically regulated, abstract linearity for over two decades, Patmore's meter—itself a symbol of order, measure, and abstraction—can look rather like a locomotive that "railroads" speech rhythm into conformity to its homogeneous mechanical movement.[27]

The growth of the railway network resulted in a homogenizing of time as well as space, and the correlations between Patmore's metrical "law" and the ordering of telegraph beats, examined below, are themselves framed by this larger narrative of temporal reorientation. The speed of telegraphic transmissions, which enabled more or less simultaneous communication between people in opposite parts of the country, and the introduction in the 1840s of "railway time," which began with the synchronizing of clocks at stations on the Great Western Railway's network and culminated with the standardizing of time across Britain, are examples of a general coordination of time associated with the regularizing impetus of industrial culture and machine efficiency. Just as the smooth iron of the railway line asserted its standardizing influence over the peculiarities of the land, so railway time organized a variety of local times into a universal "clocktime." With the introduction of railway time, isochrony (understood generally as the principle of equalized or uniform time) became the temporal cornerstone of machine modernity, and like its spatial complement isotropy (homogeneous space), it structured Victorians' everyday lives, both on and off the railway, suggesting applications for a range of "social and natural phenomena."[28] Patmore and his contemporaries could not have failed to notice the systematizing force of machine-regulated homogenous time, which governed the setting of clocks in homes and public spaces, controlled factory production, enabled the transmission of telegrams, and coordinated travel by omnibus, canal barge, and train. Planning a railway journey, in particular, involved consulting a compendious document—the railway timetable—that rendered in book form the standardizing impulses of machine temporality. "If contemporaries had to choose one item that epitomized nineteenth-century life," writes Mike Esbeter, "they might have chosen the timetable. It appeared to mesh with the tightly regulated industrial discipline of time, while signifying in print what was taken by many to be the symbol of the age: the steam locomotive and the railway system."[29]

Produced in great numbers, sold at a comparatively low price, and studied by many thousands of passengers, railway timetables—such as *Bradshaw's Monthly Railway and Steam Navigation Guide*—were available from a variety of publishers from approximately the late 1830s.[30] With their tabular organization of information, where "only quantities existed," railway timetables appeared to many a "literary puzzle," a "conglomeration of little figures, lines, and letters"—the antithesis of a fictional narrative that one might read cover-to-cover. In their presentation of material, then, and in the method of "functional reading" they demanded, timetables were not unlike the *Gradus ad Parnassum*, that infamous compendium of classical quantities, and related textbooks on Latin and Greek grammar and versification used widely in England's public schools. As we will see in "Meter Manufactories," these books demanded a skill set different from the one used in what Esbester terms "narrative reading." Using the Gradus to find a word with the requisite "long" and "short" quantities was like using the railway timetable to locate a particular "up" or "down" train. In both cases, reading is "not for leisure": rather, it is "goal-driven" and necessarily "fragmentary."[31] (Few people are likely to read a railway timetable in its entirety, just as few people—apart from prosody historians, perhaps—read a Gradus from Ā, *ăb* to *zȳthum, i.*)

This resemblance between the railway timetable and a schoolboy's classical exercises did not go unremarked by the Victorians themselves. In fact, it became something of a running joke. To understand a timetable, according to an 1850 article in *Punch*, one must have "learnt it in his early youth, for to us it is one of the dead languages . . . ."[32] Another piece in *Punch*, from 1865, depicts the railway guide as a textbook whose metrical lessons refuse to be "exhausted": "You may have tired of your favourite poet in a fortnight; but how many of BRADSHAW'S grandest lines remain unscanned?" Members of Parliament are imagined as grown-up prosody swots, eager to supplement their studies: "LORD DERBY examining [*Bradshaw's*] for opportunities for classic meter. LORD HOUGHTON making all the stations rhyme."[33] For other passengers, timetables offered more drudgery than delight, their "lessons" recalling difficult learning scenarios—for which exercises in classical prosody were a well-known byword. In his 1858 collection of poems *Belgium and Up and Down the Rhine: Metrical Memorials*, Henry Bateman, a physician and founder of the New Church College in Islington, classes *Bradshaw's* with the "Grammar, French, Latin, Algebra, and stuff" that he remembers from "early school." In the end, he finds "this popular guide and instructor" even more daunting than these philological and mathematical subjects: "'Bradshaw' beats me, out and out, at last!"[34] The "careful study of 'Bradshaw'"—as Bateman and many of his contemporaries opined—did not always leave the student of railway scheduling better equipped to navigate the "Ups and Downs of Life, from the Express to the Parliamentary."[35] Many young men, despite years of study with a Gradus, could have said much the same thing about their comprehension of the rules of Latin versification. Using either text to ascertain correct "quantities" often had as much to do with luck as with diligent study.

Because railway timetables such as *Bradshaw's* were instrumental in accustoming the Victorian popular imagination to the temporal logic of the railway and machine-ordered modernity more generally, we should consider them not only for what they have in common with elements of classical prosodic pedagogy but also as a significant point of orientation for emerging ideas about English poetics and the metrical "discipline of time" associated with Patmore and the New Prosody. As documents where synchronization and durational precision were paramount, timetables were paper instantiations of the railway's smooth, perfectly measured lines. Here the ideal "grid" of the "machine ensemble" asserted itself in its purest, most abstract form. Displaying information in rows upon rows of figures, the timetable offered readers what Barbara Adam describes as "time that is abstracted from its natural source; an independent, decontextualized, rationalized time. It is a time that is almost infinitely divisible into equal spatial units . . . ."[36] The timetable, of course, presents an "ideal," rather than a "real," image of railway movement, magnifying the logic of isotropy and isochrony. However late a train might actually start from Paddington, for example, and however much real time it may lose (or gain) before arriving at its destination (say, Exeter or Plymouth), the timetable reflects departures and arrivals only as they are scheduled. The grid may offer a standard of temporal organization to which actual journeys *should* conform, but it is not always the case that real movement is modulated in time with the regulations of *Bradshaw's* or a similar measurement index. Just as delays, those "departures" from the timetable's modulus, demonstrated that the grid's abstract timings were, like Patmore's meter, only "imaginary," so too did the abstract time-spacing of *Bradshaw's* demand a degree of compliance from real railway traffic. "Trains had to be scheduled," notes Herbert Sussman, "to move along the tracks at regular intervals so as not to collide."[37] Similarly, the driver of an "early" train may be encouraged, by a railway representative or a signalman (that enforcer of the timetable's "law"), to reduce his speed— that is, to modulate the time of his train, bringing its (real) motion back into line with the (imaginary) timings printed in the schedule.[38] As we have seen, such an exercise in spacing was also, for Patmore and several of his New Prosody successors, a theoretical concern. One element in particular of their adherence to the dialectic of rhythm and meter was a method of moderating the pacing of the former so that it aligned with the latter. To achieve a good correspondence between meter and delivery time, one might "fill up" a measure with the voice or with silence. For Patmore pauses are crucial as a means of harmonizing spoken cadences and the abstract, isochronous timing of metrical intervals.[39] In his 1880 *Elements of English Prosody*, John Ruskin endorses this theory, asserting that a reader may, "with his voice" or by observing "measured rests" in his delivery of a line, "[fill] up the time required" by the count of meter.[40]

As a machine medley that mobilized Victorian modernity in the direction of "isotropic, coordinate space and time," the railway brought the bodies and minds of millions of Victorians—some of them poets and metrists—into contact with new regimes of measurement, temporality, and abstraction. Whether gazing out of the window to count telegraph posts or checking elapsed journey times against their copy of *Bradshaw's*, railway passengers were increasingly experiencing their comings and goings in ways that encouraged a kind of spatio-temporal double-consciousness. Not only did the timetable's "matrix format" ask passengers "to work in two dimensions at the same time," reading information in horizontal rows and vertical columns to determine the timings for a given route.[41] Timetables were also part of Victorians' phenomenology of time, at the foundation of which was an experiential polyrhythmia: to move by modern machine was to possess at once an awareness of the regular, periodic spacing of guide-time and the quite possibly messy pacing of lived-time—and, of course, the slippages between the two. Such slippages were visible also in the railway's movement across the land, which rose and fell in syncopation with the engineered smoothness of the track. It is hardly surprising, then, that a new metrics, just beginning to coalesce as the age of railway travel was itself getting up to speed, should incorporate elements of this widespread spatio-temporal experience of machine culture. In February of 1857, an anonymous writer in the *Railway Record* pleaded for the introduction of a "uniformity of gauge" to resolve the practical problem of incompatible "narrow" and "wide" lines. Of course, his was not that year's only periodical contribution to the very timely question of standard measurement.[42]

Absolute Beat

Of course the railway was not the only technology that transformed Victorians' experience of time. Other nineteenth-century machines—such as the electric telegraph, itself a component of the railway "machine ensemble"—insisted upon temporal precision. The telegraph proved useful to the long-distance communication operator not least because it measured out its beats clearly. In his *Telegraph Manual*, published in 1859, Taliaferro Preston Shaffner—sometime lawyer, inventor, and collaborator with fellow American telegraphy pioneer Samuel F. B. Morse—offers the following remarks on an apparatus known as the Bright Telegraph, named after its designers, the British engineers Charles and Edward Bright:

> The needles beat against the pins, and a sound is produced sufficiently distinct to be read by the operator. . . . The operator need not depend upon the eye to see the movement of the needles. The pins may be made to produce different sounds, and those sounds can be as distinct as the beats or movements of other systems producing intelligible sounds.[43]

The "intelligible sounds" of beating telegraph needles appealed first to the operator's ear. As Rudy demonstrates in *Electric Meters*, the telegraph asserted its rhythms physiologically: "telegraphic language," as registered by operators or clerks, was a "bodily experience" that produced its own forms of "physical stress."[44] But there is a slightly different way of explicating the meters of telegraphy that I want to explore here. By giving the abstract "system" of Morse code material form, the telegraph effected what amounted to the *reification* of meter, lending material expression to the otherwise immaterial ictus, that "all-important . . . time-beater" that is among the central features of Coventry Patmore's "law" of meter. The technologies of telegraphy—like those of the coordinated communication network to which they belonged—provided a mechanical impetus not only for a "physiological poetics" but also for its contrapuntal counterpart: a burgeoning metrics of abstraction.

As many readers will know from experience, there are times when the beat of metered verse seems to force itself upon the mind's ear. In her essay "Meter and Meaning," from the 2011 compilation *Meter Matters*, Isobel Armstrong offers an anecdote about hearing a line of verse as what we might call "pure" or "absolute" beat. What plays "in [her] head" as

de de dum de de dum de dum de, de dum de de dum de dum

turns out to be the metrical "pulse" (somatic and fittingly telegraphic) of Alfred Tennyson's 1842 poem "Break, Break, Break." Armstrong's beat-memory allows her to stress a point. Meter and words do not always assert themselves as an indivisible unit: they "are not tied together." On occasion meter can exert a "somatic pressure" that is distinct from—"breaking" with and quite possibly irreducible to—what she terms the "semantic meaning" or "cognitive content" of the poem.[45] The possibility of dissociating the beat signature of meter from words is, in large part, what underpins many modern theories of versification, especially those in the New Prosody tradition that emphasize a distinction between *meter* as fixed (and abstract) pattern and *rhythm* as variable (and material) interpretation of that pattern. Patmore's metrical theory relies on this distinction, where the regular pacing of meter in the mind distinguishes itself from any possible (and possibly irregular) performance of the line, thus allowing for syncopation—an interplay between the rhythms of spoken sound and what Patmore understands as the "imaginary" spacing of beats. If meter and words are bound together tightly, then there can be no such counterpointing. "Indeed it is no small part of the poet's art," as M. A. Bayfield would declare in *The Measures of the Poets* (1919), "to see that his units of rhythm shall not correspond too frequently with the metrical feet."[46] In these elaborations of meter, we are told that there can be no threading of patterns, no possibility of "polyrhythmia"[47] where such a correspondence dominates a line, where the ideal pattern of meter and the material vocalization move as one, rising and falling, and spacing themselves, in unison. Moreover, as Patmore, Bayfield, and later historians of their metrics, such as Armstrong, assert, too much correspondence of this kind not only precludes syncopation but also produces its antithesis: programmatic, monorhythmic verse. If meter and words (or simply their phonemic values) map onto one another perfectly—for example, if a reader overemphasizes meter, subordinating speech rhythms to its regular pacing—then the "imagined variety" produced by rhythms crisscrossing is nullified; one is left with only metronomic meter: the "ticking of a clock," which, according to Patmore, is "truly monotonous."[48] This particular, though by no means universally accepted, understanding of meter has been embedded in many nineteenth- and twentieth-century theories.[49]

This one-dimensional beating can be heard in exaggerated form in the measures of telegraphy, where clicks are an example of unmitigated meter. This is, in effect, what Armstrong hears: the metronomic beat of meter, unmitigated not because the poem's words fall in line with its meter too neatly but because they have disappeared altogether. Thus beats the telegraph. Like the meter Armstrong describes, it "ask[s] for words" yet remains "independent of them and of semantic meaning."[50] And for good reason. As Victorian telegraph operators well knew, a contrapuntal dialectic between code and word is a liability, to say the least, and trustworthy devices were designed so as to preclude such confusion by prioritizing the code. Working with deliberately sounded beats, an experienced telegraph clerk counted, quite literally, on one of two phenomena: a total equation of words and beats (where the coded beat is the precise sonic surrogate for the letter or word it symbolically represents) or, for a very practiced operator, a near-erasure of words, which fall away as the code of beats accrues meaning in and of itself. Words, in this scenario, are all but superfluous. As the American linguist Edward Sapir observed in 1921, "certain [telegraph] operators may have learned to think directly . . . in terms of the tick-auditory symbolism . . . developed in sending telegraphic messages."[51] That is, they may have thought *only in beats*, so fluent in their trade that one sign system (telegraphic code registered as audible pulses) completely replaced the other (the words those pulses denote). The result is a "metrical" pulse more or less without cognitive content, or code as exact symbolic proxy for cognitive content. Either way, what distinguishes the rhythmic beating of telegraphy is the prominence of the beat: code foregrounded as code, which can stand in for words or allow operators to dispense with them entirely. Thus, in the "metrical" index of Morse—the most widely adopted telegraphic code, given material form by a panoply of electrified machines—the clerk was confronted with what might be termed absolute beat, a hyperbolic example of the metrical phenomenon that Armstrong describes in relation to Tennyson's poem.

The respective beats of meter and telegraphy keep time in some other noteworthy ways. Not only was nineteenth-century telegraphic communication essentially a technology based on "a measured rhythmic movement"[52] of clicks or beats, as a variety of contemporary sources observed; its conventional means of distinguishing among units of electrically transmitted data also had much in common with the existing conventions for prosodic notation and scansion. Morse code, invented in 1836 and by the 1840s the standard telegraphic vocabulary in use in both America and Britain, was effectively a binary system that enabled devices to send and receive messages by transmitting short and long pulses of electrical current. These "shorts" and "longs"—terms well-established in the study of classical verse as denoting the quantity (i.e., pronounced duration) of syllables—could be combined to represent the twenty-six letters of the Roman alphabet, as well as the Arabic numerals 1–10 and certain marks of punctuation. Their combinations were remarkably foot-like. One short beat followed by one long one, for example, signified the letter "A"; a long beat followed by three short ones was equivalent to "B," and so on. While telegraph machines registered long and short electrical pulses as a variety of different sounds (e.g., needle clicks, pipe tones, bell strikes), they all shared the same basic sign system. As Robert Sabine describes in *The History and Progress of the Electric Telegraph* (1869), "[t]he elementary signs of the Morse telegraph are two, a dot and a dash, produced by the recording instrument according to the time which the key at the transmitting station is held down."[53] In its graphic form (as seen in telegraphy manuals and also on the transcriptions of some so-called copying or recording telegraphs), the dot-dash chains of Morse code were similar to the groupings of macrons and breves that schoolboys, classics masters, poets, and verse theorists (among others) used to mark the quantities of Greek and Latin verse. No doubt many of those exposed to both systems of notation would have heard and seen in Morse code an echo of classical scansion. Indeed, the American Unitarian minister Edward Everett Hale, in his humorous 1858 essay "The Dot and Line Alphabet," conflates the two forms of notation when he imagines how Morse's system of longs and shorts could be used to make bells "sound intelligibly": "Daūng dĭng dĭng, — dĭng, — dĭng daūng, — daūng daūng daūng, and so on, will tell you as you wake in the night that it is Mr. B.'s store which is on fire, and not yours, or that it is yours and not his."[54] Eventually, Morse code's dots and dashes came to be expressed as the words *dit* and *dah*, respectively. A line of telegraphic code displayed with this notation (e.g., *dit dit dah*—Morse for the letter "U") would look and sound very much like Armstrong's representation of Tennyson's meter as a series of *des* and *dums*.[55]

In addition to its metrically resonant notation, telegraphic code relied on a temporal logic—at once in line with and moving beyond the prosody suggested by its quasi-quantitative classical terminology. It was time (not of syllable or word but of beats and dead-beats) that determined how operators read telegraphic patterns and divided a line of code into its constituent parts. Essential for the effective and unambiguous relay of messages in the Morse symbolic system was not only agreement about what dashes and dots and their corresponding long and short beats meant but also rules determining proportionate relationships between dots and dashes and among discrete groupings of them. First and foremost, a principle of equivalence was needed to help telegraph clerks identify letters, words, and spaces. As in classical prosody, where two short syllables are nominally "equivalent" in duration to one long one,[56] telegraphic code depended on an equation of short pulses of electrical current (dots) to long ones (dashes). "Each dot," notes George B. Prescott in his *History, Theory, and Practice of the Electric Telegraph* (1860), "requires only a single interval of time, while the dash requires two."[57] Here we begin to discern a "metrics" more in line with the temporal theory advanced by Patmore in his "Essay on English Metrical Law" than with the rules of classical quantity. Where quantitative verse takes the syllable (or simply the vowel sound) as its unit of measurement, Patmore's temporal metrics divorces time-keeping from linguistic units and links it with the abstract beating of the ictus. "The time occupied in the actual articulation of a syllable," he claims, "is not necessarily its metrical value."[58] So with telegraphy: beat-time, which is not connected to (much less coterminous with) syllable duration, is what counts. Further, the basic measurement units of Morse code—the integers of its "metrical" index—are not only temporal in organization ("the theory of *time* [is] the basis of this [telegraphic] alphabet"[59]) but also predicated, like Patmore's meter, on the principle of isochrony, or the equal spacing of beats in time. Because "any great variation in time would introduce confusion into the signals," as Schaffner observes, timings were standardized not only for code components specifically, as we have noted, but for the signaling process more generally. "We see," writes Prescott, "that intervals of equal time elapse between two dots, from one dot to the following dash, from the commencement of the dash to the first following sign." Operating a telegraph, then, was an exercise that in notation resembled the scanning of Greco-Roman verse; in practice, however, the time marked was not linguistically but electrically determined: just as only "isochronous intervals" measured by a time-beating mental ictus registered as meter to Patmore, so only the even spacing of beats and pauses mattered to the telegraph clerk. "All that is necessary to a perfect understanding of the theory of this unique and simple alphabet," one telegraph commentator remarked, "is to appreciate the difference in *time* between a dot and a dash, and a short and a long space."[60] Telegraphy's measurement logic is one that Patmore would have appreciated.

With its prosody of proportionate time-spaces in which intervals are clearly marked by a beat, telegraphy is an apt machine counterpart to the New Prosody, which began to assemble its own theoretical apparatus, as most historians of Victorian metrics have suggested, from the 1850s. By then, the "more rational and real methods" that Omond identified as defining characteristics of this "new" approach to meter had already established themselves, in principle, as the logic that made telegraphy tick: a general abstracting of measurement from semantic and syllabic values, an assertion of time as the basic measurement index, and a congruence with what Omond termed "musical structure." The "duration-related code"[61] that Morse operators listened to on a daily basis was, in keeping with meter as described by Patmore's contemporary E. S. Dallas in his *Poetics* (1852), simply "*time heard*." Similarly, though their units of measurement and their modes of delivery may not have corresponded exactly, "the thing measured" by both the telegraph and Patmore's meter "is the time occupied in the delivery of a series of words." And while he may make much of his allegiance to Hegelian idealism, Patmore's insistence on the essentially isochronous spacing of the ictus in English poetry is also in tune (and time) with telegraphy's well-established conventions of isochronously spaced bursts of electric current. Even the associations that Patmore makes between intervals of time in metered verse and bars of music—linkages that would be pursued as part of a full-blown musical metrics later in the century—had their telegraphic complement in what Dionysius Lardner, in *The Electric Telegraph Popularised* (1855), described as a diverting corollary of the Morse system's time-patterning. Lardner relates a story about a musical "experiment at New York," where clerks prevail upon one of their opposite numbers in Boston to use his machine to beat out music—to send songs such as "Yankee Doodle" and "Hail Columbia!" "by means of [their] rhythm[s]": "The instrument commenced drumming the notes of the tune as perfectly and distinctly as a skilled drummer could have made them . . . ." What the operator sends, as musically minded metrists such as Patmore would have known, was "the *time* of music"[62]—its bars rendered as audible pulses of electric current, marked on telegraph tape as uniformly spaced dots and dashes.

Jason Rudy has argued persuasively that Patmore's "insistence on meter's immateriality" is, in part, a response to the somatic shocks associated with the spread of electric telegraphy—particularly as relayed rhythmically by "the profound physicality" of Spasmodic poets such as Sydney Dobell and Alexander Smith.[63] Patmore's "imaginary" meter, he suggests, provides the poet-prosodist with a means of resisting the dangerous, embodied rhythms that the telegraph made manifest: the evenly spaced beats of his ideal ictus impose their order as a safeguard against telegraphic communication's unruly, spasmodic pulses. Yet telegraphy's measures, as we have seen, were characterized not just by a "sensational" transmission of beats but, signally, by a rule-bound, even musical and harmonious organization of them—an organization premised on temporal and specifically isochronous measurement. When Omond notes that "Patmore voiced ideas that were in the air,"[64] he may not exactly have overhead telegraph lines in mind, but he nonetheless invites us to detect a somewhat different impedance between Patmore's temporal theories and contemporary technologies of communication from the one that Rudy records. For the "new" generation of poets and prosodists—Patmore, Dallas, and their immediate successors—the "metrics" of electric telegraphs were virtually unavoidable, the everyday measures of an increasingly standardized and thoroughly mechanized modernity. If their externalized beating "initiated new ways of experiencing time and space that found their ways into the fabric of everyday life," as historians of Victorian telegraphy have asserted, then it is worth considering the New Prosody's abstracted, "imaginary" meter as another instance of how the telegraph's "new rhythms" were being "internalized" by millions of people across Europe and North America.[65] It was not only telegraph clerks who heard meaning in the messages of Morse. By the sound of it, Patmore may well have had telegraphy on the brain.

Thump and Thresh

Not all machine provocations were as easy to reconcile with the principles of meter that we typically associate with the New Prosody, specifically those we have observed in relation to the railway and telegraphy: namely, abstraction, spacing, and the contrapuntal interplay of meter and rhythm. Some mechanisms, in fact, seemed antithetical to the logic of even spacing and the clear marking of beats in time. The rhythms of telegraphs were reassuringly regular, their ictus-like beating slow and evenly spaced enough to count with the unaided ear. However, the steam thresher—another emblematic "machine in the garden"[66]—appeared to defy measurement altogether, its mechanized mastication producing a din that seemed "alien" to ears accustomed to the cadences of manual grain separation, and markedly at odds with a metric such as Patmore's. Its capacity for standardizing aspects of the harvest notwithstanding, the threshing machine suggests an alternative way of construing the effects of mechanization on prevailing understandings of metrical abstraction, as well as meter's relationship to speech rhythms and methods for describing forms of machine-generated rhythmical movement. If we can read the railway and telegraph as material counterparts to several of the abstractions that the New Prosody promoted, then we can see the steam thresher as a disruption of the isochronous, recurring beat signature associated with Patmore's imaginary ictus. The distinctive sound it generates overrides the possibility of mental marking, demanding a reconsideration of both *what* we understand meter to be and *how* we perceive its movement. Where the railway line offered up to travelers an image of perfect smoothness, the machinery of threshing presented workers with its converse: a burring roughness. As I will show, the coercive rhythms of this mechanical voice were hard to resist.

Before the invention of the threshing machine in the 1780s, grain separation was a task that had changed little for millennia. In eighteenth-century Britain, threshers were strong-armed men who used articulated wooden sticks called flails to beat the husk away from harvested grain in preparation for winnowing. As John Goodridge observes in his examination of rural occupations, this labor-intensive, noisy, and rhythmically idiosyncratic process was performed throughout the year, and as a result its beats became lodged in not only the farmer's but also the poet's imagination.[67] In two popular threshing poems, Stephen Duck's "The Thresher's Labour" (1730) and William Cowper's "The Task"

(1785), there is an attempt to mime in meter the singular sound of flailing. Duck's description emphasizes the synchronized movement of the bending and rising workers—"Down one, one up, so well they keep the Time"—while Cowper's onomatopoeia stresses the relentless sound of the beating hand-tool—"Thump after thump resounds the constant flail."[68] For both poets the description involves a small but noteworthy deviation from the lines' prevailing metrical structure. The flailing motion is signaled by what at first appears to be a trochaic substitution at the start of an otherwise regular iambic line. On closer inspection, however, it becomes clear that the mimetic element of the lines, where the movement of the threshers (in Duck's poem) or the sound produced by their flails (in Cowper's), constitutes a deliberate arc of stress that goes beyond the opening trochaic foot, falling and rising across the first *four* syllables in a marked pattern: "Dówn ŏne, ŏne úp" and "Thúmp ăftĕr thúmp." These unusual line openings—what we might read as a single foot, the Latin-derived choriambus, which comprises two stressed (or "long") syllables enveloping two unstressed (or "short") ones—begin with dactylic downbeats before rising again at the completion of the flail's "swing." In both cases, the remainder of the line, which merely comments or elaborates on the initial metrical enactment of threshing, relaxes into more conventional Augustan iambs. By the sound of it, both poets delighted not only in the "the rhythmic pleasures" of threshing but also in the distinctive distribution of beats and off-beats that gives character to the "prosody" of the threshing floor.[69]

Clearly marked periods between beats, a signature feature of the New Prosody, were also the hallmark of conventional threshing. The "charm" of premechanized threshing, as Duck's and Cowper's poems assert and as several nineteenth-century observers would concur, was linked to its rhythmical assertiveness, its symmetrically recurring beats. In 1857, the same year that Patmore was theorizing the "equal or proportionate spac[ing]" of the ictus, that "all-important . . . time-beater" of metered verse,[70] C. J. Merz was using almost identical terms to assess beats in music and, by analogy, threshing. In an essay entitled "Melody and Rhythm," printed in the *New-York Musical Review and Gazette*, Merz argues that "*the symmetrical return of certain proportions of time*," as marked by "the rise and fall of the accent," is what constitutes beauty in sounds. He goes on to posit a "fondness for measured time" as the basis of our attraction to melody in music.[71] This predisposition to "measured time" is also essentially what informs an appreciation of threshing's old rhythms.[72] As Merz writes,

> In former times, within my own recollection, before threshing-machines had superseded the primitive flail, we could hear the threshers use their instruments in a regular, symmetrical succession of strokes, so as to establish a peculiar measure of time; thus they would be able to bear the monotony of their occupation, and even turn it into an amusement, and find in it an object for ambition . . . .[73]

With the introduction of threshing machines, which derived no "amusement" from their labor and had no "ambition" to perform it more harmoniously, the hand-flail's slow "symmetrical succession of strokes" gave way to a mechanical efficiency whose rhythms were sufficiently different from the cadences of the older activity as to appear meterless—at least insofar as contemporary ears could tell.

By the early decades of the nineteenth century, threshing machines were in use across the country. From the 1830s, in the wake of the so-called Swing Riots, they became the emblems of agricultural unrest and resentment among farm workers, who worried that the machine was making their labor redundant. In this context, the unmistakable "swing" of the flail, its tell-tale beating (beating now focused not on grain but on the machines themselves, which were frequently smashed and burned in protest), was regarded by many as a radical rhythm, the calling card of "Captain Swing." But not everyone, it must be said, resisted the introduction of agricultural machinery and its new rhythms. In 1860 J. D. Bell, a Methodist minister from Weedsport, New York, advised "Literary men" to familiarize themselves "with the makers of threshing machines, locomotives, and reapers."[74] Bell's enthusiasm was shared by the English reverend and poet Charles Tennyson Turner, elder brother of Alfred Tennyson. Turner's double-sonnet "The Steam Threshing Machine" (1868) is an encomium to mechanized agriculture:

THE STEAM THRESHING MACHINE

With the Straw Carrier.
Flush with the pond the lurid furnace burned
At eve, while smoke and vapour filled the yard;
The gloomy winter sky was dimly starred,
The fly-wheel with a mellow murmur turned;

While, ever rising on its mystic stair
In the dim light, from secret chambers borne,
The straw of harvest, severed from the corn,
Climbed, and fell over, in the murky air.
I thought of mind and matter, will and law,
And then of him, who set his stately seal
Of Roman words on all the forms he saw
Of old-world husbandry: *I* could but feel
With what a rich precision *he* would draw
The endless ladder, and the booming wheel!

Did any seer of ancient time forebode
This mighty engine, which we daily see
Accepting our full harvests, like a god,
With clouds about his shoulders,—it might be
Some poet-husbandman, some lord of verse,
Old Hesiod, or the wizard Mantuan
Who catalogued in rich hexameters
The Rake, the Roller, and the mystic Van:
Or else some priest of Ceres, it might seem,
Who witnessed, as he trod the silent fane,
The notes and auguries of coming change,
Of other ministrants in shrine and grange,
The sweating statue,—and her sacred wain
Low-booming with the prophecy of steam![75]

His admiration for "the prophecy of steam" notwithstanding, Turner records the difficulty of assimilating what Bell had described as the "stentorian utterances which come from throats of wood, of iron, of brass, and of steel"[76] to conventional, especially classically inherited, meters. The sounds of mechanized threshing, as Turner's two sonnets represent them, are indeterminate: on the one hand, the machine grumbles with inarticulate cadences ("a mellow murmur"), while on the other it enunciates its periods declaratively ("booming"); it also produces a "Low-booming," an ominous, muffled sound that suggests distant cannon fire. Considering how to give metrical form to the still comparatively new soundscape of the corn harvest—no longer heard as the steady systolic plosives "up" and "keep" and "thump"—Turner implies, in the second sonnet, that the "rich hexameters" of classical antiquity may not be adequate conveyances for the "notes and auguries of the coming change" to farming practices. While the dactylic downbeat that we noticed in Duck's and Cowper's poems may have approximated the rhythm of the hand-flail (both the instrument and the meter tracing their heritage back to the classical world), did it correspond to this new technology and its loud, though somewhat indistinct, mutterings?

Almost 50 years later, questions about the mechanical thresher's metrics continued to preoccupy poets, particularly in relation to the theory of beat-spacing associated with the New Prosody. A one-time interlocutor with Patmore, whose "law" of meter she in many ways admired, Alice Meynell begins her poem "The Threshing Machine" (c. 1914) by acknowledging the gulf between the bygone world of manual husbandry and the newer (by then well-established) one of mechanized farming:

> No "fan is in his hand" for these
> Young villagers beneath the trees,
> Watching the wheels. But I recall
> The rhythm of rods that rise and fall,
> Purging the harvest, over-seas.
> No fan, no flail, no threshing-floor!
> And all their symbols evermore
> Forgone in England now—the sign,
> The visible pledge, the threat divine,
> The chaff dispersed, the wheat in store. (lines 1–10)[77]

Meditating on a nation changing utterly with the deaths of so many soldiers in the Great War (1914–18), this poem marks absences, not only absent persons but also discontinued work practices and the familiar rhythms associated with them. Gone are not only the material "sign[s]" of hand-flailing—"No fan, no flail, no threshing-floor!"—but also the rhythms they generated. But what has replaced them? Where Turner's poem looks backwards to classical meters, which may or may not resonate with the rhythms of modern threshing, Meynell's harbors doubts about whether these sounds (and some of her descriptions are reminiscent of Turner's) can be understood as metrical at all:

> The unbreathing engine marks no tune,
> Steady at sunrise, steady at noon,
> Inhuman, perfect, saving time,
> And saving measure, and saving rhyme—[.] (lines 11–14)

Meter and rhyme, these lines suggest, are unnecessary adornments for the quotidian task of grinding grain. Yet line 12, which is anything but "steady," carries what amounts to a metrical memory of the now-fading rhythms of the hand-flail, though it is unable to reproduce those cadences perfectly: "Stéadȳ ăt súnrīse, stéadȳ ăt nóon . . . ." Here, mid-line and final pauses—those in-built mechanisms for promoting a correlation between metrical spacing and the voicing of a line—function as reminders of metrical absences, effectively standing in for omitted slack syllables, which, if present, would complete the line's dactylic pattern and so "fill up" its metrical time. If the distribution of stresses at the start of the line and immediately following the caesura are any indication of the abstract timing of its meter, then a short pause (one slack syllable) would be needed after "sunrise" and a longer pause (two slack syllables) after "noon."[78] The mechanical operations that this and the immediately following lines describe seem equally at odds with the even beating of meter, dactylic or otherwise, that machines such as the telegraph exhibit. It is not absence of sound or rhythm that characterizes the threshing machine, however, only its "tuneless," "measureless" workings. The thresher's "rhythm of rods that rise and fall" is presumably visible enough to an onlooker's (or at least to an operative's) eye, but its sounds refuse to organize themselves into a regular, clearly discernible pattern that the ear can identify as its meter. The definite beating of the flail has been replaced by a "steady" machine noise. For "steady" we might be tempted to read "regular" or "uniform," but given the lines' insistence on the thresher's "saving" (that is, *obviating*) at once "time," "measure," and "rhyme," it seems more likely that "steady" does not describe a succession of beats but rather a continuous, uninflected, and incessant sound.

To those new, or at least not habituated, to the sounds of steam threshing, such a machine noise would have seemed metrically unremarkable precisely because it would have sounded *unmarked*—because it would have lacked perceivably marked periods. Though the threshing machine does have a "beat," its pulses occur too quickly to be heard distinctly. As Hermann von Helmholtz, a pioneer of nineteenth-century empirical acoustics, observes in his 1863 treatise on the physiology of musical sound, "the ear is . . . unable to follow [rapid beats] sufficiently well for counting." Instead of the familiar "thumping" beat, then, persons exposed to a threshing machine heard what Helmholtz refers to as a "rough," "unpleasant," "jarring tone."[79] This noise, as Arnold Pacey explains in *Meaning in Technology* (1999), is the rhythmic signature of engines that vibrate at a high frequency, as opposed to the easily countable "throbs" of an engine that vibrates at a low frequency. "With vibrations of higher frequency," he states, "we are no longer aware of either rhythm or throb, but instead we hear a buzz, hum, or continuous note"— what in Turner's and Meynell's poems gets expressed as the steam thresher's "murmuring" or "steady" sound.[80] The comparatively slow beats of the human thresher's flail, like the telegraph, have a frequency that human ears can hear, whereas the much quicker succession of beats accomplished by the machine's metal apparatus blends into a sound beyond humans' physiological—and therefore metrical—threshold of perception.[81] Many of those who listened to the steam thresher's hummings and buzzings may not have been familiar enough with its beat signature to hear distinctly and so count or "measure" them. Thus, especially for a poet such as Meynell—who, like Patmore, understood meter as a clearly marked timing of beats—the "rapidly beating tones"[82] produced by the threshing machine's sundry moving parts (gudgeons, beaters, pitch-chains, feeding-rollers) could not be said to mark the ictus. Furthermore, not only were the thresher's beat periods effectively indistinguishable from one another; the stentorian buzzing noise that machines such as the thresher emitted—their insistent drone—presented another problem: it did "*not admit*," to borrow Patmore's words, "*of an imagined variation*."[83] So overbearing was the steam thresher's noise that it very likely made marking the regular beats of an imaginary ictus (creating a mental melody to mitigate the job's monotony) almost impossible, its hum reverberating distractingly even inside one's head. Even as the abstract recurrence of regularly marked periods was finding expression in the machinery of telegraphy and the railway, here was a machine that seemed bent on obliterating altogether the steady pulse of the ictus.

While steam threshers did not always seem easy to reconcile with the discrete percussive beats of the metrical ictus, that is not to say they did not have an undeniable (indeed unavoidable) rhythmical energy—a voice of their own with raspy, burring rhythms. In fact, machines such as the steam thresher could assert their distinctive monotone buzz to the point of coercion, at once prohibiting other rhythms and forcibly asserting their own. What Roger Ebbatson has read, in relation to Turner's sonnet, as the threshing machine's "imposition of mechanical will-power"[84] is, in many contemporary accounts of threshing, directly linked with the device's distinctive high frequency vibrations. In both his 1891 novel *Tess of the d'Urbervilles* and an earlier essay on agricultural labor in Dorset, Thomas Hardy—who, as a poet, "realized the implications" of the New Prosody's innovations in temporality and abstraction[85]—offers a vivid account of how the threshing machine enforces its rhythmical *will* on the workers whose livelihoods demand close contact with it. We learn in *Tess*, for example, that the "inexorable," "penetrating hum" generated by the "despotic" threshing machine causes workers' bodies to vibrate in terrifying sympathy, "thrill[ing] to the very marrow all who were near the revolving wire-cage."[86] In his 1883 essay "The Dorsetshire Labourer," Hardy details an even more drastic effect of the thresher's rhythms on the body. Once the hum got into workers' bones, its vibrations could very well influence their locomotive rhythms:

> A thin saucer-eyed woman of fifty-five, who had been feeding the machine all day, declared that on one occasion in crossing a field on her way home in the fog after dusk, she was so dizzy from the work as to be unable to find the opposite gate, and there she walked round and round the field, bewildered and terrified, till three o'clock in the morning, before she could get out. The farmer said that the ale had got into her head, but she maintained that it was the spinning of the machine.[87]

Spinning involuntarily around the field, unable to control her own body, this wide-eyed woman has succumbed to the magnetic power of heavy metal, its disorienting rhythms rendering her what Karl Marx called a "living appendage of the machine."[88] In the end, it seems, the mechanized meters of the steam thresher would find their feet—however much they might appear to be out of step with the New Prosody's law.

They would find a voice as well. The same ineluctable noise that caused workers' bodies to quiver—the thresher's mesmeric murmuring—also regulated the communication of anyone working within the ambit of the engine's rapid revolutions. In *Tess* we hear that "[t]he hum of the thresher, which prevented [workers'] speech, increased to a raving whenever the supply of corn fell short of the regular quantity."[89] It turns out that the machine does, in fact, have quite determined periods of motion, whether hearers recognize them as metered or not, and its motorized "ravings" admonish workers whose bodies struggle to keep pace with its insatiable appetite for corn. In addition to these demands that a "regular quantity" be observed, the constant humming drone, as I noted above, is enough on its own to override at once mental time-marking and competing speech rhythms. The machine effectively buzzes Tess and her fellow laborers into voiceless submission to its metallic muttering. What is more, long periods of exposure to such determinative rhythms not only impose machine-measured intervals of speech and silence but also threaten to force-feed the machine's modulations into men's mouths. Standing beside the threshing machine "in a sort of trance," the engineman has a more immediate physiological connection with the engine he serves than the other workers: he is bound to it by a "long strap which [runs] from the driving-wheel of his engine to the red thresher." This material link places his body at the direct command of the machine's motive power—making him a vocal conduit for its vibrating rhythms. Like an automaton or ventriloquist's dummy, the engineman—who "holds only strictly necessary intercourse with the natives"—carries, Hardy implies, a trace of his engine in his speech. His "strange northern accent" serves as shorthand for the industrial world from which threshing machines were introduced, marking him as "alien" to the South-West world of the novel.[90] Given Hardy's awareness of prosody generally and of the ways that a machine's "meters" could find somatic expression, I like to think that the strangeness of the engineman's accent applies not only to his regional dialect but also to his voice's rhythmical inflections, which are marked by the "course kind of roughness" that Helmholtz associates with quick beats.[91] Perhaps what the workers hear when he opens his mouth is a sound modulated to the thresher's distinctive buzzing.

An Easy Flow of Language?

What does it mean to sound like a machine?[92] The threshing machine's vibratory pattern—the buzzing drone that appeared, to some auditors, to be without rhythmical periods—had itself a correlate in the physiology of human speech, which is produced by the vibration of the vocal folds or glottis. In their *Practical Phonetics and Phonology* (2003), Beverley Collins and Inger M. Mees gloss *voice* thus: "A glottal setting involving rapid vibration of the vocal folds, producing a 'buzz' which accompanies almost all vowel sounds and voiced consonants."[93] But it was not simply a case of the sounds produced in the human throat—what the physiologist Oliver Wendell Holmes called "the human *bleat*"—being *like* the distinctive buzzing of a threshing machine; rather, the human vocal apparatus itself was conceived of, by many nineteenth-century speech scientists and pioneers of sound technology, as a mechanical instrument, whose inflectionless hum, if not necessarily its complex cadences and modulations, might be successfully synthesized, by surgical or other means.[94] The inventor of the telephone, Alexander Graham Bell, for example, entitled his series of lectures on speech and vowel theory *The Mechanism of Speech*.[95] Here he describes "an artificial substitute for the larynx, made . . . of dentist's rubber," shown to him by John Gray McKendrick, Regius Professor of Physiology at the University of Glasgow. A prosthesis with "a metal reed, taken from a harmonium or small parlor organ," enabled the patient, whose own "larynx had been excised," to speak in a comparatively "natural voice," the abiding "peculiarity" of which was the tell-tale machine buzz that resulted from introducing a simple machine that replaced the organic glottis with only its most basic "voicing" function. Thus the man's voice "was monotonous and without inflection," and to achieve any vocal variety, he had to manually substitute one reed for another. As fortune would have it, the man "was a machinist by trade" and so able to spend "his spare time manufacturing reeds for himself."[96]

One obstacle frequently encountered in relation to machine-generated speech, whether produced by a prosthetic implant or by a self-contained apparatus, was the difficulty of producing sounds that more convincingly imitated human vocalizations, going beyond the mechanistic, monochromatic vowel drone. Not only the steam thresher's infectious, buzzing vernacular but machine "speech" generally, especially as embodied by the synthetic voice technologies of the eighteenth and nineteenth centuries, had a tendency to exaggerate the drone, creating vibrations that approximated spoken vowel sounds but that failed to simulate joined-up or *articulate* speech and, by extension, the prosodic modulation of phonemes and syllables. For example, Wolfgang von Kempelen's 1791 talking machine, which produced vowel sounds when the operator manipulated "a pair of organ-bellows," was unable to link the sounds of letters "into syllabic combinations and words": "the sounds of the letters would not flow into each other without a clatter or pause. If too slowly enunciated, they would seem like a child repeating his alphabet . . . ."[97] Later improvements on the device, undertaken in the 1830s by the British telegraph inventor Charles Wheatstone, would inspire Bell to investigate the possibility of a "musical telegraph," which in turn underpinned his contribution to telephony technologies. Though producing a vowel drone similar in certain ways to the rapidly vibrating buzz of the steam thresher, early speech synthesizers, in keeping with the segmented beating of the telegraph, tended to break up a message into its component parts—speech did not *flow* continuously as it would via the means of later voice recording and transmission devices such as the phonograph and telephone. The "vowel synthesizer" created by Helmholtz in the 1850s offered a modicum of flow from "one composite sound to another,"[98] using electromagnets to control the vibrations of tuning forks in order to produce vowel sounds. Yet even this device, while a sophisticated mechanizing of speech-sound harmonics, tended toward a breaking up of sounds, not emphasizing a "uniform phonetic flow" but instead "replacing the singular stream [of voice sound] with a pointillistic sound-world of discrete vibrational patterns."[99] "To make a machine that *articulates*," as Oliver Wendell Holmes would remark in 1863, "is not so easy."[100]

From "the dots and dashes of telegraphic communication" to the discrete, albeit rapid, vibrations of talking machines (a category that includes not only automatons but also the phonograph and telephone), the "modern telecommunications" of the nineteenth century, as Brian Murray has noted, were analogous with disarticulated and, at times, unintelligible speech. Murray's remark relates to the "savage-telegraphy" described by the Victorian explorer Henry Morton Stanley in his account of Congolese singing,[101] as opposed to, for example, the "distinct or intelligible syllabification" that, in Edgar Allan Poe's short story "The Murders in the Rue Morgue" (1841), distinguishes rational, educated speech from vocalizations that are "absolutely alien from humanity" (foreign voices, the raving of madmen, animal cries).[102] By contrast, another of Poe's stories, "The Man That Was Used Up" (1839), imagines how the "rapid march of mechanical invention"—namely in the field of human prosthetics—may not simply serve to reduce speech to discrete tonal values but might enable astoundingly clear and powerful articulation. Against the story's background noise of disarticulated and in places halting, telegraphic speech, exemplified aptly by Mr. Theodore Sinivate's "peculiar way of drawling out his syllables," is the eponymous used up man's "rich melody and strength" of voice. With the aid of a mechanical palate, Brevet Brigadier General John A. B. C. Smith finds a means of improving upon his impaired speech, which is described by the story's narrator as being "between a squeak and a whistle."[103] In contrast to the reality of voice-box prosthesis, as described by Bell, Poe's proto-cyborg fantasy represents technology as an aid, rather than obstacle, to melodious vocal modulation.

As Poe himself was aware, the machine age did not always produce such salutary technologies for rendering melodious speech or, moreover, for systematizing the study of verse, of which delivery intonation was only a part. When Poe examined the state of modern versification in his essay "The Rationale of Verse" (1848), which he published not long before figures such as Patmore and Dallas began to articulate aspects of the New Prosody, he lamented the absence of a "system of rhythm" and a "system of scansion"—something that Patmore's "Essay on English Metrical Law," in its attempt to promote meter as a rule-bound abstraction, would attempt to redress. Unlike Patmore, however, for whom meter was only marginally about speaking verse and more about measuring imaginary intervals, Poe proposed that versification needed to offer clear guidance not only on the principles that inform metrical measurement generally—and here he inclined toward Patmore in downplaying accent in favor of an analogy with musical temporality—but also on the practices of *enunciation* through which those principles are mediated. These two halves of the prosodic equation had become decoupled, argued Poe, to the extent that a "learned prosodist" from the future looking back on nineteenth-century metrics might draw curious conclusions about the relationship between contemporary scansions, on the one hand, and pronunciation, on the other: "because we lived a thousand years before his time, and made use of steam engines . . ., we must therefore have had a *very* singular fashion of mouthing our vowels . . . ." In particular, the orthodoxies of "scholastic scansion,"[104] which were at the core of nineteenth-century liberal education, tended to mitigate against smooth articulation and a rhythmically nuanced modulation of metrical "law," to borrow Patmore's term, and expressive verse-reading. Just as the telegraphic syllabification heard by Stanley sounded to him like so much inarticulate—literally not joined-up—"stammering,"[105] so did the application of meter to speech, particularly in nineteenth-century education scenarios, result in a form of exaggerated syllabification that did not merely counterpoint but frequently countermanded what Poe called "the rhythmical, musical, or reading flow" of verse.[106] The regular, monotonous flow of meter, in other words, might overwhelm expressive flow of speech.

Patmore himself understood a "perpetual conflict" between metrical language and linguistic expression to be essential to "the finest expressions of versification."[107] As a technology for regulating the movement of poetry—whether in the abstract, on the page, or with the voice—meter, as we have seen, was another means of controlling flow that Richard Menke has read as a hallmark of Victorian industrial society and that we have seen in operation with technologies such as the railway and telegraph.[108] Whether verses are scanned for the eye "with perpendicular lines [drawn] between the feet" or for the ear by reading in sing-song and metrically overdetermined, "the distinct marking of rhythmical flow,"[109] Poe opined, problematically disrupts the natural rhythmical (i.e., musical) flow of verse—resulting in verse-speaking where the meter, discernible in the delivery, may be, as Patmore remarked, "over-smooth and 'accurate,'" while the delivery itself is made to "*suffer from* the bonds of verse."[110] At best, "[p]ractice in scansion," as the authors of *The Art of Interpretative Speech* observed in 1927, "tends to monotonous, droning reading of poetry"[111]—as though it were voiced by a machine incapable of varying accent, pitch, or timbre. As we will see below, such a delivery style was associated not only with speaking machines but also with one of the century's most renowned poets. At worst, scholastic scansion might not only exaggerate syllabification and nullify modulation—the interplay of rhythms central to New Prosody, elements of which persisted in twentieth-century theories of counterpoint and metrical abstraction—but also render the verse unintelligible, to the point that an exercise designed to improve a pupil's understanding of prosody in fact served to further obfuscated it, leaving him trained to do little but write nonsense verses.

An irony here is that what Poe saw as a dearth of systematic prosody was, in fact, a corollary of the nineteenth century's principal prosodic systems, which, as I have been suggesting in the present chapter and as the rest of the book will examine in some detail, were at once coalescing and reconfiguring across a variety of disciplinary lines and in relation to an array of questions about bodies, minds, modes of speech, and methods of counting, computing, and expressing the rules and material instantiations of versification. That prosodic discourse was riddled for Poe, as well as many of his contemporaries, with "contradiction and perplexity,"[112] is, in part, due to the uneven practices in what was an expansive system of elementary prosodic instruction, but, moreover, a consequence of the rules on which the system itself was founded. Not unlike electric telegraphy, which rendered language as a series of discrete proxy values (dots and dashes), the pre-eminent system of versification—that which anchored nineteenth-century classical education—was predicated upon syllabic exercises, in some cases inherited from the burgeoning factory system itself. These exercises commenced with a disarticulation of the line into its component parts, and it is this system—where the conventional patterns of meter as produced in the practice of scanning determine the voice—that was largely responsible for the sing-song, robotic prosody that Poe and many of his contemporaries saw as anathema. Enshrined in pedagogical orthodoxy, the practices of scansion made their impact felt on theories of English-language versification as well, and provoked Poe and metrists to assert alternative systems that promised a less clumsy subordination of speech to scansion.

But "scholastic prosody" was not the only culprit. Under certain conditions, as I will explain in "The Automatic Flow of Verse," the body and mind could assert their own mechanistic rhythms: stammering speech where measures stick in the throat or, on the other hand, forms of metrical automatism, whereby somatic rhythms or mental aberrations resulted in meters not consciously willed by the persons uttering them—frequently these meters, too, were programmatic and unmodulated, similar to those discussed above. Whether and how meter flowed became a question, which I have begun to assess here, about the extent to which human metrical ability or proficiency was the product of living in a time of steam engines and corresponding prosodic apparatuses, as Poe jibed, or, going further, whether it was more fundamentally related to the inherently mechanistic workings of the human body and mind. The sciences that posed questions about the "human machine"—of which we will encounter various examples in the pages below—and that offered more or less tentative answers would also be responsible for initiating a return to questions of flow in the later decades of the century, when machines offered new perspectives on what measurement was and how it might be represented. But to appreciate why the tension between the idea of meter as an abstract and artificial system for marking beats and segmenting syllables, on the one hand, and its ostensible opposition to the "real" flow of speech, on the other, subtended the experimental sciences of the turn of the century, we must first explore how mainstream metrics was informed by the systems of the machine age. That exploration begins in the classroom, where processes of metrical instruction are considerably indebted to the workaday world of manufacturing and procedures of serial assembly.

Notes

1. See Thomas Richards, *The Commodity Culture of Victorian England: Advertising and Spectacle, 1851–1914* (Stanford: Stanford University Press, 1990), 17–72; Herbert L. Sussman, *Victorian Technology: Invention, Innovation, and the Rise of the Machine* (Santa Barbara: Praeger, 2009), 54–73; and James Buzzard, Joseph W. Childers, and Eileen Gillooly, eds., *Victorian Prism: Refractions of the Crystal Palace* (Charlottesville: University of Virginia Press, 2007).
2. "A Chapter or Two on Meters," *Friendly Companion and Illustrated Instructor* (Mar.–May 1857), 80+ . Some of these "meters" would have been familiar (if not perfectly understood) to Victorian readers. Thermometers and barometers had been around for well over a century, and examples of both had been on display at the Crystal Palace in 1851. John Phillips, the celebrated Oxford geologist and inventor, exhibited one of each. Gasometers—another name for large, cylindrical gas-holders—were a recognizable, if also somewhat worrying, emblem of urban modernity, their iron ribs no doubt suggesting to many observers an architectural echo of Joseph Paxton's Hyde Park structure. Electrometers (for measuring electric charge) and eudiometers (for measuring the amount of oxygen in air) had been in existence since the eighteenth century, with galvanometers (for measuring galvanic current) appearing in the early decades of the nineteenth. Such instruments had been much in circulation among Victorian readers, especially since the late 1830s when electricity—in the form of the electric telegraph—began to revolutionize communication. All three devices are mentioned in Henry Minchin Noad's popular *Lectures on Electricity* (1844), one of many texts that attempted to make that science and its developing technologies accessible to a largely non-specialist audience. Chronometers, by no means new instruments, had also been very much at the fore of the popular imagination from 1840, with the introduction of "railway time" (discussed at length below). Only two of these "meters"—the galactometer (for measuring a liquid's sugar content) and actinometer—were comparatively new inventions, dating from approximately the 1820s. Though perhaps not as recognizable to the *Friendly Companion's* target market ("children and youth," as well as "those of riper years"), these instruments, nevertheless, featured regularly in contemporary debates: the galactometer was used in the study of food adulteration (much discussed in the 1850s and 1860s); the actinometer, invented by John Herschel in 1825, belonged to the sciences of meteorology and astronomy.

3. Coventry Patmore, *Coventry Patmore's "Essay on English Metrical Law": A Critical Edition with a Commentary*, ed. Mary Augustine Roth (Washington, DC: Catholic University of America Press, 1961), 15. Unless otherwise indicated, all citations are to this version of Patmore's "Essay." I am indebted to the historical prosodists who came before me; their analyses of the role of abstraction in Patmore's verse are the modulus against which I measure my present reading. See Dennis Taylor, *Hardy's Metres and Victorian Prosody* (Oxford: Clarendon Press, 1988); Yopie Prins, "Victorian Meters," *The Cambridge Companion to Victorian Poetry*, ed. Joseph Bristow (Cambridge: Cambridge University Press, 2000), 89–113; Jason R. Rudy, *Electric Meters: Victorian Physiological Poetics* (Athens, OH: Ohio University Press, 2009); Adela Pinch, "Love Thinking," *Victorian Studies*, 50, 3 (2008), 379–397; Meredith Martin, *The Rise and Fall of Meter: Poetry and English National Culture, 1860–1930* (Princeton: Princeton University Press, 2012); and Ewan Jones, "Coventry Patmore's Corpus," *ELH*, 83, 3 (2016), 839–872.
4. Patmore, "Essay on English Metrical Law," 3.
5. Carl Mitcham and Timothy Casey, "Toward an Archeology of the Philosophy of Technology and Relations with Imaginative Literature," *Literature and Technology*, ed. Mark L. Greenberg and Lance Schachterle (Cranbury, NJ: Associated University Presses, 1992), 36–37.
6. R. Harrison Black, *The Student's Manual: Being an Etymological and Explanatory Vocabulary of Words Derived from the Greek* (London: Longman, Orme, Brown, Green, and Longmans, 1838), v.
7. The "meters" described in the *Friendly Companion* have been selected in terms of not only semantic but also lexical likeness: all are machines that measure something *and* all share a common stem word, *meter*. Alike, then, in general function and sharing a linguistic base, these "meters" are distinguished from one another by their unusual, foreign prefixes. In spite of its name, however, "A Chapter or Two on Meters" gives no guidance on how one might pronounce or correctly "measure" this terminology. Aiming to rectify this problem, a variety of etymological and pronouncing dictionaries endeavored to present in simple, accessible form the rules and conventions of syllabification and quantity, as well as related prosodical matters—offering to improve both the factual and the linguistic knowledge of not only "scholars [with] . . . only a tincture of classical learning," but also "ladies, who were not likely to pursue the study of [the Greek] language," and "the Working Class, on whose mental culture so much of our national prosperity depends." In addition to Black's text, see Joseph Worcester, *A Universal Critical and Pronouncing Dictionary of the English Language* (London: Henry G. Bohn, 1863), 843; and John Craig, *A New Universal, Technological, Etymological, and Pronouncing*

Dictionary of the English Language, Embracing All the Terms Used in Art, Science and Literature, vol. 1 (London: Henry George Collins, 1848), [iv]. In Alexander Jamieson's *A Dictionary of Mechanical Science, Arts, Manufactures, and Miscellaneous Knowledge* (1829), a reader will find entries for "metre," "prosody," "quantity," and "scanning" arranged alphabetically alongside such machines as the "steam engine," "telegraph," and "threshing machine"—three technologies that I examine below.

8. Graeme J. N. Gooday, *The Morals of Measurement: Accuracy, Irony, and Trust in Late Victorian Electrical Practice* (Cambridge: Cambridge University Press, 2004), 9; Geoffrey C. Bowker, "Second Nature Once Removed: Time, Space, and Representations," *Time and Society*, 4, 1 (1995), 49.
9. Sussman, *Victorian Technology*, 20, 19.
10. T. S. Omond, *English Metrists: Being a Sketch of English Prosodical Criticism from Elizabethan Times to the Present Day* (Oxford: Clarendon Press, 1921), 171.
11. Omond, *English Metrists*, 166.
12. Leo Marx, "Technology: The Emergence of a Hazardous Concept," *Technology and the Rest of Culture*, ed. Arien Mack (Columbus, OH: Ohio State University Press, 1997), 37.
13. Marita Sturken, "Mobilities of Time and Space: Technologies of the Modern and Postmodern," *Technological Visions: The Hopes and Fears that Shape New Technologies*, ed. Marita Sturken et al. (Philadelphia: Temple University Press, 2004), 75.
14. See, for example, Laura Otis, *Networking: Communicating with Bodies and Machines in the Nineteenth Century* (Ann Arbor: University of Michigan Press, 2001); and Friedrich A. Kittler, *Discourse Networks 1800/1900*, trans Michael Metteer (Stanford: Stanford University Press, 1990); Sturken, "Mobilities of Time and Space," 75; Richard Menke, *Telegraphic Realism: Victorian Fiction and Other Information Systems* (Stanford: Stanford University Press, 2008), 15.
15. See Wolfgang Schivelbusch, *The Railway Journey: The Industrialization of Time and Space in the Nineteenth Century* (Berkeley and Los Angeles: University of California Press, 1986); Menke, *Telegraphic Realism*, 3.
16. Patmore, "Essay on English Metrical Law," 15.
17. Yopie Prins, *Victorian Sappho* (Princeton: Princeton University Press, 1999), 149.
18. Patmore, "Essay on English Metrical Law," 15.
19. R. W. O'Brien, "Telegraph Lines," *Journal of the Telegraph*, 2, 5 (Feb. 1, 1869), 57.
20. [Anon.], "Telegraph Posts Indicators of Time and Speed," *The London Anecdotes Reader: The Electric Telegraph* (London: David Bogue, 1848),

60. Schivelbusch, who clearly sees a prosodic operation at work, cites a similar example: "[Telegraph poles] are generally erected about sixty yards apart, or thirty in the mile, so that the speed of the train is easily found by counting the number of poles passed in a minute and multiplying by two, which, of course, gives the rate per hour." See *The Railway Journey*, 31. The source he quotes is [Anon.], *Railway Appliances in the Nineteenth Century, or the Rail, Steam, and Electricity, with Illustrative Anecdotes, Engravings, and Diagrams* (London: R. Yorke Clarke and Co., 1848), 32. Anecdotes similar to these can be found in a variety of popular as well as technical texts circulating in the 1840s and 1850s.
21. *Railway Appliances in the Nineteenth Century*, 32. As Patmore himself observed: "Most people find it hard to believe what they cannot easily represent to their senses." See Patmore, "Essay on English Metrical Law," 13.
22. Prins, "Victorian Meters," 90.
23. Hazel Hutchison, "Eye Rhyme: Visual Experience and the Poetics of Gerard Manley Hopkins," *Victorian Poetry*, 49, 2 (2011), 217–233.
24. Whether the metrical correlate is construed in terms of light waves or gradations of landscape, it amounts to much the same thing: the nineteenth century's networked technologies, as Menke suggests, conveyed and paced the "information" they conveyed—so frequently conceived of in terms of a "fluid"—by means of "controlled flow." See Menke, *Telegraphic Realism*, 20.
25. Patmore, "Essay on English Metrical Law," 8, 7.
26. Rudy, *Electric Meters*, 115.
27. As Rudy has so persuasively argued, *Angel*, in its resistance to the ungoverned rhythms of the Spasmodics, reveals a very literal enactment of the regulatory force of the modulus that Patmore sets out in his "Essay." Furthermore, while versification had been conceived of in topographical terms long before the railway began imposing its mechanical will upon the landscape. Pupils embarking upon a classical education in Britain's endowed schools were compelled to scale the mountain of the muses in their daily prosodic exercises, composing and translating Latin meters with the aid of the standard companion to classical quantities, the *Gradus ad Parnassum* or "steps to Parnassus." In this chapter and in "Automaton Versifiers," I discuss the Gradus in some depth, and also the mechanistic education regime in which it was used.
28. Bowker, "Second Nature Once Removed," 48.
29. Mike Esbester, "Nineteenth-Century Timetables and the History of Reading," *Book History*, 12 (2009), 163.

30. Though several companies published railway timetables, Bradshaw's guides were arguably the most widely used, the title becoming shorthand for any such publication. *Bradshaw's* first appeared in 1839 and remained in circulation (in a number of different editions and formats) well into the twentieth century. For many years following its initial publication, *Bradshaw's* remained priced at sixpence.
31. See Esbester, "Nineteenth-Century Timetables and the History of Reading," 160. In his fascinating essay on the spatio-temporal dimensions of Victorian poetry, Herbert Tucker has commented on how the practical world of nineteenth-century commerce, to which the railway timetable belongs, "read time as space." See Herbert F. Tucker, "Of Monuments and Moments: Spacetime in Nineteenth-Century Poetry," *MLQ*, 58, 3 (1997), 269–297.
32. [Anon.], "An Educational Novelty," *Punch*, 18 (1850), 167.
33. [Anon.]. "Guide to Bradshaw," *Punch* (Aug. 5, 1865), 44.
34. Henry Bateman, *Belgium and Up and Down the Rhine. Metrical Memorials* (London: James Nisbet and Co., 1858), 44.
35. [Anon.], "An Educational Novelty," *Punch*, 18 (1850), 167.
36. Barbara Adam, *Timewatch: The Social Analysis of Time* (London: Polity, 1995), 27.
37. Sussman, *Victorian Technology*, 20.
38. In fact, this logic of train speed conforming to the abstraction of the timetable is not restricted to adjustments for comparatively "fast" or "slow" trains. Dionysius Lardner notes a distinction between a train's actual and average movement: "The actual time requisite to travel between any two points of a line of railway, does not depend so much on the speed of the train when in motion as is generally supposed; nor is there so much difference between the velocity of the first class trains and that of the slowest, when in full speed, as may be imagined. The comparative celerity with which the travelling is executed depends more upon the number of stations at which the train stops, than on its actual speed when in motion." On a given journey, a train may achieve its maximum velocity, but it will need to diminish its speed by braking as it nears a station. What the timetable reflects is the average speed that the train travels along its line, the steady pacing that it needs to arrive at its various stations and its destination on time. Though going at different speeds at different times, the train is effectively modulating its movement to this timetabled average throughout the course of its journey. As Lardner writes, "The average speeds from station to station, given in the above table, are taken from the published time-tables of the companies, and are estimated on certain average conditions; but the actual speed which is frequently attained by the express trains in motion, often

greatly exceeds even the highest given in these tables." See Dionysius Lardner, *Railway Economy: A Treatise on the New Art of Transport, Its Management, Prospects, and Relations, Commercial, Financial, and Social* (London: Taylor, Walton, and Maberly, 1850), 193, 196.

39. Periodicity and pauses were central features not only a printed document such as the railway timetable but of nineteenth-century periodical culture more generally. As Mark Turner has stated, "Built into the notion of seriality is necessarily some conceptualization of waiting. The pause is a constitutive feature of periodical-ness, of all periodicities—there must be a break in time." See Mark Turner, "Periodical Time in the Nineteenth Century," *Media History*, 8, 2 (2002), 193.

40. The metrical practice of "filling up" measures was around, albeit in different form, before the New Prosodists began to theorize it. John Carey writes that "[i]n Latin poetry, verses are not usually measured by the number of syllables, as in English, but by the number of feet, or the length of time required to pronounce them. Now, a long syllable being equal in time to two short—the word *tārdīs*, for example, to the word *cĕlĕrĭbŭs*—it becomes, in many cases, indifferent what the number of syllables is, provided that they all together fill up, but do not exceed, the time allotted for the harmonious utterance of the line." Where's Carey differs from Ruskin (or Patmore or Omond) is in his understanding of the foot as unit of measurement essentially based on syllables value ("A foot . . . contains two or more syllables"). See J. Carey, *Latin Prosody Made Easy*, new ed. (London: Longman, Hurst, Rees, and Orme, 1808), 201, 199. As we have seen, the temporal metrics that New Prosodists will develop does not link its measurement index to syllables but instead to abstract units of equal time. It is thus much more in keeping with the temporality on display in the rows and columns of *Bradshaw's*. For a discussion of abstraction, measured "rests" in verse, the New Prosody, and musical settings of meter, see Yopie Prins, "'Break, Break, Break' into Song," *Meter Matters: Verse Cultures of the Long Nineteenth Century*, ed. Jason David Hall (Athens, OH: Ohio University Press, 2011), 105–134.

41. Esbester, "Nineteenth-Century Timetables and the History of Reading," 173.

42. [Anon.], "Great Western Difficulties—And the Way Out of Them," *Railway Record, Mining Register, and Joint-Stock Companies' Reporter* (7 Feb. 1857), 85.

43. Tal[iaferro]. P[reston]. Shaffner, *The Telegraph Manual: A Complete History and Description of the Semaphoric, Electric, and Magnetic Telegraphs of Europe, Asia, Africa, and America, Ancient and Modern* (New York: Pudney and Russell, 1859), 294.

44. Rudy, *Electric Meters*, 62.
45. Isobel Armstrong, "Meter and Meaning," *Meter Matters: Verse Cultures of the Long Nineteenth Century*, ed. Jason David Hall (Athens, OH: Ohio University Press, 2011), 26, 27.
46. M. A. Bayfield, *The Measures of the Poets: A New System of English Prosody* (Cambridge: Cambridge University Press, 1919), 14. Bayfield's "new system," indebted in part to the work of Patmore and musical metrist Sidney Lanier, is based on a rejection of the iambic line as the metrical mainstay of English verse. He instead proposes "the adoption of the trochaic base" as the index of English prosody (vi).
47. Armstrong discusses "polyrhythmia" as part of her examination of "Four Epistemologies of Meter." See "Meter and Meaning," 31–34.
48. Patmore, "Essay on English Metrical Law," 16.
49. Assertions of this sort form part of not only Patmore's and Bayfield's theories, and Armstrong's latterly, but also the theories of abstraction articulated by I. A. Richards in his "practical criticism" and its American counterpart, the New Criticism. See, for example, my remarks on metrical "orientation" in chapter two of Jason David Hall, *Seamus Heaney's Rhythmic Contract* (Basingstoke: Palgrave Macmillan, 2009), 33–41.
50. Armstrong, "Meter and Meaning," 26–27.
51. Edward Sapir, *Language: An Introduction to the Study of Speech*, 1921 (Mineola, NY: Dover, 2004), 15. An 1858 article on "Telegraphic Symbols" reports on a telegraph "operator, who had become so familiar with the sound of the instrument that he could accurately read many of the common words in a message, merely by listening to its [the machine's] talking! and we doubt if it is generally known, even in this day of recorded wonders, that there is not a Morse operator, in the country worthy of the distinction who cannot interpret the sound of the instrument with as much ease as he can construe a sentence printed in bold Roman letters." See [Anon.], "Telegraphic Symbols," *American Merchant*, 1, 6 (Oct. 1858), 370.
52. George B. Prescott, *History, Theory, and Practice of the Electric Telegraph* (Boston: Ticknor and Fields, 1860), 88.
53. Robert Sabine, *The History and Progress of the Electric Telegraph with Descriptions of Some of the Apparatus* (New York: D. Van Nostrand, 1869), 63.
54. Edward E. Hale, If, Yes, and Perhaps: Four Possibilities and Six Exaggerations, with Some Bits of Fact (Boston: Ticknor and Fields, 1868), 120.
55. Alexander and Nicholas Humez remark on the "prosody" of Morse code and its anticipation of computerized binary code as follows: "[The] first message Morse actually sent was something like this: Dit dah dah, dit dit dit dit, dit dah, dah (pause) dit dit dit dit, dit dah, dah, dit dit dit

dit (pause) dah dah dit, dah dah dah, dah dit dit (pause) dit dah dah, dit dah dit, dah dah dah, dit dit dah, dah dah dit, dit dit dit dit, dah (• – – •••• • – – [pause] •••• • – – •••• [pause] – – • – – – – – •• [pause] • – – • – • – – – – •• – – – – • •••• –). This string displays in a nutshell most of what is good and bad about Morse code: The good part is that it consists of just two elements, long and short (as in classical prosody: D, for example, is the metrical equivalent of a dactyl [dah dit dit], while A is an iamb [dit dah], N a trochee [dah dit], U an anapaest [dah dit dit], M a spondee [dah dah], an R an amphibrach [dit dah dit].) As such, Morse code was tailor-made for an electronic age then still very far in the future." See their book *On the Dot: The Speck that Changed the World* (Oxford: Oxford University Press, 2008), 14–15. Confronted initially with only a pattern of beats, Armstrong, not unlike a Victorian telegraph clerk, must decide what words it signifies. Unlike the telegraph clerk, however, she has multiple possibilities among which to choose (many poems, after all, may share the same metrical code); the clerk's "scansion," by contrast, has only one correct semantic value. Over a hundred years before the publication of Marshall McLuhan's *Understanding Media* (1964), telegraphs were exemplifying the importance of attending to the form of communication. In telegraphy, beats insist—their "meter" is the message.

56. As John Russell, headmaster of Charterhouse School, informed boys, "A TIME is the time of pronouncing a short syllable. A long syllable consists of two Times." See [John Russell], *Rudiments of the Greek Language. For the Use of Charterhouse School* (London, 1826), 94.
57. Prescott, *History, Theory, and Practice of the Electric Telegraph*, 90.
58. Patmore, "Essay on English Metrical Law," 21.
59. "Telegraphic Symbols," 370.
60. "Telegraphic Symbols," 370. For more on the semiotics of spacing in telegraphy, see Winfried Nöth, *Handbook of Semiotics* (Bloomington, IN: Indiana University Press, 1990), 219.
61. Ken Beauchamp describes this innovation of Morse code—its basis in temporal pulsation—as industry changing. See his *History of Telegraphy* (London: Institution of Engineering and Technology, 2008), 48.
62. Dionysius Lardner, *The Electric Telegraph Popularised* (London: Walton and Maberly, 1855), 71. A later handbook expands on the musical features of telegraphy in relation to the Morse organ-pipe sounder (a form of acoustic semaphore): "The method devised by [Morse] was by an organ pipe so connected with a small bellows as to be opened and closed by the pen lever, in the act of writing a dot or a dash. It is at once obvious that in indicating a dot, the pipe would give a short, sharp sound, but in indicating a dash the sound would be correspondingly prolonged. The short and long intervals, therefore, by which the dot

and dash are now distinguished, in the ordinary acoustic instrument, are, by this method, more completely expressed, reducing the code to musical expression, to crotchets and semibreves." See *Examination of the Telegraphic Apparatus and the Processes in Telegraphy* (Washington, DC: Government Printing Office, 1869), 42.
63. Rudy, *Electric Meters*, 115, 122.
64. Omond, *English Metrists*, 171.
65. J. W. Harrington and Barney Warf, *Industrial Location: Principles, Practice, and Policy* (London: Routledge, 1995), 221.
66. The phrase is Leo Marx's, from his *The Machine in the Garden: Technology and the Pastoral Ideal in America* (Oxford: Oxford University Press, 1964).
67. John Goodridge, *Rural Life in Eighteenth-Century English Poetry* (Cambridge: Cambridge University Press, 1995), 45.
68. Stephen Duck, "The Thresher's Labour," *Eighteenth-Century Poetry: An Annotated Anthology*, 2nd edn, ed. David Fairer and Christine Gerrard (Malden, MA: Blackwell, 2004), 261 (line 40); William Cowper, *The Task*, *Eighteenth-Century Poetry: An Annotated Anthology*, 2nd edn, ed. David Fairer and Christine Gerrard (Malden, MA: Blackwell, 2004), 536 (Book I, line 357).
69. Goodridge, *Rural Life in Eighteenth-Century English Poetry*, 48. Years ago E. P. Thompson noted the way Duck's poem in particular offered "an obligatory set piece" about not only farming but also the distinctions between the monotonous labor "commonly ascribed to the factory system" and then "other collective rhythms" of the harvest" (62). For Thompson such texts chart the tension between the rhythms of "task orientation" and the gradual advent of "clock-time." See E. P. Thompson, "Time, Work-Discipline, and Industrial Capitalism," *Past & Present*, 38 (Dec. 1967), 56–97.
70. Patmore, "Essay on English Metrical Law," 15.
71. C. J. Merz, "Melody and Rhythm," *New-York Musical Review and Gazette* (Jun. 13, 1857) 181.
72. Patmore, "Essay on English Metrical Law," 15.
73. Merz, "Melody and Rhythm," 181.
74. J. D. Bell, *A Man* (Philadelphia: James Challen and Son, 1860), 384.
75. See Charles [Tennyson] Turner, *Small Tableaux* (London: Macmillan and Co., 1868), 62–63.
76. Bell, *A Man*, 384.
77. Alice Meynell, "The Threshing Machine," *The Poems of Alice Meynell* (London: Burns, Oates and Washbourne, 1923), 119.
78. Using a caret (^) to denote omitted slack syllables, we could represent the line's missing measures as follows: ´ ˘ ˘ | ´ ˘ ^ || ´ ˘ ˘ | ´ ^ ^ ||. Thus,

there is a ghostly (brachycatalectic) line of dactylic trimeter whose immaterial off-beats show themselves only when we attend to Meynell's pauses—that is, when we attend to the poem's in-built silences, its prosody's means of registering (threshing) sounds that are no more.

79. Hermann von Helmholtz, *On the Sensations of Tone as a Physiological Basis for the Theory of Music*, trans. Alexander J. Ellis, 2nd ed. (London, 1885), 168.
80. For details of the threshing machine's frequency, horsepower, component parts, and general mode of operation (on its own and in relation to other farm implements), see Henry Stephens, *The Book of the Farm*, vol. 2 (Edinburgh and London: William Blackwood and Sons, 1844).
81. As Helmholtz notes, "We actually [can] hear a series of pulses of tone, and are able to recognize it as such, although no longer capable of following each singly or separating one from the other." See *On the Sensations of Tone*, 168.
82. Helmholtz, *On the Sensations of Tone*, 168.
83. Patmore, "Essay on English Metrical Law," 17.
84. J. R. Ebbatson, "The Lonely Garden: The Sonnets of Charles Tennyson Turner," *Victorian Poetry*, 15, 4 (1977), 318.
85. Dennis Taylor, *Hardy's Metres and Victorian Prosody*, 59.
86. Thomas Hardy, *Tess of the d'Urbervilles* (New York: Nelson Doubleday, 1913), 301–302.
87. Thomas Hardy, "The Dorsetshire Labourer," *Longman's Magazine*, 2, 9 (1883), 268.
88. Karl Marx, *Capital: A Critique of Political Economy, Vol. I. The Process of Capitalist Production*, ed. Frederick Engels and Ernest Untermann, trans. Samuel Moore and Edwards Aveling (Chicago: Charles H. Kerr and Co., 1906), Library of Economics and Liberty, 17 Feb. 2012 http://www.econlib.org/library/YPDBooks/Marx/mrxCpA15.html.
89. Hardy, *Tess of the d'Urbervilles*, 303.
90. Hardy, *Tess of the d'Urbervilles*, 301. Raymond Williams describes the mechanical thresher as an "alien machine." See "Literature and Rural Society," *The Raymond Williams Reader*, ed. John Higgins (Malden, MA: Blackwell, 2001), 116. Zena Meadowsong recognizes the link between speech and a Northern industrial space. See her article "Thomas Hardy and the Machine: The Mechanical Deformation of Narrative Realism in Tess of the d'Urbervilles," *Nineteenth-Century Literature*, 64, 2 (2009), 236. And as Stuart Macdonald observes, there is historical evidence associating the North of England with "the first major revolution in mechanized farming" (76), as well as an initial reluctance among farmers in Southern England to accept the threshing machine. For a discussion of the introduction and use of threshing

machines in both Southern and Northern England, see Macdonald's article, "The Progress of the Early Threshing Machine," *Agricultural History Review*, 23, 1 (1975), 63–77.

91. Helmholtz, *On the Sensations of Tone*, 171.
92. There are real-life examples of industry-influenced prosody, where a person's speech patterns "incarnate," as Simon J. Charlesworth puts it, "a sonorous field of expression." One worker, for example, whose story Charlesworth records, explains "how the rhythms of the dialect he spoke were affected by the time [he] spent at work around the thresh-thresh of a mill." The threshing machine, then, might have been a formidable prosody tutor—a true grinder that offered on-the-job training, à la the schoolmasters whose scanning and reciting regimes are the subject of "Meter Manufactories." See Charlesworth, *A Phenomenology of Working Class Experience* (Cambridge: Cambridge University Press, 2000), 236–237.
93. Beverley Collins and Inger M. Mees, *Practical Phonetics and Phonology: A Resource Book for Students* (London: Routledge, 2003), 250.
94. Oliver Wendell Holmes, "The Human Wheel, Its Spokes and Felloes," *Atlantic Monthly*, 11, 67 (1863), 568; J. D. Bell, *A Man*, 384.
95. The same name was given to the chair he held at the School of Oratory at Boston University. Indeed, Bell's pioneering work in telephony—a technology predicated on rendering the vibrations of the human voice, as uttered on one end of the line, as mechanical "tremors" that can be reproduced, on the other end, by the apparatus's "diaphragm"—was, in many ways, an apt legacy of the nineteenth-century advances in the sciences of vocal mechanics that Graham Bell's father, Alexander Melville Bell, had played a central role in defining. See George M. Shaw, "The Telephone and How It Works," *Popular Science Monthly* (Mar. 1878), 561.
96. Alexander Graham Bell, *The Mechanism of Speech*, 8th ed. (New York and London: Funk and Wagnalls, 1916), 8–9.
97. See the entry for "automaton" in *The London Encyclopaedia or Universal Dictionary of Science, Art, Literature, and Practical Mechanics* (London: Thomas Egg, 1839), 314.
98. [Anon.], "The Voice, the Ear, and Music," *Dwight's Journal of Music*, 28, 22 (1869), 377.
99. Benjamin Steege, *Helmholtz and the Modern Listener* (Cambridge: Cambridge University Press, 2012), 184.
100. Holmes, "The Human Wheel, Its Spokes and Felloes," 568.
101. Brian H. Murray, "'Primitive Man' and Media Time in H. M. Stanley's *Through the Dark Continent*," *Victorian Time: Technologies,*

Standardizations, Catastrophes, ed. Trish Ferguson (Basingstoke: Palgrave Macmillan, 2013), 121.
102. Edgar Allan Poe, "The Murders in the Rue Morgue," *Selected Writings of Edgar Allan Poe*, ed. G. R. Thompson (New York and London: Norton, 2004), 260.
103. Poe, "The Man That Was Used Up," *The Selected Writings of Edgar Allan Poe*, ed. G. R. Thompson (New York and London: Norton, 2004), 193, 196, 198.
104. Edgar Allan Poe, "The Rationale of Verse," *The Works of the Late Edgar Allan Poe*, 4 vols. ed. Rufus Wilmot Griswold (New York: Redfield, 1857), 2:251, 250.
105. Murray, "'Primitive Man' and Media Time in H. M. Stanley's *Through the Dark Continent*," 121.
106. Poe, "The Rationale of Verse," 249. Poe was, of course, not the first to point out this fault of readers remaining "mechanically" faithful to scansion in their delivery of poems. Fifty years earlier, an anonymous contributor to the *Monthly Magazine* expressed the point thus: "The measure may be mechanically true, but the flow and cadence, the harmony, accent, and emphasis, so defective, that it will be verse only to the scanning, and neither verse nor prose to the ear." See [Anon.], "To the Editor of the *Monthly Magazine*," *Monthly Magazine*, 3, 16 (Apr. 1797), 258.
107. Patmore, "Essay on English Metrical Law," 9.
108. See Menke, *Telegraphic Realism*, 20.
109. Poe, "The Rationale of Verse," 249.
110. Patmore, "Essay on English Metrical Law," 9, 8.
111. Charles Henry Woolbert and Severina Elaine Nelson, *The Art of Interpretative Speech: Principles and Practices of Effective Reading* (New York: F. S. Crofts, 1927), 218.
112. Poe, "Rationale of Verse," 215.

Meter Manufactories

We find, moreover, that his Greek and Latin were "mechanically" taught....
—Thomas Carlyle, *Sartor Resartus* (1831)

Are we to go on for ever conjugating and declining, and gerund-grinding, and Latin-verse manufacturing ...?.
—F. W. Farrar, *On Some Defects in Public School Education* (1867)

In 1890, or thereabouts, at a small English boarding school called Selfton, we find one Mr. Saniter, house-master and teacher of Latin to pupils of varying abilities. His "iron-grey whiskers" and "keen grey eyes" are physiognomical clues to his teacherly temperament. Though he is "a man of fine intellectual attainments," there is something strangely machine-like about Saniter: he not only opens telegrams "mechanically" but also "hammers" Virgil "into the iron skull of the Lower Fifth." When exasperated by the boys' provoking tendency to produce false quantities in their verse compositions, their occasional recourse to collusion when faced with complicated metrical exercises, or their general prosodical dilatoriness, Saniter "heat[s] himself to boiling point." The nemesis of this steam-powered pedagogue is the "hulking" pupil Newcomen, a "good-tempered, indolent, [and] sufficiently aristocratic" young man who looks "some years over twenty." As a "big boy" who is "quite low down the class list" and unable, or at least wholly disinclined, to do his Latin verses, Newcomen coerces the "captain of the house," "a boy with [a] large intellectual nose, and a singular appetite for the composition of elegiacs and iambics," into doing them for him.[1]

These characters feature in the story "Master and Pupil," serialized in *All the Year Round* in the summer of 1890. But the educational scenario that unites them—prosodical curriculum and classical education more generally as conducted in a nineteenth-century public school—was real enough. The anonymous author was more or less drawing from life, reflecting in caricatured form a very real regime of meter that proliferated in English public and grammar schools. For much of the century, Latin and Greek grammar and meter were the principal (if not quite the only) subjects of study by which privileged boys by the thousands were prepared for "after-life": following years marked by rote, programmatic learning—for which verse composition exercises became a well-known and apt synecdoche—they were sent out into the world, prepared, above all, to scan lines of classical poetry and to pronounce the same in a deliberate, often mechanistic manner. Not only in his portrayal of scholastic life but also in his choice of charactonyms, the author of "Master and Pupil" offers an implicit indictment of this mode of instruction. Saniter, the "iron-grey" master of Latin, shares his name with E. H. Saniter— the Bessemer medal-winning chemist who, in the last decades of the nineteenth century, pioneered a method of desulphurizing iron. The mechanics of classical meter, like those of metallurgy, the author suggests, are too often administered in industrial and potentially dehumanizing ways. The pupil Newcomen has a similarly mechanical pedigree. On the one hand, his name is a nod to William Makepeace Thackeray's character Clive Newcome, who in the 1855 novel *The Newcomes* manages to all but avoid the rigors of classical education at Grey Friars' School (modeled on Thackeray's *alma mater*, Charterhouse). On the other hand, the name links him with Thomas Newcomen (1664–1729), inventor of the atmospheric steam engine—powerhouse of the eighteenth-century Industrial Revolution, before it was superseded by James Watt's "improved" model in the 1760s. While the story condemns the inflexibility of mechanical metrics, as taught by Saniter, it casts Newcomen as an adaptable engine of modernity. His disregard for verse exercises and his methods for circumventing his lessons are not hindrances; rather, they are indices of a promising, self-regulating future. By contrast, the boy who delights in the puzzles of meter and who does "all Newcomen's Latin verses," nicknamed "the Dodo," is depicted as not suited for— indeed, may not even have the prospect of—after-life. Extinction, the story implies, is the fate that awaits boys with a facility for verse composition exercises and a mind attuned to the subtleties of classical scansion.

This chapter scrutinizes the "mechanical" teaching and learning of meter that the author of "Master and Pupil" depicts in their twilight years. The systems comprising this institutional form of encounter with classical prosody—absolutely central to the shaping of the Victorian metrical imaginary—constitute one of the period's most important loci of metrical orthodoxy, as well as a site of pedagogical, philological, and ideological contention. By the mid-century, particularly in the aftermath of the Clarendon Commission's inquiry into public school curricula, Latin and Greek prosody began the long process of ceding their pride of place in this institutional matrix to English language and literature (often taught on principles inherited directly from the study of the classics) and other, more "useful" subjects, which gradually gained acceptance alongside or in place of the classical training that had asserted its dominance in British education for centuries. At its apogee, however, classroom prosody was a fact of life for boys in many ancient and some newly established schools, where lessons not only resembled but in some cases borrowed directly from the mechanistic tasks, processes, and principles characteristic of the expanding factory system and the attendant "culture of machines" that literary and cultural historians have begun to examine with renewed vigor in recent years.[2]

Covering a period of some 80 years, with a focus on the years 1810–1870, this chapter examines both well-established educational methods and experimental teaching practices, sifting through a material record of meter at the center and periphery of the nineteenth-century liberal curriculum. In the first volume of *Capital*, Marx emphasized the importance of attending to the concrete modes of production that determined the "mode of life" for workers in the nineteenth-century factory system. Here I want to underscore the extent to which "the material world of lived sensuous experience"[3] shaped those educated in what we can regard as the "meter manufactories" of Victorian Britain, educational establishments where the modes of producing and reproducing prosodic knowledge were as important as the prosodic subject matter itself. In fact, the thing studied and the specific processes by which it was transmitted—processes that were often directly indebted to contemporary regimes of factory organization—were, at times, inextricably connected. Though the general picture of metrical instruction in nineteenth-century British schools is one of uniformity of instruction and outcome, if we look in detail we find that there were in practice various "modes" of prosodic pedagogy, and the meters they produced—in terms of which rules or laws, say of accent or quantity, were observed or disregarded and which style of classical pronunciation was endorsed—at times differed significantly—both from one institution to the next (not all English public schools, for instance, were prosodically alike) and from one method of instruction to another. In some important respects, though, there was a notable cross-fertilization of techniques. From the texts used by pupils to the systems of individual or group tuition favored by educators, metrical instruction in the nineteenth century was characterized not only by a plurality of practice as well as principle but also by an exchange of ideas and activities across class lines and from one discrete institutional context to another.

The first part of the chapter concentrates on the importation of monitorial teaching methods, originally designed for application in towns with a growing population of factory workers. In the early decades of the century, this scheme of mass education was introduced, with mixed success, to classical schools, where its techniques were modified to accommodate the existing prosodic curriculum. The chapter then turns to more mainstream practices associated with metrical tuition in England's endowed schools, before assessing some of the responses to the perceived mechanistic operation of meter and scansion and their impact on, among other things, poetic recitation. There are notable parallels between these elite forms of prosodic instruction and the factory-derived monitorial methodology, but some of the differences and the experience of prosody they encouraged are also worth noting. From large-scale group exercises in syllabic reading to the lone scholar's Gradus-grinding, schoolboys' exposure to classical meter in nineteenth-century British schools was figuratively and, in many cases, materially characterized by burdensome and frequently alienating labor—how that labor looked (and sounded) in practice, however, has been more or less overlooked. By paying closer attention to the actual workings of the nineteenth-century meter manufactories, we can see in operation one of the nineteenth century's most formidable machines of meter.

Speech Factory

In the early decades of the nineteenth century, primary education in Britain was often a collective classroom experience. Tuition in reading, writing, and arithmetic was administered as part of a virtual factory system of education, where children learned *en masse*, their attention constantly engaged by one putatively edifying task after another. This was especially true in so-called monitorial schools, whose system of elementary education was founded on the methods of Andrew Bell (1753–1832) and Joseph Lancaster (1778–1838).[4] Monitorial schooling centered on the idea of teaching a great many pupils at once by utilizing pupils themselves in the place of paid adult teachers. With the help of these monitors, a single master could oversee the instruction of hundreds or, in theory, thousands of pupils.[5] The monitorial method was thus regarded as an economically efficient model of education conceived, as Eric Midwinter has observed, very much "in the factory mould."[6] Bell, in fact, likened his system to a "steam engine, or spinning machinery": "it diminishes labour and multiplies work."[7] Teaching was often conducted in "barnlike schoolrooms" that resembled great industrial mills, open-plan arrangements deemed as conducive to large-scale group learning as they were to factory processes such as cotton-spinning.[8] Significantly, this method of mass instruction not only called to mind the factory workspace; it also "forged links between the network of schools, official and otherwise, and the system of industrial factories."[9] Because its procedures could be adapted to suit the specific pedagogical aims of a given institution or class of learners, the monitorial system and variations on it would have an impact on the ways that not only young factory workers but also pupils at elite grammar and public schools learned. As we will see, many a nineteenth-century schoolboy's training in the rudiments of classical versification was closely affiliated with the pedagogical principles and classroom exercises that underpinned early efforts to extend elementary education to Britain's industrial classes.

At the start of the century, when no universal, state-administered education was available for the increasing numbers children in Britain's rapidly expanding network of manufacturing towns, many educators saw the monitorial system as an efficient means of preparing working-class boys and girls "for the various spheres of busy and useful life."[10] Whether it was provided directly by a mill owner, as a response to Factory Acts legislation,[11] or supported by subscription through a worthy body, such as the Society for Bettering the Condition and Increasing the Comforts of the Poor, the education made available to factory children was largely practical in nature. In his 1802 description of the monitorial arrangement for schools of industry at Kendal, "a populous manufacturing town in the county of Westmoreland," Thomas Bernard notes that children from the age of three upwards are taught skills relevant to factory work—for example, spinning and "preparing of the machinery for carding wool"—as well as the fundamentals of reading and writing.[12] As Andrew Bell would later assert, instruction in the elements of reading and writing could in fact benefit from modeling itself on the "teaching of the mechanical arts, [where] the apprentice is inured to do one thing well before he is allowed to go to another."[13] Bell's step-by-step approach to basic literacy did just that. And even though curricula in the majority of the so-called mutual instruction schools that based themselves on his or Lancaster's methods (or a combination of the two) were confined largely to the "Three Rs," the monitorial program of elementary education did manage to accommodate some of the basic elements of prosody—in the broadest sense of the term, at least. Signally, it became a mechanism by which certain language acquisition and recitation practices would be disseminated in some of Britain's grammar and public schools.

Children's pronunciation and their familiarity with "the elementary sounds" of language were central features of the monitorial system, in which both learner and language were rendered component parts of a larger educational apparatus that functioned along the "lines of factory production."[14] In a large class, Bell contended, the whole group's concentration could be productively engaged by requiring pupils to perform exercises "by rotation," one pupil after another executing in turn his allocated task (e.g., spelling or reading). Further, phonemic and syllabic elements were themselves presented as discrete, though interrelated, parts in a linguistic machine. At the heart of Bell's method was an activity that reproduced the division of labor characteristic of nineteenth-century factory production. What Marx would later term *serial manufacture*, which "requires the isolation of the various stages of production and their independence of each other," resembles a "process of decomposing language." Such an approach—sometimes called an "alphabetic" or "syllabic" method of reading—presents language as a series of "disconnected" units (letters, syllables, words) that children learn in isolation, only later attempting to synthesize them.[15] After children have mastered the letters of the alphabet and have become accustomed to reading monosyllables, they may be introduced to polysyllables—all by means of a group process that relied on a method of quasi-metrical "numeration," in which words, like numbers (or, indeed, lines of verse), are divided "into periods and half periods." As an aid to this mathematical approach, "words of more than one syllable" could be arranged in tabular form, "in columns to be read ... syllabically ... ."[16] Finally, children were taught to "resolve" whole words by combining consecutive syllabic units.

Lancaster's plan for elementary classes demonstrates his adherence to a syllabic method for teaching children to read:

1 Class - - - - - - - - - - - - - - - - - A, B, C.
2 - - - - - - - - - - - - - - - - - - - Words or syllables of two letters.
3 - - - - - - - - - - - - - - - - - - - Do. three letters.
4 - - - - - - - - - - - - - - - - - - - Do. four letters.
5 - - - - - - - - - - - - - - - - - - - Do. five letters.
6 - - - - - - - - - - - - - - - - - - - Reading or spelling lessons of two syllables, and Testament.

"The reading lessons" outlined here "gradually ris[e]" from individual letters to "words of one syllable ... till [children] come to words of five or six letters, or more ...." A similar arrangement governed the Lancasterian process of learning to write:

Class.

1 - Printing A, B, C.
2 - Writing alphabet, or words of two letters.
3 - Words of three letters.
4 - - - - - - - - Four letters.
5 - - - - - - - - Five and six letters.
6 - - - - - - - - Two syllables, &c.

To underscore the piece-by-piece nature of the process, Lancaster advises that "the words [be] thus di-vi-ded" into their component syllables.[17] In *The Madras School* (1808), Bell describes in greater detail how a similar mode of syllabic "division" underpins his scheme's tuition in reading:

> As spelling monosyllables ... consists in resolving a syllables into the letters of which it is composed, in order to reunite and combine their separate sounds into a single articulation; so syllabic reading consists in resolving disyllables and polysyllables into the respective syllables of which they are composed, to prepare for their future reunion and composition.

In the first instance the scholar pronounces and reads these syllables, one by one, as if they were monosyllables, pausing an instant between each syllable, and double that time at the end of each word. There is no other difference between his reading now and in monosyllables, than that he is taught to pause somewhat longer at the end of a word, than between the syllables of which the word is composed.

Thus—he—pro-ceeds—through—the—child's—book—part—first—and—se-cond—Mis-tress—Trim-mer's—spel-ling—book—part-se-cond—and—is—ne-ver—al-low-ed—to—pro-nounce—two-syl-la-bles—to-geth-er—till—he—can—thus—read—syl-la-ble—by—syl-la-ble—and—spell—e-ver-y—word—di-stinct-ly.[18]

The aim of such exercises, in which "[n]ot a letter, [or] a word ... can be passed over unknown," was to promote clear enunciation and "to prevent ... children from acquiring a vitiated pronunciation."[19] However, as some nineteenth-century elocutionists intimated, a method that disconnected the parts of language was likely to produce alienated speech because speakers so trained had little sense of how lexical parts came together to form a whole. Such a procedure, some argued, placed too much emphasis on the "unmeaning articulation" of syllables,[20] and as a consequence children often pronounced words robotically. Prefiguring the telegraph's evenly spaced pulses of linguistic data, monitorial pupils voiced syllabic units in a mechanistic, start-and-stop manner, pausing deliberately to signal breaks between syllables and words, and sounding one syllable after another in the same unmodulated monotone. What would later be deemed desirable as a mechanical means of communicating was, unsurprisingly, not regarded as a sound basis for "just articulation." According to Gilbert Austin's *Chironomia: Or, a Treatise on Rhetorical Delivery* (1806), words should not be deliberately divided, nor should they be "precipitated syllable over syllable."[21] As aspects of the Bell-Lancaster system, and the linguistic aspects of monitorial methodology more generally, were taken up and adapted in schools across Britain and North America, teachers and textbook authors attempted to mitigate mechanical mouthing among pupils.[22]

Presumably with advice like Austin's in mind, Daniel Adams, in his 1841 *Monitorial Reader*, encourages a distinction between "grammatical" and "rhetorical" reading. The former, more in line with the syllabic approach, "requires nothing but proper words, in grammatical order, to express it," while the latter "supposes *feeling*" and demands "modifications and inflections of the voice." A child trained in Bell's system, who "is—ne-ver—al-low-ed—to—pro-nounce—two—syl-la-bles—to-geth-er," would likely have fallen into a habit of "monotone" reading, assigning "a sameness of sound [to] successive syllables."[23] When, in 1836, the Glaswegian educationalist David Stow set out his so-called training system of education in a book of that title, he endeavored to improve on original monitorial reading practices, promoting "distinct articulation" and "sensibl[e]" pausing while avoiding the "monotonous tone" associated with Bell's building-block approach to syllabification. As a guard against "drawling or *singing*"—where the monotonous singling out of syllables establishes an inflexible, "sing-song" rhythm—Stow advises the pupil to "open his mouth well, and move his lips freely." Though "[e]very syllable ought to be fully articulated," the "formality" of such recitation "will quickly soften down into a clear enunciation" if the trainer correctly teaches the pupil to attend to the "motion and expansion of the mouth and lips."[24] As we will see, such an emphasis on syllable articulation and its relationship to "correct" pronunciation remained a central (if contested) feature of both conventional monitorial education and its offshoots. Even before Stow began overhauling aspects of Bell's serial method of reading and reciting, other educators were adapting it to suit their own classroom needs—particularly as part of the regime of liberal education, where syllable-timing and modulated pronunciation obtained to the teaching of classical versification.

Self-regulating Meters

Developed as a solution to educating the poor manufacturing classes, the Bell-Lancaster system was regarded by some as unsuited for "the higher branches of learning."[25] In *Elements of Tuition*, Bell admits that "[i]t is still ... made a question whether or not [his mutual instruction program of teaching] is applicable to schools of a higher description, and especially grammar schools. Indeed," he continues, "it is frequently alleged, that this mode of tuition will not apply to classical schools." The third and final installment of *Elements*, published in 1815, responds directly to this objection, offering an apology for his system's amenability to the teaching of classical languages, their grammars, and their prosodies. Bell goes as far as to assert that there is no inherent difficulty in the subject matter: provided one arranges "the Latin grammar [textbook] in such a shape, that with the long syllables being marked, it may be taught by a mother (or nursery maid) to her children."[26] Why, then, may not boy-monitors, under the guidance of a master steeped in classical learning and, ideally, using a textbook drafted according to Bell's plan, teach Latin grammar, the rules of quantity, and other aspects of versification to their peers? After all, the British "grammar system," according to some educationalists, was sufficiently "mechanical" in its own right, even in schools that did not rely on techniques of mutual instruction (a topic, as I will discuss in more detail below, that came under increasing scrutiny in the middle of the century). Bell's methods, therefore, might improve the efficiency of the schools' metrical machinery. If the recitation of verses from memory was deemed good for mental development, then Bell's procedures of mutual instruction—which involved a considerable element of "instruction by rote memorization," frequently coupled with group construing, scanning, and composing exercises that were seen to promote both good delivery and concentration—might further facilitate the classical schools' educational objective.[27] Many of the same classroom methods for imparting the basics of English grammar and pronunciation could be easily modified for the teaching of classical meters. In particular, a variation on the building-block syllable-approach was ideally conceived for teaching pupils "a progressive knowledge of Latin grammar" and prosody—which, for classical languages, was in principle (if not always in practice) a matter of the correct pronunciation and measurement of syllables.[28] After a child has mastered first syllables and then the elements of classical grammar,[29] he may attempt prosody. And after he has applied his understanding of quantity to the study of versification, he may synthesize these rudiments in the scansion of Latin or Greek verses, in the translation of the same, and in the composition of original meters (typically pentameters and hexameters).

In the early decades of the nineteenth century, when "the monitorial system of Bell and Lancaster was believed to be a panacea for all the difficulties of elementary education,"[30] its piece-by-piece pedagogical principles figured in hundreds of boys' formative encounters with Latin and Greek meter. One of the earliest attempts to conduct classical instruction along monitorial lines was pursued in Scotland, where the practice of Latin verse composition had fallen into desuetude. When James Pillans left his post as tutor at Eton to become, in 1810, Rector of the High School of Edinburgh, an old and prestigious grammar school, he reinstituted verse composition as part of his larger plan of monitorial instruction, on the grounds that the Bell-Lancaster method of teaching prosody catered well for "boys [who] differ[ed] widely both in acquirement and capacity." "The Latin class, consisting of 200 boys," he divided into "twenty divisions," each under a different monitor (one monitor looking after nine students). Using the step-by-step process that Bell was at the same time enshrining in his manuals, Pillans tasked his pupil-monitors with overseeing their peers' exercises in elementary grammar, syntax, and comprehension, as well as their ability to convey the "right meaning" of a given passage of Latin prose or verse. If a monitor heard a boy scan a line incorrectly or mispronounce in recitation, he would "mark [the error] on a slip of paper," keeping a record of "any false quantity"— a solecism that results when a long syllable is mistaken for a short one (or vice versa), thus leading to a corruption of a line's "correct" meter.[31] Should a boy admonished for so erring successfully contest the judgment of the monitor, by offering sufficient justification for his voicing of quantity or his segmentation of metrical feet (e.g., by referencing a rule in his grammar), he was permitted to assume the monitor's place.[32] Supporters of Pillans's methods were quick to point out that the monitorial system of teaching prosody had the benefit not only of allowing the master to teach "very nearly *twenty times* as much as could possibly have been done without some such contrivance" but also of ensuring against "the irksome, thankless, and unprofitable labour of licking into shape the unseemly productions of small plodders," whose metrical ability lagged behind that of their classmates.[33]

With its facility for keeping pupils constantly engaged, under the direct guidance of a peer monitor whose position they might themselves attain through scrupulous study, the ethos of the Bell-Lancaster system seemed perfectly devised to promote prosodical correctness and ensure classroom discipline. "Instead of a low drudgery, enforced by ignominious punishment," an anonymous writer for the *Edinburgh Review* acknowledged, "the writing of verses will be raised to its proper character ...."[34] Not everyone, however, felt that Pillans's monitorial methods encouraged the "salutary discipline" that verse composition, at its most effective, could impart to young versifiers. Comparing Edinburgh schoolboys' verse compositions, as collected by Pillans in *Ex Tetaminibus Metricis Puerorum in Schola Regia Edinensi Provectiorum Electa* (1812), with those of their contemporaries in English public schools (namely Eton), an anonymous writer for the *Quarterly Review*[35] is shocked to find an abundance of false quantities: "We have not the slightest idea of how Mr. Pillans scanned this line," the reviewer remarks, quoting not just one but several examples to illustrate his point. Moreover, he questions the very aspect of the monitorial system that the Scottish reviewer applauds: namely, its ability to allow the master to effectively police his pupils' composition exercises. Possible faults of such "Utopian schemes," the reviewer speculates, are "carelessness in the pupils" and a higher incidence of "plagiarisms" where a "due degree of vigilance is lacking," presumably because the master has delegated this responsibility to his monitors, thus "open[ing] a door for the grossest infringements of discipline."[36]

Proponents of the Bell-Lancaster approach to school versification insisted that issues of vigilance and discipline could be mitigated by making some adjustments to the system's usual administration. For instance, pupils might be made to perform exercises as a group. It was not enough to keep pupils constantly occupied under the guidance of monitors if their occupations failed to maintain each boy's concentration and, like the coordinated moving parts of a Jacquard loom, involve the full attention and choreographed participation of his peers. Further, while the monitorial schoolroom, like the industrial system of which it was a correlate, may have been imagined as an educational instantiation of the self-regulating machine—pupils learning *under their own steam* and with comparatively little instruction from a trained educational operative— there was concern about unsupervised verse manufacture. Whereas in the conventional Bell-Lancaster arrangement "the master [is] rather a governor than a teacher,"[37] monitors' responsibilities ought to be properly subordinated to the authority and pedagogical expertise of the master. So argues the education reformer Rowland Hill in his *Plans for the Government and Liberal Instruction of Boys in Large Numbers* (1822), explaining how at the Hazelwood School near Birmingham, where a variation on the monitorial method was in place, the "usual mechanism for classes" was well-adapted for ensuring the concentration and compelling the involvement of every individual in a class, however large. The process of identifying quantities and feet, as well as the segmentation of lines into their component metrical units—a mechanical "decomposition" of the verse line that served as a prerequisite to the composition of verses— could be taught effectively by using group instruction techniques:

> Each member of the class being furnished with a copy of the passage to be scanned, someone commences by attempting to scan a single verse; should

he fail, such questions are put to the class by the Teacher, as may best serve to point out wherein consists the error which has been committed, and the members of the class are requested to repeat the rules which have been violated; if no one offers to do this, the pupils are directed to consult their grammars, and he who first succeeds in discovering the rules reads them aloud. After this, someone again attempts to scan the verse which is before the class; if he fail, the process before described is repeated, and thus the class proceeds until the verse has been scanned without a mistake.[38]

Perhaps the *Quarterly Review* would have been pleased to see that in this arrangement the master leads the exercise directly, and repetitive scansion and the recitation of metrical rules—"recitation [being] the best method of infixing of Latin and Greek words in the recollections of our pupils"—are practiced collectively so that pupils can learn by the example of their peers. In fact, coordinated group instruction—what Hill imagines as "a machine working its numerous parts without hurry or confusion"—is prioritized over any single pupil's "mere perception" of "the laws of rhythmus." Properly conducted, group training, in which the pupil-monitor is not a substitute for but a supplement to the authority of the teacher, produces a well-ordered, correctly measured machine, useful for imparting the fundamentals of metrical verse and for teaching correct verse-speaking and elocution more generally.[39]

The Charterhouse Mode

Where verse-speaking and the "rhythmus" of Latin and Greek were concerned, the monitorial method of teaching meter exerted its most significant influence not at a comparatively new, experimental school, such as Hazelwood, but at one of England's well-established public schools: Charterhouse.[40] It was here, during the 1810s and 1820s, that the impact of Bell's pedagogical principles and techniques for teaching syllables and their metrical arrangement began to intersect with contemporary prosodical debates that radiated beyond the compass of schoolboy study. In 1811, when the Reverend John Russell (an Old Carthusian and Oxford graduate) took over as headmaster, he brought with him a willingness to prove Bell's assertion that "all composition ... might be materially aided by the Madras system; prose unquestionably, but verse also."[41] As Edward C. Mack posited in his 1938 history of the public schools, Russell's decision to reorganize the delivery of lessons at

Charterhouse according to Bell's principles of mutual instruction was, at least in part, a practical response to a socioeconomic reality of the industrial age: more and more of the aspirational middle classes were looking to raise their sons' educational prospects, and "[t]he moderately rich who patronized or wished to patronize Charterhouse," writes Mack, "desired more knowledge at cheaper prices. Russell could answer this demand only by drawing on the Madras system of Bell."[42] Whether Bell's system was in fact the *only* answer to an increase in demand is of course debatable, but enrollment did grow appreciably during Russell's tenure as headmaster, more than doubling "from 233 to 480 in seven years." With as few as eight adult masters under him, Russell (who did not even live on site) managed to oversee thirteen forms of boys, "taking the 120 top boys himself for part of the time, while they taught the lower forms for the rest."[43] It worked so well that, in 1815, Bell was able to endorse "the Charter House" as an example of a classical school where his system had "been adopted with good success." That same year he "attended the annual examination of the Charter House School," noting that "the three upper forms, taught as well as the rest of the school by monitors, were examined in the higher Greek and Roman Classics: and ... every member of these classes proved himself fully master of every book which he had read."[44] A few years later, Bell's friend, the educational patron Lord Kenyon, confirmed that the monitorial system at Charterhouse, particularly as regards its verse exercises, was both rigorous and stimulating for boys: "the whole of Horace's Odes, or a whole book of Homer, might be examined upon; and ... no boy in a class would be found deficient, either in repetition, being called upon [as in Bell's rotational regime] to go on after a few words were recited to him, or to render it straight forwards by memory ... ."[45]

Not only did Russell make use of boy-monitors to maintain a strict division of labor—"despotically drill[ing]" pupils and enforcing "the criminality of a false quantity" through a "system of boys set to govern boys";[46] he also promoted monitorial logic in a series of Latin and Greek grammars he compiled specially for Charterhouse. In *Elements* Bell objected to both the "ill-arranged course of studies" found in many of the existing Latin grammars (e.g., *Lily's Latin Grammar* or *The Eton Latin Grammar*) and the "imperfect and slovenly manner" of teaching that often accompanied them. Pupils were confronted "by the difficulty and intricacy of the initiatory lessons," which were often written in the language that boys are only beginning to study. Rather than guiding pupils' studies one simple step at a time (in the manner detailed above), these grammars put "obstacles ... in the way of some pupils," discouraging linguistic proficiency and frequently forcing advanced passages of Latin prose and poetry on pupils before they have mastered the simplest grammatical or metrical rules. Brief and to the point, Russell's Charterhouse grammars satisfied Bell's criteria for "a small initiatory grammar, consisting solely of ... essential and elementary accidents, which are easy of acquisition, and constitute the proper and necessary exercise of memory."[47] Arranged, for the most part, like many of their eighteenth-century counterparts, Russell's grammars were nonetheless responsive to Bell's proposed improvements, providing all explanations in English, with translations accompanying examples of Latin or Greek grammar. The 1812 edition of his *Rudiments of the Latin Language*—the oldest extant version I have located, and, at 48 pages, a comparatively economical text—begins with "THE LETTERS," before introducing pupils to "SYLLABLES" and "WORDS,"[48] echoing the syllabic approach promoted in the teaching of English grammar to the industrial classes. In his 1819 edition of the text, Russell added a final section on prosody, titled simply "Verses."[49] Further in keeping with Bell's plan, and in a departure from usual public school practice, Russell's grammars presented the fundamentals of quantity not as an auxiliary to but as the basis for correct pronunciation. "Vowels," we are told on the opening page of the 1822 edition of *Rudiments of the Latin Language*, "are sometimes pronounced LONG, and sometimes SHORT." Not only in the "Verses" section but in preceding ones as well, syllables are marked with a breve (˘) or macron (–) to designate them as short or long, respectively. With these basics in place, a monitor (if not a mother or nursery maid) could easily instruct the boys in his (or her) charge. Thus, from his first tuition in the sounds of vowels and the formation of syllables, right the way through to his engagement with the "*Rules to be observed in making a Verse*," a boy working with Russell's *Rudiments* (whether Latin or Greek) was—in theory, at least—accumulating piece-by-piece the components of quantitative classical meter.[50]

Emphasis on the serial mastery and eventual assembly of linguistic elements, a feature of Bell's methodology that harmonized with the organization of production in the factory system, had acute metrical significance in Russell's program. The progression from vowels to monosyllables and polysyllables and later to words and sentences was intended to leave the industrious child of the factory with a correct pronunciation of the English language; as we have seen, however, such training could impart to a learner just the opposite: an unwanted distinctiveness of utterance characterized by mechanical syllable-speak and monotonous mouthing. A similar procedural movement from, for example, Latin vowels and syllables to the principal feet and foot combinations was designed to lead the young classical scholar to a correct pronunciation of that language and to an appreciation of the quantity values of its meter. But this training, too, was organized so as to leave its distinctive trace in the mouths of schoolboys. Russell's reputed promotion of quantitative pronunciation, as I mentioned above, was out of step with standard public school practice, where quantitative recitation was reserved for exercises in scansion and not a usual feature of verse recitation. Thus the sing-song pronouncing of syllables, associated at other English grammar and public schools not with everyday recitation but strictly with "scanning aloud"[51]—an exercise in speaking verses deliberately so as to emphasize their metrical character (discussed at length below)—was, in a manner of speaking, part of the Charterhouse routine. Given the monitorial method of singling out syllables, one wonders if there would have been much distinction between ordinary recitation and the vocal partitioning of a line that scanning aloud entails, for in both cases a line is spoken so as to observe its quantities.

Beyond its potential for heightening the monotonous mouthing of verses found in other schools, Charterhouse Latin and Greek had another distinguishing characteristic. By the early nineteenth century, certain national standards of classical pronunciation had established themselves, with English pronunciation differing markedly from that of French, German, and Italian speakers, particularly in the voicing of vowels.[52] "[I]t would be an error to assume," as an anonymous contributor to the popular miscellany *Once a Week* would observe in 1871, "that the foreign pronunciation of Latin is uniform. To some extent," however, "this is the case, as in the pronunciation of the vowels *a*, *e*, and *i*—*a* being pronounced as *ah*, *e* as *a*, and *i* as *e*."[53] In what John Henry Howlett referred to as "the *usual* English mode of pronouncing Greek and Latin," by contrast, vowels retained their typical English sounds: the *a* in the name *Cato*, for example, is pronounced like the long *a* in *paper*; the *e* in *Philomela* like the long *e* in *meter*, etc.[54] While this English style of pronouncing Latin was in place in most public schools, Russell is purported to have trained his "scholars ... to enounce the vowels *a*, *e*, *i*, according to the continental method."[55] Because the manner in which a schoolboy pronounced classical vowels was directly related to his rendering of metrical quantities—a "short" or "long" vowel determining the duration of the syllable, and syllable grouping in turn determining metrical feet—not only would Russell's school have become associated, for better or worse, with a peculiar, foreign-sounding delivery, but also his pupils' verses would have had, when spoken, different quantitative values from those spoken by, for example, a boy from Eton, where the "usual" English pronunciation was in place.

Russell's decision to disregard conventions "almost uniformly adopted and patronized in our public schools"[56] set his young versifiers apart and placed his pedagogical regime, along with the metrical peculiarities it promoted, at the center of a curious debate in which Russell himself, one of his schoolboys, an elderly prosodian, and a precocious poet-in-the-making, among others, became, for a brief period in the 1820s, the unlikeliest of interlocutors. Frustrated by the modern (specifically English) pronunciation of the classical languages, Uvedale Price, an octogenarian landscape theorist, began compiling a treatise that mounted a "direct, undisguised, and unqualified attack on the whole and every part of our [current] system" of speaking the verse and prose of the ancients.[57] While working out his theories—which were printed in 1827, under the title *An Essay on the Modern Pronunciation of the Greek and Latin Languages*—Price entered into correspondence with the fledgling poet Elizabeth Barrett, who was only 20 years old at the time. Their epistolary dialog, carried on with some intensity in 1826 and 1827, reveals the extent to which Price's theories were developed and augmented in relation to Russell's monitorial experiment. Vaguely aware that a "new mode of pronouncing" had been "introduced at the Charter House,"[58] Price asked Barrett and her younger brother Edward, then a pupil at the school, to cast "a critical eye" over his manuscript and "let me know if you should discover any material errors in any of my positions." Further, he urged them to "contrive to send it to" Russell, having been advised that the headmaster "is a very liberal man, & one who would like to discuss a subject of this sort."[59] It transpired that Russell refused to enter into direct discussion with Price, but their *indirect* exchange (Russell outlined his thoughts in a letter to Elizabeth Barrett, who then relayed them to Price), coupled with hers and her brother's remarks on "the Charterhouse mode"[60] of metrical instruction, nonetheless shaped the manner in which Price marshaled his evidence against modern English pronunciation of the classics. Looking back at his essay and letters from the time, we can see that his theory fell in (as well as out of) line with Russell's practice and can assess from another vantage point the components in the metrical machine adopted at Charterhouse. Despite his ostensible adherence to the piece-by-piece pedagogical procedure of Bell, Russell's prosodic parts, as Price was keen to assert, did not always form a coherent, neatly intermeshing whole. Somewhere along the chain of production—from syllable and quantity to feet and meter—the monitorial machine appears to have broken down.

The reformation that Price proposes in his *Essay* is founded partly on the superiority of continental pronunciation. "No one," he writes, "can hear an Italian recite Latin verses, without being struck and pleased with the open sound of the vowels, and full tone and length given to the long syllables, the force and lightness of their trochees and dactyls, and the general harmony and charm of their utterance."[61] More significant, however, is the necessity of replacing the contemporary habit of "pronouncing [the classical languages] by *accent*" with the putatively more accurate one (insofar as the rules of ancient metrics were concerned) of pronouncing according "to *quantity*."[62] While quantity, as it had been taught for centuries in England's public and grammar schools, was undoubtedly observed in the making and marking of verses *on the page*, when it came to voicing the same verses quantity was more or less ignored. As Price puts it, "we are in all cases perfectly acquainted with quantity by the eye, yet we are in many [cases] quite unacquainted with it by the ear."[63] In large part, the problem hinged on a confusion between ancient and modern conventions of *accent*. Modern custom demanded that readers follow what was presumed to be a historical practice of accent placement, "that of laying our [English] accent, or acute, where the Romans laid their acute." But because ancient accent was *not*, at least in Price's assessment of Roman prosody, necessarily connected to quantity, as he maintains it to be in English, English speakers are bound to mangle the meter of Latin poetry by confounding the two accentual systems. The direct correlation that Price asserts between English accent and syllable duration complicated matters further. Whereas the Romans "laid [the accent] indifferently on long and short syllables," speakers of "English have no other way of indicating long and short syllables, but by placing the acute mark over the long [syllable]"—because "the essence of English accent ... is *quantity*."[64]

Consider, for example, the pyrrhic foot, a two-syllable foot in which "both syllables ... are equally short." If a reader were to follow the typical English practice, which demands that "[a]ll words ... of more than one syllable have an accent on one of them," then he or she must violate the true quantity value of a word by accenting and, therefore, lengthening one syllable or the other: "We accent the pyrrhic, like every other ancient dissyllable, on the first, and make it a trochee; on the other hand, were we to accent it on the last, it would be an iambus."[65] Thus, the word *cŏlŏr*, a pyrrhic in Latin, becomes the English trochee *cólor*. The consequence of applying modern English accentual pronunciation to lines of quantitative Latin verse was, of course, nothing less than the commission of "most offensive sins against quantity, metre, and rhythm." But if English speakers were to welcome "the restoration of true quantity,"[66] as Price urges, then they might rescue their recitations from the abomination of accentuation and avoid in the process an abundance of wholly unnecessary false quantities.

After reading Price's *Essay*, Hugh Stuart Boyd, neighbor of and classical tutor to Elizabeth Barrett, wrote a glowing endorsement to the editor of the *Classical Journal*, exclaiming that "if school-boys were obliged to read in this manner," pronouncing each syllable deliberately so as to call out its quantity value, "their knowledge of prosody would be much increased. They would be obliged to pay more attention to it," he writes, "for in many cases the master would perceive, at once, whether or not they knew the quantity of the syllables."[67] The Charterhouse prosodic program—with its European vowels and its method of "'quantitative' reading," designed expressly for "facilitating the acquisition of an accurate knowledge of the '*longs* and *shorts*'"—seemed perfectly suited to fulfill Price's prosodic wishes.[68] Unfortunately, however, the adoption of European vowel sounds did not, in itself, guarantee that pupils would have quantitatively "correct" verse-speech. The Italians' pronunciation of Latin may have been deemed more mellifluous, but it was also marred, according to Price, because "they laid their accent on the same syllables upon which we [i.e., English speakers of Latin] lay [ours]." Worse still, there appears to have been at Charterhouse a disconnect between pedagogical and prosodic theory, on the one hand, and their application, on the other—what Price terms Russell's "glaring vice" of "inconsistency." In spite of an ostensible adherence to continental vowels and quantitative pronunciation, classroom practice, as Edward Barrett suggests in his letters, did not differ greatly from that in place in other schools. Price is surprised, for example, to glean from Edward that the Charterhouse pronunciation of some Greek vowels contravenes Russell's own principles.[69]

Other changes that Russell effected in principle (e.g., his alteration in the placement of accents and the resulting changes to the way "the iambus and the pyrrhic" are pronounced) it seems he similarly failed to enforce (either himself or via monitors) in practical exercises.[70] Price summarizes the defects of the Charterhouse mode thus: more or less in keeping with standard English public school conventions, it is "throughout at variance with the rules of prosody and of common sense" and, therefore, characterized by a "great mass of false quantities."[71]

The method of serial assembly, as conceived by Bell in his treatises and codified by Russell in his grammars, appears to have differed markedly from what pupils administered to each other in repetitive group exercises.[72] In a monitorial verse factory such as Charterhouse—where the products of one phase of assembly became the raw materials in the next—even a small vocalic "inconsistency" was fed up the chain of instruction (from vowel, to syllable, to foot, to line); students learned to manufacture verses whose sounds were tuned to one set of rules while on paper their metrical arrangement obeyed another; as a consequence, the phonetic contours of vowels were repeatedly machined into finely filigreed metrical irregularities. In a letter to his sister, Edward Barrett describes a classmate's verses, which "were upon the whole so bad that [when] Russell read them loud out not one of them would scan."[73] It is, of course, possible that this boy (or Russell himself) simply confused the two verse systems that were in place at the school. After all, if verses were read in the way Edward himself suggests—that is, in the usual English way, without an attempt at pronouncing their quantities—then they would not comply with prevailing modes of scansion, where quantitative arrangement was everything. With its factory-inspired methods, Russell's Charterhouse seems to have become exactly what the system on which it was founded was designed to prevent: a mechanism specially suited not to the manufacture of correct pronunciation and fluent, error-free prosody but to the large-scale production of what "[Russell] himself avows and condemns as false quantities."[74] As we will see, it was not the only such meter manufactory in operation.

Gradus-Grinding

Concluding his *Essay*, Price stakes his "hopes of a practical reform" on an educational fantasy in which the principles of monitorial instruction are followed to their logical conclusion. If "some young men of acute and inquiring minds" could be "induced to try ... and to repeat the experiments of which I have given the result," then they might not only encourage "their schoolfellows or fellow collegiates" to adopt quantitative pronunciation but also humble their masters into following suit: "[W]hat would the grave masters of schools and the veteran tutors of colleges do, if they could not stem the torrent; and found that false quantities, even from their mouths, if not openly ridiculed, were laughed at *sous cape*? I hardly know, unless they took lessons from these juvenile Doctors ...."[75] In reality, a reform issuing from the mouths of an empowered multitude of young versifiers was unlikely to occur, however much the inherited pedagogies of Bell and Lancaster might conceivably enable it. At Charterhouse, as we have seen, promising methods did not translate into a complete revolution of the existing classical curriculum. Edward Barrett's letters evince a degree of prosodic confusion. Despite being drilled and examined almost daily by Russell,[76] he does not exhibit a convincing mastery of meter. On the one hand, he dutifully conveys to his sister rules of pronunciation lifted verbatim from *Rudiments*—"H is considered as no letter and therefore another vowel is cut off before it"—while, on the other, he demonstrates incorrect knowledge regarding the standard six-foot heroic line—"An Hexameter verse consists of *ten feet*, the four first may be either dactyls or spondees the fifth *must* be a dactyl [and] the last *must* be a spondee ...."[77] The prosodical recollections of his contemporaries—including Martin Tupper and Thackeray, the latter of whom fictionalizes Charterhouse and its headmaster in *Pendennis* (1848–50), *The Newcomes* (1855), and other stories—are no more salutary.[78]

In 1832, Russell left his position as headmaster of Charterhouse, student numbers having declined significantly. The monitorial mode of large-group instruction was itself falling out of favor among educators. Its boy tutors, critics asserted, did not receive guidance and tuition adequate to their responsibilities, and there was widespread interest in formalizing procedures for a new generation of trained teachers. From its establishment in 1846, the so-called pupil-teacher system—which became synonymous with its architect and principal proponent, James Kay-Shuttleworth—asserted its influence over a great many schoolchildren, as well as aspiring and qualified teachers. As described by Wendy Robinson in *Power to Teach: Learning through Practice* (2004), the new system had much in common with the monitorial model it supplanted:

> [The pupil-teaching] system was designed very much as a temporary expedient to meet an urgent need for trained teachers in a rapidly expanding elementary education system. A predominantly school-based apprenticeship model of initial teacher training, it bridged the age gap between leaving elementary school and entering training college. Bright, aspiring elementary pupils could learn on the job, through classroom observation and practical experience of supervised teaching, whilst at the same time receiving a certain amount of further personal instruction from the head teacher of the school. Pupil teachers were examined annually by Her Majesty's Inspectors (HMI) and their progress monitored.... Conceived in these terms, the pupil-teacher model of apprenticeship formed the backbone of teacher training and supply right through the remainder of the nineteenth century and into the early twentieth century.[79]

In villages, manufacturing towns, and cities across England, the pupil-teacher and Kay-Shuttleworth's teacher training system more generally came to represent a pedagogical regime that was every bit as mechanistic as the monitorial method had been. Like its predecessor, it prioritized memorization and rote learning. And though its curriculum was largely utilitarian, teachers were themselves subjected to basic training that ranged across a number of subjects, from the practical to the more classically liberal—everything being reduced to a mechanically reproducible series of "facts." This fact-oriented model of education, symbolized memorably by Thomas Gradgrind's school in Charles Dickens's 1854 novel *Hard Times*, is another apt correlate of the factory system. Along with "some one hundred and forty other schoolmasters," Mr. M'Choakumchild, the novel's caricature of the newly trained teacher, has been "lately turned at the same time, in the same factory, on the same principles, like so many pianoforte legs": "He had been put through an immense variety of paces, and had answered volumes of head-breaking questions. Orthography, etymology, syntax, and prosody," among a dozen other subjects, "were all at the ends of his ten chilled fingers."[80]

While M'Choakumchild may possess a certificated mastery of prosodic fact, his system (as his name suggests) is calculated to stifle, rather than encourage, speech—quantitative or otherwise. It is fitting that Dickens, himself a practiced public speaker, should mark the teacher's contribution to the opening chapters' "horse" exercise with a succession of caesuras: each question he puts to the baffled students is met with one "dismal pause" after another. Thomas Gradgrind, on the other hand, is from the first portrayed in terms suggesting well-marked accents. Like a seasoned reciter, elocutionist, or prosody tutor, he deliberately stresses points in his encomium to fact, using not only his voice but his forefinger, forehead, mouth, voice, hair, and clothes. He even employs his own distinctive form of textual notation, "emphasizing his observations by underscoring every sentence with a line on the schoolmaster's sleeve." His emphatic predilection for fact, we learn, obtains specifically to calculations, rules, measures, and "simple arithmetic." It is no coincidence that Gradgrind has "the multiplication table always in his pocket,"[81] for he is himself a kind of compendium, wherein all manner of expertly measured quantities are recorded. His surname, of course, has not only calculatory but specifically prosodic resonance: it combines "Gradus"— familiar shorthand for the *Gradus ad Parnassum*, a formidable index of classical quantities—and "grinder"—a well-known term for the tutor who used such a text to hammer (à la Saniter) the rules of classical quantity into his pupils. By the 1850s, "grinders of small boys" or "Gradus-grinders" were recognizable figures; they represented the arbitrary discipline, mechanical puzzlework, and alienating labor associated with a classical education in general and its metrical component in particular. In Thomas Gradgrind, then, Dickens satirizes not just the mechanistic and utilitarian educational imperatives of Kay-Shuttleworth's teacher training system but also, implicitly, the principal, if contested, method of teaching meter in the country's grammar and public schools.

The monitorial verse factory, in which boys learned their meters *en masse* from other boys, was, where the inculcation of quantity and classical versification was concerned, the exception rather than the rule. The most enduring image of nineteenth-century metrical instruction is not rows upon rows of pupils scanning out loud and in unison but the solitary—and usually silent—schoolboy poring over his Gradus in search of the correct quantity to complete his verse composition exercises. The Gradus itself—a formidable document of "fact and calculations," the prosodic analog to Gradgrind and his mathematical tables, as well as other temporal compendia, such as *Bradshaw's Railway Timetable*— was not, however, a nineteenth-century invention. Paul Aler's version, an early example of the text, circulated in various editions throughout the eighteenth century and into the nineteenth.[82] Written entirely in Latin, this nearly 800-page tome comprises, as its full title tells us, "new synonyms, epithets, poetic phrases, and verses," in which all syllables are marked with breves and macrons to indicate the immutable fact of their quantitative values. Later versions—for example, John Carey's

1818 revised and much-used edition of Aler's Gradus, often called simply "Carey's Gradus"; *Whittaker's Improved Edition of Valpy's Gradus ad Parnassum*, which had run to its seventh edition by 1847; and C. D. Yonge's 1850 *New Latin Gradus*, widely adopted in English public schools such as Charterhouse, Eton, Harrow, and Rugby (Fig. 1)— were moderately shorter, often omitting epithets (thought to clutter the text unnecessarily and confuse the learner) and offering only perfunctory introductions or forewords in English before providing more or less the same well-established list of Latin words with their fixed quantities designated. "The schoolboy told to write a Latin verse with the correct scansion," as Dennis Taylor explains, "would use the gradus"—typically on his own, outside the classroom—"and select those words and lines with the needed sets of shorts and longs."[83] Solitary Gradus-grinding such as this was a mainstay of the classical education, central to the public school "pedagogical 'method'" that Regenia Gagnier has outlined in *Subjectivities* (1991).[84] At the nine so-called Clarendon schools,[85] and many other endowed schools across the country, composing "by Gradus" constituted a boy's principal and undoubtedly most mechanical engagement with classical meter. Even at the height of Russell's monitorial experiment at Charterhouse, grinding of this kind had its place. Martin Tupper recalls both the "Lancastrian"

Ā, ăb, †abs. 1. *From.*—2. *By.* c. abl.——*A* te princĭpium, tĭbĭ dēsĭnet. V. E. 8. 11. Prīmā rĕpĕtens *ăb* ŏrīgĭne fāmam. V. G. 4. 286. *Sometimes inserted where it would be omitted in prose.* Ūstŭs *ăb* āssĭdŭŏ frīgŏrĕ Pŏntŭs. Ov. Tr. 3. 2. 8. *Abs* quīvīs hŏmĭne, **cum est ŏpus.** bĕnĕfĭcium accĭpĕre **gaudeas.** Ter. Ad. 2. 3. 1. (*Abs is almost wholly confined to comedy.*) SYN. 1. de.
ăbactus, a, um. part. from ăbĭgo, is, q. v. *Kept off, driven off.*——*A bacta* nūllā Veia conscientia. Hor. Ep. 5. 29.
†ăbăcus, i. masc. 1. *A sideboard, counter*, etc.—2. *A tablet for writing on.*—— 1. Ornāmentum *ăbăci*, nec non et parvŭlus infra Canthărus. Juv. 3. 204.—2. Nec qui *ăbăco* nŭmĕros et secto in pulvĕre mētas Scit rīsisse văfer. Pers. 1. 131. SYN. 2. tăbŭla, tăbella, cēra.
Ăbantĭădes, gen. æ or is. *A descendant of Abas. Used both of.* 1. *Acrīsius.*— 2. *Perseus.*——1. Solus *Ăbantĭădes* ab ŏrīgĭne crētus eādem Ācrīsius. Ov. M. 4. 607.—2. Quam sĭmŭl ad dūras rĕlīgātam brāchia cautes vīdit *Ăbantĭădes.* Ov. M. 4. 672.

Fig. 1 Extract from C. D. Yonge's *A Gradus ad Parnassum for the Use of Eton, Westminster, Winchester, Harrow, Charterhouse, and Rugby Schools, King's College London, and Marlborough College* (London: Longmans, Green, and Co., 1868), 1

system of large-group peer-instruction and the "pedantic scholarship" that each boy endured independently. "As for tuition," he laments, "it must have grown of itself by dint of *private hard grinding* with dictionaries and grammars ...."[86]

Ostensibly designed to encourage an "appreciate[ion] of beauty" and foster an awareness of the "mystery" of metrical "interplay,"[87] more frequently the Gradus was regarded as merely the necessary decoder for unscrambling and reconstituting Latin verses. The objective, of course, was to make verses that scanned according to the rules of classical quantity. As H. C. Adams notes in his 1878 history of Winchester College, "A boy cannot ... scribble down the first trash that comes into his head, paying no attention to idiom or grammar rules; he has not only to turn English words into Latin, but to arrange them into verses, which he must make scan."[88] Making verses scan was often regarded as a routine assembly process that discouraged independent, creative thought: the very definition of "mechanical."[89] In his 1921 book *Secondary Education in the Nineteenth Century*, R. L. Archer described such time-consuming, tedious, and repetitive exercises with the Gradus as the "brick-puzzle conception of the way to piece together Latin hexameters and pentameters."[90] A writer who identifies himself as "H" (probably a tutor in a private school at Richmond), complains in an 1866 letter to the editor of the *Times* about "the intolerable and brain-muddling task of hunting for several hours a day through the pages of a Gradus," just to find words with the requisite longs and shorts.[91] Indeed, the task could absorb boys' attention for hours on end. As the narrator of "Master and Pupil" remarks, "It is amazing how the time flies when you are making Latin verses. You twist and turn, and fit together and take to pieces again, and scour the Gradus up and down. It is absorbing work, if you have the knack of it any kind of degree."[92] But for the countless boys who did *not* have a "knack" for Gradus work, it was drudgery, where mechanistically resourcing a particular concatenation of quantities (which may not have been understood) was all—any semantic, aesthetic, and conceptual attributes being subordinated to a formula for metrical measurability. In E. J. May's 1850 novel *Louis's Schooldays*, a pupil who has spent "two hours at some Latin verses" is admonished by his tutor thus: "I have told you dozens of times that I do not want *ideas*—I want *feet*."[93]

As many a schoolboy knew, there was more than one way of filling up the quantity boxes with feet—whether they scanned or not. Just getting through verses as quickly as possible, whatever the prosodic outcome, was one option. As a Winchester pupil recalls, "Many of us ... would turn out thirty or forty lines of passable Latin, either in prose or verse, per hour," but it was "slipshod stuff."[94] The military historian Charles Oman, another Old Wykehamist, remembers that "quantities in scansion," among other things, "were my stumbling blocks." In spite of his Latin master's criticism—he "summed up my verse composition one day with 'these lines look decidedly Latin, but unfortunately there are two false concords, and four false quantities in twenty lines'"—Oman took a fairly devil-may-care approach to his verses: "If their syllabic length was convenient, I often utilized them—quantities or no. Latin verse composition indeed always seemed to me like a perverse jigsaw puzzle, in which one had to use words that fitted into a pattern, rather than words which rendered the proper meaning."[95]

In *Tom Brown's School Days* (1857)—a fictional narrative about Rugby School under the headmastership of Thomas Arnold, and probably the most widely read example of the popular school-novel genre—Thomas Hughes presents four ways of doing one's "vulgus," a common verse composition assignment. First, there is Tom's "traditionary method":

> He carefully produced two large vulgus-books, and began diving into them, and picking out a line here, and an ending there (tags as they were vulgarly called), till he had gotten all that he thought he could make fit. He then proceeded to patch his tags together with the help of his Gradus, producing an incongruous and feeble result of eight elegiac lines, the minimum quantity for his form, and finishing up with two highly moral lines extra, making ten in all, which he cribbed entire from one of his books, beginning "O genus humanum," and which he himself must have used a dozen times before, whenever an unfortunate or wicked hero, of whatever nation or language under the sun, was the subject.

Second, there is "the dogged or prosaic method" of verse composition, as exhibited by the character Martin, who works mechanically from English to Latin: "Martin proceeded to write down eight lines in English of the most matter-of-fact kind, the first that came into his head; and to convert these, line by line, by main force of Gradus and dictionary into Latin that would scan." Third is Arthur's "artistic method":

> He considered first what point in the character or event which was the subject could most neatly be brought out within the limits of a vulgus, trying

always to get his idea into the eight lines, but not binding himself to ten or even twelve lines if he couldn't do this. He then set to work, as much as possible without Gradus or other help, to clothe his idea in appropriate Latin or Greek, and would not be satisfied till he had polished it well up with the aptest and most poetic words and phrases he could get at.

Finally, there is the "vicarious method" preferred by "big boys of lazy or bullying habits," such as Flashman: it "consisted simply in making clever boys whom they could thrash do their whole vulgus for them, and construe it to them afterwards ...."[96] As we noticed at the chapter's outset, this method is also adopted by the big boy Newcomen in "Master and Pupil."[97]

The great majority of boys, however, did not have recourse to the Flashey-Newcomen "vicarious method," and for them Gradus-grinding was a deliberate process of manufacturing verses whose quantities, it was to be hoped, might at least turn out to be correct on the page. How they were spoken, as we have noted, was another matter entirely. Not only at Charterhouse but generally in public schools, the relationship between written scansion exercises and verse-speaking was characterized by paradox. On the one hand, because written verses did not conform to prevailing methods of classical pronunciation, which as we have seen tended to disregard quantity, what was "correct" on the page was frequently "false" in the mouth. Recalling his days at Eton, where he was a pupil from 1826 to 1833, Alexander J. Ellis, the eminent philologist and translator of Helmholtz, describes this conundrum:

> [A]s an Eton boy, I had been taught to feel a holy terror for "false quantities," yet also as an Eton boy, I had been perpetually making false quantities in common with all the Eton masters themselves. In *sīc vōs nōn vōbīs nīdificātis avēs*, it was usual, in my day, to pronounce *sīc* like English *sick*, *nōn* to rhyme with *on*, *vōbīs* with the last syllable like the first in *biscuit*, *nīdificātis* with the syllables as far as the *a* like English *nid"ifica'tion*, and *avēs* with *av* as in *aviary*, so that five false quantities were made in one short line. Of course *opus op'eris, sō'lus sŏl'itūdo*, and the like, furnished thousands of others. Since the place of the Latin accent is dependent on the quantity of the last syllable but one, in words of more than two syllables, if the accent were placed right there, the speaker was held to have made no "false quantities"; and if in his verses he followed the laws in his "gradus" which were at utter variance with the custom of his speech, he was also held to have made no "false quantities." That he did not

pronounce a single vowel correctly by intention, that he did not understand the nature of long and short vowels or syllables, or the rhythm that they made in verse (except as by "gradus" aforesaid), that he had no conception of what the nature of Latin accent was, and that Latin as he uttered it (not as he saw it) was pure *vōx et praetereā nihil*, sound without any sense at all to a Roman's ears, of this he had no conception whatever, though in his ignorance he did not hesitate to laugh at a Frenchman's or German's English, which, however poor, would be at any rate properly intended, and at least intelligible.[98]

It was not only Russell's pupils who were subjected to a confusing regime of mixed metrical messages, where theory and practice were at odds with one another.

On the other hand, Gradus-assisted exercises in scansion could positively one-dimensionalize spoken verse, encouraging a robotic, hyper-quantitative scansion-speak—not unlike the overdetermined syllabification associated with Bell's "alphabetic" mode of reading—that educators, elocutionists, linguists, and theorists of the emerging science of acoustics argued was not only unduly pedantic but actively harmful to young boys, who were being turned into verse-speaking machines. For example, Francis Newman, the Latinist and translator of *The Iliad* into ballad meters, complained in 1846 about the practice of "*read[ing] by scansion*" and "the debasing process of *learning artificial rules for right pronunciation, without the least intention of ever pronouncing aright* ...."[99] Later in the century, when phoneticians, physiologists, and psychologists were assiduously experimenting on the rhythms of speech, Edmund Gurney, author of *The Power of Sound* (1880), would also object to mechanical recitations designed to exhibit verbally, and in exaggerated form, the "ideal stress" that was graphically available in written verse compositions. "A school-boy who is just beginning the study of classical verse," states Gurney, "and who scans the lines aloud in order to get the metre into his head, will invariably read each hexameter of Homer and Virgil with six regular stresses at equal distances, the first falling on the first syllable, the sixth on the last syllable but one, of the line."[100] In the 1860s, Alexander Melville Bell, elocutionist and inventor of "visible speech," explicitly cast the scanning schoolboy as a machine:

> Like the pins in the barrel of an organ, his accents come precisely in the same place at every revolution of a sentence, striking their emphasis,

at one turn, upon a pronoun or conjunction, and, at another, impinging sonorously on an article or an expletive.... The little green twigs in the Grammar School are sedulously bent into the organ-barrel shape, and pegged to play their destined tune by the systematic teaching of the school; and when the tiny twig-barrel has swelled into a full-grown cylinder, and rolls forth its cadences in far-sounding pitch, the old pegs are still there, striking the old chords in the old way.

By training pupils in the "monstrous" practice of scanning, where lines are spoken so as to call out their metrical divisions, schools, Bell averred, are erecting "barriers of nonsense in the way of sense," turning boys into unthinking, gibberish-producing devices.[101] As we will see in the following chapter, the notion of an automaton versifier had more than just metaphorical currency.

Bricks and Egyptian Bondage

For many Victorians, Gradus-oriented classroom exercises were anathema, and pedagogical reforms were deemed urgent. Around the middle of the nineteenth century, the place of prosody in the public schools was frequently debated and zealously assaulted by some of the most eminent Victorians. As early as the 1830s, for example, John Stuart Mill had made his position clear regarding the metrical dimensions of poetry. In his essay "Thoughts on Poetry and Its Varieties" (1833), Mill channels Jeremy Bentham as much as Wordsworth when he states: "It has often been asked, What is Poetry? And many and various are the answers which have been returned. The vulgarest of all—one with which no person possessed of the faculties to which poetry addresses itself can ever have been satisfied—is that which confounds poetry with metrical composition."[102] With such a view in mind, Mill engaged in the educational reforms of the 1860s, when the public schools and their curricula were in the spotlight as a result of the Clarendon Commission. Set up to examine the educational structures, financial situations, and disciplinary procedures at nine of the country's well-established public schools—Charterhouse, Eton, Harrow, Merchant Taylors', Rugby, St. Paul's, Shrewsbury, Westminster, and Winchester—the Royal Commission did not recommend, as some had hoped it might, a sweeping abolition of the classical curriculum. Instead, it advised maintaining Latin and Greek, but not to the exclusion of other subjects:

Assuming, therefore, for the present at least, that the course of study is to run mainly—we do not say undeviatingly—in one track, we are of opinion that the classical languages and literature should continue to hold, as they now do, the principal place in public school education. We are equally convinced that they ought not to be studied solely and exclusively.

Hardly a frontal assault on the status quo, the 1864 *Report* nevertheless did criticize the "assiduous practice of repetition" and mechanical, habit-forming nature of verse composition exercises.[103] It also recommended the adoption of a standard grammar. More important, perhaps, the publication of the *Report* precipitated an educational controversy, exercising textbook authors, schoolmasters, grinders, and others affiliated with the instruction of youth on questions relating to new and existing grammars and primers, pronunciation (in many cases recapitulating debates mentioned above), and, of course, the practice of "verse-making." In 1866, following the publication of Benjamin Hall Kennedy's *Public School Latin Primer*, the *Times* newspaper became a forum for the evolving fracas,[104] and in 1867 Mill entered the fray with his *Inaugural Address Delivered to the University of St. Andrews*, where he asks, "To what purpose should the most precious years of early life be irreparably squandered in learning to write bad Latin and Greek verses?"[105] It is an interesting question, especially coming from the man who claimed to have learned Greek by the tender age of three.

Published the same year as Mill's *Inaugural Address*, Frederic William Farrar's compilation *Essays on a Liberal Education* gathers some of the more considered writing on the subject of public school reform and the classics. In the volume's opening essay, Charles Stuart Parker, a Fellow of University College, Oxford, casts the debate in terms of "natural" versus "artificial" education. The former "teaches a boy things in which ... he will be likely to take an interest in after life," while the latter is narrowly commercial or instrumental. If a liberal education is designed to deliver a rounded, "natural" education, then the question remains: is that system of education, as it is actually delivered, suited to fulfill its stated objective? On the one hand, the Gradus-grinding central to the classical curriculum appears too rigidly mechanical to provide the "full, vigorous, and harmonious" culture to which a truly liberal education aspires.[106] On the other, in spite of its patently mechanical character, the metrical component of classical education is regarded as particularly unsuited to the "artificial" training associated with a professional career. These questions had been percolating for some time. In 1830, for instance, George Long, in his "Observations on the Study of the Latin and Greek Languages," stated flatly that "[a] knowledge of these languages would be of no use to persons employed in laborious bodily occupations and in many mechanical arts ...."[107] Parker follows up this line of thinking, considering arguments for the supposed relevance of the classics to careers in the church, law, and medicine. While he identifies certain reasons why Latin and Greek may be more or less beneficial to persons pursuing such occupations, there is little to suggest that verse manufacture of the kind discussed above constitutes an appreciable advancement of "useful" learning.

Just as proponents of monitorial instruction had drawn on factory logic and procedures in the orchestration of their metrical curricula, so did opponents of public school prosody turn to the industrial workplace to formulate their critique. Farrar's own contribution to the volume he edited, "Of Greek and Latin Verse-Composition as a General Branch of Education," is unequivocal in its conclusion: "I will say at once that the reform which will here be advocated is the immediate and total abandonment of Greek and Latin verse-writing as a *necessary or general* element in liberal education, and the large diminution of the extravagant estimation in which this accomplishment as hitherto been held." His rejection of public school prosody is founded on many of the complaints we have encountered already: it occupies too much space in the syllabus, squeezing other subjects to the margins (or excluding them altogether); it "degrade[s] education into a mere discipline," rather than a process of nurturing moral, responsible young men; and it inflates the importance of grammatical and metrical conventions, establishing them as proxies for gentlemanly character and upper-class affiliation. Related to these drawbacks is the enervating and "absurd" effect of this "system of education" on the minds of youth.[108] At the heart of Farrar's essay is an extended conceit that the author employs to hammer home the harmful nature of the contemporary metrical regime and the debasing manner in which masters and grinders impose it upon boys. Drawing on the vocabulary of political economy and contemporaneous critiques of industrial labor as organized in the factory system, Farrar casts the public school as a prison-like mill that discourages what John Ruskin, only a few years later, would describe as the "thoughtful labour of true education";[109] in its place, such a system promotes a "long and laborious" form of indentured servitude—or, worse still, a counterpart to estranging wage-labor as conducted in the "cash nexus," which Marx theorized that same year in the first volume of *Capital*. Where Ruskin would decry the dangers of "the increasing mechanization of labor, and the way in which, in the new industrial economics, the worker was becoming indistinguishable from a machine,"[110] Farrar condemns a "miserable drudgery" that is "worse than Egyptian bondage." By "sending its sons to Public Schools," the "English nation" is "dooming them to seven or eight years of this weary mill-wheel" of verse composition, where "mechanical" teaching produces "mechanical" pupils. Faced, for example, with the task of writing a line such as "Where *something* Acheron rolls *something* waters," the schoolboy's

> one object is to get in the "something" which shall be of the right shape [i.e., quantity] to screw into the line. The epithet may be ludicrous, it may be grotesque; but provided he can make his brick, he does not trouble himself about the quality of the straw, and it matters nothing to him if it be a brick such as could not by any possibility be used in any human building.

Even if he performs his routinized task correctly (we have seen the confusion among experts, not to mention schoolboys, about what distinguished a "correct" line of verse from a "false" one), he is producing a material for which there is no market. Thus, the public school verse factory-*cum*-prison, with its pointless work, "alienate[s]" the otherwise "robust minds" of youth. One cannot but hear echoes of Factory Act legislation—which established limitations on the number of hours children could be employed in factories—behind Farrar's plea to "emancipate English boys from [the] yoke" of "compulsory verse-making," or at least find a means of "curtail[ing] ... the hours at present squandered on Latin and Greek verse."[111]

A Working-Class Eton?

Farrar's critique of the public school verse "economy" found several backers—among both apologists for liberal education, who dreamed of a more intellectually stimulating classroom, and utilitarians, who were clamoring to dismantle its outdated apparatus. T. H. Key, headmaster of University College School, actually went as far as to drop verses from his school's curriculum.¹¹² But Farrar's attack on mechanical metrical instruction also encouraged ire in the same camps. One of the more curious ripostes to *Essays on a Liberal Education* came from the Reverend Stephen Hawtrey, who was determined not only to make a case for verse-making as part of a liberal education that did *not* replicate the mechanistic systems of the factory but also to contemplate extending the prosodical franchise in an experimental school he envisaged as a "working-class Eton."¹¹³ In his pointedly titled *A Narrative Essay on a Liberal Education, Chiefly Embodied in the Account of an Attempt to Give a Liberal Education to Children of the Working Classes* (1868), Hawtrey outlines his attempt to effect what amounts to the converse of the monitorial system as depicted earlier in this chapter. Whereas the Bell-Lancaster method had been conceived with the factory in mind and then adapted for the teaching of meter to boys in elite institutions, St Mark's School, founded by Hawtrey at Windsor in 1847, adapted the best features of a public school liberal education for the cultivation of those directly involved in "the arts and manufactures of the country." While Hawtrey is "flatter[ed]" by a school inspector's observation that the institution "reminded him of nothing so much as of a paper mill" that turns "rags" into "clean white paper," he is nonetheless adamant that his system conceives of boys as "moral agents, not as so many parts of a great educational mill which is to be kept in good working order." Though his pupils go "but a little way… in Latin," Hawtrey speculates that verse composition and exercises in scansion could be so taught as to fulfill his school's objectives. Unlike Farrar and other gainsayers of classroom metrics, Hawtrey imagines that prosody could very well function as a promoter of "general mental acumen": "Are we quite sure that the Remove and Fourth-form boy is not deriving intellectual profit from that 'worry and torture of the brain' which makes him knit his brow, bite his pen, and turn from Gradus to Dictionary and back again from Dictionary to Gradus?" Moreover, he objects to one of the frequently suggested alternatives to verse exercises, tuition in practical subjects:

> Suppose them [schoolboys] freed from verse-making, … and allowed, instead, to learn about the electric telegraph, the lightning conductor, the electric light, the Davy Safety Lamp, chloroform, and vaccination … would there not be a great danger of the boys becoming less vigorous-minded than they are?

Even the mechanics his school has been set up to teach, who are not "exceptional" but "whose weak or dormant faculties we have called out" with careful study, could conceivably benefit more from the mechanics of prosody than other, more directly mechanical and putatively useful varieties of instruction.[114]

As we will see, Hawtrey was not alone in his thoughts about what we might call widening prosodic participation. Only 2 years before he established St Mark's School, another plan to bring the mechanics of meter to "the million" captured the public imagination and broadened debated about verse composition. That is the subject of "Automaton Versifiers." Looking further ahead—beyond the immediate radius of the meter manufactories, across the second half of the nineteenth century and into the early decades of the twentieth—we can glimpse in outline many of the issues that this chapter has examined: questions about the use-value of versification, about the appropriateness of exposing it to the youth of different classes, about sing-song syllabic recitation, about the boundary between the human versifier and the speaking or writing machine. These and related matters of meter will resurface, in other contexts and in relation to other manifestations of the period's machine culture, in the analyses below.

NOTES

1. See [Anon.], "Master and Pupil," *All the Year Round* (Aug. 2, 1890), 117–120; (Aug. 9, 1890), 141–144; (Aug. 16, 1890), 164–168; and (Aug. 23, 1890), 185–192. As this is a chapter almost entirely about school*boys*' exposure to "verses in the process of manufacture," it is only fitting that I should point out the prosodic proficiency of Janet Jerome, the unofficial "pupil" of the story. Her curious place as an expert outsider in an otherwise exclusive world of men and meters can be compared with the case of a real-life young woman discussed below in "The Charterhouse Mode" section.
2. The phrase "culture of machines" is taken from Erin O'Connor, *Raw Material: Producing Pathology in Victorian Culture* (Durham, NC: Duke University Press, 2000), 201. Ketabgian and Sussman discuss similar conjunctions of mechanics and culture. See Tamara Siroone Ketbagian, *The Lives of Machines: The Industrial Imaginary in Victorian Literature and Culture* (Ann Arbor, MI: University of Michigan

Press, 2011); and Herbert Sussman, *Victorian Technology: Invention, Innovation, and the Rise of the Machine* (Santa Barbara, CA: Praeger, 2009).
3. Tim Dant, *Materiality and Society* (Maidenhead: Open University Press, 2005), 14.
4. Bell and Lancaster in fact developed their respective educational models independently and disagreed on several points. In practice, their methods often mingled, and many contemporary sources refer simply to the "Bell-Lancaster system," a composite pedagogical model that drew on aspects of both men's writing. See, for example, Eric Midwinter, *Nineteenth-Century Education* (Harlow: Longman, 1970), 28–29.
5. The following contemporary extracts describe Lancaster's flagship school in Borough Road, Southwark: "It was necessary to devise plans of economy in order to teach the greatest number at the smallest expense— this he [Joseph Lancaster] effected by a judicious system of Monitors, by making one book serve for a whole school however large, and by causing the Children to write upon slates, together with other ingenious contrivances, by which means *one* Master may teach 500 or 1000 Scholars in one Schoolroom, and in a large School the yearly expense for each child is only from 5 to 6 shillings." "During the years 1809, 1810 & 1811 the [Lancasterian] plan spread through the Country— towards the close of 1811 a rival Institution was set up at the head of which Dr Bell, who had introduced some improvements in a school at Madras, was placed." [Anon.], Account of starting schools, Joseph Lancaster Papers, J.T. 317, 1, 3, Library of the Religious Society of Friends.
6. Midwinter, *Nineteenth-Century Education*, 26. As the social reformer Thomas Bernard remarked in 1796, "The principle in schools and manufactories is the same." Bernard is cited in Peter Gordon and Denis Lawton, *A History of Western Educational Ideas* (Oxford: Routledge, 2002), 117.
7. Andrew Bell, *The Madras School, or Elements of Tuition: Comprising an Analysis of an Experiment in Education Made at the Male Asylum, Madras; with Its Facts, Proofs, and Illustrations* (London, 1808), 36. Not only did Bell's school resemble aspects of the factory system that it was intended to benefit; it also promised to ameliorate the damaging effects of machine culture. As Bell observes, "In *prison-houses*, work-houses, and in manufactories, as well as in school-rooms, it [the Bell system] has already ... begun to operate with considerable effect. And, it seems, as if providentially occurring, at this time, to counteract

the growing evils of a recent date, arising from the material machinery for the multiplication of power and division of labour in manufacturing and commercial world, to which it bears so striking a resemblance in its mighty operations, in the multiplication of power and division of labour in the intellectual and moral world." See Andrew Bell, *The Wrongs of Children; Or, a Practical Vindication of Children from the Injustice Done Them in Early Nurture and Education; Addressed to Parents, Tutors, Guardians, and Masters; and to Legislators and Governors; Setting forth the Source of Much Human Misery, and Pointing Out the Remedy* (London, 1819), 13. N.B. I have modernized Bell's spelling, replacing his long s (f) with the modern standard short s.

8. Elizabeth Gargano, *Reading Victorian Schoolrooms: Childhood and Education in Nineteenth-Century Fiction* (New York: Routledge, 2008), 14; see also Nanette Whitbread, *The Evolution of Nursery-Infant School: A History of Infant and Nursery Education in Britain, 1800–1970* (London: Routledge and Kegan Paul, 1972), 6. As Whitbread explains, "In one large schoolroom hundreds of children of various ages and standards of attainment were taught with only one master in charge, as child monitors taught ten to twenty children each. These monitors were the older children of nine or above, and only they were taught by the master. Children sat in serried rows on wooden benches, learning by heart what their monitors taught them. This was the factory system of mass production applied to instruction."

9. John G. Richardson and Justin J. W. Powell, *Comparing Special Education: Origins to Contemporary Paradoxes* (Stanford: Stanford University Press, 2011), 298 n7.

10. Universal, state-provided elementary education did not arrive until 1870 with the Forster Education Act. As David Wardle notes, "Given the fact that a state system was out of the question in the early nineteenth century, cheapness was bound to be of the utmost importance in elementary schooling, and one has to look no further for the reason for the enthusiastic welcome given to the monitorial school. Of course it had other attractions. The division of labour and the mechanical organization appealed to businessmen and industrialists who saw in it the factory system applied to education." See David Wardle, *English Popular Education, 1780–1975* (Cambridge: Cambridge University Press, 1976), 18. Bell's ideas about "mutual instruction" had grown out of his work at an orphan asylum in India, and Lancaster's experiments in large-group teaching with monitors had been conducted first at his free school for the "industrious classes" in London. See Bell, *The Madras School*; and Joseph Lancaster, *Improvements in Education, as It Respects*

the *Industrious Classes of the Community: Containing a Short Account of Its Present State, Hints towards Its Improvement, and a Detail of Some Practical Experiments Conducive to that End*, 2nd edn (London, 1803).

11. The Factories Act of 1802, for example, made nine the minimum age that a child could be employed in a factory and insisted that factories provide rudimentary education for children under nine.
12. Thomas Bernard, "Extract from an Account of the Schools of Industry at Kendal," *The Reports of the Society for Bettering the Condition and Increasing the Comforts of the Poor*, vol. 3 (London, 1802), 249–250.
13. Andrew Bell, *Elements of Tuition, Part III. Ludus Literarius: The Classical and Grammer School; Or, An Exposition of an Experiment in Education, Made at Madras in the Years 1789–1796: With a View to Its Introduction into Schools for the Higher Orders of Children, and with Particular Suggestions for Its Application to a Grammar School* (London, 1815), 371.
14. David Vincent, *Literacy and Popular Culture: England 1750–1914* (Cambridge: Cambridge University Press, 1989), 77.
15. Karl Marx, *Capital*, vol. 1 (London: Penguin, 1990), 463. See Vincent, *Literacy and Popular Culture*, 76–77. As Vincent notes, this method draws considerably on "[l]ong-established techniques" that had been handed down through the primers of the seventeenth and eighteenth centuries.
16. Bell, *Elements of Tuition, Part III. Ludus Literarius*, 196. The tabular method of learning syllables was in fact based on an element of Bell's procedure for mathematical instruction, his "lessons in forming the digits, and exhibiting the progression of numbers by unity." See, for example, Andrew Bell, *Mutual Instruction and Moral Discipline; Or, Manual of Instructions for Conducting Schools through the Agency of the Scholars Themselves*, 7th edn (London, 1823), 113.
17. Joseph Lancaster, *The British System of Education: Being a Complete Epitome of the Improvements and Inventions Practised at the Royal Free Schools, Borough-Road, Southwark* (London, 1810), 3, 13, 4, 13.
18. Bell, *The Madras School*, 64–65. It is possible that "Mistress Trimmer's spelling book" is either *The Little Spelling Book for Young Children*, second edition published in 1786, or *The Charity Spelling Book*, published in 1798. The latter is the more likely source: it is divided into two parts, the second of which (as Bell mentions) "Contain[s] Words Divided into Syllables, Lessons with Scripture Names, &c." The first part "Contain[s] the Alphabet, Spelling Lessons, and Short Stories of Good and Bad Boys." Both texts, which ran to several editions and remained in use in the early years of the nineteenth century, are by Sarah Trimmer (1741–1810), author of children's books on many subjects.

19. Bell, *Elements of Tuition, Part III. Ludus Literarius*, 157, 215.
20. William Russell, *Orthophony; Or, the Cultivation of the Voice, in Elocution: A Manual of Elementary Exercises, Adapted to Dr. Rush's "Philosophy of the Human Voice," and the System of Vocal Culture Introduced by Mr. James E. Murdoch*, 5th edn (Boston: William D. Ticknor and Company, 1848), 219.
21. Gilbert Austin, *Chironomia; or, a Treatise on Rhetorical Delivery* (London, 1806), 38.
22. John Ruskin was among the Victorians who considered seriously the pros and cons of syllabic reading. His early tuition in reading took place at home—possibly along the lines of the "the *method maternelle*" (see note 26 below)—and according to a very different scheme from the one associated with monitorial instruction. Ruskin states in *Fors Clavigera* that he "absolutely declined to learn to read by syllables" and instead "learn[ed] words in their collective aspect," recalling that he "would get an entire sentence by heart with great facility, and point with accuracy to every word in the page as I repeated it." Not altogether impressed by his own experience, however, he admits that he "might consent, in the process of years, to adopt the popular system of syllabic study," particularly in relation to the schools affiliated with the Guild of St. George, which he founded in 1871. It is interesting to see him considering for this quasi-medieval project (an attempt to roll back the industrial clock to an ostensibly simpler time) methods so closely associated with the factory system. Also worth noting is the role that the "measure" of syllables plays in the metrical theory he outlined in a short text designed with this project in mind, though he does not explicitly reference syllabic reading/writing in this book. See John Ruskin, "Humble Bees," *Fors Clavigera*, vol. 3 (London: George Allen, 1896), 42; and *Elements of English Prosody for Use in St George's Schools* (Orpington: George Allen, 1880).
23. Daniel Adams, *The Monitorial Reader, Designed for the Use of Academies and Schools* (Concord, NH: Roby, Kimball, and Merrill, 1841), no page.
24. Adapting the Bell-Lancaster model of group instruction, Stow emphasizes what he terms a "simultaneous gallery method," whereby children are arranged in tiered rows and time-saving exercises involve every child at once: "whatever one reads, all read; and each and all may in less time read audibly." See David Stow, *The Training System of Education, for the Moral and Intellectual Elevation of Youth, Especially in Large Towns and Manufacturing Villages*, 7th edn (Glasgow: Blackie and Son, 1846), 135, 136, 134, 137, 129, 137. Lancaster's own mechanism for discouraging sing-song reading was founded on humiliation: "When a boy gets into a singing tone in reading, the best cure that I have hitherto found

effectual, is by force of ridicule.—Decorate the offender with matches, ballads, &c. and, in this garb, send him round the school, with some boys before him, crying 'matches,' &c. exactly imitating the dismal tones with which such things are hawked about the streets in London, as will readily occur to the reader's memory." See Lancaster, *The British System of Education*, 36.

25. Cited in John Griscom, *Monitorial Instruction: An Address, Pronounced at the Opening of the New-York High-School, with Notes and Illustrations* (New York, 1825), 114.
26. Bell, *Elements of Tuition, Part III. Ludus Literarius*, 247, xix. This assertion is worth considering in light of Friedrich Kittler's analysis of literacy and "maternal instruction" at the start of the nineteenth century. See Friedrich A. Kittler, *Discourse Networks 1800/1900*, trans. Michael Metteer (Stanford: Stanford University Press, 1990), 25–69. For the relationship between "the *method maternelle*" and classical curriculum as it was being critiqued in the nineteenth century, see Charles Stuart Parker, "On the History of Classical Education," *Essays on a Liberal Education*, ed. F. W. Farrar (London: Macmillan and Co., 1867), 56–57.
27. "The memory," as H. C. Adams writes, "is a machine." See Adams, *Wykehamica: A History of Winchester College and Commoners, from the Foundation to the Present Day* (Oxford and London: James Parker and Co., 1878), 357. Thomas William Heyck, "Educational," *A Companion to Victorian Literature and Culture*, ed. Herbert F. Tucker (Malden, MA: Blackwell, 1999), 206. For Bell, there was a direct correlation between "improvements" in mechanics and manufacture, on the one hand, and classical learning, on the other: "If after the discovery of the properties of steam, and the invention and improvement of the steam engine, and the various contrivances for the multiplication of power, and division of labour, to which late years have given birth, the commercial and manufacturing classes had not availed themselves of these invaluable inventions, what would now be the state of this kingdom, and its rank, compared with other nations? And if our learned men do not avail themselves of the improvements, which have been suggested [by Bell's method] to the use of Lilye's Grammar, as well as to the other branches of the scholastic art ..., what will be the relative attainments, and powers of our future statesmen, orators, and citizens, compared with those of such nations, as, not having the same obstacles, from established institutions, shall avail themselves of the obvious, manifold, and interesting benefits, which are now presented to general acceptance, without patent and without cost?" See Bell, *Elements of Tuition, Part III. Ludus Literarius*, 441–442.
28. Bell, *Elements of Tuition, Part III. Ludus Literarius*, 256, 267.

29. Bell's plan for a classical school did not differ so much in the order in which pupils learned: first came accidence (declining nouns and conjugating verbs), then vocabulary, and finally syntax (which involves some construing, translating, and parsing). But he objected to the way existing grammars too often ask a pupil to anticipate lessons that they will not be taught in detail until much later in the program. Also, he disagreed with the practice of giving early instructions in Latin, which pupils, at the outset of their studies, were unable to comprehend. Like the authors of most grammars in circulation in the eighteenth and nineteenth centuries, Bell places prosody at the end of the pupil's studies. The "rules of prosody," notes Bell, "will fall to be taught in the last place, before the scholar quits his grammar books; unless the master should prefer postponing them, till the scholar is going to read a Latin poet." See Bell, *Elements of Tuition, Part III. Ludus Literarius*, 339–418.

30. R. L. Archer, *Secondary Education in the Nineteenth Century* (London: Cass, 1921), 67.

31. So serious was a false quantity, that a boy who introduced one was often subjected to corporal punishment. Here is an observation contemporary with the development of the monitorial system: "To write a false quantity is a fault: to read a quantity false is also a fault. The former is a fault in the memory; the latter, if in verse, betrays a want of ear, that is, of good breeding. A boy may deserve a flogging, for making a false quantity in writing, because it may originate in carelessness; but surely a carelessness in reading is equally culpable. A compromise therefore seems highly desirable, to which the boys at least cannot object: and this is to lay it down as a rule of the school, that, if the master flogs the boys for making a false quantity in writing, the boys shall flog the master, if he makes false quantities in reading their Latin verses." [Anon.], "Answers to the Historical and Philosophical Questions," *Universal Magazine*, 4 (1805), 427. It is worth remembering that flogging (as Swinburne and many other Victorians have noted) continued throughout the nineteenth century. As I mention below, proponents of the monitorial system argued that mutual instruction could in fact mitigate the need for such punitive measures. Students were encouraged to listen to and correct each other, and the monitor, acting on the master's authority, was often responsible for addressing metrical, as well as general disciplinary, lapses. The subject of false quantities continued to provoke heated debate across the nineteenth century. See, for example, F. W. Farrar, "Of Greek and Latin Verse-Composition as a General Branch of Education," in *Essays on a Liberal Education*, 221–222.

32. [Anon.], "Memoir of James Pillans, Esq. F.R.S.E., &c. &c., Professor of Humanity in the University of Edinburgh," *Imperial Magazine*, 11 (Feb. 1829), 99, 100.
33. [Anon.], "Musæ Edinenses," *Edinburgh Review*, 20, 40 (1812), 395.
34. [Anon.], "Musæ Edinenses," 394, 395; see also Walter Scott Dalgleish, *Memorials of the High School of Edinburgh Containing a Historical Sketch with Portraits of the Present Rector and Four of the Classical Masters and Biographical Notices* (Edinburgh: Maclachlan and Stewart, 1857), 27.
35. One surmises that the author of this review is motivated as much by a willingness to represent Scottish classical education unfavorably in comparison with its English counterpart as by a desire to address the technicalities of meter.
36. [Anon.], rev. of *Ex Tentaminibus Metricis Puerorum*, by James Pillans. *Quarterly Review* (Dec. 1812), 401, 404, 395, 401.
37. Rowland Hill, *Plans for the Government and Liberal Instruction of Boys in Large Numbers; Drawn from Experience* (London: G. and W. B. Whittaker, 1822), 124. The schoolmaster's role, according to Andrew Bell, "is to direct and conduct the system in all its ramifications, and to see all the subordinate offices carried into effect." Bell, *Elements of Tuition, Part III. Ludus Literarius*, 87.
38. Hill, *Plans for the Government and Liberal Instruction of Boys in Large Numbers*, 42–43.
39. Hill, *Plans for the Government and Liberal Instruction of Boys in Large Numbers*, 170. "Frequent opportunities for exercises in the open air with companion of his own age,—a system which regulates his actions without harshly coercing them,—the spectacle of a machine working its numerous parts without hurry or confusion;—these appear to us to be circumstances more than commonly favourable for placing the pupil in a state of body and mind to receive the lessons of the master with profit…. [T]he pupil is constantly witnessing the measured movements of others, and is trying to act in concert with them. To learn to march he finds indispensable to his comfort. The motive to exertion thus obtained, his daily practice, and the effect of example, soon overcome any natural inaptitude for making the acquisitions [of rhythm and measured movements in time]." Hill's description of the students working together like the coordinated parts of machine under the careful guidance of master echoes the definition of a machine, as given by Charles Babbage, inventor of the Analytical and Difference Engines: "The union of all these tools, actuated by one moving power, constitutes a machine." See Charles Babbage, *On the Economy of Machinery and Manufactures*, 3rd edn (London: Charles Knight, 1833), 174.

40. Charterhouse was founded in London in 1611. It is worth noting the distinction between the Lancaster-Bell monitorial system and a pre-existing system of pupil governance, also called "monitorial," that was in place in English public schools. While the former is an educational experiment developed at the close of the eighteenth century and only in succeeding years applied to classical education, the latter is a long-standing tradition of peer-discipline (also known as the "prefect" or "præpostor" system) that existed, in various forms and under different names, in many of the public schools. Thus, when the 1864 report of the Clarendon Commission observes that "Winchester [College] undoubtedly produced the earliest type of what is called the monitorial system," it is referring to this arrangement and not to the Lancaster-Bell method of large-group mutual instruction—though a degree of peer-instruction obtained in this pre-existing system. As Howard Staunton notes: "The monitorial system, which exists in full vigour at Winchester, may be traced to the statutes framed by [the school's founder] William Wykeham himself. 'In each of the lower chambers let there be at least three Scholars of good character, more advanced than the rest in age, discretion, and knowledge, who may superintend their chamber-fellows in their studies ....'" In fact, in schools such as Charterhouse, Bell's monitorial pedagogy mingled with aspects of the prefect monitorial system, and in some of the other schools (e.g., Rugby), though to a lesser degree, elements of the two systems (including the much-debated institution of "fagging") co-existed. See *Report of Her Majesty's Commissioners Appointed to Inquire into the Revenues and Management of Certain Colleges and Schools, and the Studies Pursued and Instruction Given Therein; with an Appendix of Evidence*, vol. 1 (London, 1864), 152; Howard Staunton, *The Great Schools of England: An Account of the Foundation, Endowments, and Discipline of the Chief Seminaries of Learning in England* (London: Sampson, Low, Son, and Marston, 1865), 92–93; and [Anon.], *The Public Schools* (Edinburgh and London: William Blackwood and Sons, 1867), 302–303.
41. Cited in Charles Cuthbert Southey, *The Life of the Rev. Andrew Bell*, vol. 3 (London: John Murray, 1844), 282.
42. Edward C. Mack, *Public Schools and British Opinion, 1780–1860* (London: Methuen, 1938), 225; see also Stephen Porter, *The London Charterhouse* (Stroud: Amberley, 2009), 92–94. Christopher Stray points out how the aspirational nineteenth-century "bourgeois parent," who was "torn between the quest for profit and the search for status," might find in public schools, where classical texts were at the "curricular core" and formed part of the regime's means of fostering "mental discipline," a way "to transform their profits into their sons' status,

and economic capital into cultural capital, by sending their offspring to public schools." See Stray, *Classics Transformed: Schools, Universities, and Society in England, 1830–1960* (Oxford: Clarendon Press, 1998), 21–22, 35, 32.

43. Archer, *Secondary Education in the Nineteenth Century*, 67; see also W. H. G. Armytage, *Four Hundred Years of English Education*, 2nd edn (London: Cambridge University Press, 1970), 91. In a later history of the school, William Haig Brown (headmaster from 1863 to 1897), remarks on Russell's adoption of Bell's Madras methods: "A few years after his [Russell's] election [to the position of headmaster] he introduced into the School the plan of teaching devised by Dr. Bell, and known as the Madras system, which as in great vogue in England during the early part of the century. For some time the popular acceptation of the system, and still more the personal vigour and ability of Dr. Russell, and his 'indefatigable and excellent teaching' gave such a measure of success to the change introduced by him, that the School grew rapidly in numbers. In 1825 it had reached the unprecedented total of 480. According to the plan of Dr. Bell the work of the Master consisted mainly in supervision, and a great portion of the teaching devolved upon the boys themselves. These childish pedagogues were called 'præpositi,' and it may be supposed that they were not always equal to the task imposed upon them. 'There was,' says Dr. Saunders, 'a præpositus of one form, who, being a little mite but a very clever scholar, was put by Dr. Russell at the head of his class, but he said it was torture to him above everything. Dr. Russell would call out, "Fifth form, where is your præpositus?" "Please, Sir, here he is," and they would hold him up by the neck.' The popularity of this system was necessarily short-lived; not even the power of Dr. Russell could avail to make it efficient or durable." See William Haig Brown, *Charterhouse Past and Present* (Godalming: H. Stedman, 1879), 149–150.
44. Bell, *Elements of Tuition, Part III. Ludus Literarius*, xxi, 249.
45. Cited in Southey, *The Life of The Rev. Andrew Bell*, 283.
46. This is how Martin Tupper, a pupil at Charterhouse between 1821 and 1826, recalls his time at the school. He did not appreciate the monitorial method or the "passive servility and pedantic scholarship" it promoted. "I think the system was called Lancastrian," he remarks, asserting that he found the "efforts of memory" and prosodic exercises in particular "almost useless in afterlife." See Martin Farquhar Tupper, *My Life as an Author* (London: Sampson, Low, Marston, Searle, and Rivington, 1886), 14–17.
47. Bell, *Elements of Tuition, Part III. Ludus Literarius*, 257–259, 293. Often Russell's Latin grammar is bound together with his *Rudiments*

of the Greek Language. For the Use of Charterhouse School, which is similarly arranged. (The first copies I consulted were from 1822 and 1825, respectively, and belonged to Isaac Atkinson, a pupil at Charterhouse from 1823 to 1826.) Not everyone considered the abridged nature of Russell's grammar to be an improvement. One reviewer is sceptical of the "mere skeleton and outline," which is "to be filled up by that oral instruction" central to monitorial learning. See [Anon.], review of Russell, *Rudiments of the Latin Language. For the Use of Charterhouse School, British Critic, and Quarterly Theological Review* (Oct. 1840), 327. Two years earlier, however, Walter Powell, an Old Carthusian and master of the Free-Grammar School of Queen Mary in Clitheroe, had used Russell's grammar as a model for his own, remarking that it "will be used with the greatest advantage, if ... the pupils are required to spell out aloud, and *write on slates as they are spelling* ...; and it is quite astonishing to perceive the readiness and accuracy of the very youngest boys, attained by corrections among themselves .... I would not, however, wish to be understood as desiring to arrogate to myself any merit from this plan, which I have pursued constantly for the last 8 years; since I feel bound to acknowledge having derived much benefit from it, while a boy at Charter-House under the Rev. Dr. Russell." Powell also recommends those choosing to adopt his text to employ large-group teaching in the monitorial fashion: "the larger he can form his class, the better." See Walter P. Powell, *A Simplified Latin Grammar* (London: John Murray, 1838), xiii, xvi (emphasis original).

48. [John Russell], *Rudiments of the Latin Language, with Short Vocabularies. For the Use of Charterhouse School* (London, 1812), 3.
49. All subsequent editions of Russell's *Rudiments* conclude with a short section on "verses." In the 1866 edition, brought out by William Allan and Co. of London 3 years after Russell's death, this section has been retitled "Prosody."
50. [John Russell], *Rudiments of the Latin Language. For the Use of Charterhouse School* (London, 1822), 11, 136 (emphasis original). In a letter to Uvedale Price, Elizabeth Barrett conveys Russell's determination "as a teacher" to adopt "the best mode of communicating a knowledge of the Quantity at the same time with the word itself." See EBB to Uvedale Price, 30 Dec. 1826, *The Brownings' Correspondence*, vol. 1, ed. Philip Kelley and Ronald Hudson (Winfield, KS: Wedgestone Press, 1984), 278. Russell's decision to unite instruction in quantity and basic language acquisition—whereby the boy learned to pronounce Latin with its quantity values in mind—was out of line with standard public-school practice. For centuries, as Derek Attridge has shown, pronunciation and quantity were taught separately, and the rules of

the latter did not shape the former. Only after boys had been taught to pronounce Latin, typically "in accordance with English speech-habits," would they be introduced to the rules of quantity, by which verses might be scanned (if not necessarily pronounced). See Derek Attridge, *Well-Weighed Syllables: Elizabethan Verse in Classical Metres* (Cambridge: Cambridge University Press, 1974), 67. In his 1826 edition of *The Eton Latin Grammar*, T. W. C. Edwards would recommend a similar attention to quantity, which might help to ameliorate the "very vitiated pronunciation of the Latin tongue [that exists] in many, if not most of the schools in this realm." See T. W. C. Edwards, *The Eton Latin Grammar, a Plain and Concise Introduction to the Latin Language; Being Lily's Grammar Abridged, for the Use of the Young Gentlemen of* Eton College: *But with the Addition of Many Useful Notes and Observations, and Also of the Accents and Quantity* (London, 1826), v. Given their respective dates of publication, it is possible that Russell's grammars—and obliquely Bell's methods—informed revisions to Edwards's well-known and widely used grammar.

51. Attridge, *Well-Weighed Syllables*, 37.
52. For background regarding the "correct" pronunciation of the classical languages as a topic of longstanding debate, see Françoise Waquet, *Latin, Or, the Empire of a Sign*, trans John Howe (London: Verso, 2001), 152–172.
53. [Anon.], "Table Talk," *Once a Week* (Jan. 28, 1871), 118. It is possible that the contributor is the magazine's editor, the prosodist E. S. Dallas.
54. John Henry Howlett, *Instructions in Reading the Liturgy of the United Church of England and Ireland* (London, 1826), 217. My examples are borrowed from John Walker. As he remarks in his well-known pronouncing manual, the ordinary pronunciation of English vowels determined, in general, the way English speakers sounded Latin vowels, but syllable placement and accent also mattered. See John Walker, *A Key to the Classical Pronunciation*, 9th edn (London, 1830), 2–4.
55. P. A. Nuttall, "London University," *The Gentleman's Magazine* (Dec. 1828), 482 (emphasis added).
56. [Anon.], *Anti-Scepticism; Or, An Inquiry into the Nature and Philosophy of Language, as Connected with the Sacred Scriptures* (Oxford, 1821), 74.
57. Uvedale Price, *An Essay on the Modern Pronunciation of the Greek and Latin Languages* (n. pub., 1827), vii.
58. Price, *An Essay on the Modern Pronunciation of the Greek and Latin Languages*, 222.
59. Uvedale Price to EBB, 20 Dec. 1826, *The Brownings' Correspondence*, 1: 275.

60. Uvedale Price to EBB, 11 Jan. 1827, *The Brownings' Correspondence*, 2: 2.
61. Price, *An Essay on the Modern Pronunciation of the Greek and Latin Languages*, viii.
62. Price, *An Essay on the Modern Pronunciation of the Greek and Latin Languages*, ix.
63. Price, *An Essay on the Modern Pronunciation of the Greek and Latin Languages*, 25.
64. Price, *An Essay on the Modern Pronunciation of the Greek and Latin Languages*, 13.
65. Price, *An Essay on the Modern Pronunciation of the Greek and Latin Languages*, 32.
66. Price, *An Essay on the Modern Pronunciation of the Greek and Latin Languages*, 38.
67. H. S. Boyd, letter to the editor, *Classical Journal*, 37, 74 (1828), 327.
68. Attridge, *Well-Weighed Syllables*, 38. Howlett, *Instructions in Reading the Liturgy of the United Church of England and Ireland*, 217.
69. For a summary of Price's understanding of Russell's inconsistency, including his remarks on Edward Barrett's information about Charterhouse pronunciation of the *u* in the Greek word κμνε, see Uvedale Price to EBB, 11 Jan. 1827, and 16 Feb. 1827, *The Brownings' Correspondence*, 2: 1–5.
70. Russell's reluctance to enter into dialogue with Price suggests that he may have been aware that his principles and practice were at odds.
71. Uvedale Price to EBB, 16 Feb. 1827, *The Brownings' Correspondence*, 2: 24.
72. It is worth noting that the record of commentary on this subject presents differing views. For example, James Commeline rejects Price's assertion and backs Russell's Charterhouse mode, which he finds perfectly consistent and prosodically sound. See James Commeline to EBB, 1 Dec. 1827, *The Brownings' Correspondence*, 2: 87–90.
73. Edward Moulton-Barrett (Brother) to EBB, 12 Oct. 1822, *The Brownings' Correspondence*, 1: 166.
74. See Uvedale Price to EBB, 16 Feb. 1827, *The Brownings' Correspondence*, 2: 28. In a letter to his sister, Edward Barrett describes one of his classmate's verses, which "were upon the whole so bad that [when] Russell read them loud out not one of them would scan." One wonders whether the fault with the verses had been introduced by the boy or if it was simply incompatible with the in-built faults of Russell's system. See Edward Moulton-Barrett (Brother) to EBB, 12 Oct. 1822, *The Brownings' Correspondence*, 1: 166.

75. Price, *An Essay on the Modern Pronunciation of the Greek and Latin Languages*, 242–243.
76. Insofar as the Charterhouse "Blue Books" (records of admissions, forms, and monitors) provide a correct record, Edward did not serve as a monitor during his years at the school. It is possible that the examinations he mentions in his letters are either a general aspect of school procedure or an indication that he was in need of more direct tuition from Russell (possibly because he lagged behind in his verse compositions).
77. Edward Moulton-Barrett (Brother) to EBB, 22 Jun. 1823, in *The Brownings' Correspondence*, 1: 188 (emphasis added); cf. Russell, *Rudiments of the Latin Language* (1822), 136 and 142: "*H* is considered as no letter"; and, regarding the dactylic hexameter (a "VERSE OF SIX FEET"), "The Four first feet either Dactyls or Spondees, the FIFTH foot a DACTYL, the SIXTH foot a SPONDEE." Possibly Edward, writing in haste, has penned "ten" by mistake; or possibly he means to describe the hexameter as a ten-syllable (rather than ten-foot) line, though even if all of the spondaic substitutions permitted by Russell were observed, the line would still contain no fewer than thirteen syllables.

$$(--\,|\,--\,|\,--\,|\,--\,|\,-\,\smile\smile\,|\,--).$$

78. The "Blue Books" for 1816–1832 show that Thackeray himself served as a monitor at Charterhouse in 1828.
79. Wendy Robinson, *Power to Teach: Learning through Practice* (Oxford: Routledge Falmer, 2004), 33.
80. Charles Dickens, *Hard Times. For These Times* (London: Bradbury and Evans, 1854), 10.
81. Dickens, *Hard Times*, 8, 3–4.
82. The title *Gradus ad Parnassum* translates as "the steps to Parnassus"—Parnassus being the mountain associated with Apollo, god of poetry. As Françoise Waquet observes, "It was … in the seventeenth century (1659 to be exact) that the famous *Gradus ad Parnassum*, that indispensible tool of all school versifiers, made its first appearance. Originally the work of an anonymous Jesuit but attributed to a fictitious 'Father Chastillon,' then reattributed to the German Jesuit Paul Aler in the early eighteenth century, the manual enjoyed enormous success …." See Waquet, *Latin or the Empire of the Sign*, 35.
83. Dennis Taylor, *Hardy's Metres and Victorian Prosody, with a Metrical Appendix of Hardy's Stanza Forms* (Oxford: Clarendon Press, 1988), 66.

84. Gagnier draws on "a world of testimony to the futility of this 'method'"—citing the remembrances of Anthony Trollope, Charles Darwin, Edward Lyttleton, and others. See Regenia Gagnier, *Subjectivities: A History of Self-Representation in Britain, 1832–1920* (New York: Oxford University Press, 1991), 177.
85. The nine public schools whose practices were scrutinized by the Clarendon Commission in the 1860s (they are mentioned by name later in this chapter).
86. Martin Farquhar Tupper, *My Life as an Author* (London: Sampson Low, Marston, Searle, and Rivington, 1886), 15 (emphasis added).
87. Taylor, *Hardy's Metres*, 67.
88. H. C. Adams, *Wykehamica: A History of Winchester College and Commoners, from the Foundation to the Present Day* (Oxford and London: James Parker and Co., 1878), 350.
89. The *OED* cites William Hazlitt's definition of "versification"—"a thing in a great degree mechanical"—as an example of "mechanical" in the following sense: "Of a person or action: working or operating like a machine; acting or performed without thought; lacking spontaneity or originality; automatic, routine." See also William Hazlitt, *Lectures on the English Poets* (London, 1818), 64.
90. Archer, *Secondary Education in the Nineteenth Century*, 86.
91. This letter, dated 5 September 1866, is collected, along with others in the same chain of correspondence, in Christopher Stray, *Grinders and Grammars: A Victorian Controversy* Reading: Colloquium on Textbooks, Schools, and Society, 1995), 32.
92. "Master and Pupil," *All the Year Round* (Aug. 16, 1890), 166.
93. E. J. May, *Louis's Schooldays: A Story for Boys*, 2nd edn (Bath: Binns and Goodwin, 1852), 10 (emphasis original). Exercise books from Russell's years at Charterhouse further evidence the importance placed on scansion. Above one boy's Latin composition, a tutor or monitor (there is no way of determining which) has written in pencil, "These verses would be more beautiful if they would scan." In another example, a line is underscored and "scan" is scrawled above it in an exasperated hand. See 1st Form Musae Carthusianae, 1821–1822, 34/1, Charterhouse School Archive, Godalming, Surrey.
94. Quoted in M. L. Clarke, *Classical Education in Britain 1500–1900* (Cambridge: Cambridge University Press, 1959), 89.
95. Charles Oman, *Memories of Victorian Oxford and of Some Early Years* (London: Methuen and Co., 1941), 54–55.
96. [Thomas Hughes], *Tom Brown's School Days* (Cambridge: Macmillan and Co., 1857), 288–290.

97. "Vicarious" composition such as this is presumably what a tutor or monitor has in mind when he writes "Nicholson cribbed these March 28th 1832" above a boy's verse exercises. See Liber Aureus: Exercises, 1822–1824, 34/2, Charterhouse School Archive, Godalming, Surrey.
98. See Alexander J. Ellis, *Quantitative Pronunciation of Latin. For the Use of Classical Teachers and Linguists* (London: Macmillan and Co., 1874), vii-viii.
99. Francis William Newman, "On the Pronunciation of Greek," *Classical Museum: A Journal of Philology, and of Ancient History and Literature,* 3 (1846), 403.
100. Edmund Gurney, *The Power of Sound* (1880; New York: Basic Books, 1966), 434. What Gurney has in mind seems to be a so-called stressed-ictus reading, where the "imaginary" time-keeping beat of the ictus translates into a spoken accent on the first syllable of each foot. As we have seen, such a distinctive mode of delivery—"scanning aloud"—could be used to impart to a pupil an awareness of a line's metrical structure. In 1855, one contributor to the debate about classical pronunciation suggested that a person may "read the lines [of a poem] aloud half-a-dozen times, laying a strong emphasis on the first syllable of each foot, and giving to each long syllable twice the time of utterances of a short one. His ear by that time will be so drilled into the beat (ictus) of the metre, that he will be able, as most schoolboys are, to scan hexameter verse without a thought of quantity"—an appreciation for metrical movement having been rendered "a mere mechanical feat." The writer nonetheless warns against too strict an adherence to this habit of reading: "I do not recommend such a practice; it is merely serving poetry as some annoying people serve music, by beating or kicking time to it, and so adding an accompaniment the very reverse of pleasing to a musical ear." See B. S., "Latin Pronunciation and Poetry," *British Controversialist, and Imperial Inquirer,* 6 (1855), 74.
101. Alexander Melville Bell, *The Elocutionary Manual. The Principles of Articulation and Orthoepy, the Art of Reading and Gesture; Illustrated by Tables, Notations, and Diagrams; with Exercises in Expressive Delivery, and a Copious Selection of Emphasized Extracts, Embodying the Language of the Passions,* 3rd edn (London: Hamilton, Adams, and Co., 1860), xxi–xxii; see also J. Edmund Barss, "A Few Pedantries in Classical Teaching," *School Review,* 10, 4 (1902), 290–291.
102. John Stuart Mill, "Thoughts on Poetry and Its Varieties" (1833), in *Autobiography and Literary Essays,* ed. John M. Robson and Jack Stillinger, vol. 1 of *Collected Works of John Stuart Mill* (Toronto: University of Toronto Press, 1981), 343. Bentham loathed the

prosodic instruction he received at Westminster School, and he generally "bemoaned the longevity of the classical curriculum in England's grammar schools." See Elissa S. Itzkin, "Bentham's Chrestomathia: Utilitarian Legacy to English Education," *Journal of the History of Ideas*, 39, 2 (1978), 304.
103. *Report of Her Majesty's Commissioners*, 30, 14.
104. See Stray, ed., *Grinders and Grammars*.
105. John Stuart Mill, *Inaugural Address Delivered to the University of St. Andrews, Feb. 1st 1867* (London: Longmans, Green, Reader, and Dyer, 1867), 20.
106. Parker, "The Theory of Classical Education," 86–87.
107. George Long, "Observations on the Study of the Latin and Greek Languages," *The Schoolmaster: Essays on Practical Education*, vol. 2 (London: Charles Knight, 1836), 269.
108. F. W. Farrar, "Of Greek and Latin Verse-Composition as a General Branch of Education," in *Essays on a Liberal Education*, 206–207, 230, 209, 205.
109. John Ruskin, *Fors Clavigera: Letters to the Workmen and Labourers of Great Britain*, vol. 2 (Orpington: George Allen, 1872), 7.
110. Sara Atwood, *Ruskin's Educational Ideals* (Farnham: Ashgate, 2011), 137.
111. Farrar, "Of Greek and Latin Verse-Composition as a General Branch of Education," 215, 218, 214, 233, 217, 208.
112. See M. L. Clarke, *Classical Education in Britain 1500–1900*, 93. Clarke describes Key as "an exception among schoolmasters."
113. See Evelyn E. Cowie, "Stephen Hawtrey and a Working-Class Eton," *History of Education*, 11, 2 (1982), 71–86.
114. S. Hawtrey, *A Narrative-Essay on a Liberal Education, Chiefly Embodied in the Account of an Attempt to Give a Liberal Education to Children of the Working Classes* (London: Hamilton, Adams, and Co., 1868), 3, 13, 23, 29–30.

Automaton Versifiers

> Full many a thought, of character sublime,
> Conceived in darkness, here shall be unrolled.
> The mystery of number and of time.
> is here displayed in characters of gold.
> Transcribe each line composed by this machine,
> Record the fleeting thoughts as they arise;
> A line, once lost, may ne'er again be seen,
> A thought, once flown, perhaps for ever flies.
> —lines inscribed on the Eureka Latin Hexameter Machine (c. 1845)

> [T]he works of some poets we could name would sound very well from a machine, if any new Babbage could give a machine voice.
> —*Tait's Edinburgh Magazine* (1854)

Through the gloom of a darkened room in one of London's premier venues of spectacle and curiosity, the Egyptian Hall in Piccadilly, paying customers of 1846 beheld a "weird figure, rather bigger than a full-grown man, with an automaton head and face" that was affixed to an apparatus made of "metal, wood, and india-rubber."[1] By manipulating "a complex amalgam of pedals, bellows, whistles, tubes, diaphragms, pulleys, and shutters, connected to a seventeen-note keyboard," the curiosity's exhibitor, one Professor Faber, brought forth from the figure's waxen lips "a hoarse sepulchral voice."[2] This talking automaton had much in common with the speech synthesizers of Kempelen, Wheatstone, and Helmholtz, as discussed in "Measurement, Temporality, Abstraction." Its "various pieces of mechanism" imitated "more or less successfully the movement and action of mouth, lips, teeth, tongue, palate, glottis, lungs, & c."[3] There was, however, an ostensible difference between Faber's device and these other speaking machines; the clue was in its name: Euphonia. Its pleasing tones were not limited to vowel sounds, as the other machines already described largely were; rather, Faber's automaton speaker was "euphonic" in that it uttered pleasing sounds "in combinations of words in sentences."[4] A reminiscence from 1870, published in *All the Year Round*, describes the machine's operation thus:

> When any word or sentence was spoken out, either by Faber or by one of the audience, the exhibitor mentally divided all the syllables into as many distinct sounds as they embodied; he pressed upon a particular key for each particular sound, which admitted a blast of air to a particular compartment, in which the mechanism was of the kind to produce the sound required; there were thus as many pressures as there were elementary sounds.[5]

While capable of producing sounds that approximated the flow of speech by linking sounds and syllables to form phrases and clauses, Faber's Euphonia, like other eighteenth- and nineteenth-century speaking machines, in fact relied on a mechanical process of vowel synthesis that resembled the serial assembly educational methods examined in "Meter Manufactories." Indeed, a familiarity with the rudiments of scholastic prosody would have been an asset to Faber and any apprentice working under him, for essential to the machine's successful mimicry of flowing speech was the ability of its human operator to quickly "scan" what he or she had heard, decomposing its phonemic values before combining them again as a series of "pressures on the properly selected keys."[6]

The Euphonia was not unique among contemporary automata—neither in its general mechanics of serial assembly nor in its specific method of decomposing and reconstituting language by a process of mechanized "scansion." In a certain sense, Faber's machine, with its uncanny face, was really more of an *android*—from the Greek ἀνδρο (man) and εἰδης (like)—than an *automaton*—properly a self-acting device—though these terms were not mutually exclusive during the nineteenth century.[7] While the Euphonia automated speech by mechanizing language production, the device nonetheless depended both on human input (it could not compose the sentence it spoke or even determine how the combination of sounds could be arranged to make grammatical sense) and impulse (it could not "speak" without a constant human motive force, in this case the pressing of keys to produce successive sounds). By contrast, another language synthesizer of the period, John Clark's Eureka machine, exhibited at the Egyptian Hall a year before Faber's device and at least once confused with the talking machine, not only functioned under its own power but also varied, to an extent, its linguistic productions according to a set of predetermined rules. "[U]nique among the exhibited inventions of the time in its union of the mechanic and literary arts," the Eureka was properly a "permutation" or "composition" device.[8] Though capable of making sounds, its primary function was not auditory but visual, generating in random order a sequence of words that, when displayed together, formed a unique line of poetry.[9] The Eureka's "program" enabled it to combine the letters of the alphabet, manufacturing not just a complete sentence but a sentence in that heroic measure known well to nineteenth-century schoolboys: the dactylic hexameter.

This chapter pays particular attention to the role Clark's Eureka machine (Fig. 1) played in a number of significant mid-century metrical debates, as well as wide-ranging discussions about work, diversion, automation, and intelligence. The Eureka belonged not only to a discourse of diversion and spectacle that included Faber's speaking machine but also to a program of technological innovation that attempted to incorporate "thinking" mechanisms into quotidian labor processes. The Eureka was thus situated at the intersection of curiosity and utility, leaning in one direction toward a mechanics of playfulness and, for some, absurdity and in the other direction toward an earnest attempt to pioneer useful business machines.[10] Like many other devices examined in *Nineteenth-Century Verse and Technology*, however, the Eureka collapses these distinctions, just as it problematizes the division between the creative capacities of humans and machines. There is in the operation of Clark's machine, as well as in the constitution of the meters it produced, an extension of the meditation on metrical segmentation and step-by-step assembly that we examined in relation to contemporary instantiations of scholastic prosody. In many ways, the Eureka was regarded as a mechanical schoolboy, performing what amounted to verse composition exercises with a facility that might inspire surprise or provoke consternation. Was the machine a programmable prosodic prodigy? Or were schoolboys arranging their hexameters merely robots? In determining

Fig. 1 Eureka as depicted in the *Illustrated London News* (July 19, 1845), 27

that his machine would produce hexameters, Clark positioned himself in the middle of both professional and popular debates about the mechanical praxis on which much classical education was founded, as we saw in "Meter Manufactories," as well as at the center of a contemporaneous hexameter controversy. This measure, thought by some to be as amenable to modern as to ancient poetry, could at once accommodate extreme variation and encourage an arbitrary assembly of prosodic parts. As produced by machine, hexameters only magnified debates about the measure's relevance to both modern poetics and pedagogy. Not only for elite boys, whose educational experience was characterized by hours of tedious hexameter manufacture, nor only for the many poets, prosodists, and philologists who acted as the official arbiters of metrical propriety, but also for "the million," those persons for whom the Eureka—whether via exhibition or discussion in the pages of a popular periodical—might constitute their one and only encounter with the subject of Victorian versification, there was focused in this unique example of machine poetry an imagined metrical community where a familiarity with the rules and laws of prosody—however much they might be disputed—was by no means taken for granted.

Automata, Labor, and Computation

John Clark's "machine for making Latin verses"—sometimes he called it simply "The Automaton"—was one among many automata, calculators, and arithmetical substitution devices that captured the popular imagination in the eighteenth and nineteenth centuries. Indeed, the Eureka belonged to a well-established tradition of mechanizing both physical and mental tasks. On the one hand, there were "ingenious" spectacles and curiosities, which, in addition to Faber's speaking machine, included inventions such as Jacques Vaucanson's Flute player, exhibited in Paris in the 1730s; Kempelen's automaton chess player from the 1760s; the 1774 Jaquet-Droz androids, who, respectively, played music, drew, and wrote; and the Maillardet brothers' Magicians, from the early nineteenth century, whose "tricks" included answering a series of predetermined questions.[11] The mid-nineteenth century offered similar diversions: alongside the Eureka and Euphonia were Van Noorden's Polyharmonicon, a machine that composed polkas and capitalized on the "polkamania" of the 1840s and 1850s. Simon Schaffer has identified also "the Prosopographus and the Corinthian Maid, machines shown in the Strand in the early 1830s which could apparently copy the likeness of any sitter."[12] These latter two devices, much like Kempelen's chess playing Turk, belonged to what some contemporaries, for example the renowned mechanical engineer Robert Willis (1800–1875), deemed to be lesser classes of automata: namely "the compound" and "the spurious."[13] These devices, though mechanical to a greater or lesser degree, owed a significant portion of their operation to human intervention, though frequently this fact was not disclosed to observers. The Euphonia, as we have noticed, was a "compound" automaton in that it could speak by means of "communication ... with human agency"—that is, by compounding or combining mechanical apparatus with the input of a keyboard player. These other devices were properly "spurious": they functioned "under the semblance only of mechanism" and were in fact "wholly directed and controlled by a concealed human agent."[14] For example, in the case of the chess playing automaton, Willis was not alone in speculating that its complex calculations were performed not by mechanical means at all but by a person hiding within a secret compartment. Clark's Eureka, though it belonged to the same milieu of showroom spectacle, conformed legitimately to what Willis termed the "simple" category of automata: "those insulated Automata whose movements result from mechanism alone; by the aid of which they perform certain actions, and continue them, so long as moving force is kept in an active state."[15] Once set in motion, Clark's automaton versifier produced Latin hexameters, one after the other, until its motive force—a descending lead weight that powered a system of gears, pulleys, and flywheels—wound down.

In his *The General History and Description of a Machine for Composing Hexameter Latin Verses* (1848), a self-published account of the principles on which the Eureka functioned, John Clark himself acknowledged the connection between his device and certain curious automata. He mentioned specifically "a Flute Player" that was "exhibited at Paris" in 1738 and "a fine collection of Mechanism, by *Messrs. Phillipsthal & Maillardet*, [that] was publicly exhibited in the principal towns of England" in 1810. Further, he not only discussed in his prefatory remarks on the Eureka's manufacture the relative difficulty of making a "Chess playing Automaton" but also provided "An Account of Some of the Principal Androides [*sic*] and Automatic Figures, Which Have Hitherto Been Designed and Constructed."[16] Unacknowledged by Clark, however, was another class of automata, arguably more "useful" in their workings and applications than the curiosities discussed immediately above, whose mode of operation was in keeping with the Eureka's piecemeal manufacture of verses. Indeed, as characterized by Andrew Ure in his 1835 *The Philosophy of Manufactures*, the whole of Britain's factory system was fundamentally "automatic" in that it effected production by machines, "with little or no aid of the human hand."[17] "It is in our modern cotton and flax mills," remarked Ure in another text, "that automatic operations are displayed to most advantage."[18] Ure even posited a basic connection between the nineteenth-century factory and amusing automatons: both "may be employed, to give portions of inert matter, precise movements resembling those of organized beings ...." Just as "cords, pulleys, toothed-wheels, nails, screws, levers, [and] inclined-planes" allow the Euphonia or a Jaquet-Droz draftsman to perform its diverting functions, so too do these and similar mechanical compilations make possible large-scale "organizations [such] as cotton-mills, flax-mills, silk-mills, woollen-mills, and certain engineering works." Indeed, the factory system was for Ure "a vast automaton, composed of various mechanical and intellectual organs, acting in uninterrupted concert for the production of a common object, all of them being subordinated to a self-regulated moving force."[19] Organized on the principle of the division of labor, where increasingly specialized and sometimes self-regulating machines often replaced the skilled work of human artisans, the factory system was not simply structurally akin to an automaton. Because the division of labor, as envisaged by the economist Adam Smith (1723–1790) and several subsequent theorists of economics and industry, propelled mechanical innovation, focusing working practices that in turn promoted tool refinements in line with increasingly specialized tasks, some feared that it actively transformed the men and women working alongside its vast looms and engines into automata themselves. It was not just characters such as the threshing machine operator from Hardy's *Tess*, as discussed in "Measurement, Temporality, Abstraction," who became more mechanical as a result of their first-hand experience of nineteenth-century industrial culture.

The division of labor that underpinned the factory-system-as-automaton had much in common with the workings of both the Eureka, as we shall see below, and other automata, as well as the classroom methods discussed in the previous chapter. It depended upon a segmentation of processes, breaking down complex mechanical operations into a series of simpler tasks that could be performed in isolation from one another. As Karl Marx noted, the factory separates the "process of production into its various successive steps." Marx understood that the structural logic on which the "division of labour, that distinguishing principle of manufacture," depended on what, in *Capital* (1867), he termed serial manufacture: "the isolation of the various stages of production and their independence of each other."[20] Along with the machine refinement and segmentation of tasks that the division of labor encouraged, came what Marx viewed as a curbing of human input: fewer skills were required from workers, who became merely machine operators, their functions simply an extension of the machines they served. As he observed memorably in his *Economic and Philosophical Manuscripts* (1844), the worker in the modern factory system was alienated from the production process, reduced to "the condition of a machine."[21] However, not all of Marx's contemporaries took this view. The mathematician and engineer Charles Babbage (1791–1871), for example, "considered the division of labour a key element in reducing production costs" because it promoted "the invention of machinery able to perform ... simple activities," thereby reducing the cost of human labor and presenting the possibility of freeing up workers from "the duller, more repetitive activities" that industrial manufacture necessitated. By "breaking a complex labour process down into simple operations," the division of labor on which the factory system was organized at once diminished the reliance on "less qualified workers" and stimulated technological innovation. In Babbage's estimation, then, the factory's mode of operating did not turn human workers into automatons, as Marx feared; on the contrary, it spared them that fate, purposely deploying machines, specially designed to function in line with the division of labor's segmentation of tasks into "elementary components," to reduce human drudgery while at the same time improving productivity—long before the "scientific management" theories associated with Taylorism would promote a systematizing and standardizing of industrial manufacturing "workflows."[22]

Babbage is probably best remembered for his work to extend these principles to include a "division of mental labor," particularly through his design of calculating machines "based on the principle of breaking down any computation into its elementary components, for which it is easier to substitute the mind of a man with a standard process that can be performed by a machine."[23] Believing machines might help to relieve the tedium of "computers" —a term, in Victorian usage, that denoted not machines but human clerks whose job involved basic reckoning or computation—Babbage conceived of a "Difference Engine" that would both ease the "drudgery of endless calculations [that] degraded the mind" of those tasked with compiling them and "reduce the extremely complex business of tables calculation to its simplest essentials."[24] Like other contemporary calculating devices, such as Thomas de Colmar's Arithrometer (conceived in the 1820s but not properly introduced for commercial use until 1851), Babbage's automaton calculator built on existing calculation technologies—such as the Leibniz wheel, a cogwheel "milled in steps"—that broke down mathematical calculations into simple, repeatable functions. Essentially "synthetic," or capable of mere calculations where a process of simple and predictable actions could be mechanized, the Difference Engine, a prototype for which Babbage produced in 1822, "consisted of an elaborate clockwork mechanism with a cast-iron frame":

> Using the decimal system, numbers are represented on geared brass wheels called figure wheels. Each wheel is turned to a specific gearing to represent

a number, e.g., a wheel will be turned two teeth to represent the number 2. The wheels are arranged on columns centered on brass rods with the place of the wheels on the column representing their place in the decimal system. For example, for the number 246, the wheel turned to six for units would be at the bottom, with the figure wheel for four in tens above it, and at the top the wheel turned to two for hundreds. ... Babbage imagined figure wheels piled for as many as twelve digits on a single column and a total of six adjoining columns.[25]

With its system of gears and wheels, Babbage's Difference Engine (Fig. 2) promised to economize the calculation process, offering a mechanical "simplification of the arithmetical processes to repeated addition and subtraction."[26] By rendering calculation as a "systematic method" that assigns to discrete components of the apparatus values that can be synthesized, the automaton calculator—which Babbage never managed to construct in full during his own lifetime—promised a solution to time-consuming numerical calculation and the production of reliable tables of logarithms, which nineteenth-century modernity's impetus toward standard measurement methods, particularly in relation to accurate marine-navigation and ordinance-survey data, demanded.[27]

Babbage eventually abandoned the Difference Engine, instead devoting his attention to an even more ambitious project: the Analytical Engine, "a machine capable of executing not merely arithmetical calculations, but even all those of analysis, if their laws are known." While the Difference Engine could execute a predetermined program, offering correct calculations that would be both time-consuming and tedious for a human "computer," not to mention liable to error, it was, in essence, not much more of a legitimate "thinking machine" than a Jacquard Loom or a Jaquet-Droz android.[28] Where Babbage's device automated a numerical formula, the others automated a sequence of physical movements—all were predetermined, and none of the machines could "think" beyond the formula or program (whether a punch-card or notched drum) they were given by their respective inventors. As L. F. Menabrea wrote in his 1842 *A Sketch of the Analytical Engine Invented by Charles Babbage*, translated by Ada Lovelace, the Difference Engine's calculations were limited to "merely the expression of one particular theorem of analysis; ... its operations cannot be extended so as to embrace the solution of an infinity of other questions included within the domain of mathematical analysis."[29] Babbage's Analytical Engine, by contrast, promised to

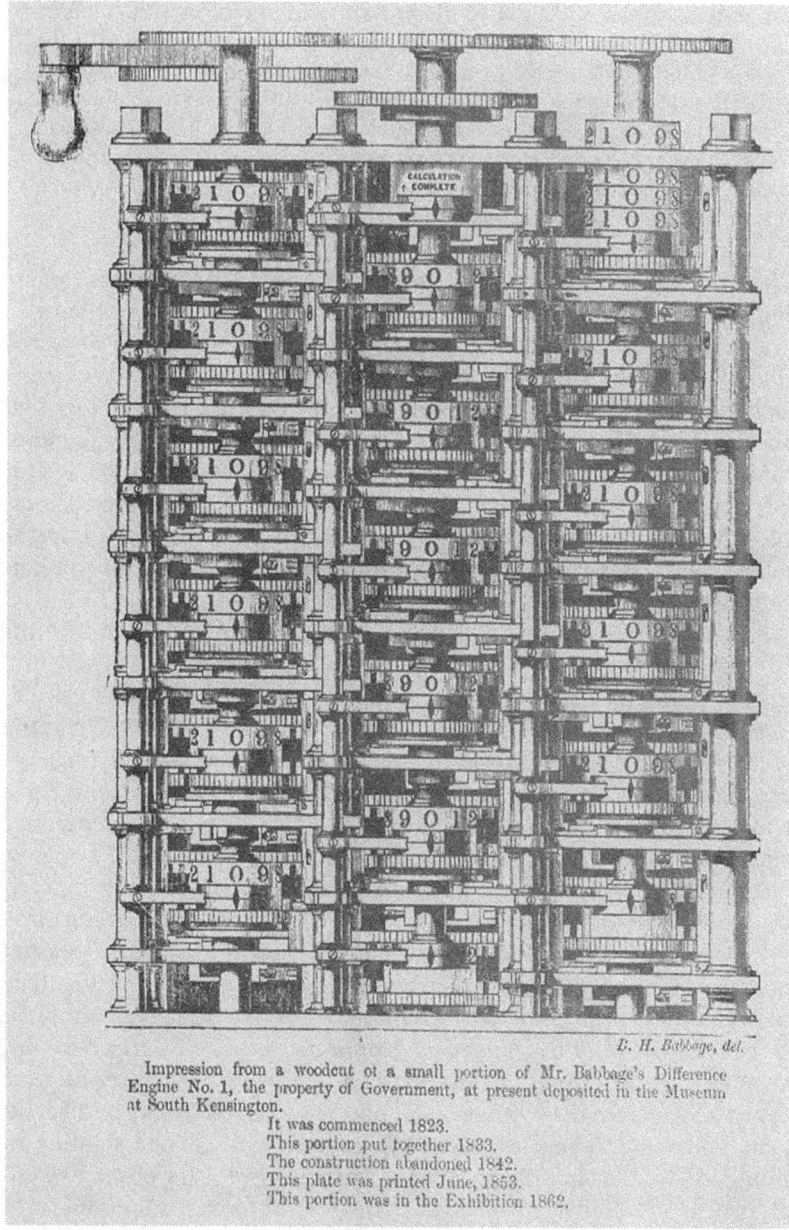

Fig. 2 Illustration of the Difference Engine No. 1, frontispiece of Charles Babbage's *Passages from the Life of a Philosopher* (London: Longman, Green, Longman, Roberts, and Green, 1851)

do more than calculate according to a predetermined formula or "program." As Niran Abbas points out in *Thinking Machines* (2006), "the Difference Engine's successor ... was a machine that not only calculated, but also decided what formula to use in order to do so."[30] In this regard, the Analytical Engine came closest, among the devices mentioned so far in this chapter, to fulfilling the automatic fantasy that the machine age promised: a machine that offered to substitute its workings not only for merely "mechanical" activities—those performed by human "computers" or factory operatives, which, as I will discuss in more detail below in "The Automatic Flow of Verse," were deemed "automatic" insofar as they are not directed by conscious human agency or informed by discriminating intellect—but also for the very opposite of such mechanistic activities: the imaginative capacities of the human mind itself. In this sense Babbage's Analytical Engine appeared to deliver what a device such as Kempelen's automaton chess player could only imitate by "spurious" means—that is, a mechanics of deliberative action and intelligent discrimination, a demonstrable ability to think about and decide upon a course of action without recourse to regular human input, either in the form of manual manipulation or via a pre-established formula or program. For this reason, Babbage's Analytical Engine is often regarded as an antecedent of modern artificial intelligence devices.[31]

Whether by means of deception or legitimate mechanical innovation, both the "diverting" and "serious" automata discussed here, as exemplified by Kempelen's and Babbage's devices, focused contemporary questions about the relationship between *mind* and *machine*. At this meeting point, where what Stephen P. Rice has called "the self-regulatory difference between humans and machines" begins to "blur,"[32] is also where John Clark positioned his Eureka Hexameter Machine, itself an amalgam of showroom curiosity and putatively earnest endeavor. On the one hand, Clark imagined his device alongside Kempelen's chess player as an automaton that can "calculate" an "uncertainty" and then correctly mechanize a response to it. Instead of the moves of chess, however, Clark proposed an automaton that accomplished "a far more complex work ... in a mechanical formation of Latin hexameters ...." The Eureka, as described by Clark, was able to mechanize the discriminating powers of the human versifier—schoolboy, poetaster, or prosodic prodigy—who possessed not only an awareness of "the several kinds of verse," namely "the several *measures* or *Feet*," but also an understanding how best to combine these prosodic values to form a "poetical composition."[33] On the other hand, however, and more in keeping with the calculating automata conceived by Babbage, Clark was clear that his automaton versifier was not to be understood as involving any sleight of hand or other "spurious" mechanics: there was no human hidden behind its "bureau-bookcase" exterior. Rather, Clark asserted that the Eureka could "*produce the effect by mechanical means.*" "It is a fact," he wrote in 1848, "that *the Rules of verse*, the measured syllables, and the measured time, of dactyls, spondees, trochees, & c., which acts as fetters of confinement to the *writers* of verses, much increasing their difficulties, have an *opposite effect* when applied to *a machine*...."[34] But as we will see, there is a considerable element of showmanship in Clark's estimation of his machine's compositional abilities. Though the Eureka did, in fact, employ *bona fide* mechanical means to manufacture its hexameters—a combination of appropriated and purpose-built technologies that operated under the tension provided by a lead weight—its meters were not as "calculated" and discriminating as Clark suggested, gesturing in only a basic way toward the arithmetical and *synthetic* processes of the Difference Engine, much less the *analytical* "intelligence" of Babbage's later venture. What may have appeared, particularly to the metrically uninitiated among Clark's audiences, to be a mechanical feat involving skills of linguistic and prosodic deliberation—a knowledge of Latin vocabulary and syntax, an awareness of quantitative prosodic values, an ability to combine foot varieties to compose a metrically "correct" hexameter line—was, in fact, a formulaic process where values were predetermined and their combination invariable. While there was in the operation of the Eureka an element of randomness, aligning it to an extent with Babbage's work and its legacy in the modern discourse of machine intelligence, there was also something fundamentally *mechanistic* in its verse manufacture, a quality that aligned it more with the unthinking and segmented automatic labor of the factory floor that a critic of industrial capitalism such as Marx regarded as contributing to a mechanic's alienation from the mode of production in which he or she was engaged. Rather like the schoolboys discussed in "Meter Manufactories," whose daily regime of scholastic prosody consisted of manufacturing nonsense hexameters one after the other, Clark's Eureka was an automaton versifier, a meter robot that had no real understanding of the meters it manufactured. Further, if the verse compositions of the schoolboy were deemed by many to be lacking in any demonstrable utility, then there might be, paradoxically, a supreme usefulness in Clark's Hexameter Machine in that it could relieve them, in a way similar to that imagined by Babbage, from that notoriously tedious task: their Latin verse composition homework.

Fixed Mixed Verse

The year 1845, when John Clark's Eureka was "grinding out" hexameters for visitors to the Egyptian Hall, was at the mid-point of a turbulent decade for prosody. Classical metrics, and hexameters in particular, as Yopie Prins and Joseph Patrick Phelan have demonstrated, were central to the imbroglio.[35] In 1844 Lancelot Shadwell's translation of the *Iliad* into English hexameters had sparked a controversy regarding the possibility of reproducing classical metrical properties in English. This debate was thickened by the publication of experimental English hexameters, such as the American poet Henry Wadsworth Longfellow's *Evangeline* (1847) and two narrative poems by Arthur Hugh Clough: *The Bothie of Toper-Na-Fuosich* (1848) and *Amours de Voyage* (1849). In 1850 Walter Savage Landor came out against English hexameters in his (hexameter) poem of that title, singing the praises of an ostensibly more home-grown meter, the pentameter: "We have a measure/Fashion'd by Milton's own hand, a fuller, a deeper, a louder."[36] Also keen to assess the hexameter's suitability as a "national" measure, Charles Kingsley not only assayed the meter in 1858 with the publication of *Andromeda and Other Poems*, described by one contemporary as containing "the finest English hexameters ever written," but also inserted a fictionalized debate on the subject of English hexameters—between Walter Raleigh and Edmund Spenser, no less—in *Westward Ho!*, his 1855 historical romance. In the 1860s these contributions to what was by then clearly a mounting "hexameter controversy"[37] would be complemented by Alfred Tennyson's "On Translations of Homer. Hexameters and Pentameters" (1863) and Algernon Charles Swinburne's "Hymn to Proserpine" (1866).[38] Among the more interesting interlocutors in that decade's hexameter debate was Matthew Arnold, who endorsed the hexameter as a measure of modernity. His *On Translating Homer* (1860–1861) initiated a heated exchange with Francis W. Newman, whose 1856 "ballad-poetry" translation of the *Iliad* Arnold dismissed as not "noble enough."[39] As Yopie Prins has noted, Arnold, in his 1857 lecture "The Modern Element in Literature," had associated modernity in literature with poets' "ability to take the measure of their own time"; the hexameter was not only an apt "measure" of the heroic age of Homer but also a meter "that might adequately represent and comprehend the multiplicity of the modern age," both as a template for modern translations of the classical epics and as a medium of original English compositions. Thus, as Prins writes, the "hexameter became Arnold's measure of, and for, the present time."[40]

The hexameter's enduring appeal and amenability to modernity might be explained, in part, by its metrical plasticity, in particular its capacity for accommodating a variety of feet besides the dactyl that gives the measure its name and the differing modes and moods of address that such a rhythmically versatile line affords. As John Seely Hart would remark in his 1871 *A Manual of Composition and Rhetoric*, in contrast to the "prevailing law of English verse," which states "that the feet in any one line shall all be of one kind" (e.g., lines of iambic pentameter tend to be all, or at least predominantly, iambic), the dactylic hexameter is characterized as a "mixed" measure, where "feet of different kinds are mixed together freely in the same line." In a standard hexameter line, some, though by no means all, of the six feet may be dactyls. "The Dactylic Hexameter consists, as its name imports," wrote William Ramsay in the 1859 edition of his *A Manual of Latin Prosody*, "of six feet; in the first four places, Dactyls or Spondees may be used at pleasure; the fifth foot is usually a Dactyl, the sixth foot invariably a Spondee" (Fig. 3). Several classical primers set out even stricter rules governing the kind and placement of feet and permissible substitutions. For example, John Russell's *Rudiments of the Latin Language for the Use of Charterhouse School*, examined in "Meter Manufactories," asserted six laws concerning syllable count for given feet, their relationships, and the number as well as placement of caesurae.[41] Other prosodians, however, were less inclined to limit the line's metrical possibilities by imposing too many rules. Some authorities, for example, permitted a trochee in the final foot. Ramsay favored imparting to "the composer" the responsibility of determining an artful arrangement of feet. "With regard to the comparative number of Dactyls and Spondees which ought to constitute a line," wrote Ramsay, "or the order in which they ought to succeed each other, no

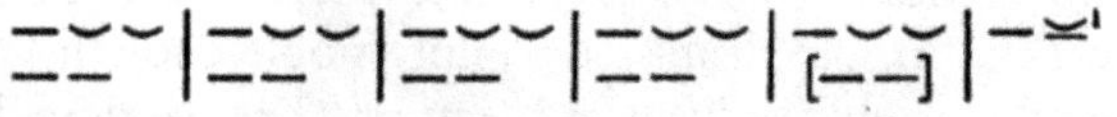

Fig. 3 Dactylic hexameter foot patterns, from William Ramsay's *A Manual of Latin Prosody*, 2nd edn (London and Glasgow: Richard Griffin and Company, 1859), 162

positive rule can be laid down." What mattered most was the versifier's ability "to vary the arrangement of the constituent parts of the verse, in such a manner as to avoid uniformity and monotony."[42]

Composers of both Latin and English hexameters, made clear just how versatile the line could be. An adept versifier—what many a prosody grinder hoped his pupils, by dint of repetitive hexameter assembly exercises, might become, though demonstrably few did—appreciated how a change in the proportion and placement of dactyls and spondees (or the occasional substitution of other foot varieties) could alter not only the line's metrical constitution but also the tone and character of what it expressed, lending it, on the one hand, loftiness or gravity and, on the other, levity or apparent spontaneity. "A preponderance of dactyls [gives] a rapid movement to the verse, suitable to a light, gay, or beautiful subject," noted Hart, whereas a "preponderance of spondees ... [makes] the movement of the verse slow, stately, and solemn." For example, the "rapid movement" of dactyls in "the familiar line [from the *Aeneid* of] Virgil describing the horse-race" mimes galloping hoof-beats:

| Quādrŭpĕ|dāntĕ pŭ|trēm sŏnī|tū quătĭt | ūngŭlă | cāmpŭm. |[43]

In a contrasting example that Hart cites from Virgil, a succession of spondees "describes the slow, heavy motion of the Cyclops at work on the anvil":

| Ōll' īn|tēr sē|sē māg|nā vī|brāchĭă |tōllūnt. |[44]

This flexibility—whether expressed quantitatively in Latin or English, or in a much-disputed English accentual equivalent—was doubtless part of the measure's appeal to translators of the classic epics and exemplars of innovative English hexameters, frequently described as logœdic.[45] Indeed, as Hart observed, the hexameter in English might comprise "a free intermixture of iambuses, trochees, anapæsts, and spondees," as in the following example from Longfellow's *Evangaline*:

Thīs ĭs thĕ	fŏrĕst prī	mēvăl. Thĕ	mūrmŭrĭng	pīnes ănd thĕ	hēmlŏcks,
Bēardĕd wĭth	mŏss, ănd ĭn	gārmĕnts	grēen, ĭndĭs	tīnct ĭn thĕ	twīlĭght,
Stānd līke	Drŭīds ŏf	ōld, wĭth	vōicĕs	sād ănd prŏ	phētĭc.

Hart himself was not certain that Longfellow had managed to "[reconcile] the English ear to this kind of verse,"[46] whose long lines and miscellaneous meters diverged significantly from the usual pentameters and ballad measures of the English tradition. And he was not alone. Some intimated that the metrical unevenness of English hexameters resulted in an overly clumsy movement. "In America," noted a writer in the *Westminster Review*, the hexameter's "rhythm has been described as somewhat similar to the noise of pumpkins rolling over a barn floor."[47] Others, however, such as Kingsley, insisted that by making the most of the hexameter's mixable measures, poets might anglicize it quite readily: "As to hexameters being foreign to our language, if you will mind the cæsura, and split your sense at that as often as convenient, you can talk prose in hexameters just as easily as in blank verse."[48] Indeed, as Clough would demonstrate adroitly in *Amours de Voyage*, it was entirely possible to compose talkable "prose" hexameters in English. This epistolary poem is replete with colloquial monologues, such as the following one addressed by Claude, an English tourist in Rome, to his friend Eustace:

> Rome disappoints me much; I hardly as yet understand, but
> *Rubbishy* seems the word that most exactly would suit it.[49]

Clough's management of miscellaneous foot combinations, his caesura placement, and his use of enjambment, not to mention his ear for how the dactyl can accommodate slang (*Rŭbbĭshy̆*), ensures that his English hexameters "avoid uniformity and monotony." They exhibit not only a conversation ease—at times more akin to the popular fiction of the period than to Longfellow's hexameters—but also what James Williams has called an "assured seriocomic balance."[50]

In the case of Clough, arguably among the more accomplished exponents of the English hexameter, such a mixed meter, with its comparative openness to substitution and amenability to license, provided ample opportunities to vary the inflection of verses, to formalize compositions in direction of high epic or enliven them with an eminently speakable prosiness—quite the opposite of the monotonous, droning meters that, as noted elsewhere in this book, frequently attend a uniform succession of regularly alternating quantities or accents. On the other hand, however, as a mixed measure where one foot might be changed without necessarily impacting on the next one in sequence or on the overall metrical constitution of the line, the hexameter ran the risk of being as remote from "good" poetry, where deviations from a metrical template might mitigate against rhythmical monotony, as it was susceptible to an arbitrary, and nonetheless mechanical, combination of feet, particularly when the versifier is less aware of or motivated by an awareness of the rhythmical nuances that such a mixed measure promised. There was a difference, in other words, between capitalizing on the mixed metrical character of the hexameter, combining miscellaneous feet to achieve a balanced and rhetorically dynamic line, and merely mixing its feet at random because such an approach satisfied, however loosely, the most basic of rules of versification associated with the measure. The latter, as we saw in "Meter Manufactories," was often the case with scholastic prosody: classroom exercises in verse composition, which frequently focused on hexameters, involved a form of metrical assembly with correlates in the modes of production identified by contemporaries such as Marx as the mainstay of industrial manufacture and its segmentation of labor into discrete, repetitive tasks. Using his *Gradus ad Parnassum* to identify words that will fit into each metrical segment, a schoolboy might well find the hexameter's mixing of measures, coupled with certain prosodians' relative laxity about their arrangement, a positive aid to composition. In the examples of "Gradus-grinding" already considered, we often find a subordination of metrical subtlety to "correctness"—whether an ostensibly metrical line made sense or, harder still, made an attempt at linguistic or rhythmical beauty might matter a great deal less to its composer (or, indeed, his prosody tutor) than whether it could be demonstrated to scan, however ineptly. C. J. Ellingham's recollection of the schoolboy at work, taken from his 1935 "Apology for the Practice of Latin Verse Composition," makes precisely this point:

> We can picture him, with Dictionary and Gradus and a small store of juvenile cunning, embarking upon a rendering of "Welcome, wild northeaster." He draws his seven vertical lines to mark the limits of the six feet, fills the last space with the obliging Eurus, eight points at most off the required bearing, consults the Gradus and helps himself to *turbidus* for the fifth foot and *ingenti strepitu* to start the line sonorously, pads the middle with *flabat iam* .... It looks somewhat diffuse ... but at least it scans.[51]

While Ellingham claims to have enjoyed this sort of activity for its own sake, it nevertheless adequately conveys the puzzle-like nature of the enterprise—for which the mixed feet of the hexameter seemed perfectly predisposed.

The compositional mechanics of "dactyls, spondees, trochees" might represent, as John Clark speculated, so many metrical "difficulties" for a boy versifier, but was it really the case, again as Clark suggested, that the same "*Rules of verse*" would "have an *opposite effect* when applied to a *machine*"? Clark confidently portrayed the Eureka as a device that managed with comparative ease the complicated metrical grinding of scholastic prosody that baffled and often alienated the schoolboy. Yet while his machine, like the calculating engines of Babbage, may have appeared to relieve humans of prosodic drudgery by substituting a mechanical versifier that performed more or less the same hexameter exercises, capitalizing on a mixed measure like the hexameter in a mechanized feat of combinatory skill and prosodical prowess, the Eureka was in fact even more limited in its compositions than the most haphazard of schoolboys. Clark might insist, in his "General Description of the Hexameter Machine," that it is the variety both of feet—"Each *foot* consists of a *certain number* of Long and Short Syllables"—and of their combination to form a variety of hexameters—"this *variety of measure* constitutes the *variety of cadence* in poetical composition"—that the Eureka automates,[52] but in practice the machine reduced the measure to but one variation on the dactylic hexameter. One particular distribution of quantities across the line's six feet became a mechanically reproducible pattern, where words of the requisite quantitative values could be selected from among the machine's limited store of Latin vocabulary (its in-built Gradus of 105 words), enabling it to manufacture lines differing considerably in content but not at all in form—each one conformed to the same invariable, though irregular, metrical structure. By first mixing but then resolutely fixing the machine's hexameters, Clark achieved an apparently ingenious spectacle of automated prosody. As a meter automaton—a machine that appeared to make decisions about versification using its own discriminating prosodic processes—the Eureka worked not by understanding versification generally or even the discrete metrical properties of the dactylic hexameter in particular but by reducing the prosody of this mixed measure to a predetermined, fixed, and readily repeatable series of data.

Artificial Versifying

For many contemporary observers of the Eureka, its compositional abilities were noteworthy, even inspired. Babbage, who saw it in operation, regarded the machine and its creator as equally "curious." As Richard D. Altick notes in *The Shows of London* (1978), Clark's device "purported to realize a long-standing English ambition: the production of a limitless number of Latin hexameter verses unassisted by any muse."[53] But if Clark's automaton metrist did not have a muse, or even a metrically inclined schoolboy, tucked away inside, as with Kempelen's chess playing automaton, and if it did not require the exhibitor himself to perform any on-the-spot mental scansion, as Professor Faber had done when overseeing the mechanization of speech sounds with his Euphonia, then how did the Eureka effect such a feat of prosodic ingenuity? As I suggested above, it worked by stripping out all possibility of variety afforded by the dactylic hexameter, leaving only one iteration of that otherwise highly mixable measure. For even though the pattern of the hexameter as produced by the machine was fixed, the number of semantically different hexameters the machine could produce, by substituting words of identical metrical value for one another, remained vast. But the simplification did not stop there. Indeed, the Eureka's metrical capacity was even further fixed. A skilful human versifier might well engage with his or her metrical composition by taking into account the interplay between the grid of meter, its sequentially occurring quantitative values (patterns of longs and shorts), and the words that might be arranged variously across this grid. The number of words might vary from line to line, even if the meter, as with Clark's device, did not. The hexameter's six feet might accommodate fewer polysyllables or more monosyllables, depending on the desired meaning and rhythmical or rhetorical effects. A more perfunctory and arguably more *mechanical* approach, however, as we have seen in relation to scholastic prosody, might simply regard the verse line as a series of discrete metrical boxes that must be filled with words of the requisite quantitative values: a foot for each box and a word for each foot. Clark's automation versifier, like the schoolboy, began by first fixing the relationship between semantic and metrical values—following the principle of diaeresis, "the division made in a line when the end of a foot coincides with the end of a word."[54] Such a direct correspondence between metrical and linguistic units further emphasized the serial assembly element in the Eureka's verse manufacture. The production of each component in the series could be divorced from the production of surrounding segments, thereby effectively negating any sense of composing a unified line of verse. It might be more fitting, then, to describe the Eureka not as a Latin verse machine but as a fixed-foot fabricator. In keeping with the "technical division of labour—in which the production process is divided into isolated tasks to be reintegrated in the product itself"[55]—Clark's mechanical versifier operated by distinguishing the process of making feet and the product, a metrically complete dactylic hexameter, which was merely the sum of the component parts as perceived by someone viewing the machine. The machine itself had no capacity for conceiving of hexameters in their entirety. Each foot was produced in isolation from the next, and no change in one foot impacted on the properties (either metrical or semantic) of the surrounding feet.

A final element of simplification involved a transposition of values that placed the Eureka's machinations at an even further remove from the prosodic or even linguistic composition that constituted the "product" offered up to paying customers at the Egyptian Hall. According to a contemporary report in the *Illustrated London News*, the Eureka's

> process of composition is not by words already formed, but from *separate letters*. ... The machine contains *letters* in alphabetical arrangement. Out of these, through the medium of *numbers*, rendered *tangible* by being expressed by indentures on wheel-work, the instrument selects such as are requisite to form the verse conceived; the *components* of words suited to form hexameters being alone previously calculated, the harmonious combination of which will be found to be practically interminable.[56]

As we have seen, Clark's device was in no legitimate sense "a machine for composing Latin verses," verses being merely the accumulation of the foot-long words its mechanism generated. Further, its true "medium" was not the foot, the word, or even a measure of duration such as the quantity; rather, it was the numerical integer. The Eureka had no knowledge of Latin or meter, though such signs and values could readily be assigned to its computations. All it really did was combine a limited array of integers, uniting predictability (all values were determined beforehand) with unpredictability (the order in which the values might be arranged was not). Indeed, the Eureka's significance was less a consequence of its capacity to mechanize composition in any linguistic or prosodic sense than a result of its ability to introduce a considerable element of randomness to its production of outputs. The most ingenious feature of Clark's automaton was not its apparent fluency in manufacturing Latin hexameters but the mystery surrounding which one might appear next in sequence. Like a true cousin of Babbage's calculating mechanism, the Eureka was a machine that specialized in generating numerical *differences*.

Babbage's and Clark's respective machines not only shared a medium of computation; both also participated in the mechanizing of a particular form of data representation and evaluation that was central to the production of knowledge in the nineteenth century: namely, the presentation of numbers in tables.[57] The Eureka functioned according to what Clark himself called a *"tabular principle."*[58] Just as Babbage had designed his Difference Engine to automate the calculations used to produce tables of logarithms, so did Clark take pre-existing tables as the inspiration—and basic "program"—for his device. Where Babbage envisaged a mechanism that could produce tables more quickly than a human "computer," as well as with a greater degree of accuracy, Clark both imagined and, unlike Babbage, realized a way to *"produce the effect* [of existing tables] *by mechanical means"*[59]—thus offering a similarly quick and ostensibly error-free alternative to the mechanical computation of the schoolboy or, more precisely, a system of hexameter composition even more formulaic and mechanistic than that associated with scholastic Gradus-grinding. The "astonishing" mathematical principles of verse computation on which the Eureka was designed had, in fact, been around for well over a century, though no one before Clark, it seems, had attempted to automate them. As early as 1677, John Peter's *Artificial Versifying, Or, the School-Boy's Recreation* set out "A New Way to make Latin Verses." By following Peter's step-by-step process, which involved selecting letters in sequence from a set of prearranged "Versifying Tables,"

> Any one of ordinary Capacity, that only knows the A.B.C. and can Count 9 (though he underſtands not one word of *Latin*, or what a *Verſe* means) may be plainly taught, (and in as little a time as this is Reading over,) how to make Hundreds of *Hexameter Verſes*, which ſhall be True *Latin*, True *Verſe*, and good *Senſe*[.][60]

Similar tables were in circulation throughout the eighteenth and nineteenth centuries. Under the entry for "Hexameter" in his *Universal Etymological English Dictionary*, published in 1727, Nathan Bailey provided "a curious and admirable Contrivance"—"Tables for making Hexameter *Latin* Verses" and a detailed explanation of how to use them.

Another table, this one also titled "Artificiall [sic] Versifying," accompanied Edward Manwaring's 1737 treatise *Stichology, Or a Recovery of the Latin, Greek, and Hebrew Numbers*. In an echo of Peter's earlier text, Manwaring explains "how any person shall make both hexameter and pentameter Latin verse which shall be both good Latin and good sense ... although he understand not the Latin tongue."[61] Such tables, following more or less the same set of instructions, appeared throughout the nineteenth century, the latest example consulted for this project being *Tables for Making Hexameter and Pentameter Latin Verses* from 1878 (Fig. 4).

To an extent, these verse tables were parodies of the alphabetic literacy methods discussed in "Meter Manufactories." These systems of reading instruction, associated with the monitorial methods of Andrew Bell and Joseph Lancaster, insisted, particularly when embellished to underpin prosodical instruction, that pupils first learn letters before graduating to syllables and, eventually, the combination of these elements in the application of the principles of versification. Tabular prosody allowed users to circumvent most steps in this process, dispensing with all but the most rudimentary element, "the A.B.C." Magnifying the disaggregating tendencies of the Bell-Lancaster approach, which relied on a decomposition of words into their discrete graphemic values, verse tables required users to engage solely the "numeration" function of the reading regime, counting to select letters and trusting the formatting of the table to supply the most important part of the process: the combination or "resolution" of letters to produce a complete word. Tables of letters, which Bell himself had advocated for the teaching of syllables, might also allow would-be versifiers, regardless of their knowledge of classical languages or metrics, to make selections from among a pre-established group of letters arranged in rows and columns. Each such table represents one word/foot of the eventual hexameter line, there being six tables in total and multiple possible words (though only one foot variety) for each table. The user begins by selecting, from the numbers 1–9, six integers (one for each table); these numbers determine the starting places in each table. The remainder of the process involves counting boxes and recording the letters in the ninth box of each count, until the word has been formed. For example, if the number corresponding to the first table is determined to be 3, then the user begins by counting horizontally to the right from the first box (designated 4) until arriving at 9: the letter in that ninth box (m) is the first letter of the word. Nine boxes further

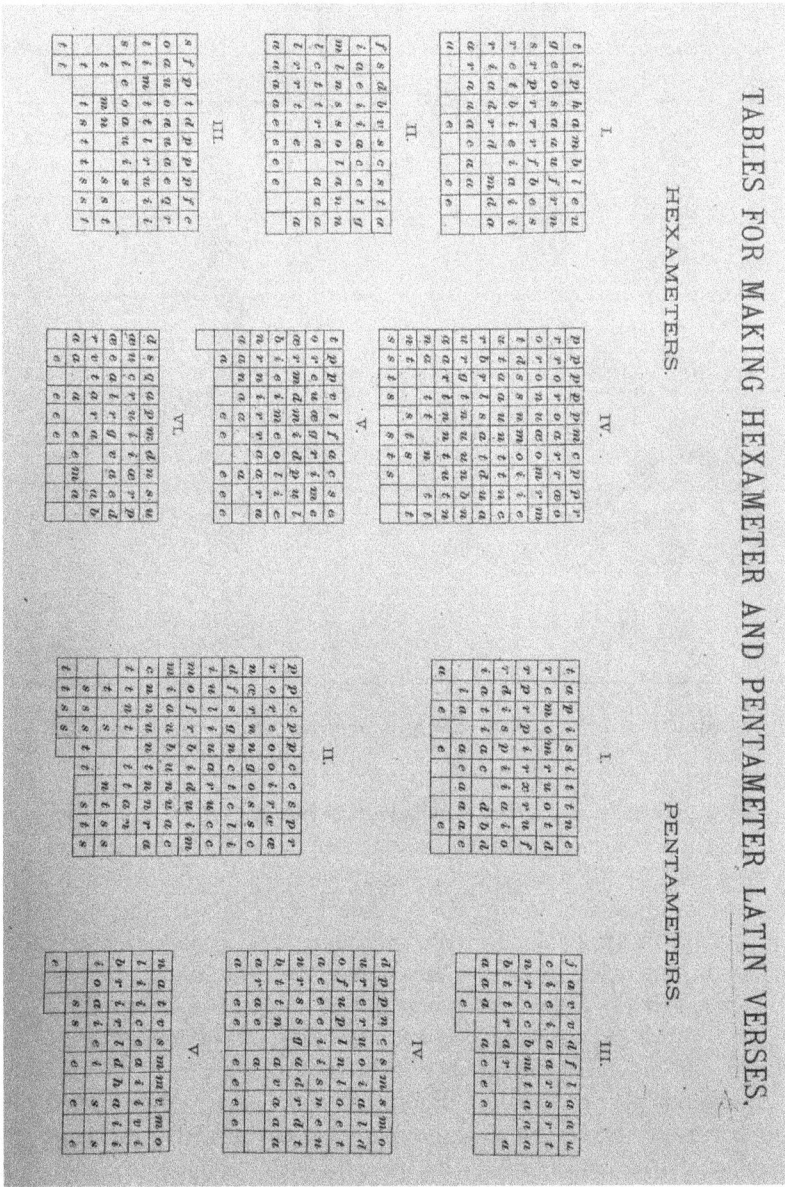

Fig. 4 *Tables for Making Hexameter and Pentameter Latin Verses* (London [?], 1878)

t	i	p	h	a	m	b	l	e	u
g	e	o	s	a	a	u	f	r	n
s	r	p	r	r	r	f	b	e	s
r	e	t	b	i	e	i	a	i	i
r	i	a	d	r	d		m	d	a
a	r	a	a	a	e	a	a		
a				e			e	r	

Fig. 5 Example of word selection from hexameter table

along, which in this case is in the second row down the table, the user reaches the second letter (a), and so on until the word (*martia*) has been formed (Fig. 5). By choosing a different number for the first table, the user can produce a different word. For example, by selecting the number one for the same table, the user produces *lurida*; two yields *barbara*, and so on. There are nine possible words in this table, and all are dactyls. Once the user has followed the process through all six tables, he or she will have produced six words, six feet, and, thus, a complete hexameter—though the only activities actually undertaken are the random selection of numbers and the recording of letters from the relevant boxes. As the authors of such tables promise, the user need not be able to read or scan the line of Latin verse he or she has produced. Yet however alienated the user might be from the product of this pseudo-metrical labor, the hexameter that results will nonetheless be a "true" one. Moreover, it is one among a great many that can be produced by this process. Because each of the six tables is capable of producing nine words, there are a total of 9^6 or 531,441 hexameter variations, all of them with exactly the same arrangement of metrical feet.[62]

In effect, the Eureka mechanizes this process, using a medley of repurposed and purpose-built contrivances. Some, such as an ornate brass spit engine, Clark appropriated from its everyday use at a domestic hearth; others—including the wooden staves printed with letters, drums fashioned from segments of an apple-tree trunk, and a hand-made star-wheel for controlling the machine's compositional impulse—he fabricated specially for the purpose making meters (Figs. 6 and 7). By pulling a lever (or "a small rope," as one report maintained),[63] either Clark himself or possibly a visitor to the Egyptian Hall could set this curious contraption into motion, its multi-teeth gears, flywheels, and cams clicking away in concert to grind out a line of Latin verse.[64] In the place of a table of letters, such as the ones described above, the Eureka offered a

Fig. 6 View of gears from Clark's Eureka Latin Hexameter Machine. Photograph by author, 2015

Fig. 7 Detail of lettered staves from Clark's Eureka Latin Hexameter Machine. Photograph by author, 2015

wooden drum—not dissimilar in operation to a stepped Leibniz wheel—radiating from the circumference of which were so-called stop wires of varying lengths; each wire determined how far a stave would descend and, thus, which letter among the many printed on it would be visible to viewers. The motive force of the machine caused each drum to revolve on a central axis—the distance of each drum's revolution depending variously on friction, weight, and balance. Thus, an element of randomness, corresponding to the user's selection at random of a number with which to begin his or her tabular calculation, was introduced into the Eureka's composition process. When all six drums completed their turns, and the staves came to rest (having been suspended, during the machine's "composing" phase, above the turning drums), a horizontal row of letters was visible to viewers in a series of six windows on the front of the machine.[65] This interconnected system of staves, wires, and drums was needed to produce "a large number of randomly worded" verses. In fact, Clark's Eureka promised considerably more possible lines than the hexameter tables discussed above because its drums accommodated between fifteen and twenty words each, totaling 27,907,200 permutations.[66] In keeping with the tabular logic on which it works, though, variability of combination is the machine's only means of asserting difference. To keep lines "true as to scansion and perfect as to sense,"[67] the Eureka's "compositions" were of necessity "highly determined."[68] All lines of dactylic hexameter it produced were arranged in the same order:

No. of drum .	.	1	2	3	4	5	6
Metrical pattern	.	−∪∪	−∪	∪−	−−−	−∪∪	−∪

There is never any elision, and never any variation in scansion. The verb is always a molossus (e.g. *prōmūlgānt*) and never a lesser ionic (e.g. *mănĭfēstānt*), which would be a possible alternative.[69]

Neither did the lines vary in syntax; the arrangement of words follows the same pattern in each line generated: adjective, noun, adverb, verb, noun, adjective.[70]

The Eureka's capacity for grinding out a seemingly endless number of formulaic, mechanical meters made it more than a mere spectacle, whose curious hexameters constituted a diversion for mid-Victorian consumers of showroom spectacles. As we saw in the previous chapter, amid the climate of education reform the study of the classics—and prosody as part of that study—became highly contested and thoroughly politicized, and as such prosody became a site of political contest between reformers who wanted to expand and modernize the curriculum and the *ancien regime*, for whom prosody was at the humanizing core of an anti-utilitarian idea of liberal education. How one pronounced or scanned lines of classical verse, whether one believed in the possibility of English dactylic hexameters, and what one thought about quantities versus accents—all of these prosodic questions were becoming deeply ideologically invested by the time the Eureka was exhibited in the Egyptian Hall. With its serial assembly process, where meters are produced by a mechanical process of numerical substitution, some contemporary observers of its hexameters or second-hand commentators saw in Clark's machine a parodic indictment of the lamentable state of classical education and the centrality of verse composition exercises to it. While its creator may have preferred to promote its powers of "conception" and "composition," assigning a quasi-literary intelligence to the Eureka's mechanical verse transports, what others perceived in its inflexible meters, where every line resembles the next in an apparently interminable chain of prosody, was a mechanical emblem of current metrical instruction. Babbage's Difference Engine may have been an automaton noteworthy for its *utility*, offering to lighten the load of "computers" whose calculations were demonstrably useful to the workaday world of Victorian commerce and exploration. Clark's Eureka, by contrast, seemed to some to be characterized not only by supreme uselessness but by downright absurdity.

Prosody for the Million

The fractiousness of mid-century debates about classical prosody and education, in which hexameters figured centrally, both focused on and extended beyond the immediate politics of the public schools and the Oxbridge system, where the professional philological franchise was itself in a state of transition. In these debates, which we touched on in "Meter Manufactories," are the contours of the more comprehensive epistemological redistributions that are often regarded as characterizing the nineteenth century. For example, Michel Foucault's paradigm of "modern" historicity posits that from the end of the eighteenth century new disciplines emerged and organized knowledge into new discursive economies.[71] At the beginning of the nineteenth century, philology was just such a new field, and over the course of the century, it set about demarcating its territory and establishing its own discursive taxonomies and methodologies in an attempt to confirm its existence as what Max Müller, first Professor of Comparative Philology at Oxford, called a "science of languages."[72] What is important to note here is that the whole of the philological franchise was, in fact, undergoing a series of discursive reconfigurations in which disciplinary boundaries and subdivisions were being contested and reconfigured. Of course, prosody was among these subdivisions, and it too was in flux, moving, as Yopie Prins has noted, "toward the codification of numerical modes of analysis."[73] During the 1840s, as Joseph Patrick Phelan has pointed out, philologists like the University of Aberdeen's John Stuart Blackie were engaged in attempts to "rethink the whole subject of prosody from first principles." Blackie's reconsiderations—themselves indicators of discursive transition—are threaded into the education debates taking place in and around the English educational establishment, and in this context they enable what is for Phelan a prosody that is "radical" in its borrowings from German philology, whose New-Humanist ethos—characterized by an attempt "to bring the Classics back into living contact with the real world"—was rejected by the Oxbridge establishment. Of course, Blackie's "radical" prosody—which promoted the viability in English of so-called accentual hexameters in which the *ictus*, or stress, replaced the *longa* of quantitative Latin verse—played a significant part in the mid-century's hexameter frenzy.[74] What becomes apparent is the interpenetrating nature of these debates: prosodical theories, reform politics, and disciplinary (re)organization are in fact complexly interrelated.

Phelan's research has highlighted some of these discursive linkages; in particular, he examines how scholarly journals such as the *Classical Museum*—which featured essays by Blackie, Francis Newman, John Oxenford, and Arthur Hugh Clough, among others—became sites of political contact, where discussions of meter merged with "the ongoing debate about the stultifying effect of the ancient universities on British intellectual life."[75] In the 1850s, 1860s, and beyond, after the collapse of the *Classical Museum* in 1848, prosody debates continued to circulate: in major philological organs; in the reports of the Newcastle Commission, the Taunton Commission, as well as in Matthew Arnold's school inspector reports and his essays arising from these; in treatises on metrics published by Coventry Patmore and others; in a raft of putatively scientific enquiries into the principles of (increasingly English) versification. The contributions of these texts to prosodic debates have been well documented by Phelan and others and several have been discussed already in *Nineteenth-Century Verse and Technology*. The narrative they construct is, of course, central to prosody's institutional history. But what is less well known, perhaps, is the popular narrative that exists on the margins of the prosody and philology establishment. The politics of Victorian versification was not confined exclusively to scholarly organs and professional manuals; on occasion it spilled over into more popular fora, such as "improving" periodicals. Here it came into contact with Clark's Eureka machine, which became a powerful material embodiment—and served as a useful anchor for indictments—of the institutional practice of Victorian verse composition, particularly as it featured the Latin hexameter line.

Commentary on the Eureka machine featured in a range of widely circulating periodicals, including cheap weeklies such as *Chambers's Edinburgh Journal* and more upmarket magazine such the *Athenæum* and the *Illustrated London News*. Like the Eureka itself, these magazines effectively provided a popular forum that constituted an intervention in prosodic discourse, one comprising not only aesthetic or philological observations regarding syntactic and metrical explication but also politicized contributions to broader mid-century questions regarding the specialized nature of meter, its rules or laws, and their role in Victorian society. The exchanges in these periodicals were not only comments on the Eureka machine itself. They were often the expressions of broader preoccupations with meter that either invoked the Eureka as a convenient material anchor for their critiques or eerily anticipated its automatic versification in their examination of schoolroom practices. Thus, the Eureka spectacle became the fulcrum on which both earlier and later popular prosodic debates pivoted, enabling access to a discursive space that was otherwise institutionally regulated, restricted to scholars, educators, and other professionals. The intertext of popular prosody emanating from and surrounding the Eureka extended to debates regarding well-established pedagogical practices—namely, the Gradus-oriented regime—and fundamental questions of nineteenth-century education reform, as expressed by Frederic William Farrar and others. Specifically, discussions of Clark's Latin Hexameter Machine overlap with a powerful improving agenda that involves the role of the classics in schools. What will become clear is that there existed an intertextual dialectic in which the Eureka can be seen to operate synecdochically. Much more than spectacle, Clark's metrical automaton facilitated a link between the worlds of private diversion and utilitarian application, between the leisure space of the Egyptian Hall and the institutional space of the classical schools, where the technologies of verse were becoming increasingly entangled in a national conversation about Greek and Latin instruction, as well as more comprehensive education reforms.

Curiously mechanizing one process that was absolutely central to scholastic prosody—the manufacture of Latin hexameters—Clark's Eureka delivered the technology of versification to a mass audience, many of whom, not having been privileged enough to receive a classical education, would have understood neither the Latin tongue nor its meters—making many among them ideal users of the versification tables on which the machine's compositions were based and, furthermore, no more knowledgeable about prosody than the machine itself. (One presumes that Clark would have been on hand to supply translations, as and when requested by paying visitors to the Egyptian Hall.[76]) But as a meter-making spectacle situated at the intersection of popular culture and scholarly specialization, the Eureka did not only supply uncanny classical meters to the masses. What is particularly fascinating about Clark's machine is how it operated as much more than just a curious, "recreational" device that existed freakishly at the margins of the mid-nineteenth-century prosody orthodoxy. Some observers of Clark's machine were understandably dazzled by, and consequently content to limit their commentary to, the machine's rate and volume of data combination—with the *Illustrated London News* remarking that, if left running for "a whole week (Sundays included)," it would generate "about 10,000" verses.[77] More often, however, it was the Eureka's relative metrical sophistication that caused observers to marvel at—but also to engage dialogically with—the more serious implications of its poetic productions. As such, this kitsch device was, as A. S. Gratwick gleefully noted in the 1990s, a "more fun" way to engage with versification "because you got your hexameter one tantalizing word at a time,"[78] but it also made otherwise comparatively circumscribed Victorian debates about, for example, Latin and English hexameters, the status of prosody as a specialized and rarefied academic discipline, as well as the function of prosody as a pedagogical tool at once immediately visible and accessible.

As Bernard Lightman, Joss Marsh, and others have shown, spectacle, commerce, and education were closely linked in Victorian Britain.[79] The Eureka intertext—a constellation of commentary, particularly contributions to general-interest and educational miscellanies, in which we can situate the machine—clearly demonstrates that visitors to the Egyptian Hall were keen not only to remark with wonder on this prosodic device, observing it as mere entertainment, but also to engage intellectually and critically with it and by extension the prosodic discourse in which it was curiously embedded. Popular periodicals such as *Chambers's Edinburgh Journal* "made the benefits of science visibly tangible for the masses."[80] Among the benefits made visible was the controversy surrounding scholastic prosody and classical metrics more generally. The laws and rules of mid-century metrics were on display not only as and when visitors to the Egyptian Hall stepped up to pull the Eureka's lever and "grind out" Latin hexameters, but also—for a much wider public, many of whom would not see Clark's mechanical versifier—when readers encountered the Eureka, or discussions that brought its mechanical composition process to mind, in the pages of *Chambers's* and other "popular improvement" publications that aimed at a "mass" or working-class readership.[81] Like the Eureka itself, these magazines effectively provided, as the title of one article put it, "Latin Versification for the Million," and, in the popular forum they enabled, there emerged a parallel prosodic discourse that included the Eureka phenomenon. By engaging with the machine's principles of composition as well as its verse product, contributors—both paid journalists and interested readers—participated in topical, and often highly politicized, prosodic debates. As its Latin hexameters were transcribed, explicated, and aesthetically judged, the Eureka figured briefly as the material signifier of a popular prosody that was characterized by the reform agendas circulating not only in the improving pages of popular print media but also in Victorian society more generally. This popular prosody extended authorship to amateur prosodists well outside the specialized scholarly franchise, and, further, it constructed an imagined community of prosody consumers for whom entertainment was mingled with both education and indoctrination in a politics that was, by and large, hostile to the centrality of prosody in Victorian pedagogy.

As by Machine

When the Victorian classical scholar P. A. Nuttall brought out his edition of Virgil's *Eclogues* in 1826, he attempted to provide an alternative to the arbitrary and poorly taught "prosodical rules" that, in his estimation, featured so centrally in public-school education. That most pupils, in spite of hours spent working with Latin meters, remained "utterly ignorant of their true principles" was, for Nuttall, a condition that might be remedied by simplifying the teaching of Latin metrics. To this end, he included in his edition an interlineal translation—where an English version is given under each line of Latin verse—and a "Treatise on Latin Versification," thus providing rules that are grounded in examples in the hope that the versification of Virgil will appeal more readily to the learner's ear. Nuttall was not at all in favor of practices—which Clark's Eureka and the hexameter tables on which its mechanics were based more or less replicate—of verse composition exercises that asked pupils to produce poetry before they had a good working grasp of the language in which it was written: "To attempt to write [Hexameter verse] by poring over a Gradus, before he can read it fluently, is as absurd as a foreigner attempting English poetry before he understands the accentuation of common words."[82] It is little wonder, then, that Nuttall regarded Clark's mechanical versifier as "little better than a mere puzzle, which any schoolboy might perform by a simpler process."[83] And he was not alone. Clark's mechanical versifier figured significantly in a prosodic intertext that radiated outward—beyond the immediate discursive radius of "professional" prosody that included classicists such as Nuttall and into the more expansive Victorian social terrain, which was characterized, as Joseph Bristow demonstrates, by a culture of systemic reform.[84]

When Nuttall commented on the Eureka's "curious and instructive" relationship to the prosodic education of "school-boys and Latin students," his words resonated beyond the Egyptian Hall.[85] One hears in the link he establishes between school and spectacle an indictment of a mechanistic pedagogy grounded in prosodic exercises. In this equation the Gradus provides a formulaic principle for composing Latin verses that "can be as readily performed … as by machine." A similar line of thinking was doubtless behind the inclusion by an anonymous contributor to *Chambers's Edinburgh Journal* of a set of prosodic "Tables" to illustrate "the secret of the [Eureka] machine"[86]—the contributor has not only correctly grasped the program on which Clark's machine functioned but also implied a critique of the kind of verse-by-numbers on which both versifying tables and the Eureka operate.[87] His presentation of a table that he "found" in "an old arithmetical school-book" reads very much as a sly swipe at institutional prosody, particularly his remark (an echo of Peter and Manwaring) that "any one of ordinary capacity, though he understands not one word of Latin, may be taught immediately to make hexameter and pentameter verses—true Latin, true verse, and good sense!" It appears that the author is suggesting that both the arcane, "arithmetical" system of rules and the machine that computes them are equally absurd and, consequently, of little practical use to "the million." Indeed, he concludes: "'What is the use of all this?' I can only reply, that the construction of these tables helped to wile away from me some tedious hours of lassitude and ill health."[88]

In the early 1860s, when the Clarendon Commission's suggestions for public-school reform brought these debates to a head, attacks on classroom prosody and "sticklers for *Gradus ad Parnassum*" were not uncommon in popular periodicals. As one contributor to *Chambers's* remarked, a "young gentleman with his head full of Latin verses would lag behind the other [young man] (of equal powers), who has received a more general, although not necessarily superficial education."[89] Indeed, Françoise Waquet has pointed out in *Latin or the Empire of a Sign* (2001) that this sort of adversity to classical instruction on the grounds of its (lack of) usefulness had been circulating throughout Europe since the eighteenth century. In France as much as in England, many men of property, as well as educators, felt that "Latin was not of the slightest use to the son of a peasant or artisan whose life would be spent behind a plough or bent over a counter or workbench, while for a merchant's son mathematics would serve better than Latin verse."[90] Such a position was by no means uncommon in the English educational debates of the 1840s, when it converged with the intertext that incorporates the Eureka. This convergence is particularly visible in an anonymous 1840 article (again in the reform-minded *Chambers's*) titled "View of a Classical School," whose author staunchly indicts the fetishizing of Greek and Latin:

> The extent to which classical education, as it is called, has long been carried in this country, to the almost entire exclusion of instruction of every other kind, has been more than once commented on in this periodical, and the injurious consequences of the practice pointed out. While admitting the standard writings of Greece and Rome to be fair adjuncts to an elegant education, or, in other words, to constitute an agreeable branch of the belles letters, the custom of imbuing the mind of youth with that species of knowledge alone, and neglecting all those departments of it calculated to be of use in after-life, was reprobated as alike absurd and deleterious.[91]

The emphasis on the neglect of "useful" knowledge in whose place one finds an "absurd and deleterious" training in the classics resonates with other reforms proposed around mid-century, most of which wanted to redress the narrow emphasis on Greek and Latin. Also, this "View" expresses criticisms that will re-emerge later in the decade in relation to Clark's Eureka machine, described by one commentator as a "curious" device without "immediate utility."[92] Several commentators also suggest that there is something "absurd" about the machine's function: the Eureka's verses, which as Blandford later notes "never [accommodate] any elision, and never any variation in scansion,"[93] are rendered wonderfully empty—a kind of meter for meter's sake. There is a fitting irony, then, in "[a]n inscription on the machine itself [that] describes [the verses] as 'eternal truths'—such as might be found in a book of moral maxims."[94] Like the perceived impracticality of a classical education centered on mechanical prosodic exercises, the Eureka, with its randomly generated "truths," appeared to many observers absurd in the extreme; its "moral maxims," likewise, are undoubtedly "deleterious" if acted upon.

Many Victorians, as we have seen, shared the opinion of the author of "View of a Classical School" regarding the pointless or at best stiflingly pedantic approach favored in the classical schools, and even in the early decades of the twentieth century the problems of nineteenth-century classical education continued to exert themselves.[95] Dorrance S. White, writing in the *Classical Journal* in 1930, explained the protracted "practical process" of Latin textbook reform and welcomed a series of what she calls "vitalizing" or "humanizing" improvements.[96] It is a "vitalizing," if not exactly "humanizing," fervor that motivated the author of "View of a Classical School," who claimed to see nothing but rote inculcation in the educational practice of "one of the most ancient and distinguished schools of England."[97] The curriculum in this institution is far from "liberal": in the exercises of the sixth form, "we find but one *half hour* (Thursday) given to modern history! ... With the exception of a sprinkling of mathematics, all the rest is Latin and Greek, Greek and Latin, over and over again, without pause or change." But what is most troubling is the emphasis on Latin and Greek poetry: "Poetry! all this time spent upon poetry!"[98] In order to "enable ... readers to judge for themselves," the author then quotes several weekly plans similar to the one reproduced below:

> "MONDAY.—Repetition of Friday's *Horace*, Satires or Epistles, 50 lines; *Latin lyrics* or *Greek verses* of Thursday looked over—hour for this half-past 7 A.M. ... WEDNESDAY.—Repetition of Friday's *Greek* play, 30 lines; *verses* of Friday looked over—hour half-past 7. ... *Musa Græca* (Greek verse), 40 or 50 lines, according to author chosen. ... THURSDAY.—Repetition of Monday's *Horace*, odes, 60 or 70 lines. ... FRIDAY.—*Latin verses*, hexameter, or hexameter and pentameter. SATURDAY,—."[99]

The presentation of these schedules has rhetorical import. Clearly, they are included as evidential ripostes to proponents of an anti-utilitarian conception of "liberal education" who broadly believed, in the words of John Henry Newman, that "the intellect ... is disciplined for its own sake."[100] That position at its most general is targeted in "View of a Classical School"; more narrowly the author's rhetoric is leveled at apologists for conventional prosodic instruction. As articulated years later by Ellingham in his "Apology for Latin Verse Composition," this position affirms that "while [the schoolboy] is learning to write Latin verses he is doing other valuable things, which are ignored in much of our utilitarian curriculum."[101] Yet this is certainly not what the *Chambers's* schedule is meant to illustrate. On the contrary, the message that the author is sending is clear. Engaged in a repetitive and potentially alienating educational regime that included reciting, memorizing, scanning, translating, and composing with the aid of the Gradus, the pupils eerily anticipate Clark's Eureka. They perform "as by machine," churning out predetermined sequences of verses in formulaic repetition.

Even the week's plan itself, as arranged for inclusion in "View of a Classical School," transmits the monotony and inflexibility of the pedagogical model it presents. The densely typed schedules, containing sequences of Arabic figures and studded with Graeco-Roman diction, appear almost impenetrable (certainly difficult to scan). Their typographic layout suggests, in another echo of the Eureka, extreme mechanical compression and the generation of material on a quasi-industrial scale. Moreover, many readers of *Chambers's Edinburgh Journal* were likely also to have been readers of the *Penny Magazine*, which circulated from 1832 to 1845 and attracted roughly the same readership as *Chambers's*. If so, then they would have been familiar with Charles Knight's "The Commercial History of a Penny Magazine," published in 1833. Indeed, it is highly likely that, in what John Plunkett and Andrew King have demonstrated was a "media-saturated society,"[102] the graphic display of school exercises would have achieved resonance with Knight's descriptions of compositors, moveable types, "stereotyping," and other features of nineteenth-century printing technology. The schoolboys' routine, in fact, provides little to distinguish them from compositors working in the *Penny Magazine*'s print-office, which Charles Knight describes:

> [W]e enter a very long room, in which from fifty to sixty compositors are constantly employed. Each man works at a sort of desk called a frame, and in most instances he has the desk or frame to himself. ... They are ... intelligent-looking, active artisans; not much thinking about the matter of

the work they have in hand, but properly intent upon picking up as many letters in the hour as may be compatible with following their copy correctly, and of producing what is called a clean *proof*,—that is, a proof, of first impression, with very few mistakes of words or letters.[103]

Algernon Charles Swinburne, for one, was well aware of the similarities in these kinds of mechanical endeavor. Well trained in classical verse composition at Eton, Swinburne once remarked to John Morley: "I am half blind and half dead with correcting all these proofs in a space of 4 days. Was not that (in schoolboy parlance) a *grind?*" Swinburne himself was indefatigable in correcting errors in his proofs, and his exasperated letters to friends and publishers convey his ire at "the intolerable drudgery of toiling after the steps of blunderers and idlers to do their proper work for them," not to mention his dissatisfaction with the quasi-metrical labor of the printers: "These are the things that men whose whole business is orthography and the setting up of sentences arranged in order ought to know without giving authors the trouble to instruct their ignorance and teach them their trade."[104]

Further, the tasks of compositors and schoolboys were similar also to those of the boy computers, whose "intolerable labour and fatiguing monotony" Babbage had suggested an automaton such as his Difference Engine might ameliorate. Babbage himself imagined that his device could speed up and reduce errors in both the calculation and copying processes—"becoming at the same time a substitute for the compositor and the computer."[105] Clark's Eureka extended a similar promise: it could offer hexameters that were unfailingly "correct" and always rendered letter-perfect by the display of preprinted letters on its wooden staves. His machine's serried rows of staves, with their letters and ligatures carefully adhered to their front surface, resemble blocks of printed typeface. Instead of providing a printed impression made from these letters, however, Clark determined that his device would display each hexameter output through a sequence of six horizontal windows. They remain visible just long enough for an observer to read them, though, in theory, a series a brakes and levers allowed Clark to pause the machine's verse production so that a line might be transcribed. That the Eureka's inventor himself deemed the "*visible Display* of the Lines produced [by the machine] … not essential," the process of perpetual verse production "during the night, or in the intentional absence of all Intelligent Beings, or Spectators,"[106] both subordinates the significance of any particular hexameter to a process of mass metrical production and reinforces that kind of unthinking and repetitive mechanical labor that contemporaries identified in the work of computers and compositors.

We see this position clearly in "View of a Classical School," which conveys its author's worry (shared by many others) that a pupil in such an educational regime was in real danger of becoming, if he had not already been reduced to, a "calculating" machine—or, more precisely, to borrow the words of one Eureka observer, "an automaton Latin versifier"[107]—as a consequence of classical instruction that foregrounded not merely Latin and Greek but more specifically poetry and prosodic exercise. Indeed, as the rigid weekly schedule quoted above is constructed to suggest, there was very little by which to distinguish a week's prosodic exercises in the schoolroom from other forms of mechanical activity, from working at a compositor's frame to pulling the lever of Clark's apparatus in the Egyptian Hall.[108] (John Clark, the inventor of the Eureka machine, was himself a printer by trade.)[109] The difference is in the ratio of (relatively) comfortable physical exertion to stultifying mental exertion. As one commentator remarked in 1859, thinking retrospectively about the Eureka, "All inspired poets were invited to lighten their labours by merely putting a few words into a box, turning a handle, and grinding out a Latin hexameter ready made."[110] Another, unimpressed by the Eureka mechanism's ability to rapidly "shuffle" grammar and prosody, found little application for it inside the classroom, where it might constitute an "amusement—but nothing more."[111] Given the context of education reforms and debates regarding a classical curriculum that emphasized attention to meter and scansion, such textual engagements with the Eureka acquire a political resonance. With Clark's Latin Hexameter Machine, education reform outlets such as *Chambers's* had a grotesque parody of classical education, and in representations of the machine—in which it is cast as supremely useless, an "oddity"—it effectively serves as a convenient material anchor for their reform agendas. Accounts of the machine itself, as well as the metrical computation "Tables" designed for someone who "understands not one word of Latin,"[112] went beyond engagements with the spectacle; they operated intertextually in contemporary debates about prosody and education, and as such can be seen as instances of a potentially disruptive meta-prosody, whose aim was actually thoroughly to dismantle prosody in the name of utilitarian pedagogical reconfiguration. If that did not work, one imagines, then at least there was a ready-to-hand solution to the "pristine defectiveness" of the educational system:[113] schoolboys (the bone-idle or merely metrically disinclined) could do worse than get their hands on an "Artificial Versifying" table, or, better still, they could have their poetic labors mechanically lightened by Clark's curious device.[114] According to William Makepeace Thackeray, writing anonymously in *Punch*, such a device was just what was needed. He satirically reports of an exhibition of the machine at work: "That notable invention, the Eureka, or Latin Verse-grinder, was tried yesterday before a committee of young gentlemen from the public schools, who are anxious to have their exercises done with the least possible trouble." Following this display, naturally, "Several double-barrelled Eurekas were ordered for Eton, Harrow, and Rugby...."[115] With the aid of their mechanical Gradus, schoolboys would be free to get on with instruction more immediately relevant to what the *Chambers's* school reformer calls "the business of after-life, and … their worldly success or happiness."[116]

Random Measures

Possibly with Professor Faber's Euphonia or a similar "Speaking Automaton" in mind, John Clark entertained the idea of improving upon the process of voice synthesis "actuated by a performer": "if it were combined with the Hexameter Machine, it would produce its sentences *spontaneously*."[117] Such a device, which married sound generating capabilities with a mechanics of self-powered composition, would be a step in the direction of both utility and intelligence. Clark concludes his pamphlet on the Eureka with the following words: "Every *new thing* is an intellectual *accession*, and every *accession* may, *possibly*, be of important use."[118] This unflinching belief in advancement or "accession" though the technologies of speech synthesis and prosodic composition belies a recognition that machines, if correctly conceived and constructed, might well be capable of feats of ingenuity that once had been regarded as arising from uniquely human (also typically educated and privileged) powers of intellectual agency and mental acuity. Even if Kempelen's chess playing automaton had been a hoax, there might still be a way of imagining and realizing a legitimate thinking machine, one that could perform a specific range of tasks as good as, or possibly even more efficiently than, its human counterpart. Yet even Babbage, who arguably came closer than any of his contemporaries to achieving such a mechanization of intellectual labor, was more modest in his claims for the discriminating powers of technology. He was clear that his calculating engine, however sophisticated, was only automating the most basic function of the human mind. In an 1822 letter to Humphry Davy, the eminent chemist and then president of the Royal Society, Babbage remarked that his Difference Engine "should become a substitute for one of the lowest operations of the human intellect": "a continued repetition of ... arithmetical calculations."[119] As we have seen, some reformers contended that the Eureka offered a similarly rudimentary substitution, automating only the "lowest operations" of the boy verse-computer. There was, they held, a paucity of intelligence and use-value evident in the hexameters manufactured by the Latin verse machine.

But not necessarily so. In a way, Clark was prescient in seizing upon the "spontaneous" element of the Eureka's operation. While its hexameters, as we have seen, were fixed in their metrical and grammatical patterns, they were nonetheless mixable in their combinations of words. After each line was produced and then decomposed, the process would begin again as the machine acted under the impetus of its descending lead weight. With the lettered staves drawn up, the built-up force of the mechanism would send an impulse to the drums, causing them to spin on their axes. Where they came to rest determined which length of stop wire would project in a given position to support a stave as it fell again to reveal a letter. But how much each drum revolved was a consequence of many unplanned factors: how heavy a drum was and how (un)balanced it was (the arrangement of stop wires produced an uneven distribution of weight on some drums), how freely a drum could spin on its axis, how much "play" there might be in the brake that stopped drums from spinning. These mechanical factors meant that neither the machine's inventor nor its observers could ever be certain where the drums might come to rest and, consequently, which letters would form the next hexameter in sequence. Thus, not only was the Eureka capable of a vast number of hexameters, but also it offered an element of randomness in their composition—in spite of its prosodic limitations, the machine was truly "spontaneous" in that the determination of each line, unlike the prescanned pronouncements of Faber's Euphonia, had nothing at all to do with the operator, who could neither guess nor accurately determine what line the machine was about to produce. Each line was produced independent of any external agency, making the Eureka a legitimately self-acting versifier. It is this capacity, however limited, for producing unplanned results that lent Clark's machine not just an unpredictably spectacular quality, which doubtless enhanced its curious appeal among visitors to the Egyptian Hall, but also a modicum of what we would now term machine intelligence.[120] Randomness and related nondeterministic capacities are, for some theorists of machine intelligence, a sign of commensuration between human brains and thinking machines. For example, the British computer scientist Alan Turing (1912–1954) thought that the human mind had an inherently "random element," and devices that display a similar degree of randomness, whether "a genuinely random element [or] a quasi-random one," might in some scenarios be described as showing signs of intelligence.[121] As Elizabeth Wilson observes, the surprise generated by randomness suggested for Turing "the capacity for unexpected behaviour ... [which is] a necessary component in any intelligent machine."[122]

But would such an intimation of intelligence offer any appreciable advantage to the Eureka in a now famous measure of machine intelligence? The Turing Test, proposed by Turing in "Computer Machinery and Intelligence" (1950) and since widely popularized, provides a means of gauging the ability of a machine to demonstrate signs of thought. The test involves a series of textual exchanges in which a human evaluator attempts to determine if his or her interlocutor is another human or a machine. If the evaluator is unable to distinguish person from computer, the test is deemed "passed," and the device in question regarded as "intelligent." Randomness and the surprise it can produce in an observer can play an important role in this kind of evaluation—not least because of the capacity for defamiliarization. On the one hand, a violation of what was anticipated might be perceived as a mark of thoughtful deviation from pattern or convention, while, on the other, it might be read as an indication of absurdity. In any case, the question of the Eureka's random "intelligence" is somewhat complicated by Clark's decision, discussed above, to fix its hexameter pattern. Clark's choice of an irregular hexameter, with freely mixed feet (dactyl | trochee | iamb | molossus | dactyl | spondee), might well enhance the semblance of imagination that the randomness of the word choice exhibits—until, of course, one realizes that every line is formed on the *same* irregular pattern. For Turing, what ultimately mattered was the unsettling mimesis of human behavior that randomness excites. The ability to be surprised by a machine was, for Turing, a remarkable instance of the blurring of boundaries between machine and mind, where we can witness both what we have in common with machines and what distinguishes us from them and them from us. Notably, Turing imagined this thought-provoking aspect of randomness as "the unexpected (and child-like) character of machines."[123] Thus, in the Eureka's mechanization of an intellectual pursuit typically performed by young versifiers, there is perhaps a fitting anticipation of the man-machine dynamic that continues to captivate computer scientists and theorists of artificial intelligence well over a century after Clark's automaton versifier amazed audiences in 1845. As we will see in "The Automatic Flow of Verse," these and related questions about machines and minds, as well as bodies, were impacting on the Victorian metrical imaginary in a number of ways. The Eureka was only one among many metrical machines where components were deliberately segmented and produced in isolation from one another. While the Eureka's random production of meters might suggest a glimmer of thought, its rigid and highly determined versification was mechanical in the extreme. But what did it mean when similar qualities— for example, rigidly patterned, robotic prosody or, in other cases, apparently random, unplanned metrical utterance—characterized the metrics of living persons? If one might speculate about the ghost of intelligence in a meter-making machine, then might one also need to entertain the possibility of metrical mechanization in an apparently intelligent creature?

Notes

1. John Hollingshead, *My Lifetime* (London: Sampson, Low, Marstan and Co., 1895), 68–69. [Anon.], "Talking Machines," *All the Year Round* (Sept. 24, 1870), 396.
2. David Lindsay, *Madness in the Making: The Triumphant Rise and Untimely Fall of America's Show Inventors* (New York: Kodansha, 1997), 87. Hollingshead, *My Lifetime*, 68–69. As Thomas L. Hankins and Robert J. Silverman note, Faber's Euphonia—"probably the most loquacious pneumatic speaking machine ever made"—should be understood in the context of nineteenth-century investigations into acoustics. This and other "ingenious demonstrations of phonetic theory"—as conducted by Hermann von Helmholtz, Charles Wheatstone, Edward Scripture, and others—were the popular expression of a serious science of sound that would turn its scrutinizing ears toward meter during the second half of the century. I will explore this subject in detail below in "The Automatic Flow of Verse." See Hankins and Silverman, *Instruments and the Imagination* (Princeton: Princeton University Press, 1995), 214, 216.
3. "Talking Machines," 395.

4. See definition of *euphony* in *OED*: http://www.oed.com/view/Entry/65042?.
5. "Talking Machines," 396.
6. "Talking Machines," 396.
7. Translation of *android* from *OED*. See, for example, *Ure's Dictionary of Arts, Manufactures, and Mines*, 6th edn, ed. Robert Hunt, 3 vols (London: Longman, Green, and Co., 1867), 3: 260.
8. Richard D. Altick, *The Shows of London* (Cambridge, MA: Belknap Press of Harvard University Press, 1978), 356. See [Anon.], "Latin Versification for the Million," *Chambers's Edinburgh Journal*, 13 (1850), 205. The author confuses the Eureka and the Euphonia, discussing the functions of the former in relation to the creator of the latter.
9. See [Anon.], "The Eureka," *Illustrated London News*, 19 July 1845, 37. This source claims that the Eureka "perform[ed] the National Anthem" while producing verses, and "as soon as the verse is complete, a short pause of silence ensues." It continues: "On the announcement that the line is about to be broken up, the cylinder performs the air of 'Fly not yet,' until every letter is returned into its proper place in the alphabet."
10. See, for example, Peggy Aldrich Kidwell, "Calculating Machine," in *Instruments of Science: An Historical Encyclopedia*, ed. Robert Bud and Deborah Jean Warner (New York and London: Garland, 1998), 75–77.
11. For a more detailed account of some of these early androids, see Jessica Riskin, "The Defecating Duck, or, the Ambiguous Origins of Artificial Life," *Critical Inquiry*, 29 (2003), 599–633.
12. Simon Schaffer, "Babbage's Dancer and the Impresarios of Mechanism," *Cultural Babbage: Technology, Time, and Invention*, ed. Francis Spufford and Jenny Uglow (London: Faber, 1996), 64–65.
13. [Robert Willis], *An Attempt to Analyse the Automaton Chess Player, of Mr. De Kempelen* (London: n. pub., 1821), 9.
14. Willis, *An Attempt to Analyse the Automaton Chess Player*, 10.
15. Willis, *An Attempt to Analyse the Automaton Chess Player*, 9–10.
16. John Clark, *The General History and Description of a Machine for Composing Hexameter Latin Verses* (Bridgwater: Frederick Wood, 1848), 19–22.
17. Andrew Ure, *The Philosophy of Manufactures: Or, an Exposition of the Scientific, Moral, and Commercial Economy of the Factory System* (London: Charles Knight, 1835), 1.
18. Andrew Ure, *A Dictionary of Arts, Manufactures, and Mines*, 3rd edn, 2 vols (New York: D. Appleton and Co., 1844), 82.
19. Ure, *Philosophy of Manufactures*, 9, 13–14.
20. Karl Marx, *Capital: A Critique of Political Economy*, vol. 1 (1867; New York: Modern Library, 1906), 371, 378.

21. Karl Marx, *Economic and Philosophical Manuscripts of 1844*, trans and ed. Martin Milligan (Mineola, NY: Dover, 2007), 24.
22. Alessandro Roncaglio, *The Wealth of Ideas: A History of Economic Thought* (Cambridge: Cambridge University Press, 2005), 231. For more context on Babbage, Ure, and antecedents to twentieth-century Taylorism, see John Bellamy Foster's "New Introduction" to Harry Braverman's *Labor and Monopoly Capital: The Degradation of Work in the Twentieth Century* (New York: Monthly Review Press, 1998), ix–xxiv.
23. Roncaglio, *The Wealth of Ideas*, 231.
24. Laura Otis, *Networking: Communicating with Bodies and Machines in the Nineteenth Century* (Ann Arbor: University of Michigan Press, 2001), 31. James Essinger, *Jacquard's Web: How a Hand Loom Led to the Birth of the Information Age* (Oxford: Oxford University Press, 2004), 62.
25. See Doron D. Swade, "Calculating Engines: Machines, Mathematics, and Misconceptions," in *Mathematics in Victorian Britain*, ed. Raymond Flood et al. (Oxford: Oxford University Press, 2011), 239–260. Brian Winston, *Media, Technology, and Society—A History: From the Telegraph to the Internet* (London: Routledge, 1998), 157. Herbert Sussman, *Victorian Technology: Invention, Innovation, and the Rise of the Machine* (Santa Barbara: Praeger, 2009), 41.
26. Doron David Swade, "Calculation and Tabulation in the Nineteenth Century," PhD thesis, University of London, 2003, 71.
27. See Jeremy M. Norman, "From Gutenberg's Press to the Foundations of the Internet," *From Gutenberg to the Internet: A Sourcebook on the History of Information Technology*, ed. Jeremy M. Norman (Novato: historyofscience.com, 2005), 50–51.
28. For an overview of the link between Babbage's devices and other technologies, such as the Jacquard loom, see Essinger, *Jacquard's Web*.
29. L. F. Menabrea, *A Sketch of the Analytical Engine Invented by Charles Babbage*, trans Ada Lovelace, *From Gutenberg to the Internet: A Sourcebook on the History of Information Technology*, ed. Jeremy M. Norman (Novato, CA: historyofscience.com, 2005), 234.
30. Niran B. Abbas, *Thinking Machines* (Berlin: Lit Verlag, 2006), 52.
31. See, for example, John Haugeland, *Artificial Intelligence: The Very Idea* (Cambridge, MA: MIT Press, 1985), 125–132; George F. Luger, *Artificial Intelligence: Structures and Strategies for Computer Problem Solving*, 5th edn (Harlow: Pearson Education, 2005), 10.
32. Stephen P. Rice, *Minding the Machine: Languages of Class in Early Industrial America* (Berkeley and Los Angeles: University of California Press, 2004), 36.
33. Clark, *General History*, 2, 4.
34. Clark, *General History*, 3.

35. See Joseph Patrick Phelan, "Radical Metre: The English Hexameter in Clough's *Bothie of Toper-Na-Fuosich*," *Review of English Studies*, 50 (1999), 173.
36. Walter Savage Landor, "English Hexameters," *Fraser's Magazine for Town and Country*, 42 (1850), 62.
37. See George Saintsbury, "The Prosody of the Nineteenth Century," *The Cambridge History of English Literature*, vol. 13, ed. A.W. Ward and A.R. Waller (New York: Putnam's Sons, 1917), 250–282. A compelling and more recent account can be found in Yopie Prins, "Metrical Translation: Nineteenth-Century Homers and the Hexameter Mania," *Nation, Language, and the Ethics of Translation*, ed. Sandra Bermann and Michael Wood (Princeton and Oxford: Princeton University Press, 2005), 159–174.
38. Tennyson's poem expresses his worries about English hexameters— "a most burlesque barbarous experiment. / When was a harsher sound ever heard, ye Muses, in England?" Alfred Tennyson, "On Translations of Homer, Hexameters and Pentameters" (1863), *The Poems of Tennyson in Three Volumes, Second Edition, Incorporating the Trinity College Manuscripts*, ed. Christopher Ricks (Berkeley and Los Angeles: University of California Press, 1987), II, 651, ll. 2–3. For an interesting discussion of Swinburne's use of the measure in his "Hymn to Proserpine," see Martin J. Duffell, *A New History of English Metre* (London: Legenda, 2008), 182.
39. See Matthew Arnold, *On Translating Homer*, *On the Classical Tradition*, ed. R. H. Super, vol. 1 of *The Complete Prose Works of Matthew Arnold* (Ann Arbor: University of Michigan Press, 1960), 124. See also Phelan, "Radical Metre," 174. As Yopie Prins remarks, Arnold "prescribed hexameter not only for future translators of Homer but also for the future of English poetry." See Prins, "Metrical Translation," 231. To William Whewell, Arnold remarked that "[t]he Hexameter is just as well fitted to the English ear as any of our common measures, *when* we have got rid of the fancy of scanning by Latin rules ...." Nevertheless, he did have reservations. Earlier that same year (1861) he had written to Herbert Hill, his one-time classics master at Rugby, that a quantitatively accurate rendering of English hexameters (here he alludes to the experiments of his friend Arthur Hugh Clough) could countermand rhythmical "naturalness." See Matthew Arnold, *The Letters of Matthew Arnold*, vol. 2, ed. Cecil Y. Lang (Charlottesville and London: University Press of Virginia, 1997), 68, 56.
40. Prins, "Metrical Translation," 231.
41. Russell specifies not only that "the LAST word must be either of TWO or of THREE syllables" but also that its number of syllables typically

determines the number of syllables of "the preceding word." Further, while the "Dactylic Hexameter must have at least ONE caesura," it may have as many as many as three." See John Russell, *Rudiments of the Latin Language for the Use of Charterhouse School* (London: R. and A. Taylor, 1822), 142.
42. William Ramsay, *A Manual of Latin Prosody*, 2nd edn (London and Glasgow: Richard Griffin and Company, 1859), 162.
43. John S. Hart, *A Manual of Composition and Rhetoric: A Text-Book for Schools and Colleges* (Philadelphia: Eldredge and Brother, 1871), 227. Though Hart presents the final foot as a trochee, others have suggested this line, from Virgil's *Aeneid* (8.596), is a textbook example of the hexameter pattern of five dactyls followed by a spondee. See, for example, G. Braden's entry for "Hexameter" in *The Princeton Encyclopedia of Poetry and Poetics*, 4th edn, ed. Roland Greene, et al. (Princeton: Princeton University Press, 2012), 627.
44. Hart, *A Manual of Composition and Rhetoric*, 227.
45. Worth mention here is a later contribution to the debate on English hexameters: Robert Bridges, *Ibant Obscuri: An Experiment in the Classical Hexameter* (Oxford: Clarendon Press, 1916). For a more recent critical appraisal of Victorian experiments with English hexameters, see Jospeh Phelan, *The Music of Verse: Metrical Experiment in Nineteenth-Century Poetry* (Basingstoke: Palgrave Macmillan, 2007), 45–87. As Andrew Barker points out, the term *logaoedic* "seems to mean 'between prose (*logos*) and verse or song (*aoidē*).'" See Barker, *Greek Musical Writings: II, Harmonic and Acoustic Theory* (Cambridge: Cambridge University Press, 1989), 452 n243. Logaoedic verses are sometimes defined, loosely, as verses in which different feet are mixed.
46. Hart, *A Manual of Composition and Rhetoric*, 227. The extract from Longfellow's *Evangeline* is reproduced from Hart, with his own scansion.
47. [Anon.], "Belles Lettres," *Westminster and Foreign Quarterly Review* (Jan. 1, 1866), 288.
48. Charles Kingsley, *Letters and Memories: Novels, Poems, and Letters of Charles Kingsley* (New York: Cooperative Publication Society, 1899), 298.
49. Arthur Hugh Clough, *Amours de Voyage*, in *The Poems and Prose Remains of Arthur Hugh Clough*, 2 vols, ed. [Shore Smith] (London: Macmillan and Co., 1869), II:301.
50. James Williams, "The Jokes in the Machine: Comic Verse," *The Oxford Handbook of Victorian Poetry*, ed. Matthew Bevis (Oxford: Oxford University Press, 2013), 822. The word "rubbishy," an unusual poeticism, appears here and there in the popular prose fiction of the period. Examples include Frederick Marryat's *Joseph Rushbrook, or The Poacher*

(1841), Sheridan Le Fanu's *The Tenants of Malory* (1867), and the anonymous *Laura Erle* (1873). Le Fanu's novel describes one character as "writ[ing] long, rambling, rubbishy letters to his attorneys in London." What is interesting about Clough's usage is that gets added comic mileage by fusing the two senses of the word: (1) "covered with rubbish; full of rubbish, rubble or debris," denoting the actual state of the Roman ruins he is beholding, and (2) "worthless, of poor quality; contemptible," conveying Claude's disregard for the picturesque beauty of crumbling Roman antiquities. See *OED* entry for "rubbishy," www.oed.com, accessed 20 October 2015.

51. C. J. Ellingham, "Apology for the Practice of Latin Verse Composition," *Greece and Rome*, 4 (1935), 151–152.
52. Clark, *The General History*, 3, 4.
53. Altick, *Shows of London*, 356.
54. John Strachan and Richard Terry, *Poetry* (Edinburgh: Edinburgh University Press, 2000), 174.
55. Matt Davies, "Works, Products, and the Division of Labour: Notes for a Cultural and Political Economic Critique," *Cultural Political Economy*, ed. Jacqueline Best and Matthew Paterson (Abingdon: Routledge, 2010), 59.
56. "The Eureka," *Illustrated London News*, 37.
57. See Mary Poovey, *A History of the Modern Fact: Problems of Knowledge in the Sciences of Wealth and Society* (Chicago and London: University of Chicago Press, 1998).
58. Clark, *General History*, 3.
59. Clark, *General History*, 3.
60. See John Peter, *Artificial Versifying, Or, The School-Boy's Recreation* (London, 1677). n. pag. Jonathan Swift may have had such tables in mind when he wrote, in *Gulliver's Travels*, about a thinking machine that allowed "the most ignorant Person at a reasonable Charge, and with a little bodily Labour, [to] write Books in Philosophy, Poetry, Politicks, Law, Mathematicks and Theology, without the least Assistance from Genius or Study." See Jonathan Swift, *Gulliver's Travels*, ed. Paul Turner (Oxford and New York: Oxford University Press, 1971), 183.
61. See Edward Manwaring, *Stichology, Or the Recovery of the Latin, Greek, and Hebrew Numbers* (London, 1737). n. pag.
62. I am extremely grateful to Richard Everson, Professor of Machine Learning in the University of Exeter's Department of Computer Science, for explaining to me—and subsequently verifying—the process these verse tables describe.
63. [Anon.], "Odds and Ends," *Nelson Examiner and New Zealand Chronicle* (Apr. 18, 1846), 25.

64. See [Anon.], "Oddities in Music," *Chambers's Journal of Popular Literature, Science, and Arts*, 12 (1859), 313. The verb "grind" here can, of course, denote the physical activity of pulling the machine's lever, but from the mid-1830s it had another meaning: "to work hard at a subject of study under the direction of a tutor or 'grinder.'" See *OED* entry for "grind," www.oed.com, accessed 20 October 2015. These two meanings are fused in the educational debates that surround and incorporate Clark's Eureka.

65. This process is described in detail, with particular attention to the specific mechanics of the machine and accompanied by helpful illustrations of the various parts, in a 1963 essay by D. W. Blandford:

> Externally the machine resembles an automatic vending machine, with a word appearing in each of six slots. The mechanism works like a grandfather clock, by weights, pulleys, and gear wheels. From time to time it needs winding up (with a clock key) but it does not require any further setting. Words are formed by a series of lettered staves which rest on stop wires projecting from revolving drums....
>
> ... There are six drums in all—one for each slot—resembling so many mechanical hedgehogs....
>
> At present the six drums turn independently of each other, at different speeds, and irregularly.

See D. W. Blandford, "The *Eureka*," *Greece and Rome*, 10 (1963), 73–77. Blandford's description is based on his viewing of the machine subsequent to its restoration in 1950, so it may not precisely reflect the workings of the Eureka at the time of its 1845 exhibition.

66. See A. S. Gratwick, "The Latin Hexameter," *Classical Review*, n.s. 40 (1990), 341; and Blandford, "The *Eureka*," 71. In an 1845 letter to his sister, written when he was exhibiting the Eureka in London, John Clark remarks excitedly: "A most astonishing discovery has been made with the Hexameter Machine. It would make so many millions of verses that to produce *all* will not be done for a century or more, but we have discovered that if we take 100 or so of its productions that these will produce thousands & millions of *other* verses, by another machine, & so on. It has opened a new field of scientific speculation." See John Clark, letter to his sister, Sarah (Clark) Metford, August 1845. Clark Archive, Street, Somerset.

67. "Odds and Ends," 25.

68. Gratwick, "The Latin Hexameter," 341.

69. Blandford, "The Eureka," 77.

70. Blandford, "The Eureka," 77.

71 See Michel Foucault, *The Order of Things: An Archaeology of the Human Sciences* (London and New York: Routledge, 1973).

72. See Max Müller, *Lectures on the Science of Language: Delivered at the Royal Institution of Great Britain in April, May, and June, 1861*, 2nd ed., revised, 2 vols. (London: Longman, Green, Longman, and Roberts, 1862), I, 23. See also Tony Crowley, *The Politics of Discourse: The Standard Language Question in British Cultural Debates* (Basingstoke and London: Macmillan, 1989), 13–90.
73. Prins, "Victorian Meters," *The Cambridge Companion to Victorian Poetry*, ed. Joseph Bristow (Cambridge: Cambridge University Press, 2000), 106.
74. Phelan, "Radical Metre," 172.
75. Phelan, "Radical Metre," 166.
76. According to Richard Bellon, "The Egyptian Hall had been one of the capital's most popular attractions since its opening in 1812.... It accommodated everything from live orangutans to exotic cheese. Featured among the countless shows in the decade before the Great Exhibition were a speaking automaton [i.e., Professor Faber's Euphonia], a machine for composing hexameter Latin verse, models of ancient and modern Jerusalem, and nine performing Ojibwa Indians in native costume". See Richard Bellon, "Science at the Crystal Focus of the World," *Science in the Marketplace: Nineteenth-Century Sites and Experience*, ed. Aileen Fyfe and Bernard Lightman (Chicago and London: University of Chicago Press, 2007), 318. Joss Marsh notes that the Egyptian Hall was "the most successful of London's show-places throughout the century." See Marsh, "Spectacle," *A Companion to Victorian Literature and Culture*, ed. Herbert F. Tucker (Oxford: Blackwell, 1999), 278. According to Steven Connor, the Egyptian Hall was "a venue which would establish itself as a home of wizardry and wondrous mechanics." See Connor, *Dumbstruck: A Cultural History of Ventriloquism* (Oxford and New York: Oxford University Press, 2000), 354. By and large, visitors to the Hall came to consume diversions, oddities, and mechanical curiosities, but while the context may encourage us to think of these devices as merely popular "amusements," Connor reminds us that at the same time they figure importantly in the development of more conventionally scientific technologies such as telephones, phonographs, and loudspeakers. Indeed, he traces Alexander Graham Bell's development of the telephone to the inventor's early attempts to reproduce effects of Professor Faber's Euphonia machine (356).
77. "The Eureka," *Illustrated London News*, 37. As it happens, these words are taken almost verbatim from Clark's own *General History*, 5.
78. Gratwick, "The Latin Hexameter," 341.
79. See Bernard Lightman, *Victorian Popularizers of Science: Designing Nature for New Audiences* (Chicago and London: University of Chicago

Press, 2007), 167–218; Marsh, "Spectacle," 276–288; and Bellon, "Science at the Crystal Focus on the World," 301–335.
80. Marsh, "Spectacle," 285.
81. See [Henry Brougham], "Progress of the People—The Periodical Press," *Edinburgh Review*, 57 (1833), 240. Brougham was involved in the Society for the Diffusion of Useful Knowledge, which distributed Charles Knight's "improving" *Penny Magazine* (1832–1845); another penny weekly was the *Saturday Magazine of the Society for Propagating Christian Knowledge*. *Chambers's Edinburgh Journal*, a commercial and slightly more expensive periodical (1 1/2d.), competed for roughly the same largely working-class market. See also Jonathan Topham, "The *Mirror of Literature, Amusement and Instruction* and Cheap Miscellanies in Early Nineteenth-Century Britain," *Science in the Nineteenth-Century Periodical*, ed. Geoffrey Cantor et al. (Cambridge: Cambridge University Press, 2004), 37–66.
82. P. A. Nuttall, *P. Virgilii Maronis Bucolica* (London: Simpkin and Marshall, 1826), xi–xii.
83. P. A. Nuttall, "The Eureka," *Littell's Living Age*, 7 (1845), 214.
84. See Joseph Bristow, "Reforming Victorian Poetry: Poetics after 1832," *The Cambridge Companion to Victorian Poetry*, ed. Bristow (Cambridge: Cambridge University Press, 2000), 1–24.
85. Nuttall, "The Eureka," 214.
86. "Latin Versification for the Million," 205.
87. A later contributor to the journal *Notes and Queries*, perhaps recalling the earlier *Chambers's* piece, draws an explicit connection among the Eureka, versification tables, and the *Gradus ad Parnassum*. See W. Pinkerton, "Machine Hexameters," *Notes and Queries*, 3 (Jan. 19, 1856), 57–58.
88. "Latin Versification for the Million," 205.
89. [Anon.], "The Public Schools *v.* Belvidere House," *Chambers's Journal of Popular Literature, Science and Arts*, 15 (1861), 9, 10.
90. Françoise Waquet, *Latin or the Empire of a Sign*, trans. John Howe (London and New York: Verso, 2001), 218.
91. [Anon.], "View of a Classical School," *Chambers's Edinburgh Journal*, 9 (1840), 207.
92. [Anon.], "A Latin Hexameter Machine," *The Athenæum*, no. 921 (Jun. 21, 1845), 621.
93. Blandford, "The Eureka," 76–77.
94. Blandford, "The *Eureka*," 77.
95. See Gagnier, *Subjectivities*, 175. Timothy Steele has suggested that the Modernist rebellions against conventional meter in English verse were connected to the lingering presence of a classically informed approach

to English poetry in schools and universities. See Steele, *Missing Measures: Modern Poetry and the Revolt against Meter* (Fayetteville: University of Arkansas Press, 1990), 59–60.
96. See White, "Humanizing the Teaching of Latin: A Study in Textbook Construction," *Classical Journal*, 25 (1930), 507–520.
97. "View of a Classical School," 207.
98. "View of a Classical School," 208. See also Adamson, *English Education*, 239. Indeed, there is more than rhetorical venom in this reformer's insistence on the primacy of classics in public-school curriculum. Herbert Branston Gray, who spent much of life directly involved in classical education, recalls the 1860s and 1870s thus: "Out of the thirty-two 'period' (or hours) in the week devoted to study in class-rooms (*i.e.* exclusive of preparation time, which was mainly appropriated to classics), about twenty to twenty-four were given up to Latin and Greek, the remaining twelve or eight being distributed between Mathematics, Scripture, French, and German (the last-named a later importation)." See Herbert Branston Gray, *The Public Schools and the Empire* (London: Williams and Norgate, 1913), 111.
99. "View of a Classical School," 207–208.
100. See John Henry Newman, *The Idea of a University, Defined and Illustrated*, ed. I. T. Ker (Oxford: Clarendon Press, 1976), 135. The anti-utilitarian position is of course not simple and one-dimensional; Matthew Arnold's stance is not interchangeable with Newman's, but it suffices to recognize the general thrust of the "View of a Classical School" author's invective. Also not straightforward is the supposed utilitarianism of this position. Isobel Armstrong has explored the complex relationship between the utilitarianisms of Mill and W. J. Fox and the poetry of Tennyson and Browning, drawing attention to Fox's "conscious and deliberate effort to develop a *Utilitarian* and radical aesthetics" that endorsed a poetics that is both dialogic and thoroughly engaged with objective reality through its vivid images. See Isobel Armstrong, *Victorian Poetry: Poetry, Poetics and Politics* (London and New York: Routledge, 1993), 142 (esp. 112–161). In this context we can understand the reactions of the author of "View of a Classical School" to Gradus-oriented prosody: the necessarily solitary pursuit countermands any democratic possibility, and, further, the acutely technical linguistic and prosodic nature of the classical-school exercises precluded the pupils' ability to recognize or engage with any potentially sustaining "physical experience of the senses" (Armstrong, *Victorian Poetry*, 144). A similarly politicized assault on the insular narrowness of classical studies, this time in the universities, appears in J. S. Blackie's

contributions to the *Classical Museum*. See Phelan, "Radical Metre," 173.
101. Ellingham, "Apology for the Practice of Latin Verse Composition," 156.
102. Andrew King and John Plunkett, "Introduction," in *Victorian Print Media: A Reader*, ed. King and Plunkett (New York: Oxford University Press, 2005), 1.
103. [Charles Knight], "The Commercial History of a Penny Magazine.— No. III," *Penny Magazine of the Society for the Diffusion of Useful Knowledge*, 2 (1833), 466.
104. See Algernon Charles Swinburne, *The Swinburne Letters*, ed. Cecil Y. Lang, 6 vols. (New Haven: Yale University Press, 1959), II: 295, 319. (Numerous other letters convey the same sentiment.)
105. Charles Babbage, *A Letter to Sir Humphry Davy ... On the Application of Machinery to the Purpose of Calculating and Printing Mathematical Tables* (London J. Booth, 1822), 3, 5. These topics enjoyed a similarly popular circulation. Commentary on the combination of calculation and copying, often reproducing elements of Babbage's own text, appears in a number of miscellanies aimed at "the million," among them *Chambers's Journal*, the *Mechanics' Magazine*, and the *London Encyclopædia, or Universal Dictionary of Science, Art, Literature, and Practical Mechanics*.
106. Clark, *General History*, 16–17.
107. "Oddities in Music," 313.
108. While these comparisons no doubt did not escape the author of "View of a Classical School," the complications they introduce to the macrodynamics of his argument—would it be better to labor repetitively and automatically with a Gradus or with compositor's frame?—are never considered. In a highly class-conscious and market-driven society, however, there is no doubt about the relative drudgeries of the two tasks. Anyone who is familiar with Ruskin's contemporary assessment of the manufacture of glass beads will know that, though many varieties of task offer "the smallest occasion for the use of any single human faculty," some are more enervating than others. See John Ruskin, *The Stones of Venice* (1851–1853), *The Complete Works of Ruskin, Library Edition*, ed. E. T. Cook and Alexander Wedderburn, 39 vols. (London: George Allen, 1903–1912), X, 197.
109. See Blandford, "The *Eureka*," 71.
110. "Oddities in Music," 313.
111. Nuttall, "The Eureka," 214.
112. "Latin Versification for the Million," 205.
113. "View of a Classical School," 208.
114. [William Makepeace Thackeray], "The Eureka," *Punch*, 9 (1845), 20.

115. [Thackeray], "The Eureka," 20. The remainder of his treatment of the Eureka is given over to politics that extend well beyond classical education. Invented lines satirizing the Peel government and policies in Ireland are attributed to Clark's machine, and the article ends with a verse epigram praising mechanized poetry:

> Such an invention were, indeed, a treasure
> Since there would be no longer a pretence
> For PEEL's not bringing in a perfect measure,
> And for poor SIBTHORP's never talking sense.
>
> How ministers would hail it in due season,
> If by its potent aid they could but reach
> The art of putting either rhyme or reason—
> Or both together—in a royal speech!

116. "View of a Classical School," 208. Well into the twentieth century, public schoolboys still had the occasional encounter with the Eureka. See "Public Schoolboys Test Latin Verse Machine," *Clarks Courier*, 148 (1963), 7.
117. Clark, *General History*, 17.
118. Clark, *General History*, 17.
119. Babbage, *Letter to Sir Humphry Davy*, 3.
120. It is worth considering also how Clark's mid-century contribution to "structures based on randomness and combinatorics," as discussed by Friedrich Kittler, both anticipates the "discourse network" of 1900, where machines "produce discourses without sense or thought," and the residuum of a previous network of syllabic decomposition. See Kittler, *Discourse Networks 1800/1900*, trans. Michael Metteer (Stanford: Stanford University Press, 1990), 210, 229.
121. B. J. Copeland, "A Lecture and Two Radio Broadcasts on Machine Intelligence by Alan Turning," *Machine Intelligence 15: Intelligent Agents*, ed. K. Furukawa et al. (Oxford: Oxford University Press, 1999), 452.
122. Elizabeth Wilson, *Affect and Artificial Intelligence* (Seattle: University of Washington Press, 2010), 48.
123. Elizabeth Wilson, "Imaginable Computers: Affects and Intelligence in Alan Turing," *Prefiguring Cyberculture: An Intellectual History*, ed. Darren Tofts et al. (Cambridge, MA: MIT Press, 2004), 45.

The Automatic Flow of Verse

> Physically, a human being is a machine .... The perfect action of the steam-engine depends upon the quality, form, and adjustment of its several parts. These conditions being defective, the action of the machine is imperfect. The same principle applies to man.
> —D. P. Butler, *Butler's System of Physical Training* (1868)

> Mark time with the hand and foot, march in time, count time both verbally and mentally, in short periodicize every moment of the body and mind, in harmony with all the varieties of English versification .... The speech-apparatus should be disciplined by going through a course of rhythmical training for the voice ....
> —"Stammer," *The Penny Cyclopædia of the Society for the Diffusion of Useful Knowledge* (1842)

Central to the question of meter's role in nineteenth-century education were dilemmas surrounding the prosodic capacities of learners. Some, as we have seen, wondered what a pupil might do with prosody later in life, and others wondered if there were people who might not be able to learn the fundamentals of versification in the first place. The Victorian industry advocate Andrew Ure categorically refused to endorse prosodic education, on the grounds that it served no demonstrably useful purpose for Britain's future leaders. "Grandees may be allowed freely to waste their early years in the pastime of scanning Greek and Roman metres," he writes in *The Philosophy of Manufactures*

(1835), "provided they do not fancy themselves thereby, albeit ignorant of the principles of Science, Art, and Trade, qualified to scan the measures and regulate the affairs of empires at their will."[1] Whatever a boy might glean from his Gradus, it would not be sufficient to prepare him for "after-life"—the workaday world beyond school and university. And if the study of prosody could not be said to prepare elite boys for careers, then what about their less privileged counterparts? Unlike Stephen Hawtrey, for whom verse-making could be beneficially incorporated in the curriculum of a "working-class Eton," Ure believed metrical exercises were particularly unsuited for the Sunday and factory schools set up to provide basic education for thousands of Britain's working children. Taking a similar position in an 1836 address, the Reverend Robert Jones, a Middlesex vicar and outspoken supporter of "practical" education and matters of "self-tuition," advised his audience that he would not "mislead the future scholar into the by-gone fallacy, that there is neither merit nor fame but in scholastic prosody."[2]

This argument found expression in America, as well. Writing under the pseudonym Christopher Crowfield, Harriet Beecher Stowe, whose abolitionist novel *Uncle Tom's Cabin* (1852) was still a bestseller in both the USA and Britain, put the case even more forcefully in her 1866 book of instructive anecdotes, *Little Foxes*. In particular, she warned against dooming a "born mechanic" to an education wholly incompatible with his ability and inclination. If a boy who "understands machinery at a glance" is forced into "the Latin School," rather than an apprenticeship or manual trade, "and spend[s] three or four years in trying to learn what he never can learn well," he will soon become "disheartened by always being at the tail of his class, and seeing many a boy inferior to himself in general culture, who is rising to brilliant distinction simply because he can remember those hopeless, bewildering Greek quantities and accents which he is constantly forgetting ...."[3] While Stowe implies that no amount of hard labor and scholastic inculcation will ever make a metrist out of a person whose mind is naturally inclined toward practical, mechanical matters, others were prepared to concede that perhaps such persons could at least hope to grasp the basics of versification—provided they had the right set of instructions. The wherewithal to turn metrical skills into poetry, however, was another matter altogether. As a reviewer for the *Educational Reporter* admonishes the "many young versifiers" who might be eager to teach themselves using Robert Frederick Brewer's popular 1869 *A Manual of English Prosody*, "Ponder well the motto, 'Poeta nascitur non fit.'"[4]

Is one born with a knack for meter—which might include an ability to grasp its rules or a fluency in verse recitation or a capacity for metrically sound verse composition? Or, if not, can one be "made" into a competent versifier (if not exactly a poet) through rote school exercises or autodidactic diligence? In the previous chapters, I canvassed some pedagogical perspectives on this question as regards modes of instruction and specific classroom exercises: public school boys, at least, could be made to scan, if not always pronounce, verses with a degree of proficiency, and the means of encouraging such skills were associated with similar practices used among working-class children. As we have seen, classical meter may have served as a proxy for elite affiliation, but the fundamentals of its tuition were by no means exclusive to elite institutions. This chapter looks elsewhere: not to the organization of learning technologies but to the would-be metrist him- or herself. The nineteenth-century understanding of the human as machine informed not only discussions about physical culture or physiology but also assessments of the rhythms produced by the "man-machine." In particular, then, this chapter approaches meter in relation to the fundamentals of nineteenth-century debates about body and mind, examining how some contemporary "sciences of man" addressed ideas about somatic and mental "machinery," volition, and automatism as they impacted on questions of metrical inclination, aptitude, and fluency. Not only was versification considered by many a "mechanical" skill prerequisite to the composition of poetry "by those who are born with the *gift*";[5] it might also depend upon "mechanistic"—that is, apparently involuntary—somatic and cognitive processes. To understand the truth of "the mechanical versifier's art,"[6] therefore, it was necessary to examine the functions of the human mechanism itself: the instruments of speech, the rhythms and cadences of bodily systems, and the conscious and unconscious mental processes that were themselves grounded and even localized in the materiality of the human machine. Meter was thus a matter not simply of prosodic, literary, or philological debate; rather, it was a subject of often controversial scientific scrutiny. As experimental, materialist methods began to redefine the various motive forces of the human organism and the mechanical properties, functions, and outputs associated with them, a new breed of prosodists—among them phrenologists, physiologists, physicians, and psychologists—played an active role in the nineteenth century's evolving metrical discourse. Though their methods and aims often differed, they all attempted to answer more or less the same set of questions. Exactly how was a person's capacity for meter formed? Did metrical ability originate in the mind or the body? Was there an explanation for the variety of speakers—from the well-educated, practicing poets to the unlettered prosodic ingénues—who found themselves capable, sometimes to their own surprise, of manufacturing metrical verses? And what of those who could not? In some of the cases examined below, meters seem to issue automatically from the body or mind, without the voluntary control of the speaker and not always informed by his prior exposure to meters or prosodic training. In other cases, however, the flow of meter, because of a defect in the vocal mechanism or from an insufficient exercise of the will, might be impeded. This chapter examines some of the theories that such scientists, to use the term broadly, advanced about what lay behind and made possible the ability or inability to versify. While some attested to a prosodical "ghost in the machine,"[7] others advocated a purely physiological explanation. For them, the Eureka was by no means the only automatic meter-maker the nineteenth century had to offer.

Prosodic Protuberances

Years before he would make his major contribution to Victorian metrical theory with his "Essay on English Metrical Law," a teenage Coventry Patmore visited a phrenologist while in Paris. Reading Patmore's cranium, the phrenologist "pronounced it to be that of a poet." His confidence bolstered by the phrenological diagnosis, Patmore "determined seriously to [begin] cultivat[ing] the art of verse ...."[8] According to Patmore's biographer Basil Champneys, the author of *The Angel in the House* would pay at least one more visit to a phrenologist, this time in London and in the company of Alfred Tennyson. The two poets, as this possibly apocryphal story goes, "went together to visit [a phrenologist ...] who had no means of knowing who they were"—we are told that they go incognito, though Champneys does not describe how they disguised their identities. This bump-reading practitioner vindicated his French counterpart's assessment of Patmore, reassuring the poet of his suitability for his chosen vocation; he also confirmed, to Patmore's great delight, "that he was equally qualified to succeed in business."[9] Tennyson, by contrast, presented a singularly poetic head—"one of the finest [the phrenologist] had ever seen." The outside of his skull told the fundamental truth of his character: that he was a poet through and through, "and of the grandest poetic type."[10] Tennyson and Patmore were not alone. Many nineteenth-century poets were at least curious, if a little skeptical, about the controversial science of phrenology, which promised to explain—"via physiognomical head reading"—the secrets of the poetical mind.[11] As a matter of fact, the dimensions of poets' heads (and in some cases the heads themselves) were very much coveted by enterprising phrenologists. In 1834 George Combe, founder of the Edinburgh Phrenological Society, published a pamphlet entitled *Phrenological Development of Robert Burns*, which describes how a plaster cast of Burns's skull was taken in 1834, when the poet's grave was opened for the burial of his widow. Combe quotes Archibald Blacklock, a surgeon involved in the procedure:

> [N]othing could exceed the high state of preservation in which we found the bones of the cranium, or offer a fairer opportunity of supplying what has so long been desiderated by Phrenologists—a correct model of our immortal Poet's head; and in order to accomplish this in the most accurate and satisfactory manner, every particle of sand or other foreign body was carefully washed off, and the plaster-of-Paris applied with all the tact and accuracy of an experienced artist. The Cast is admirably taken, and cannot fail to prove highly interesting to Phrenologists and others.[12]

To the phrenologists' great delight, the skull plainly divulged Burns's poetic temperament. The brain was "large"—"exceed[ing] the average of Scotch living heads"—and its protuberances indicative of "great Intellectual power."[13]

Under the interpretive fingers of phrenologists, heads living or dead might be made to reveal the nature of the poetic mind. But what, exactly, did a "poetic" head look like? What "bumps" or "organs" were prominent, and to which mental "faculties" did they correspond? Combe remarks that Burns's skull "spreads wide in the region of Ideality," the organ most often identified as the center of poetic expression (or aligned with what Edgar Allan Poe, himself a poet-prosodist with an amateur interest in phrenology, called the "sentiment of Poesy"[14]). The organ of ideality was typically located on or near the forehead, the general prominence of which was often equated—in phrenological and also physiognomical writing—with a shrewd intellect and a pronounced capacity for imagination. As Franz Joseph Gall, the developer of "craniology" (phrenology's eighteenth-century Continental forerunner), had observed, "the heads of great poets were enlarged above the temples, in a direction backward and upward."[15] This area of the cranium indicated a person's possession (or lack) of the powers of "imagination" or "fancy," two qualities often deemed "essential to the poet."[16] Here *bigger* really did mean *better*. While a "small" or underdeveloped organ of ideality signified imaginative deficiency—"coarse," "vulgar," "uncouth," and "awkward" are words that crop up often—and promised little in the way of poetic achievement—"little relish for poetry or oratory, or fine writing, and ... but a miserable judge of anything of the kind"—a "large" one was, by contrast, not only a signifier of taste in its most general form but also the mark of a discerning poetic temperament. O. S. Fowler, the American popularizer of phrenology, notes that "One having ideal[ity] *Large*, will possess refinement and exquisiteness of taste and feeling, a lively imagination, and a brilliant fancy; an admiration of the elegant, the beautiful, the gorgeous, the ornamental, the perfect, and the sublime; of the fine arts and polite literature; of poetry if of a high order, and of eloquence; and will relish everything fanciful and exquisite wherever it is to be found." If the organ of ideality be "very large" indeed, then the person will be not only highly responsive to poetry but also capable of "mak[ing] poetry of a high order."[17]

Making poetry of a high order, of course, required more than just "brilliant fancy" and a finely tuned aesthetic disposition; it also presumed a familiarity with the rules of prosody and versification. Early phrenologists such as Gall had accepted the existence of a generic poetry organ as a given, but was it possible for a trained phrenologist to read in the shape of a poet's head something as specific as an inclination toward and facility for composing in measured language (or, beyond that, even a predilection for specific foot varieties, such as the iambus or the dactylic hexameter)? Certainly it was possible, as Combe had speculated in his popular book *A System of Phrenology* (first published in 1825), that a "taste" for prosody was cerebrally encoded and that it had an identifiable and measureable physiological bump. But was a single faculty on its own responsible for metrical acuity? Was it simply a fact that a propensity for prosody had a corresponding protuberance? Or did contemporary phrenological thinking posit that multiple faculties worked in concert to produce a mind attuned to the modulus of meter, which Patmore and other nineteenth-century poet-prosodists were at the same time actively attempting to define theoretically?

The organ of ideality, the source of a poet's imagination, was suggested as this locus of metrical preferences. As we have seen, from the 1850s, with the rise of the New Prosody, idealist conceptions of English meter, such as those propounded by Patmore and E. S. Dallas, emphasized "the abstract nature of metrical form."[18] Phrenology, which concentrates its attention on the materiality of the brain and cranium, would seem to be poorly placed in relation to such idealist abstractions, yet there are noteworthy correlations between this science and contemporary prosodical thinking. Both phrenologists and New Prosodists, for example, read meter as emanating from the mind—and a particular kind of mind at that. The way that Patmore, in particular, distinguishes the "imaginary" modulus of meter from the "real" rhythms of speech has parallels with phrenological thinking about aesthetic perception. If the "mentalizing of meter" that one finds in Patmore's essay is distinct from "what you actually hear or say aloud,"[19] then the prosodically minded individual, who possesses a developed faculty of metrical appreciation and organization, may not need to hear verses aloud to follow their metrical movement. Meter, in other words, may not depend upon the physical properties of sound or the physiology of the ear but, rather, upon the extent to which the poet or metrist is fully attuned to meter as an abstract measurement, the extent to which his mind "craves measure in everything"—or, as a phrenologist might express it, it depends on the subtlety of his organ of ideality (that organ of elegance, perfection, and order). As a member of the Phrenological Society of Paris remarked in the early 1830s, one should not confuse a well-tuned ear with a well-tuned brain faculty or organ:

> When we would wish to designate a musician of high taste, &c., we are in the habit of saying, "He has an exquisite ear;" but this manner of appreciation is quite erroneous. When Beethoven placed himself before a piano, his fingers ran along the notes, but never struck them; that would have been useless, as he had completely lost the sense of hearing: he was perfectly conscious of what he executed, through the internal organ of the brain, although the instrument remained as much without sound, as the player himself was deaf.[20]

Just as Beethoven did not need to strike the keys to perceive the notes, so too the adept poet or prosodist would not need to read the line aloud (or hear it intoned) to infer its metrical movement. The ability to scan, like the ability to read and interpret musical notes, could be understood to proceed from an "internal organ of the brain."

Or possibly multiple organs. Several phrenologists were ready to admit that a responsiveness to the technical dimension of both music and poetry involved organs besides ideality. As Johann Gaspar Spurzheim details in his *Phrenology, Or the Doctrine of Mental Phenomena* (1832), while "some authors ... write in prose, and yet their expressions are highly poetical; ... others make verses which contain no tinge of poetic feeling."[21] A "highly poetical" sense and an ability to "make verses," in other words, were not necessarily the same thing. Verse-making, in particular, involved specific competencies that might (or might not) be present in a person with a well-developed organ of ideality. For example, a pronounced organ of form, which predisposes persons to "such objects as written language, arbitrary symbols, [and] outline drawings,"[22] would seem beneficial to the prosodic individual or the musician, whose stock-in-trade is a set of arbitrary symbols associated with classical quantitative verse or musical notation. The organ of order, which corresponds to a person's sense of "method" and "regularity," would also seem apposite for dealing with meter's repeating patterns of stress or duration, as would the organ of number (or calculation), which is described as the seat of arithmetic and algebra.[23]

In particular, though, as Combe asserted in his *A System of Phrenology*, the organ of time "is essential to [both] music and versification,"[24] something that Dallas and Patmore, whose verse theories were informed by a conception of meter as a uniform measure of time elapsed, might have appreciated. Like Dallas's definition of meter as "time heard," Patmore's temporal metrics instates duration, instead of accent, as the "integer" of the verse line. Lines of English poetry, as we have seen, are divided into units of equal time, or "isochronous intervals."[25] Thus, "[t]he special faculty [that] seems to be the power of judging time, and of intervals in general,"[26] presumably would make an individual more predisposed to a time-measuring metrics such as the mental and musical one that Patmore elaborates in his "Essay on English Metrical Law." "By giving the perception of measured cadence,"[27] time enables the metrist to distinguish one metrical interval from another, to judge whether intervals are in fact isochronous, and to determine the placement of the "ictus" or "beat".[28] In noting the role played by a sense of time in versification, the phrenologists are much more kindred with Patmore's conception of meter than, for instance, Alexander Bain, the pioneer of British psychology whom Jason Rudy has discussed in relation to the materialist contexts for Patmore's theory.[29] Though prepared to accept some of the general positions of phrenology—for example, "the phrenological localization of a number of cerebral organs"—Bain, as Robert M. Young has pointed out, had "various objections to details of the phrenological faculties themselves."[30] In his 1861 book *On the Study of Character, Including an Estimate of Phrenology*, Bain finds himself "at a loss to understand" the relevance of time to versification. As he writes, "it may be questioned whether versification has much to do with this peculiar sensibility. It does not seem essential either to the composition or the enjoyment of verse that we should have a very nice appreciation of intervals of time."[31]

Not everyone, however, was of the same mind. Patmore shared with many phrenologists of his day a conception of the mind developed so as either to "crave" and appreciate meter or to not understand it at all. There were other phrenologically inclined commentators on versification who speculated—contra George Combe, who insisted that verse-making undertaken simply by "learning quantities" but without any "natural talent" for poetic composition would result in "a mere mechanical facility of placing words in metrical apposition, utterly without value"[32]—that an aptitude for prosody might depend less on the faculty-specific hardwiring and more "on acquired [metrical] knowledge and the ability to apply it."[33] Attentive to phrenology's general recognition that "[c]ertain strong sensibilities, must be at the foundation" of a person's appreciation of poetry, Bain still sees how exposure to verse composition and meter inform the mind's prosodical constitution. Verse-making begins with a mind tuned to poetic expression and replete "with apt materials":

> No man can compose songs [i.e., lyric poetry] without having, in the first instance, a strong susceptibility to the metrical cadence; not merely a pleasure in it, but a pleasure bound up with delicate discrimination, and accompanied with strong retention in the memory .... But let a man have an intense ear for metrical form, shown in a strong abiding presence of the examples of it, and he will, out of his recollection of prose, cast words in metrical mode. Should he have a surpassing sensibility on this head, he has a chance to devise new and superior cadences, being all the better able to do so if he is also largely versed in language.[34]

A "surpassing sensibility" and a good memory, capacities that might be phrenologically locatable, will allow a person to find verse even in ordinary prose. But being "versed in language"—through study or training, for example in a classical school—is nonetheless an aid to composition. Writing in the *Phrenological Journal* in 1846, Richard Cull, a tutor in elocution who had joined the Phrenological Association 6 years earlier, anticipated Bain's distinction between intuitive abilities (that is, those that a person might be predisposed to as a result of having a well-developed faculty or organ) and learned ones (those that a person has acquired through study or training, for example at school). Interestingly, however, Cull is more convinced than Bain that a facility for meter, as he construes it, might be less about a particularly susceptible protuberance (e.g., the "organ of Time") and more about one's prosodical education. "The heads of metricians do not necessarily present a good field for observation," he writes,

> Because a man may be a good classical metrician without a nice perception of the temporal value of syllables, if he possesses a good memory of rules and has a facility in their application .... It will be found, on inquiry, that most classical scholars determine syllabic quantity by rule and not by ear.[35]

For Cull "by ear" seems to mean both physiological perception and also a large time organ. Either way, he suggests that it might be more important to enlarge one's familiarity with the *Gradus ad Parnassum*, if a mastery of "longs" and "shorts" is really the end in sight.

Cull was not alone in stressing the importance of being habituated to the rules of verse. Nineteenth-century phrenology's flirtation with the mechanics of meter gives us a glimpse into the structure of metrical debate as it would evolve during the second half of the nineteenth century, when questions of versification were framed by developments taking place among materialists in the new fields of physiology and psychology. If meter "has its place in the mind," as Patmore held, and if "[t]he brain," as Fowler pointed out, "is the organ of the mind, or the physical instrument of thought and feeling,"[36] then the immateriality of meter takes on a markedly material aspect and falls, along with a variety of other mental phenomena, within the remit of the brain scientist and his rapidly methodizing scrutiny of the human machine. Locating a capacity for meter in the bumps of the brain, phrenology grounded poetry's mechanical aspect in the body. External factors might well influence one's metrical abilities, as Cull maintains, but there is nonetheless a somatic determinism that was, for some, "disturbingly materialist" in the questions it raised about conscious volition and the agency of the will or, for some, spirit.[37] Later in the century, advocates of cerebral localization—for which early psychologists such as Bain found antecedents in a faculty science like phrenology—and related theories such as cerebral automatism would go even further than phrenologists had done, postulating that metrical acuity, like other forms of mental activity, might not only be associated with parts of the cerebrum but simply be the irreducible consequence of brain functions. These sciences of the body and the embodied mind, detailed below, continued to ask questions about metrical learning and cognition, exploring the mechanics of meter in relation to brain functions and other somatic factors, such as respiratory rhythms, speech pathologies, and cerebral diseases.

THE MAN-MACHINE

Nineteenth-century psychology's ideas about mechanistic bodies and minds, as well as the exchanges between materialist sciences and meter that issue from them, have a prehistory that it is worth pausing to examine. As Laura Otis remarks in *Networking: Communicating with Bodies and Machines in the Nineteenth Century* (2001), "Organic systems have been compared to technological ones since ancient times."[38] The *locus classicus* of modern thinking about the body-machine is the work of the seventeenth-century philosopher René Descartes. In works such as *Discours de la Méthode* (1637) and the posthumously published *L'Homme* (1662), Descartes outlines an influential, albeit controversial, mechanistic physiology in which the body is imagined as an automaton. For example, in his theory of optics, as Nancy L. Maull notes, Descartes imagines the eye "as a mere mechanical device—as a *camera obscura*. The transferal of information contained in the retinal image to the pineal gland"—where he thought the soul to reside—"is accomplished by way of a baroquely conceived optical plumbing: a kinematics of fluids."[39] For Descartes animal and human bodies alike are mechanistic in their function; it is only the soul that sets humans apart: "but for the soul"—and its corollaries, reason and a capacity for language—"the body is nothing but an automaton."[40] As we will see, there are echoes of Descartes's mechanistic philosophy in the distinction made by some prosodic commentators of the period between, on the one hand, the machinery of speech (tongue, palate, teeth, etc.) and, on the other, the soul that commands these apparatuses to produce articulate language generally and metered poetry in particular.

By the middle of the eighteenth century, philosophical materialists such as Julien Offray de La Mettrie, a French physician and author of the controversial pamphlet *L'Homme machine* (1748), had already begun to advance alternatives to the standard Cartesian division between the material, mechanical body and the immaterial soul. For La Mettrie the soul could not be said to exist independent of the body-machine. In intellectual dialogue with not only Descartes but also some of the makers of eighteenth-century automata (as mentioned in the previous chapter)—and paving the way for the physiologists and psychologists of the nineteenth century—La Mettrie's works "emphasize the physiological basis of human life," from feelings to thoughts—even "the soul's various states," he contends, "are always correlated with the body's."[41] Around the same time, another French thinker, Etienne Bonnot de Condillac, would take up the question of the human machine in his *Traité des sensations* (1754), in which he "illustrates the radical empiricist position that no cognitive abilities, such as will, desire, and judgment, were innate; instead, all derived exclusively from sensation."[42] In contrast to Descartes's "ghost in the machine" formulation, the philosophies and physiologies developed as part of the Enlightenment project of empirical materialism and later inherited by nineteenth-century physicians, physiologists, and laboratory scientists prioritized a body-as-machine whose functions were the seat of cerebral and linguistic ability, including, as we will see, the power to versify. For some scientists the human was indeed a kind of automaton, as Descartes had posited, but it did not necessarily follow that consciousness, will, or the soul was operating the levers and gears. The basis for versification was decidedly physiological. Not unlike a kind of organic Eureka, the man-machine itself—not some intelligent and immaterial "ghost" inside it—was the source of meter. For others, however, there was a reluctance to disavow the will entirely. Physiology might explain meter to an extent, but it could not account for everything.

By the middle decades of the nineteenth century, materialist energies had thoroughly transformed the science of physiology, not only in France but also in the German-speaking states, Britain, and the USA. German physiologists, in particular, were among the pioneers of a new "radical empiricism" that, from the 1840s, was associated with the experimental laboratory work of figures such as Johannes Müller and Hermann von Helmholtz. As Anson Rabinbach explains, Helmholtz, who had trained under Müller, and some of his contemporaries working in the fields of biology, chemistry, and physics "adopted the industrial machine as their model of the universe ...."[43] In contrast to the watchwork automata envisaged by Descartes and eighteenth-century materialists such as La Mettrie, Condillac, and Vaucanson (the well-known inventor of automata), nineteenth-century materialist physiologists, especially in France and the German states, increasingly construed "the analogy of the human or animal machine" in terms of a self-motivating machine that functioned along the lines of industrial processes associated with an expanding factory system.[44] Among the "so-called 'automatists'" that Anne Stiles discusses in *Popular Fiction and Brain Science in the Late Nineteenth Century* (2012) are figures such as Thomas Henry Huxley, William Kingdon Clifford, and Shadworth Hodgson, who "extended Descartes's idea that 'brute animals are mere machines or automata' to human beings."[45] Huxley would argue, in his 1874 treatise "On the Hypothesis that Animals Are Automata, and Its History," that the "explanation" of Descartes, whom he rebrands "a physiologist of the first rank," is vindicated by "[m]odern physiology, aided by pathology," in establishing "the brain [a]s the seat of all forms of consciousness."[46]

Certain British physiologists were not as keen as their German counterparts to assert a materialist, mechanistic explanation for human functions. Some of Huxley's contemporaries preferred to temper such a materialist understanding of "the working of the Physiological Mechanism" (i.e., the body) so as to accommodate the discriminating powers of the will. Among the group of scientists who were unwilling to fully endorse the "biological determinist views of brain function,"[47] were the British physiologist William Benjamin Carpenter and the American physician-physiologist Oliver Wendell Holmes. Refusing to dispense with the agency of will as a determinative feature of human consciousness, they nevertheless contributed to the elaboration of a mental physiology that would reorient debates about human automata and their capacity for metrical composition and analysis. To an extent, metrical cerebration might be unconscious or "automatic," a corollary of our bodies' physical processes; yet the exercise of will might be beneficially superadded, so to speak, in certain circumstances. Willing meters—or invoking the metrical mind and mouth to ameliorate the matters of the body—is not only a subject bound up with what was "central to the Victorian sense of self," as Matthew Campbell has suggested, but also where "poetic practice" joins dialogue with the sciences of physiology, psychology, elocution, and speech therapy.[48]

I *Would* that My Tongue Could Utter

In 1846, while Clark's Latin Hexameter Machine was still the subject of discussion in popular periodicals, Alexander Melville Bell—father of the telephone inventor and an authority on the related sciences of philology, phonetics, and elocution—published *The Tongue: A Poem in Two Parts*. Praising this "organ of the soul," whose powers are languishing because the "art of graceful speech has found no place" among the British "lib'ral arts," Bell not only extols the virtues of proper elocutionary training but also devotes lengthy passages of verse to the functions and malfunctions of the vocal apparatus—what he terms the "articulative parts": "The lips, the teeth, the palate, and the tongue."[49] Working in concert, these instruments of what Bell would later describe, in his 1867 book *Visible Speech*, as the "speaking machine"[50] transform the sounds of respiration—or "mere voice"—into "the elementary sounds of speech," thus forming the building blocks of both prose and verse. "The motion of the lips" modulates the breath; the teeth "divide the streams of air/Into the complicated parts of speech" (e.g., syllables); and the tongue presses against parts of the palatal arch to form vowel or consonant sounds. In all of these compound actions, the "mechanism" of speech is subordinated to the "art" of delivery, which can be perfected through elocutionary training (what Bell preferred to call "vocal physiology") but which is ultimately subject to the agency of the immortal soul: "The human voice is man's immortal part/Made audible."[51] The correct delivery of verse, in particular, depends not only upon the proper functioning of the "speaking machine"—beginning with the "mechanical vibration" of air in the glottis—but also, as Bell and his collaborator (also brother) David Charles Bell explain in *Bell's Standard Elocutionist* (1878), upon the speaker's ability to control that machine so as to preclude "discord between the reader's voice and the poet's rhythm."[52] Thus, the mechanical operations of the "labial parts" are subordinated not only to the speaker's elocutionary skills, which have been acquired through instruction and practice (Bell's texts are replete with examples of "oral gymnastics" for the lips, teeth, and tongue), but also to his "power over all the processes concerned in the management of [his speaking machine]." In other words, the articulation of metered verse is, first and foremost, not a physiological exercise but an exercise of the speaker's will—an act predicated upon a conscious governing of the tongue.[53]

Bell's insistence on the speaker's active marshaling of speech (in verse or otherwise) is very much in keeping with an emphasis, common among nineteenth-century elocutionists, on the possibility of self-improvement. A similar conviction in the power of an individual's mind over matter (and meter), for example, can be found in John Thelwall's earlier writings on elocution and the "Rhythmus." In his 1810 *The Vestibule of Eloquence*, Thelwall not only states that any pupil who follows his plan of study is capable of refining his or her enunciation—of speaking prose or verse more sonorously—in only a "*few weeks*"; he also observes "that the prosodies of the Greek and Latin languages," which "are made to co-operate with demonstrated principles of [the] English Rhythmus," may indeed be regarded as aids, rather than obstacles, to elocutionary improvement.[54] In matters of meter, Thelwall refused to accept that meter was out of an ordinary mechanic's (or woman's) reach; instead, he championed, as Simon Jarvis has noted, the reader's "voluntary power" and rejected conventional prosodic doctrine, with its tendency to "dogmatize," as a hindrance to this spirit of individual empowerment.[55] Though there may be truth in Stowe's assertion, mentioned at the start of this chapter, that an orthodox classical school may not be the most conducive place for a working-class boy to master meter, elocutionists such as Thelwall and Bell (along with dozens of their ilk) were adamant that just about anyone—even a "born mechanic"—could acquire the fundamentals of versification, if only he *would*—that is, if only he had the conscious inclination to learn metrical rules and apply them to the speaking of verse.

But what about the tongue that *will not*, that refuses to be governed by the will? The speaker of Alfred Tennyson's 1842 lyric "Break, Break, Break"—which Isobel Armstrong has described as "a poem about finding words"[56]—is in exactly this position, seeking a metrical arrangement to express his grief but unable to bring his "speaking machine" under the control of his will: "And I would that my tongue could utter/The thoughts that arise in me."[57] The poem itself, whose meters have presented a "conundrum" for various readers,[58] is an exercise in metrical blockage, an enactment of "an obstruction to the very phonetics of loss."[59] Surrounded by the unconstrained ebb and flow of sea water and the corresponding vocal ease exhibited by the "fisherman's boy" who "shouts" and the "sailor lad" who "sings,"[60] Tennyson's speaker finds that flowing sounds are precisely what he cannot produce. While there is undoubtedly a "correlation [between] the breaking surf" and "the observer's sense of broken life," as Thomas McFarland has suggested,[61] the world all around the speaker is by no means a straightforward objective correlative for his dilemma of speech. The stressing, in line 3, of *would*, the subjunctive form of the verb *will* (in the sense of *intend* or *demand*), underscores precisely the inability to speak troubling thoughts in metrical language. The poem's halting refrain—"break, break, break"—enacts the tongue's sticking on a sound, its refusal to comply with the speaker's will. Indeed, there is something frustratingly involuntary about the repetition of the word "break" that impedes the "flow" of metrical movement before the poem has even properly begun. What Armstrong describes as the "crushing ictus"—the pronounced beat on each of the first line's three monosyllables—and "'vanished' offbeat[s]", implying that "the second part of a trochee ... has been eliminated or thwarted," are indicative of a lack of compliance from the speaking machine—possibly due to incorrect tongue or labial placement, or perhaps respiration.[62] The plaintive, panting plosives, coupled with the unspecified pauses between successive "breaks," convey a breathlessness suggestive of the "discord" between reading and rhythm that Bell warns against, as though the speaker cannot correctly measure his breathing. As Yopie Prins has suggested, there is a "problem of voicing *in* and *of* the poem that provokes so many nineteenth-century readings";[63] her attention to the histories of voice has given us a fuller picture of how both prosodists and musicians (e.g., Sidney Lanier) attempted to find appropriate scansions and musical settings for Tennyson's poem, struggling with and interpreting variously the refrain's pauses or "interval[s] of silence," which interrupt "the continuity of the utterance." For example, speakers' attempts to measure the sounding of words and regulate their breathing (acutely important when singing) might well be inhibited by the line's indeterminate pauses or rests.[64] Like the speaker of Tennyson's 1855 "monodrama" *Maud*, whose strong feeling "made my tongue so stammer and trip," the tongue-tied talker of "Break, Break, Break" seems to suffer from a "natural defect of utterance" in which, as Bell writes, "the letters"—and in this case the meters—"*will not out.*"[65] It may be the case that with "energetic practice"—that is, a combination of will power and hard work—such a problem can be remedied, returning the vocal apparatus to full functionality. For Bell, at least, stuttering measures can be made to flow freely once vocal impediments have been removed by the use of articulations designed to free the tongue and open the mouth, allowing it to "emit" vowels and consonants correctly.[66]

Bell's system of vocal physiology—like some other systems promoted by contemporary phoneticians, speech pathologists, and instructors of elocution—was intended to help not only those who simply wanted to improve their enunciation but also stammerers whose words, like Tennyson's "spasmodic" rhythms in "Break, Break, Break," would not flow freely.[67] Indeed, stammering, as one mid-Victorian medical practitioner put it, is when "the wished-for words will not flow, [and] the very thought of the words is enough to cause spasmodic action of the articulative muscles ...."[68] Bell himself was adamant that what was often described as the jerky, "spasmodic" speech patterns typically associated with stammering were nothing more than the manifestations of a "habit" that could be overcome through education and careful training of the vocal apparatus. Rejecting more invasive surgical means of "curing" stammering—for example, "divid[ing] the frænum linguæ with a view to reliev[ing] an impediment of speech"[69]—Bell, at times cagey about revealing the details of his professional methods, nonetheless suggests that the "regulation of the breathing is the most important part of the process of cure."[70] If stammering results from a "derangement of the respiration during the effort to speak,"[71] then attention to the rhythms of respiration might allow the spasmodic utterances of the stammerer to settle into a smoother, more articulate cadence. The ear, nose, and throat specialist James Yearsley, founder in 1838 of London's Ear Infirmary and Orthophonic Institution, offered similar suggestions in his assessment of stammering. His article "On Stammering, Its Causes, Varieties, and Treatment," published in the *Lancet* in 1843, discusses, among other speech impediments, respiratory stammering, and Yearsley recommends methods for "giving sustained power to the breath." In particular, he advocates a practice that instills "in the patient's mind the rhythmical precision in which he is ... deficient."[72] "This idea of respiratory scanning," as Yearsley terms it, effectively introduces an immaterial modulus, not dissimilar to the one that Patmore would theorize the following decade, that works by "caus[ing] the inspirations and expirations" of the patient "to follow each other in the same intervals of time."[73] Patmore's "law" of meter, based on rhythmically recurring intervals marked by the ictus, was itself a response, as Jason Rudy has persuasively argued, to the unruly metrics of mid-century poets such as Sidney Dobell, whose "celebration of the physical principles of sound" represented a form of spasmodic utterance in need of metrical regulation.[74] With a "rhythm ... run[ning] at an irregular, spasmodic canter,"[75] a poem such as Tennyson's *Maud* or "Break, Break, Break" might well benefit from a treatment conceived in metrical terms, whether the application of Patmore's "ideal" modulus or the "respiratory scanning" described by Yearsley and Bell.

In addition to measured respiration, several Victorian remedies for stammering encouraged a form of metrical speaking not dissimilar to the overdetermined practices of prosodic recitation that featured centrally in the public school curriculum. Scanning poems aloud, as we saw in "Meter Manufactories," was thought by some educators to promote an awareness of a line's correct metrical character. For others, it amounted to a mechanistic mangling of a poem's music. In spite of the frequently encountered, albeit avoidable, antagonism that poet-prosodists such as Edgar Allan Poe perceived between "rhythmical flow," on the one hand, and "scholastic scansion," on the other, where the latter arbitrarily breaks up the verse line (typically designated by drawing "perpendicular lines between the feet") and so interrupts the movement of the former,[76] in some cases the deliberateness of scanning was observed to produce a salutary effect upon a speaker whose words will not flow out by other means. As a form of reading that "regulate[s] the pronunciation by the volition," scanning aloud might be used as an "exercise" for the stammerer. A contributor to Charles Dickens's *Household Words* advocated precisely this method in 1857. Like Bell and others, the author begins with the assumption that stammering is at once "the insubordination of the pronunciation to the volition" and perfectly "curable." He describes how he overcame his own stammer by making a conscious effort to modulate his speech to the measures of classical poetry: "Scanning and reciting verses in the dead languages implies habitual regulation of the voice by the will, and cured me of the disease of stammering."[77] The medical establishment entertained similar remedies. In 1871 the *Medical and Surgical Reporter* includes a personal anecdote submitted by Lute A. Taylor, an American newspaper editor turned tax assessor, who informs stammerers that "keeping time" and speaking words syllable by syllable will "cure the habit."[78] This method recalls the Bell-Lancaster process of "singling out" or "singing" syllables, used not only in working-class schools but also by John Russell as a means of inculcating an awareness of meter in boys at Charterhouse. As Taylor states, "Let the stammerer take a sentence, say this one, 'Leander swam the Hellespont,' and pronounce it by syllables, scan it, keeping time with his finger, if necessary letting each syllable occupy the same time, thus Le—an—der—swam—the—Hel—les—pont, and he will not stammer."[79] Professionals such as Yearsley also recommended—for example in the case of a laryngeal stammer—an "application of rhythm to the voice." Scanning in speech, as well as in breathing, might help to ameliorate "the violent spasmodic action of the larynx." Further, like Taylor, Yearsley advocated beating time with the body to accentuate the rhythmical modulation of the voice, noting that metrical delivery "may be still more facilitated by marking time with the foot, the hand, or the head."[80]

In his 1852 book *Poetics: An Essay on Poetry*, E. S. Dallas, who shared with his contemporary Patmore a belief in the nominally mental character of meter, mentions how a similar practice of marking meter might inspire movement in the body: "if [the reader's] thoughts are very livelily engaged, he will beat time with his fingers or with his feet."[81] At the same time, however, Dallas lamented that "recourse to modulated expressions" in actual speaking, whether the speech is accompanied by bodily movement or not, rendered a speaker's utterances overly "mechanical": a "poor speaker" who gets carried away with modulation lets "his voice [lift] into an unchanging sing-song, ding-dong ...."[82] The problem for Dallas is when this inclination to modulated speech presents itself "unconsciously," not only exaggerating the metrical features in the recitation of a poem, as in a schoolboy's scansion exercises, but also in a delivery not intended to be in verse in the first place. *Contra* Bain, as mentioned above, one might "unwittingly"—and for Dallas unfortunately—slip into sing-song speech, reading ordinary prose as if it were "an attempt at blank verse."[83] For a similar reason, Bell, though he shared with some of his contemporaries a willingness to consider the role of rhythm in the regulation of the stammerer's respiration, refused to endorse "systems for the cure of stammering [based on] the adoption of a drawling or singing tone of voice ... or some other unnatural expedient,—such as whistling between the words, stamping with the foot, &c."[84] Fearing that "the *cure* must often have been as bad as the malady," Bell is reluctant to encourage too much modulation, whether by methods of vocal scansion or their somatic auxiliaries. There was a fine line, for him, between the conscious management of the speaking machine and the possibility of establishing other equally bad habits, where a metrical "cure" might turn into a "derangement" of its own.[85] As we will see, there were not only times when a person might drift into meter without making a conscious effort to do so; in other scenarios unwilled or "automatic" meters might themselves be symptoms of a condition "where the mechanism of articulation is fatally deranged."[86]

Unconscious Metrical Actions

While meter may have been administered to persons as a means by which they could learn to assert their will over their bodies, there were other instances in which meter seemed to flow out of the body without any assertion of or interference from the will at all. If the former scenario finds expression in the metrical blockage experienced by the speaker of Tennyson's "Break, Break, Break," where the tongue refuses to respond to the will, then the latter presents itself in a passage from *In Memoriam*, where the tongue responds of its own accord, as if unconsciously. As Tennyson well knew, not all thoughts lie too deep for versified lamentation. There are times, as the familiar lines quoted below have it, when both our bodies and our minds move mechanically through meters:

> But, for the unquiet ear and brain,
> A use in measured language lies;
> The sad mechanic exercise,
> Like dull narcotics, numbing pain.[87]

Though both poems explore "the painful discrepancy between expressive need and expressive resources," as Timothy Peltason has suggested,[88] the "expressive need" in "Break, Break, Break" struggles to find adequate resources and, as a consequence, the flow of meter is impeded, while the expression described in section V of *In Memoriam* finds in meter a "mechanic exercise" that automatically address itself to the grieving poet's "need"—or, specifically, to the needs of his "ear and brain." Falling into verse-speech was, as we have seen, a subject considered by both metrists such as Dallas and scientists of the mind such as Bain. For some it represented an aptitude for or heightened awareness of meter, an awareness that might be encouraged by educational exposure to prosody. Given the extent to which repetitive metrical exercises featured in a schoolboy's daily routine (Tennyson, though mostly educated at home, was not undrilled in classical scansion, recitation, and composition), it is hardly surprising that, in times of mental or emotional anguish, "measured language" should assert itself as a form of subconscious distraction.[89] Tennyson was not alone, of course.[90] A similar pattern is at work in Emily Dickinson's 1862 poem "After great pain a formal feeling comes": "The feet"—podiatric and prosodic alike—"mechanical, go round— ...."[91] As Annie Finch has observed, "[t]he pain appears to have weakened the poet's resistance to the hypnotic, 'mechanical,' 'Wooden way' of the traditional meter."[92] Meter asserts itself automatically when the mind is otherwise distracted by "pain."

It is worth pausing to unpack the locomotive slant Dickinson gives to the metrics of grief. As another Massachusetts native, the physician-poet Oliver Wendell Holmes, Sr., would observe in the opening paragraph of his 1883 essay "The Physiology of Walking," these forms of articulation (with the vocal apparatus or the legs) have much in common: "The two accomplishments common to all mankind are walking and talking. Simple as they seem, they are yet acquired with vast labor, and very rarely understood in any clear way by those who practise them with ease and unconscious skill."[93] The "vast labor" involved in learning to walk and talk occurs so early that we might not even recall learning at all. By contrast, the acquisition of metrical knowledge, as discussed in "Meter Manufactories," was by dint of hard labor in the classroom, yet while prosodic attainment might be a process remembered (even regretted) later in life, it too might provide the basis for an "unconscious skill," whereby meter comes easily to a mind trained in repetitive scansion and composition exercises. Once someone knows how to put one foot in front of another, so to speak, the activity might become automatized. Above the title of Holmes's essay, there is an illustration (Fig. 1) that corresponds as well to Dickinson's mechanics of mourning as to the subject of perambulation. This line-drawing of an octopod with shoes—an effective literalizing of Dickinson's legs that "go round—/Of Ground, or Air"[94]—expresses Holmes's point that "[w]alking ... is a perpetual falling with a perpetual self-recovery"—a somewhat frightening process, but one that goes largely unnoticed in everyday life. As a result of "continual practice from a very early period of life," what Holmes calls "*ordinary walking*,"[95] like routinized speaking or even composing in familiar meters, can happen almost without our conscious awareness—to borrow Finch's term, it becomes "hypnotic." A physiologist anatomizes such an activity, breaking it down into its various musculoskeletal actions, just as

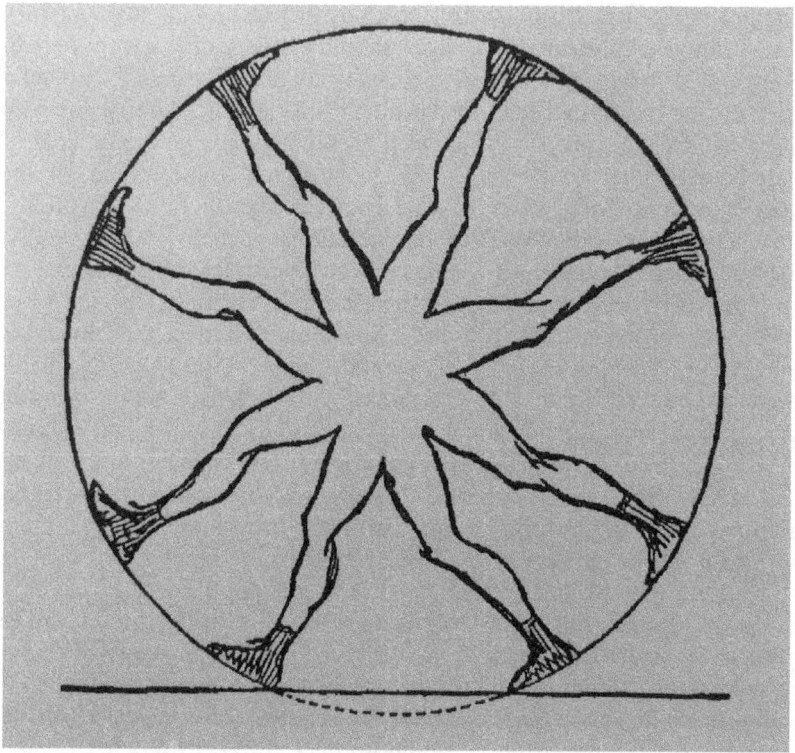

Fig. 1 Illustration from Oliver Wendell Holmes's "The Physiology of Walking," from *Pages of an Old Volume of Life: A Collection of Essays, 1857–1881* (Boston and New York: Houghton, Mifflin, and Company, 1892), 121

a prosodist's explications divulge the structure of a line of verse, thereby making us consciously aware of segmented movements and complex cadences and articulations of which we may be, in the process of performing them, unconscious. Once the material has been "scanned," we perceive clearly the feet going around; we notice the falls, the rises, the repetitions and rhythms that our bodies perform without any apparent input from our minds.

Such an involuntary, automatic metrics is at once subvolitional and inherently physiological, and in the elegiac poems quoted above it is specifically associated with strong emotion. The mechanical measures that sustain Tennyson in *In Memoriam*—expressions Gregory Tate has read in relation to the involuntary "noise[s] made by the brain, and the body in general"—and that carry Dickinson like a somnambulist through "great pain" were, for some nineteenth-century contributors to metrical discourse, not the exception but the rule, and not just in cases of bereavement. But what we hear in these poems, and in other examples mentioned below, seems not so much a conscious attempt, as Tate proposes regarding Tennyson's elegy, to "silence the unquiet heart and brain" by the application of metrical "form," intentionally superimposing the regular structure of meter on the disorganized rawness of grief as an elocutionist or surgeon might recommend scanning exercises to a stammerer, but rather an involuntary expression of the body itself, whose "audible noises" are externalized in the "metrical consistency" that we have seen, in other instances, to represent a concerted attempt to subordinate "visceral corporality" to the authority of the speaker's will.[96] What is more, not only meters such as these, which assert themselves as an unconscious coping mechanism, but metrical expressions more generally might, according to Holmes, be the compositions of "the internal organs" of the human body, which "have a will if not a voice of their own."[97] As we will see, if our organs were to will a voice into existence, it might well be metrical.

Holmes's own contribution to nineteenth-century verse theory was directly informed by his medical training. His physiological methods, shaped in Paris at the *École de Médecine* in the 1830s, were very much grounded in "the sort of scientific materialism" that grew out of *L'Homme machine*.[98] As regards theories of mind and human mechanics more generally, what William C. Dowling has termed Holmes's "'Parisian' allegiance" is particularly visible in an 1870 address to the Phi Beta Kappa Society of Harvard University, published the following year as a treatise entitled *Mechanism in Thought and Morals*.[99] Outlining Holmes's thinking about materialist explanations for intellectual capacities and process and their dubious or "false" application to "the sphere of moral self-determination" (he never did entirely forsake will in favor of physiological determinism), this text provides a conceptual framework for his later work on meter and somatic functions. Its conclusion—that more of our mental processes than we might imagine depend upon "automatic, unconscious action of the mind"—is indicative of Holmes's affiliation with generally accepted physiological psychology of the nineteenth century, which upheld the materialist assertion that mental activity was ultimately based in physiology. For such scientists—among them not only Holmes but also Alexander Bain, William Carpenter, George Henry Lewes, and Henry Maudsley—the mechanics of the human system and its related "intellectual machinery" can be inspected and understood with relative clarity by someone prepared to pause and "clink some of the wheels." In the first place, urges Holmes, we must accept not only that the mind depends "upon its organ," the brain (a basic principle of the burgeoning discourse of psychology that Bain, for example, had traced to a faculty science such as phrenology), but also that "the machinery of consciousness" is itself complexly bound up with the most "mechanistic" of bodily processes—those that he identifies as "automatic." Automatic processes or actions, for Holmes, are those that are not controlled by our conscious will:

> I call that part of mental and bodily life mechanical which is independent of our volition. The beating of our hearts and the secretions of our internal organs will go on, without and in spite of any voluntary effort of ours, as long as we live. Respiration is partially under our control: we can change the rate and special mode of breathing, and even hold our breath for a time; but the most determined suicide cannot strangle himself without the aid of a noose or other contrivance which shall effect what his mere will cannot do. The flow of thought is, like breathing, essentially mechanical and necessary, but incidentally capable of being modified to a greater or less[er] extent by conscious effort.[100]

Walking and talking are both more or less automatic activities, and versification, as Holmes would theorize in 1875, owes much to the involuntary, "mechanical" functions of the body.

In "The Physiology of Versification," Holmes focuses on the "two great vital movements pre-eminently distinguished by their rhythmical character,—the respiration and the pulse." While his remarks on cardiac rhythms are a bit more speculative,[101] he is convinced that his arguments about the body's respiratory functions are sound and, further, that "rhythmical action has an intimate relation with the structure of metrical compositions." Not only in states of heightened emotion but in our everyday lives, the somatic rhythms "conditioned by economy of those muscular movements which insure the oxygenation of the blood" predispose us to certain modulations of speech and breath—a premise that provides a physiological context against which one might gauge the proposed efficacy of the rhythmical breathing exercises discussed above in relation to stammering. Because our inhalations and exhalations occur at certain demonstrable periods—he suggests a "natural rate of respiration" to be "sixteen to twenty-four times per minute"—and because "breathing takes care of itself" there is what amounts to a somatic imperative for a reader to fall into vocal delivery that segments his speech so that it conforms to the "patterns of respiration." In other words, rhythms in breath promote meter in speech. Normal breathing, Holmes posits, is particularly conducive to the production of an octosyllabic line, which "follows more exactly than any other measure the natural rhythm of respiration":

> In reading aloud in the ordinary way from the "Lay of the Last Minstrel," from "In Memoriam," or from "Hiawatha," all written in this measure, the first two in iambics, or short-longs, the last in trochaics or long-shorts, it will be found that not less than sixteen nor more than twenty-four lines will be spoken in a minute, probably about twenty. It is plain, therefore, that if ones reads twenty lines in a minute, and naturally breathes the same number of times during that minute, he will pronounce one line to each expiration, taking advantage of the pause at its close for inspiration.[102]

Holmes proffers this physiological rationale as an explanation for the "fatal facility of the octosyllabic meter." Because tetrameter verses are so compatible with the body's respiratory rhythms, "eight syllable verse is ... singularly easy to read aloud." There is thus a problematic or "fatal" ease in pronouncing them in a deliberately metrical manner: "octosyllabic lines ... slip away too fluently, and run easily into a monotonous sing-song."[103] The unconscious meters of the body, in this case, are "mechanical" not only in that they are facilitated by our biomechanics but also in their tendency to promote mechanical, sing-song delivery.

That Tennyson's "measured language"—presented in the form of the *In Memoriam* stanza, an envelope (abba) quatrain in iambic tetrameters—should assert itself as if without conscious intervention is, by the logic of Holmes's physiology of versification, indicative of the body's "automatic" response to the rhythms of breathing; it is also suggestive of a somatically induced metrical response to grief. Such mechanical meters are particularly suited to moments of grief. As Robert Pogue Harrison has noted in *The Dominion of the Dead* (2003), meter and other forms of "rhythm and repetition—whether in the swaying and rocking of the body or in ... lamentation chants"—provide mourners with a medium for "mastering the chaotic impulse at the heart of grief."[104] In her recent book *Heartbeats: Everyday Life and the Memorized Poem* (2012), Catherine Robson discusses how the very rhythmical fabric of memorized poems "lurk[s] deep within the self, ready to be called up not so much by a conscious act of rational retrieval, as by simply allowing the body to utter what the body stored, in a state that approached something like a trance."[105] The physiological metrics that Holmes posits takes this logic a step further. It is not simply that familiar metrical patterns, as well as familiar poems, memorized early in life might be "stored" in the body, which can "utter" them unconsciously at a later date. Holmes's physiological metrics does not imagine the body as merely a storage facility with a replay function that works by activating learned but subconsciously cataloged versification: instead, the body itself participates in generating, as well as uttering, the meters. This "sad mechanic exercise," the composition of meters "not even demanding a thought," thus represents a kind of physiological consolation mechanism in which the poet "instinctively" entrains his prosody to his respiration and in doing so effectively calms the "unquiet" rhythms bereavement has encouraged. Where a stammerer might be prescribed meter to modulate a "spasmodic" speech mechanism, here the body seems to possess an inbuilt, self-regulating metrical function.

Dickinson's "Regardless" metrics similarly "come" of their own accord.[106] Indeed, there is a grimly appropriate "fatal facility" to the octosyllables of the line "The féet mechánicál go róund," which invites sing-song delivery: the body's autometrics recur with monotonous, and potentially palliative, regularity. It is well-known among scholars that Dickinson was drawn to tetrameter lines—whether derived from hymn or ballad meters, as has frequently been suggested.[107] But "a consistent tetrameter," as Helen Vendler observes, often gives way to "meaningful variations."[108] Further, the layout of Dickinson's poems in their original fascicle form often "break[s] up established metrical lines."[109] It is, therefore, worth noting that the manuscript for "After great pain" presents this particular line as an unbroken octosyllable. Whether or not Dickinson's body suggested it is, of course, impossible to say. In any case, the majority of Dickinson's poetic corpus would eventually fall into line, quite literally, with this measure. When R. W. Franklin brought out his *The Poems of Emily Dickinson: Variorum Edition* in 1998, he standardized much of the poetry, rejecting the poet's idiosyncratic lineation in favor of a more conventional tetrameter division of lines. Franklin's editorial intervention regulates Dickinson's measures, not only giving them a more recognizable "poetic" shape on the page but also providing what Lena Christensen has called an "aural code" based on "the tetrameter line,"[110] the measure that was, for Holmes, best tuned to the regular inspirations and expirations of normal human breathing. Was Franklin instinctively responsive to his own body's respiratory rhythms or perhaps cannily alert to the pulmonary preferences of readers? We may never know. But his assertion of tetrameters may well ensure that Dickinson's verses, some metrical eccentricities notwithstanding, will, for generations of readers to come, harmonize as much as possible with the automatic rhythms of the body.

SCANNING SPEECH

In *The Principles of Mental Physiology* (1874), William Benjamin Carpenter discusses a different variety of mechanical meters, ones not elegiac in character but instead an automatically supplied resource for diversion in which measured language provides a vehicle for storytelling that needs little direction from the conscious mind. Carpenter's example is the "practice of the Italian *improvisatori*, who, without preparation, compose and utter a long series of verses upon any given subject." These improvised meters arise from persons with "a special gift for versification."[111] For Carpenter, a mental "gift" for meter and an ability to improvise in such a way were manifestations of the unconscious or automatic processes of the brain (he was interested in, among other things, dreaming and mesmeric trances), not just the rhythmical fluctuations of the lungs or other organs, though in a sense the activities of thought and breathing are similar in that both are merely "reflex actions" of the brain. Presupposing a thoroughly physiological insistence on the derivation of "Thought and Feeling" from cerebral activity, he admits that "intellectual products," including improvised meters, are more or less like "muscular movements" or, in keeping with Holmes, "the ordinary movements of Respiration." What Carpenter calls "Brainchange" is responsible for much of what might otherwise be attributed to conscious thought processes. For such "automatic *Mental* activity" he coins the term "unconscious cerebration," which "encompass[es]," as Helen Groth and Natalya Lusty explain, "any cognitive process that [takes] place while the will [is] suspended."[112] However, Carpenter, like Holmes, concedes that the "unconscious" actions of the mind are not incompatible with the existence of will: "both," he notes, "are equally true" phenomena. The will is a more or less autonomous if "*indirect power*" that exerts its influence over our otherwise automatic processes "through the *habitual discipline* by which it gives shape to the intellectual fabric ...."[113] When Carpenter turns to a discussion of meter as part of his examination of "imagination," he recognizes automatic processes at work, but the compositions he discusses are not strictly unconscious: they are mediated both by prior metrical training and by the will's "constructive power." In some instances, the improvisatore's "unpremeditated verse" might be truly *creative*, as opposed to merely a mechanical composition. Without the guidance of the will, however, such "extemporaneous versification" would be merely doggerel (not unlike the nonsense verses composed by schoolboys in their Latin exercises) and would hardly "bear perusal."[114]

The semiautomatic meters composed by the Italian improvisatori might be regarded not only as products of the brain's biomechanics, as Carpenter proposed, but possibly as signs of cerebral disorder. An 1832 article from the *London Medical Gazette* describes a lecture given at the Royal Institution by an improvisatore called "the Count," who explains for listeners the art of "extemporaneous verse," offering "anecdotes and illustrations" drawn from his own experience. Of particular interest to the publication's readership, notes the author, is the speaker's assertion that "the power of improvisation is a symptom of mania": "Most of the improvisatori named, appear, from our lecturer's account, to have died apoplectic or mad." The Count himself claims to have suffered from a mental malady, which he reputes to have been confirmed by an eminent phrenologist:

> "Thirty years ago," continued he, "I was myself an improvisatore and a madman; when the fit was coming on, I felt a great internal commotion, trembled, seemed to be swelled, as if a large ball or barrel was within me; my sight failed me, my throat was irritated, I had singing in my ears, and subsequently fell to the ground convulsed." He was ill afterwards for three or four days, and his physician recommended a keeper, and pronounced him mad. In 1811, [Franz Joseph] Gall examined the configuration of his skull, and declared that if he had not known him to be a soldier, he should have thought him a poet, and that he could detect many indications of madness, which, he quaintly observed, "was another consolation."[115]

The correlation between extemporaneous versification and madness, as diagnosed by the phrenologist, is taken by the Count as a vindication of his belief that his poetic propensities are the result of a "disease" of the brain. Specifically, it suggested a localization of both madness and metrical activity. As noted above, phrenology presupposed not only a crudely materialist "connexion between mind and matter"[116] but also a correspondence between a particular faculty and "a certain portion of the brain."[117] Verse-making ability, like madness, is, therefore, the product of a derangement of particular parts of the cerebellum. As the phrenologist Hewett C. Watson had proposed in his 1836 book *Statistics of Phrenology*, "[t]he perversion in madness ... of certain faculties, cannot otherwise be explained, than by supposing that [it] ... has a [specific] locality in the brain." So too might the metrical acuity of the improvisatore be traced to disease in "a portion of the brain."[118]

The development of neurophysiology in the second half of the nineteenth century at once confirmed and complicated phrenology's attempt to establish a "correlation of faculties with organs," suggesting surgically demonstrable links between forms of mental "derangement" and metrical predisposition. As Robert M. Young has observed, Victorian brain scientists asserted theories of cerebral localization that replaced the phrenologists' faculty science, premised on "psychological faculties with no precise designation of the related material processes," with a laboratory-tested "physiology of sensory motor processes."[119] In the 1860s and 70s, figures such as Pierre Paul Broca, a French surgeon and anatomist, and David Ferrier, a Scottish neuropathologist who had studied psychology with Bain at Aberdeen, began to produce work based on the analysis of animal and human brains. Broca's interactions with living stroke patients, and his postmortem examinations of their brains, revealed how certain functions were associated with particular regions of the brain. Ferrier's work to establish detailed cortex maps was performed in his research laboratory at the West Riding Lunatic Asylum in Yorkshire and grounded in vivisection—principally the electrical stimulation of dog, monkey, and other animal brains. Their respective contributions marked a turning point in the developing science of neurophysiology, offering demonstrable cerebral localizations for various motor and visual functions (Ferrier), as well as linguistic ability (Broca). As Broca would announce definitively in 1865, "We speak with the left hemisphere" (*Nous parlons avec l'hémisphère gauche*).[120] Further, not only could one's ability to speak be identified with activity in a particular region of the brain, but also damage to a region associated with language and speech, as Broca discovered in relation to left frontal lobe lesions, could result in distorted speech. In certain cases, for example, a stroke might produce damage that manifests itself as a form of "spasmodic," stuttering speech, while in other cases it might present as an overly mechanical, quasi-metrical form of enunciation. It might not be only respiratory rhythms of the lungs, as Holmes had suggested, that could produce an unconscious fatal facility for mechanical, sing-song speech. Indeed, the automatic meters produced by damage to parts of the brain were an outward sign of a condition that could be, in certain instances, legitimately fatal.

If speaking in verse could be an instance of "[t]he unconscious adaptation of voluntary life to the organic rhythm"[121] that was, in certain circumstances, capable of offering forms of rhythmical recuperation, for instance in persons experiencing intense grief, then under other conditions, metrical speech was the symptom of a severe malfunction within the human machine. One pathology that nineteenth-century neurophysiologists such as Broca began to document and investigate was dysarthria: a motor speech disorder caused by an injury to the brain. Broca's own examinations on the subject of language and communication were based principally on both pre- and postmortem examinations (the former through clinical interaction and the latter involving brain biopsy) of two patients, Louis Victor Leborgne and Lazare Lelong, who suffered from damage to a region of the brain now known as the inferior frontal gyrus (commonly designated "Broca's area"). As a result, Leborgne could utter only the sound *tan* or *tan-tan*, while Lelong could speak a few words such as *oui* and *non*. These cases enabled Broca not only to postulate that speech function might be localized in this particular area of the brain but also to offer a diagnosis of aphimia (or "Broca's aphasia")—a condition characterized by a disruption or loss of speech. What these patients had in common was not merely a severe loss of speech but the loss of *articulate* speech: both could utter one or more words but of only one or two syllables. Fluid articulation, for example when linking syllables to form polysyllables, and prosody, the ability to correctly intone words and modulate cadences across a sentence, were severely affected. In *On Aphasia, Or Loss of Speech and the Localisation of the Faculty of Articulate Language* (1870), one of the earliest English-language examinations to engage with Broca's work on cerebral localization and aphasia, Frederic Bateman, a British physician specializing in diseases of the brain, describes Lelong's condition thus: "he had neither lost the general faculty of language nor the movement of the muscles concerned in phonation and articulation; ... he had only lost the faculty of articulate language."[122] Language no longer flows; rather it halts, in some cases similar to a stammer, with the speaker's tongue sticking on a word. In other cases, when "the muscles of phonation and articulation" do not "obey the mandates of the will,"[123] prohibiting articulate language in the manner Bateman documents, an impairment may manifest itself in the form of unconscious syllabification. Here the speaker can in fact speak, if in a similarly *un*fluid, segmented way. This expression of brain disease, however, is not so much similar to stammering as to the syllable-speak cure for it as proposed by Yearsley and others, where the speaker is advised to pronounce "by syllables" as though he were scanning poetry, "pronouncing only one syllable at a time, much as the schoolboy scans his hexameters." While "grammatical and semantic competence" is unaffected, "the prosodic quality" of the utterance, "particularly rhythm and inflection, ... are disrupted."[124] As with the forms of speech impediment studied by Broca, such a decomposition of articulate speech into discrete syllables, aptly named "scanning speech," does not originate with the vocal mechanism itself, as in the cases of stammering assessed by Bell and Yearsley, but with the mechanism that *wills* the speech apparatus in the first place: the embodied mind, specifically as affected by multiple sclerosis.

By the 1880s and 90s, there was a considerable literature devoted to brain and related nervous system diseases, including ones causing impaired speech. William Gowers's well-known *A Manual of Diseases of the Nervous System* (1886–1888) distinguishes between "defects of articulation," caused by damage to "a mechanism of the nerve-nuclei situated in the pons and medulla," and "cerebral defects," which "result from disease of the cerebral hemisphere." Disarthria and scanning speech, where "syllables are unduly separated," belong to the former category.[125] In his 1895 *A Handbook of Medical Diagnosis for Students*, James Herrick, an American physician later known for his work relating to sickle-cell disease and myocardial infarction, discusses scanning speech in a section on multiple sclerosis. When "sclerotic plaques develop irregularly in the brain, spinal cord, and peripheral nerves," certain pathognomonic signs occur that are indicative of the disease's severe inhibition of a sufferer's agency—that is, his or her conscious control over motor and speech functions. "The diagnosis of the disease," writes Herrick, "is based very largely upon the existence of what is known as the intention or voluntary tremor." When attempting to perform a volitional act, a marked tremor sets in. A "change in the manner of speech" is likewise an indicator of the condition: "There is an interruption of the continuous and smooth flow of speech, the patient separating words or even syllables and being obliged to speak slowly and deliberately in order to enunciate the words distinctly." Thus, scanning speech—which, in other contexts, might be read as the unfortunate "symptom" of a particularly mechanistic educational practice (scholastic prosody) or even used as a means of alleviating a pathology (e.g., a stammer)—becomes for brain scientists merely an aid to the "discovery of multiple sclerosis."[126] Under certain circumstances, meter might be too much on one's mind.

Mind Over Meter

When Edward William Cox, a lawyer with an interest in the developing science of psychology, published the second volume of his *The Mechanism of Man* in 1879, he admitted, as had several contemporary scientists whose work we have examined in this chapter, that automatic functions of the human mechanism were, in many instances, directed by an "intelligent agent." Even though the brain might ultimately control these functions, as materialists such as Huxley had argued and as neurophysiological experiments had begun to confirm, there might well be "another independent force" worth taking into account—one directing the material process of the brain and that we might not yet be able to explain using conventional scientific methods.[127] Eleven years earlier, Cox's curiosity about the relationship between will and neurophysiological determinism was already percolating in his contribution to Victorian metrics, "How To Read Poetry," a chapter from his 1868 *The Art of Writing, Reading, and Speaking*. Learning to read poetry well involved, first, an exercise of the will to assess one's strengths and weaknesses and, second, a conscious, willed attempt to bring one's utterance into line with certain rules of articulation. There is a line to tread between delivering verse in the manner of ordinary prose and "singing" it. While Cox exhibits a preference for a more musically informed, singing delivery—he cautions against monotony as "the gravest danger in the reading of poetry"—he nonetheless worries about too much singing. Though, ideally, one might learn to read so as to make verse sensible to the ear without overemphasizing its metrical character, there remains a danger, particularly among those for whom "[t]he *singing* of poetry is the ...

most frequent fault," of lapsing "unconsciously" into "that regular swell and fall of the voice in accordance with the metre." Cox advises speakers predisposed to such involuntary sing-song delivery to attempt to forget "the metrical arrangement of the words." Pitting the concentrated powers of the will against the automatic urges of the body (one's "natural impulse"), expressed via the vocal apparatus in its delivery of "the mechanical part" of poetry, may provide, with practice, a check against "relapsing into the old habit."[128] Here mind over matter was also mind over *meter*.

As we have seen, the extent to which a speaker asserts meter or, by contrast, the extent to which meter asserts itself is framed during the nineteenth century by investigations into the relationship between the mind and body and the ability of an individual to exert—or not—control over the components of the human mechanism, whether the "articulative parts," as focused on by Alexander Melville Bell, or a brain lesion, as in the case of the aphasiacs diagnosed by early proponents of cerebral localization. At times, a consciously directed application of meter might ameliorate defects of the vocal apparatus, such as stammering, while at others an involuntary, automatic metrics might issue from the body or mind, variously imparting recuperative rhythms or permanently distorting articulation. Meter might be brought to bear on the body by the mind with positive effects, or it might be an embodied assertion uncontrollable by conscious intervention. In all of the examples discussed above, the "fact" of meter's manifestation—whether intended or not—was a productive site of analysis at the intersection of literary and scientific perspectives. As the final chapter of the book will show, a similarly fruitful and multidisciplinary process, equally focused on the extent to which meter could be explained in terms of embodied experience, was aided by emerging scientific methods and mechanical technologies; here, as we will see, questions of meter were answered with apparently indisputable data amassed by "prosodists" from a variety of disciplinary backgrounds, particularly in relation to the experimental agendas of physiology and psychology.

NOTES

1. Andrew Ure, *The Philosophy of Manufactures: Or, an Exposition of the Scientific, Moral, and Commercial Economy of the Factory System of Great Britain* (London: Charles Knight, 1835), 404.

2. Robert Jones, *An Address, Delivered at the Opening of the Literary and Scientific Institution, at Staines, on Tuesday, January 12th, 1836* (Staines: J. Smith, 1836), 16.
3. [Harriet Beecher Stowe], *Little Foxes* (Boston: Ticknor and Fields, 1866), 196.
4. [Anon.], rev. of *A Manual of English Prosody*, by Robert Frederick Brewer, *Educational Reporter*, 1, 3 (1869), 10.
5. [Anon.], "The Step from Versification to True Poetry," *Lloyd's Magazine*, 7, 2 (1879), 124.
6. "The Step from Versification to True Poetry," 124.
7. This now commonplace phrase was coined by Gilbert Ryle in his 1949 book *The Concept of Mind*. It signifies the mind-body dualism associated with the Cartesian tradition, which Ryle sets out to disprove. See Ryle, *The Concept of Mind* (London: Hutchinson's University Library, 1949).
8. See Edmund Gosse, *Coventry Patmore* (New York: Charles Scribner's Sons, 1905), 13. Basil Champneys reproduces a letter from the poet's father, P. G. Patmore: "'Touching poetry,—if you have any of it in you it will be pretty sure to come out—whether you will or no—but do not *entice* it out—for of all follies there is none so foolish in its results as the habit of mere *verse* writing. There is no harm in the Charivari man's phrenological prognostic about your head. But if there is anything in it (in the *prognostic* I mean)—or if you *think* there is anything in it—it is a reason the more for eschewing verse-making: for I verily believe there never yet was a *poetical* genius that was not cursed rather than blessed by the possession—unless it was Shakespeare.'" Champneys himself remarks that "The 'Charivari man' alluded to is obviously a phrenologist. There was, I am told, one of some eminence practising in Paris about this time, whose name was Deville." See Basil Champneys, *Memoirs and Correspondence of Coventry Patmore*, vol. 1 (London: George Bell and Sons, 1901), 39–40, 43.
9. Champneys, *Memoirs and Correspondence of Coventry Patmore*, 43.
10. Gerald Massey, "Thomas Hood, Poet and Punster," *Eclectic Magazine of Foreign Literature, Science, and Art* (June 1855), 169.
11. John van Wyhe, *Phrenology and the Origins of Victorian Scientific Naturalism* (Aldershot: Ashgate, 2004), 15. See Ilana Kurshan, "Mind Reading: Literature in the Discourse of Early Victorian Phrenology and Mesmerism," *Victorian Literary Mesmerism*, ed. Martin Willis and Catherine Wynne (Amsterdam and New York: Rodopi, 2006), 17-38.
12. George Combe, *Phrenological Development of Robert Burns, from a Cast of His Skull, Moulded at Dumfries, the 31 Day of March 1834* (Edinburgh: W. and A. K. Johnston, 1834), 4–5.

13. Combe, *Phrenological Development of Robert Burns*, 6, 7. See also Kurshan, "Mind Reading: Literature in the Discourse of Early Victorian Phrenology and Mesmerism."
14. [Edgar Allan Poe], "Critical Notices: Drake-Halleck," review of *The Culprit Fay, and Other Poems* by Joseph Rodman Drake and *Alnwick Castle with Other Poems* by Fitz-Greene Halleck, *Southern Literary Messenger*, 2, 5 (April 1836), 328.
15. J. G. Spurzheim, *Phrenology, Or the Doctrine of Mental Phenomena*, vol. 1 (Boston: Marsh, Capen, and Lyon, 1833), 237.
16. O. S. Fowler, *Fowler's Practical Phrenology* ([no publisher], 1840), 165.
17. Fowler, *Fowler's Practical Phrenology*, 166, 167.
18. Dennis Taylor, *Hardy's Metres and Victorian Prosody* (Oxford: Clarendon Press, 1988), 22.
19. Adela Pinch, *Thinking about Other People in Nineteenth-Century British Writing* (Cambridge: Cambridge University Press, 2010), 135.
20. [Anon.], "Phrenological Society of Paris—Annual Meeting, Aug. 1834," *Annals of Phrenology*, vol. 1 (Boston: Marsh, Capen, and Lyon, 1834), 406.
21. Spurzheim, *Phrenology, Or the Doctrine of Mental Phenomena*, 238.
22. Alexander Bain, *On the Study of Character, Including an Estimate of Phrenology* (London: Parker, Son, and Bourn, 1861), 147.
23. Bain, *On the Study of Character*, 157.
24. George Combe, *A System of Phrenology*, 6th American edn (Boston: Benjamin B. Mussey and Co., 1851), 407.
25. Patmore, *Coventry Patmore's "Essay on English Metrical Law": A Critical Edition with a Commentary*, ed. Mary Augustine Roth (Washington, DC: Catholic University of America Press, 1961), 15.
26. Combe, *A System of Phrenology*, 407.
27. Combe, *A System of Phrenology*, 407.
28. Patmore, "Essay on English Metrical Law," 15.
29. See Jason R. Rudy, *Electric Meters: Victorian Physiological Poetics* (Athens, OH: Ohio University Press, 2009), 76–136.
30. Robert M. Young, *Mind, Brain, and Adaptation in the Nineteenth Century: Cerebral Localization and Its Biological Context from Gall to Ferrier* (New York and Oxford: Oxford University Press, 1990), 104.
31. Bain, *On the Study of Character*, 160.
32. George Combe, *Education: Its Principles and Practice*, ed. William Jolly (London: Macmillan and Co., 1879), 463.
33. Richard Cull, "On the Perception of Metre and Rhythmus, Both in Language and in Music," *Phrenological Journal*, 19, 86 (1846), 5.
34. Bain, *On the Study of Character*, 330-331
35. Cull, "On the Perception of Metre and Rhythmus," 5.

36. Fowler, *Fowler's Practical Phrenology*, 6.
37. Anne Stiles, *Popular Fiction and Brain Science in the Late Nineteenth Century* (Cambridge: Cambridge University Press, 2012), 11.
38. Laura Otis, *Networking: Communicating with Bodies and Machines in the Nineteenth-Century* (Ann Arbor: University of Michigan Press, 2001), 5.
39. Nancy L. Maull, "Berkeley on the Limits of Mechanistic Explanation," *Berkeley: Critical and Interpretive Essays*, ed. Colin Turbayne (Minneapolis: University of Minnesota Press, 1982), 100.
40. Jonathan Sterne, *The Audible Past: Cultural Origins of Sound Reproduction* (Durham, NC: Duke University Press, 2003), 73.
41. Julien Offray de La Mettrie, *Man-Machine*, trans Jonathan Bennett, http://www.earlymoderntexts.com/assets/pdfs/lamettrie1748.pdf (2010-15), 7. For a good explanation of La Mettrie's thoughts on language, particularly in relation to Descartes, see Keith Gunderson, *Mentality and Machines*, 2nd edn (Minneapolis: University of Minnesota Press, 1985), 1-38.
42. Adelheid Voskuhl, *Androids in the Enlightenment: Mechanics, Artisans, and Cultures of the Self* (Chicago: University of Chicago Press, 2013), 24.
43. Anson Rabinbach, *The Human Motor: Energy, Fatigue, and the Origins of Modernity* (Berkeley and Los Angeles: University of California Press, 1992), 49.
44. Rabinbach, *The Human Motor*, 52.
45. Stiles, *Popular Fiction and Brain Science in the Late Nineteenth Century*, 52.
46. Thomas Henry Huxley, "On the Hypothesis that Animals Are Automata, and Its History," *Methods and Results: Essays* (New York: D. Appleton and Company, 1899), 201, 205.
47. Stiles, *Popular Fiction and Brain Science in the Late Nineteenth Century*, 54.
48. See Matthew Campbell, *Rhythm and Will in Victorian Poetry* (Cambridge: Cambridge University Press, 1999), 19.
49. Alexander Bell, *The Tongue, a Poem, in Two Parts* (London: W. J. Cleaver, 1846), 1, 7, 41, 42.
50. Alex[ander] Melville Bell, *Visible Speech: The Science of Universal Alphabetics; or Self-Interpreting Physiological Letters, for the Writing of All Languages in One Alphabet* (London: Simpkin, Marshall, and Co., 1867), 11.
51. Bell, *The Tongue*, 68.
52. David Charles Bell and Alexander Melville Bell, *Bell's Standard Elocutionist* (London: William Mullan and Son, 1878), 28.

53. As Anne Stiles notes, the terms "Will," "Ego," and "Consciousness" are often used as alternatives for the more theologically inflected word "soul." See Stiles, *Popular Fiction and Brain Science in the Late Nineteenth Century*, 55.
54. John Thelwall, *The Vestibule of Eloquence* (London: n.p., 1810), 3, 7. Around the same time, in his preface to his 1815 *Poems*, William Wordsworth addressed the "spirit of versification" in relation to the reader's "*voluntary* power to modulate." See William Wordsworth, "Preface to the Edition of 1815," *The Poetical Works of William Wordsworth*, vol. 5, ed. Edward Dowden (London: George Bell and Sons, 1893), 287 (emphasis added).
55. Simon Jarvis notes the exchange of letters between Wordsworth and Thelwall on this topic and discusses their difference of opinion regarding the abstract "law" of meter. See Jarvis, *Wordsworth's Philosophic Song* (Cambridge: Cambridge University Press, 2007), 11.
56. Isobel Armstrong, "Meter and Meaning," *Meter Matters: Verse Cultures of the Long Nineteenth Century*, ed. Jason David Hall (Athens, OH: Ohio University Press, 2011), 41.
57. Alfred Tennyson, "Break, Break, Break," *Tennyson: A Selected Edition*, rev. edn, ed. Christopher Ricks (Harlow: Longman, 2007), 165.
58. Derek Attridge, "Beat," *The Oxford Handbook of Victorian Poetry*, ed. Matthew Bevis (Oxford: Oxford University Press, 2013), 36. Attridge notes that the poem "presents a metrical puzzle," and he quotes Dana Gioia's remarks about the difficulty of scanning a poem that is "tangibly metrical" yet "misleading." See Gioia, "Meter-Making Arguments," *Meter in English: A Critical Engagement*, ed. David Baker (Fayetteville: University of Arkansas Press, 1986), 93.
59. Armstrong, "Meter and Meaning," 37.
60. Tennyson, "Break, Break, Break," 165.
61. Thomas McFarland, *Romanticism and the Forms of Ruin: Wordsworth, Coleridge, and the Modalities of Fragmentation* (Princeton: Princeton University Press, 1981), 274.
62. Armstrong, "Meter and Meaning," 39. Attridge's beat scansion of the first line places a beat on each "break," with intervening off beats and a final "virtual beat" at the line's end: **B** O **B** O **B** O B.
63. Yopie Prins, "'What Is Historical Poetics?,'" *Modern Language Quarterly*, 77, 1 (2016), 17.
64. Yopie Prins, "'Break, Break, Break' into Song," *Meter Matters: Verse Cultures of the Long Nineteenth Century*, ed. Jason David Hall (Athens, OH: Ohio University Press, 2011), 112, 117.

65. Alfred Tennyson, "Maud," *Tennyson: A Selected Edition*, 535. Alexander Melville Bell, *A New Elucidation of the Principles of Speech and Elocution* (Edinburgh: W. P. Kennedy, 1849), 136.
66. Bell, *A New Elucidation of the Principles of Speech and Elocution*, 189. In *Bell's Standard Elocutionist*, Mellville and David Charles Bell include a short section "On the Reading of Verse" among "Miscellaneous Directions for Reading," "Miscellaneous Directions for Recitation," and "Miscellaneous Exercises" designed to improve articulation (27-34).
67. As Jason Rudy has argued, Tennyson's "vocalization by way of bodily disintegration" in "Break, Break, Break" brings him into dialogue, via the poetics of sensation as theorized by Arthur Hallam, with the spasmodic poetry of the 1850s. For Rudy, though, Tennyson only ever really "gestures" toward the physiological poetics on which spasmodic verse is founded, "disavowing [it] as too extreme, too extravagant, and ultimately, in a time of national unease, too dangerous." See Rudy, *Electric Meters*, 73-75.
68. [Anon.], *On Stammering and Its Treatment* (London: John Churchill, 1850), 10.
69. James Yearsley, "Stammering, Its Causes, Varieties, and Treatment," *Lancet* (Dec. 2, 1843), 289.
70. Bell, *A New Elucidation of the Principles of Speech and Elocution*, 22.
71. Alexander Melville Bell, *Observations on Speech; the Causes and the Cure of Stammering, Mal-Articulations and Defects; and on the Principles of Elocutionary Instruction; with Numerous Cases Systematically Arranged* (Edinburgh: W. P. Kennedy, 1853), 26.
72. Yearsley, "Stammering, Its Causes, Varieties, and Treatment," 290.
73. Yearsley, "Stammering, Its Causes, Varieties, and Treatment," 291, 290.
74. Rudy, *Electric Meters*, 115.
75. Rudy, *Electric Meters*, 106.
76. Edgar Allan Poe, "The Rationale of Verse," *The Works of the Late Edgar Allan Poe with a Memoir by Rufus Wilmot Griswold and Notices of His Life and Genius by N. P. Willis and J. R. Lowell*, 4 vols. (New York: Blakeman and Mason, 1859), II, 249, 250.
77. [John Robertson], "My Ghosts," *Household Words*, 15, 360 (Feb. 14, 1857), 168.
78. [Anon.], "How To Cure Stammering," *Medical and Surgical Reporter* (Jul. 29, 1871), 111.
79. "How To Cure Stammering," 111. The same text is reprinted in the *Maine Journal of Education*, 7, 8 (1873), 318.
80. Yearsley, "Stammering, Its Causes, Varieties, and Treatment," 291.
81. E. S. Dallas, *Poetics: An Essay on Poetry* (London: Smith, Elder, and Co., 1852), 171, 159.

82. Dallas, *Poetics*, 158, 159, 160.
83. Dallas, *Poetics*, 158, 160.
84. Bell, *Observations on Speech*, 41.
85. Bell, *Observations on Speech*, 41. Others involved in the teaching of elocution and rhetoric shared Bell's worries. Ebenezer Porter, an American minister who wrote several books on rhetorical delivery, eloquence, and style, warns in *The Rhetorical Reader* (which had reached its 116th edition by 1842) against forming overly metrical reading habits: "in aiming to acquire a distinct articulation, take care not to form one that is *measured* and *mechanical*. The child, in passing from his spelling manner, is ambitious to become a swift reader, and thus falls into a confusion of organs, that is to be cured only by retracing the steps which produced it. The remedy, however, is no better than the fault, if it runs into a *scanning, pe-dan-tic for-mal-i-ty*, giving undue stress to particles and unaccented syllables; thus, 'He is *the* man *of* all *the* world whom I *re*joice *to* meet.'" See Porter, *The Rhetorical Reader* (New York: Dayton and Newman, 1842), 26.
86. [Anon.], "Remarkable Disorders of Speech," *Otago Witness* (Feb. 21, 1889), 31.
87. Alfred Tennyson, In Memoriam A. H. H., *Tennyson: A Selected Edition*, 349.
88. Timothy Peltason, *Reading* In Memoriam (Princeton: Princeton University Press, 1985), 41.
89. See A. A. Markley, "Tennyson," *The Oxford History of Classical Reception in English Literature*, vol. 4, ed. Norman Vance and Jennifer Wallace (Oxford: Oxford University Press, 2015), 539–557. Pat Jalland has discussed how recourse to verse, including the practice of reading aloud, was promoted during the nineteenth century as a way of "sooth[ing] mourners" and "bereaved people." See Jalland, *Death in the Victorian Family* (Oxford: Oxford University Press, 1996), 281.
90. The usefulness of measured language, according to David McAllister, extended beyond the poet himself and into Victorian mourning culture more generally. As metered lines appeared on mourning cards and other *memento mori*, mourners were provided with another example of how meter mediates grief: "The 'use in measured language' for many Victorian readers was that it screened the terrifying absence behind diverting and familiar cultural texts." See McAllister, "'A Use in Measured Language': Poetic Allusion and the Victorian Culture of Death," *Modern Language Studies*, 49, 3 (2013), 230.
91. Emily Dickinson, "After great pain," *The Poems of Emily Dickinson*, ed. R. W. Franklin (Cambridge, MA: Harvard University Press, 1998), 170.

92. Annie Finch, *The Ghost of Meter: Culture and Prosody in American Free Verse* (Ann Arbor: University of Michigan Press, 1993), 29. According to Finch, the weight of metrical convention is difficult for poets, even those composing in putatively free verse, to avoid; thus, "ghosts," to borrow T. S. Eliot's expression, of the "metrical code" haunt apparently verse-less poems.
93. Oliver Wendell Holmes, "The Physiology of Walking," *Pages from an Old Volume of Life, The Works of Oliver Wendell Holmes*, 15 vols (Boston: Houghton, Mifflin and Co., 1892), 8: 121.
94. Dickinson, "After great pain," *The Poems of Emily Dickinson*, 170.
95. Holmes, "The Physiology of Walking," 124.
96. Gregory Tate, *The Poet's Mind: The Psychology of Victorian Poetry 1830–1870* (Oxford: Oxford University Press, 2012), 94.
97. Oliver Wendell Holmes, "The Physiology of Versification: Harmonies of Organic and Animal Life," *Pages from an Old Volume of Life: A Collection of Essays 1857–1881* (Boston and New York: Houghton, Mifflin, and Co., 1892), 315. The essay was first published in the *Boston Medical and Surgical Journal* in January of 1875.
98. William C. Dowling, *Oliver Wendell Holmes in Paris: Medicine, Theology, and* The Autocrat of the Breakfast Table (Lebanon, NH: University of New Hampshire Press, 2006), xi.
99. Dowling, *Oliver Wendell Holmes in Paris*, xii.
100. Oliver Wendell Holmes, *Mechanism in Thought and Morals* (Boston: James R. Osgood and Co., 1871), 48, 10, 29, 6–7.
101. For more on the exchange between Victorian versification and the heart, see Kirstie Blair, *Victorian Poetry and the Culture of the Heart* (Oxford: Clarendon Press, 2006), 63–102.
102. Holmes, "The Physiology of Versification," 316.
103. The "fatal facility" of octosyllabic lines was first suggested by Lord Byron in his preface to "The Corsair" (1814). See the entry for "Octosyllable" in *The Princeton Encyclopedia of Poetry and Poetics*, 4 ed., ed. Roland Greene et al. (Princeton: Princeton University Press, 2012), 970.
104. Robert Pogue Harrison, *The Dominion of the Dead* (Chicago: University of Chicago Press, 2003), 171.
105. Catherine Robson, *Heart Beats: Everyday Life and the Memorized Poem* (Princeton: Princeton University Press, 2012), 112.
106. Dickinson, "After great pain," 170.
107. See Christanne Miller, "Nineteenth-Century U.S. Literary Predecessors," *Dickinson in Context*, ed. Eliza Richards (Cambridge: Cambridge University Press, 2013), 119–128.

108. Helen Vendler, "Introduction: Dickinson the Writer," *Dickinson: Selected Poems and Commentaries*, ed. Helen Vendler (Cambridge, MA: Harvard University Press, 2010), 5.
109. Fred D. White, *Approaching Emily Dickinson: Critical Currents and Cross Currents since 1960* (New York: Camden House, 2008), 89.
110. Lena Christensen, *Editing Emily Dickinson: The Production of an Author* (New York: Routledge, 2008), 106.
111. William B. Carpenter, *Principles of Mental Physiology, with Their Applications to the Training and Discipline of the Mind, and the Study of its Morbid Conditions* (London: Henry S. King and Co., 1875), 492. According to an 1855 article in a popular magazine, *improvisatori* was a name "given in Italy to poets who compose and declaim extemporaneously on any given subject, accompanying their voice with an instrument." The improvisatori were active from the Renaissance, but their numbers were dwindling by the middle decades of the nineteenth century. See [anon.], "Improvisatori," *Arthur's Home Magazine* (Jan. 1855), 9.
112. Carpenter, *Principles of Mental Physiology*, ix, 32, ix. Helen Groth and Natalya Lusty, *Dreams and Modernity: A Cultural History* (Abingdon: Routledge, 2013), 43.
113. Here Carpenter's "emphasis ... on ... social norms and acquired habits," as Michael Davis has observed, results in a "limited volitional autonomy" at best. Not only is the will capable of intervening in the spontaneous activity of the brain; further, the will itself is shaped by social and cultural factors such as education. See Davis, *George Eliot and Nineteenth-Century Psychology: Exploring the Unmapped Country* (Aldershot: Ashgate, 2006), 123.
114. Carpenter, *Principles of Mental Physiology*, 492, 493.
115. [Anon.], "Royal Institution," *London Medical Gazette, Being a Weekly Journal of Medicine and the Collateral Sciences* (Mar. 10, 1832), 888.
116. Fowler, *Fowler's Practical Phrenology*, 407. In this section Fowler discusses the objections to phrenology as a materialist science.
117. Hewett C. Watson, *Statistics of Phrenology: Being a Sketch of the Progress and Present State of That Science in the British Islands* (London: Longman, Rees, Orme, Brown, Green, and Longman, 1836), 24.
118. Watson, *Statistics of Phrenology*, 24-25.
119. Young, *Mind, Brain, and Adaptation in the Nineteenth Century*, 209.
120. Pierre Paul Broca, *Sur le siege de la faculté du langage articulé*. Bulletin de la Société d'Anthropologie 6 (1865), 384.
121. Holmes, "The Physiology of Versification," 319.

122. Frederic Bateman, *On Aphasia, Or Loss of Speech and the Localisation of the Faculty of Articulate Language* (London: John Churchill and Sons, 1870), 10–11.
123. Bateman, *On Aphasia, Or Loss of Speech in Cerebral Disease* (London: J. E. Adlard, 1868), 33.
124. Medical science has followed up nineteenth-century links between brain pathology, for example multiple sclerosis, and scanning speech, though disputing whether there is sufficient "evidence to specify a cerebellar localization for scanning speech." See D. Frank Benson and Alfredo Ardila, *Aphasia: A Clinical Perspective* (Oxford: Oxford University Press, 1996), 289.
125. William Gowers, *A Manual of Diseases of the Nervous System*, vol. 2 (London: J. and A. Churchill, 1886), 101, 102.
126. James B. Herrick, *A Handbook of Medical Diagnosis for Students* (Philadelphia: Lea Brothers and Co., 1895), 408.
127. Edward W. Cox, *The Mechanism of Man: An Answer to the Question, What Am I? A Popular Introduction to Mental Physiology and Psychology*, vol. 2 (London: Longman, 1879), 5, 6.
128. Edward W. Cox, *The Arts of Writing, Reading, and Speaking* (London: G. W. Carleton, 1868), 143, 139, 146.

Instrumental Prosody

> Metre and Rhythm are too closely conjoined ... to be separated in poetry, though they may be separated in theory....
> —"Hints on Dramatic Versification," *Monthly Chronicle* (1840)

> Metrical form, ... that is to say the rhythm inherent in the sequence of the actual sounds in verse, the rhythm that appears in the records of the kymograph, is very important.
> —I. A. Richards, *Practical Criticism* (1929)

Whether "metrical form" and "the rhythm inherent in ... the actual sounds in verse" are one and the same thing and the related question of whether they can "be separated" in practice or theory have been a subject of much speculation—long before the advent of the "practical" mode of criticism associated with I. A. Richards. During the nineteenth century the debate went back and forth. "The ancient grammarians," as an anonymous reviewer wrote in an 1839 issue of the *Foreign Quarterly Review*, "knew very well that rhythm was one thing and metre another; they knew also very well that rhythm was the continual controller and modifier of metres ...."[1] This author's proposition about classical meters appears to differ significantly from Richards's about English versification. Five years later, however, an English translation of the German classical scholar Edward Munk's *The Metres of the Greeks and Romans* (1844) promoted a position more in keeping with the one Richards would later espouse: that rhythm and meter are fundamentally alike in character. Rhythm, Munk stated, "is a succession of portions of time perceptible to the senses," in which the alternation of arsis and thesis "divides the uninterrupted flow of time into proportions of time," while meter "*is a definite succession of longs and shorts.*"[2] Both of these nineteenth-century texts agreed that time, specifically in relation to the structures of ancient Greek and Latin poetry, was the principal prosodical index—because classical poetry, originally a form of song, could be understood to adopt the same basic temporal structure as music. Both texts were also more or less in agreement on the subject of rhythm as *flow*, though for the author of the 1839 text, this emphasis on flow as *embodied* was what distinguished rhythm from meter: "Rhythm exists only in living and breathing things," as opposed to "the abstract idea of succession," which too often characterized contemporary assessments of classical meter.[3] As we saw in the previous chapter, the rhythms of the body (recall Oliver Wendell Holmes on respiration) provided an organic time signature that, as the anonymous author of 1839 proposed, "run[s] on in a continuous flow." While the flow of rhythm *should* "control" meter, it was often the case that metrical theorists posited meter as the controller of rhythm, interrupting the flow, breaking it up into "fixed and unbending" segments. By letting the abstraction of meter dominate organic rhythms, there was a risk, the author speculated, of divorcing poetry from somatic experience and from its origins in music. That the "arbitrary" and "artificial system of metrical feet and monotonous quantities" was allowed to constrain the "plastic principle of rhythm" was an unfortunate consequence of modern metrical culture, which was dominated "by the pedantry of the Prosodians" whose methods, as we observed in previous chapters, favored segmented, telegraphic, unflowing prosody.[4] Richards himself, writing about English meters, would later assert a similar worry about how "[t]he notion that verses must conform to metrical patterns" constitutes "the most damaging enemy to good reading"—resulting in "mechanical reading."[5]

The focus of the previous chapter was on the flow of meter in direct relation to embodied experience. Whether meters flowed out, or did not, from a function of the brain or an impulse of the body—for example, the lungs or the vocal apparatus—was, at times, an act of will, of the individual's control over his or her body and the meters it produced, while, under other circumstances, metrical utterances came forth "automatically," without the conscious direction of the speaker. This chapter extends the previous one's grounding of meter in corporeal experience, but it reorients notions of flow in relation to a rhythm-meter dialectic that, while already a subject of discussion much earlier in the century, was itself adapting to materialist procedures not only as applied to the body, as we have seen, but as focused specifically on the physical properties and aesthetic dimensions of sound, music, and versification. By the 1880s, a methodical verse science was exerting its empirical energies. Gripped by the thought of articulating an objective, fact-based metrics, verse scientists brought to bear on the traditional English verse line principles of observation and later full-blown experimental practices—as well as curious instruments such as the kymograph mentioned by Richards. By the turn of the century, metrical verse was being subjected to a rigorous measurement regime, which employed techniques and apparatuses derived from the new disciplines of experimental physiology and psychology. Proponents of this newly mechanized metrics pitched themselves enthusiastically into the turn-of-the-century prosody fray, believing they could resolve, once and for all, some of the fundamental dilemmas of nineteenth-century versification. For them establishing the reality of meter involved a thoroughly technologized examination of sound and, specifically, speech flow, as well as an attempt to render in more accurate, visible form the movement and measurement of verse. Would the records of machines, whose data purported to offer up the "facts" of versification, be able to resolve questions about the relationship between the "continuous flow" of rhythm, on the one hand, and the abstract "systems" of metrical representation, on the other? When a poem was given voice, was its meter audible and measureable? Or was meter merely an abstraction, as Patmore asserted, that no machine could capture, no matter how sensitive and ostensibly objective it was?

Do You Not Hear It?

How can the movement of meter be represented? It is a question this chapter will take up in relation to a burgeoning science of versification. Signally, it is a question about materiality *versus* immateriality, as well as about what notation or media can best capture or substitute for the truth of meter's modulations. To begin this assessment, it is worth pausing to scrutinize some of the visual and auditory positions on meter that were circulating before and as late-Victorian verse science set its machines to take their measure. To anchor this examination, we can focus attention on the versifying of Alfred Tennyson, whose meters constitute one of the main examples for this chapter's history of mechanical metrical representation. So let's begin by looking at Tennyson's verse. If meter, as Patmore theorized, is imaginary, then maybe one does not even need to hear it to understand its movement. Perhaps *seeing* a poet read is sufficient for us to imagine his measures. So imagine a large, mostly empty room. Now position two figures opposite one another: a poet and a monarch. In the bottom left-hand corner of the frame, Tennyson intones his 1850 elegy, *In Memoriam*. Separated from him by an expanse of patterned carpet, is the diminutive Victoria, who listens in inscrutable silence. While she sits bolt upright, looking into the middle distance, he lounges, legs outstretched. In both of their bodies—his reclining toward the horizontal, hers respectably upright—one might imagine a grimly comic suggestion of *rigor mortis*. There is a fireplace in the center background, between the two figures. Above the mantelpiece, deaf to the scene taking place in the immediate foreground, a portrait of the Prince Consort in profile completes a compositionally balanced triangle of death.

This is the scene offered to us in Max Beerbohm's 1904 cartoon "Mr. Tennyson Reading In Memoriam to His Sovereign" (Fig. 1). We can glimpse here the complex interplay between audition and vision, between meters in the ear and in the eye, to borrow John Hollander's terms,[6] that is central to this chapter's argument about what metrical analysis and measurement are and how they might be undertaken. Much of irreverent comedy of Beerbohm's caricature derives from its spatial arrangement. Viewers see, but do not hear, a metrical performance: they *see* Tennyson's metrical delivery. But viewers can *only* see, for illustration, as the Greek maxim goes, "is *silent* poetry."[7] The picture's viewers remain outside audition, shut out from the very thing the picture purports to represent: the vocal immediacy and peculiarity of Tennyson's reading. In an extension of the image's geometry, viewers become Albert's opposite numbers. And because their position is, like his, outside the diegetic frame, their ears, too, are effectively dead to Tennyson's elegiac strains. Quite possibly, this *unhearing* is part of Beerbohm's joke: "Be glad I've spared you the deadening, monotonous drone," the artist seems to say. For though lookers do not hear it, Tennyson's idiosyncratic, at times stupefying, style of delivery is nonetheless communicated—signed by his posture. With his head tilted slightly back, his text held aloft, and his free arm raised in elocutionary emphasis,

Mr. Tennyson, reading "In Memoriam" to his Sovereign.

Fig. 1 "Mr. Tennyson Reading 'In Memoriam' to His Sovereign," from Max Beerbohm's *Poet's Corner* (London: Heinemann, 1904). Hulton Archive. Photo by The Print Collector/Print Collector/Getty Images

the cartoon-Tennyson mimes his real-life counterpart's well-known reading affectations. Dante Gabriel Rossetti's well-known 1855 sketch of *Tennyson Reading Maud*, for example, offers a similar glimpse of the poet intoning. Though less of an exaggeration, Rossetti's Tennyson, like Beerbohm's, is sufficiently slouchy. He holds the book in front of him as though to declaim from it, yet his eyes appear closed. His left arm, stretched at his side, waits in readiness to make the characteristic quasi-mesmeric passes, which, in hypnotic concert with the poet's distinctive reading voice, will likely fascinate his auditors. So well-known, in fact, was Tennyson's reading pose that his contemporaries could often hear well enough with their eyes when they beheld images such as these. Gilbert Haven, for example, offered the following remarks on looking at "a sketch of Tennyson reading 'Maud,'" which he claimed to have seen on Robert Browning's mantelpiece:

> It represents him lounging in an easy-chair, with one leg drawn up on the cushion, and held in its place by a nursing hand, while he holds the little

volume in the other (hand, not leg); and the tall, bearded, repellant, yet all-fascinating poet, is slowly chanting, in an unheard but not unfelt monotone, his song of songs. Do you not hear it?[8]

Some listeners did hear Tennyson's chanting first-hand, and their recollections resonate with Haven's imagined audition. William Michael Rossetti remarked on the "sonorous and emotional" quality of Tennyson's delivery. Not a few speak of sitting "rapt" or "spell-bound" throughout his readings[9]—which could go on for hours.[10] Almost without exception, his hearers attest to the singularity of his pronunciation. Part of what enthralls Rossetti, for instance, is Tennyson's "slightly chanting intonation."[11] William Allingham remembers the poet's habit of "lingering with solemn sweetness on every vowel sound."[12] Indeed, Tennyson himself, in his poem "The Epic," bestows this elocutionary affectation on his poetic avatar, Everard Hall, who deliberately "mouth[s] out his hollow oes and as." Not all listeners, of course, appreciated such distinctive declaiming—as Tennyson seemed to know. The parson Holmes, a member of the listening party in "The Epic," is promptly "sent to sleep with sound,"[13] and drowsing sometimes accompanied Tennyson's real-life readings, as well. One of the poet's contemporaries, Edmund Gosse, remembers finding an 1877 recital overly soporific, stating that Tennyson "hangs sleepily over the syllables, in a rough monotonous murmur."[14] Francis Turner Palgrave thought this murmuring made Tennyson's reading "too little varied or emphatic, his voice and delivery monotonous." At the same time, however, Palgrave speaks favorably of Tennyson's "power of modulation," and Allingham observes approvingly that the poet "modulates his cadences with notable subtlety."[15] These recollections reveal a plurality of sound effects—from sonorous and solemn to muffled and muted. Were Tennyson's listeners hearing different things? Were his readings, as some suggest, monotonous, or were they powerfully modulated?

The examples mentioned above stretch across several decades—from the late 1830s, when a comparatively young Tennyson depicts his stylized surrogate in "The Epic," to the late 1870s, when Gosse heard the poet, who was by then almost 70 years old. Nevertheless, there are unifying factors worth noting. First, let's pause to examine some features of nineteenth-century elocutionary and orthophonic practice, namely orotund speech and the monotone. As Jed Rasula has pointed out, the "oracular declamatory style" of poetry reading popular in the Victorian period is exemplified by Tennyson's distinctive "mouthing."[16] Orotund reading or *ore rotundo*—literally, speaking with a "round mouth"—was associated with stage acting, political oratory, and sermonizing from the pulpit; it was characterized by a sonorous "fullness of tone" and a resonant musical quality, in which can be heard a rich, throaty sound reminiscent of the "vibrations made by the reed" of a wind instrument. The orotund thus allows the bleating or buzzing of the glottis to resonate, "combining the 'purity' of the 'head tone' with the reverberation of the chest."[17] Intense and expressive, orotund speech was regarded as particularly suitable for the delivery of "the *bolder* forms of *poetry*."[18] Yet it could also produce stultifying monotony. In the 1848 edition of his book *Orthophony; Or the Cultivation of the Voice in Elocution*, William Russell, discussing "effusive" and "expulsive" orotund as two profoundly poetic modes of utterance, reminded his readers that orotund reading in fact falls under "the monotone" category of speech. Not necessarily signifying "mere monotony," which is the result of "an accidental fault of the ear and habit," the monotone style denotes "a long, and even protracted, vowel sound, with a peculiarly full 'median stress,' which absorbs the attention, and occupies the ear, to the exclusion of... differential sounds ...."[19] However resonant and expressive, this "low-pitched, solemn utterance"[20] was, for both novice and well-trained speakers alike, capable of degrading into a mechanical evenness of tone. For the unpracticed speaker, *ore rotundo* was "at first...monotonous" not only for want of practice but also because it was typically acquired by means of a step-by-step syllabic process, similar to the verse-reading practices examined in "Meter Manufactories": "As soon as single words can be uttered, of a pure orotund character, let attempts be made to sound sentences, and by degrees this voice will be heard upon successive syllables."[21] The process of learning to sound one's vowels sonorously thus lent itself to an undesirable scanning speech. Further, even "professional speakers" who had much practice in "correct" monotone delivery might not be immune to such infelicities: as a result of "habitual" use, they might fail to notice that their tones had lapsed into "the wearisome sameness of school reading."[22] Given that the monotone style could range from the expressive to the droning, it is possible that Tennyson's readings fluctuated not only across his life but also across the monotone scale, here elevating in the direction of poetic solemnity and there falling into the "monotonous murmur" that Gosse recalled. As we saw in the previous chapter, the poet was susceptible to "automatic," mechanical measures—not least in

In Memoriam, described by a contemporary as "one long monotone of grief."[23]

These questions about the monotone and modulation have metrical implications, particularly as regards the poet's performance of his versification, how he speaks *in verse*, to use Yopie Prins's expression.[24] For Prins, Tennyson's distinctive intoning is the result of a "meticulous reinscription of the meter": she suggests that the poet was striving to convey with his voice something of the page-bound "trueness" of his poems' metrical patterns—to the point where listeners hear in Tennyson's readings a deliberate attempt *to speak the modulus of meter itself*.[25] It is worth remembering that, for many educated Victorians, for example the poet-prosodist Coventry Patmore, the word *modulus* in fact meant "metrical structure or pattern."[26] Reading aloud so as to make the metrical pattern audible was, as we have seen, one object of scholastic scansion. Here an elocutionary style such as the monotone—"usually distinguished by [a] horizontal mark,"[27] not unlike the macron placed above long vowels in school books devoted to the subject of classical quantity—was particularly well adapted. The elocutionary methods used to teach orotund speech and the piecemeal syllabic system that underpinned prosodic education were, in fact, designed to achieve more or less the same end: a mode of pronunciation that builds on "successive repetitions" of vowel sounds, pronounced in a conventional, stylized way, so as to produce "a partial sameness of voice on several, or on many words, in succession."[28] In the case of Tennyson's delivery, it is not surprising that his auditors were more or less united not only in their attention to his predilection for vowel-proud delivery but also in their sensitivity to how Tennyson's *rhythms* dominated his readings. Both Rossetti and Palgrave, for example, responded to Tennyson's tone in terms that suggest vocal elevation (accent or pitch, for example): what the one perceived as the poet's only "slightly changing intonation," the other heard as a lack of variety or emphasis ("a rough monotonous murmur"). Tennyson's metrical orations, they implied, sounded "monotonous" because he did not "vary the tone, pitch, or strength" of his voice. Yet Palgrave stated that Tennyson in fact modulated his verses powerfully (or with "notable subtlety," according to Allingham). So while he may not have offered his auditors much diversity in terms of *accent*, Tennyson, a poet well-versed in classical prosody, nevertheless intoned them with the correct attention to syllabic "*measure or duration*." Indeed, as one hearer suggested, the peculiarity of Tennyson's pronunciation is very much a consequence of his habit of "sacrificing everything to quantity."[29] So devoted was Tennyson to communicating the proper lengths of his syllables that he neglected in the process the relative degrees of speech stress that otherwise might have added variety to and so enlivened his parlor performances.[30] The monotone and the modulus could work in concert to produce a formidable—if, on occasion, unfortunate—mouthed measuring of syllables.

Thus, Gilbert Haven's leading question—*Do you not hear it?*—might be a good one to ask about a poet's spoken meters. Certainly it can help us focus our attention, as it might well have done for Haven's contemporaries, on what was in the nineteenth century a controversial topic: the presence of meter in spoken verse. Does the voice of the poet (or one of his many reciters) *reinscribe* meter, as Prins contends? Or does voice remain fundamentally distinct from meter even while engaging with it on some level? Moreover, *should* it? For many Victorian poets and verse theorists, as well as their immediate heirs, there were both theoretical and practical questions associated with meter as a determining factor in voicings of verse, as well as in the way meter might be communicated (or not) by the printed poem and orthographic systems of metrical notation. *Should meter really be heard at all?* Or, more specifically, how much should the metrical line as a distinct unit—or the component units of it for that matter (whether syllables, feet, or musical periods)—audibly inform the delivery of poems? Some nineteenth-century prosodic hardliners insisted that the line and its metrical organization be foregrounded in readings; they objected to overly "natural" delivery in which the modulus all but disappeared. This is particularly noticeable in relation to discussions of so-called final or end-of-line pause (a close cousin to medial pause, or caesura). The 1825 edition of Lindley Murray's popular *English Reader*, for instance, asserted that we "ought" to read poetry "so as to make every line sensible to the ear: for, what is the use of melody or for what end has the poet composed in verse, if in reading his lines, we suppress his numbers, by omitting the final pause; and degrade them, by our pronunciation, into mere prose?"[31] Noah Webster, in his 1843 *An Improved Grammar of the English Language*, commented that the "final pause marks the close of a line or verse, whether there is a pause in the sense or not.... [T]he final pause, when the close of one line is intimately connected with the beginning of the next, should be merely a suspension of the voice without elevation or depression."[32] Coventry Patmore went as far as to make final pause a central feature of his mid-century verse theory. By moving along too quickly from one line to the next, readers run the risk of negating the effect of the poem's metrical movement, of compromising what Patmore understood as the immutable "law" of meter. On this point, several contemporary readers and elocution manuals were clear: poetry *should* be read as poetry, with attention to the modulus. Here, for example, is how one text, Epes Sargent's *The Standard Fifth Reader* (1867), advises pupils to read section CVI ("Ring out, wild bells") of In Memoriam:

> Delivery. The tone should be a pure orotund, animated and expressive, with imitative modulation, mostly in the middle pitch. The falling inflection should be used at nearly all grammatical pauses, and at the end of every line. In the last, there should be a reverential pause after *in*.[33]

The author not only recommends a fittingly Tennysonian monotone ("pure orotund") and expressive, yet even, modulation ("in the middle pitch") but also communicates the importance of observing mid-line and final pauses, thus ensuring that the reading audibly preserve both the metrical patterning as the voice moves across the line and the aural distinction of the line as a self-contained metrical unit.

Even proponents of final pause were aware that the law of meter could be applied with a regrettable lack of subtlety. In making every line sensible to the ear, the reader risked subjecting his or her auditors to a form of mechanical scansion-speak. Caution was urged by mainstream prosodists and elocutionists, as well as non-specialist writers, including the well-known sensation novelist Wilkie Collins. The relentless march of the modulus is something that Collins, in his 1870 novel *Man and Wife*, conveys with characteristic good humor. Allowing one character to deliver the opening verses of John Milton's *Paradise Lost* so that "every line [ends] inexorably with a full stop," Collins pokes fun at those who demanded that meter be asserted by main force (Fig. 2).[34] Collins's representation of these lines—he deliberately prints the full stops—seems, in the context of Victorian metrical discourse, more than just a comic touch. For how we *see* poetry, some would claim, often directly correlates to how we are likely to *sound* it. According to the elocutionist and "visible speech" popularizer Alexander Melville Bell, a reader too mindful of the modulus of meter is unduly inclined toward "singsong" recitation. To guard against a "too rhythmical delivery," Bell suggested displaying verse so that it did not look like verse at all. If only we

"Of Man's first disobedience and the fruit.
Of that forbidden tree whose mortal taste.
Brought death into the world and all our woe.
With loss of Eden till one greater Man.
Restore us and regain the blissful seat.
Sing heavenly Muse—"

Fig. 2 Endstopped lines from Milton's *Paradise Lost*, as printed in Wilkie Collins's novel *Man and Wife* (Leipzig: Bernhard Tauchnitz, 1870), 265

LXI.—TIME AND THE SEA-TIDE.—TENNYSON.

Break! break! break! on thy cold grey stones, oh Sea! And I would that my tongue could utter the thoughts that arise in me. Oh well for the fisherman's boy, that he shouts with his sister at play! oh well for the sailor lad, that he sings in his boat on the bay! And the stately ships go on to their haven under the hill; But oh for the touch of a vanished hand, and the sound of a voice that is still. Break! break! break! at the foot of thy crags, oh Sea! But the tender grace of a day that is dead, will never come back to me.

Fig. 3 "Time and the Sea-Tide—Tennyson" ["Break, Break, Break" in prose], from David Charles Bell and Alexander Melville Bell's *Bell's Standard Elocutionist* (London: William Mullan and Son, 1878), 297

could get beyond *seeing* meter asserted by "metrically printed LINES," he argued, then there would be less chance of pronouncing poems in an artificially metrical manner. So, "as an assistance to the habitual use of pauses and tones in strict accordance with the SENSE," Bell, in his *Standard Elocutionist* of 1878, displayed many poems—including extracts from Milton and Tennyson—"PROSAICALLY."[35] Figure 3 shows how Bell renders Tennyson's "Break, Break, Break" for readers. If an intoner like the one Collins imagines were to see a poem in prose blocks instead of in visually distinct lines, then he might offer a more mellifluous sounding.

Tennyson himself, dedicated as he seems to have been to the voicing of the modulus, might not have been overly impressed by this prosified version of his lyric. But as we shall see, questions about how meters—quite often Tennyson's own—were or were not represented visually became, especially in the latter decades of the nineteenth century when these questions began to interest not only those involved with elocution but also scientists of sound and speech, a subject investigated with redoubled scrutiny. The emerging sciences of rhythm and scansion were less interested in the possibility of reinscribing printed meter; instead, they devoted their efforts to capturing by other visual means and, in some cases, with new graphic mechanisms the rhythmic data of the voice itself. Their aim was nothing short of establishing definitively the *real* basis of verse. Rather than looking at examples of voice *in verse*, starting with the cues of the printed page to understand how the voice might adapt itself to the patterns of meter, the verse scientists who conducted their prosodic experiments in laboratories instead started with the voice and embodied rhythmic phenomena, utilizing measurement and graphing machinery to *see*, quite literally, what they could find out about modulations of verse *in voice*.

Signs of Sounds

Beerbohm's illustration of Tennyson's metrics is framed by attempts to present meter in clearer, visually distinctive ways, and these attempts would lead, ultimately, to the laboratory. But the turn toward the mechanized measurement of meter at the end of the nineteenth century did not take place exclusively in laboratories. It began with and, throughout the period under examination here, continued to enjoy less instrumental—and more conventionally literary—expressions of scientific analysis in a broader sense, where prosodic practice appropriated, at times loosely, methods and principles from the natural and physical sciences in an attempt to firm up, disambiguate, and otherwise rationalize the study of verse form.[36] In 1885, for example, Francis Gummere, writing in his *A Handbook of Poetics for Students of English Verse*, lamented that the existing prosody manuals were "aesthetic and vague," arguing that "there is really no established standard by which we can try true poetry, as a chemist tries gold." Calling for a "science of verse" that "aims to formulate, as far as it can, the principles of poetic expression," Gummere adumbrated a prosody that was at once "historical and analytical."[37] Thinking along similar lines, Mark H. Liddell, in *An Introduction to the Scientific Study of English Poetry* (1902), proposed a "method of study... like that of biology."[38] Like Gummere and Liddell, Sidney Lanier, author of *The Science of English Verse* (1880), held that because the study of verse "involves mainly the observation of sensible appearances" it can "be carried on with the confidence attaching to the methods of physical science." "[T]he basis of a science of verse," Lanier insisted, was the need "to recognize verse as in all respects a phenomenon of sound."[39] Indeed, as Edmund Gurney maintained in *The Power of Sound* (1880), a physics of sound would provide a firm grounding for prosodic study: the material properties of the verse line—rhythm, pitch, color, etc.—could be established, like those of music more generally, on a methodical, "scientific basis" by an expert verse scientist.[40]

For these and other late nineteenth-century verse theorists, emphasis on a more analytical and ostensibly scientific prosody was bound up with a desire to rethink one of the fundamental preoccupations of versification: how to conceptualize, measure, and represent the English verse line. As Emily Harrington and others have demonstrated, disputes about prosody's "origins and rules" figured significantly in nineteenth-century metrical discourse, and throughout the century variant theories emerged regarding the function of accent, the role of time or quantity, and the part played by classical terminology in the definition of metrical effect.[41] As we have seen, in the 1830s Edwin Guest had attempted to establish a provenance for accent as the rhythmical "index" of English poetry.[42] However, as we noticed in "Measurement, Temporality, Abstraction," from the 1850s prosodists such as Dallas and Patmore were theorizing English meter not in accentual but rather in temporal terms. Patmore's "Essay on English Metrical Law" asserted that meter was properly a measurement of time, and his "law" divided lines into "isochronous intervals."[43] Central to these debates about accent and time was what Gummere termed the "difficult matter of nomenclature."[44] In the second half of the nineteenth century, prosodists were growing increasingly skeptical about the "application ... of classic [i.e., Greek and Latin] prosody to English rhythms."[45] While Patmore felt that the "word *foot* ... may be usefully retained in the criticism of modern verse, inasmuch as it indicates a reality, though not exactly that which is indicated by it with regard to classical metre,"[46] later metrists struggled to accommodate what Liddell called a "wrong and misleading"[47] vocabulary within their new "scientific" methodologies. Somewhat hesitantly, Gummere, for example, advised weighing "the old [classical] terms" against a putatively new vocabulary, which "substitute[s] the '*rising*' foot of two or three syllables (iamb, anapaest), and the '*falling*' foot of two or three syllables (trochee, dactyl)."[48] Others, Liddell and Lanier among them, took a more radical approach. Pushing beyond conventional foot-based metrics, they set out a nomenclature and a notation that not only extended existing temporal theories but also posited new modes of scansion.

Patmore had conceived of meter as being principally a mental phenomenon: it is, as he writes, "imaginary." Later generations of prosodists, however, whose "science" of verse demanded not only something concrete to quantify and analyze but also a correlative metrical schema, were more inclined to assert the "material and external existence" of meter.[49] It is perhaps not surprising, then, that their systems of notation often rely on "an appeal to the eye."[50] Objecting that conventional prosody's notations were "not particularly graphic" enough, Liddell proposed a new method for representing the rising and falling "rhythm-waves" that comprise a line of verse. English lines, he argues, combine to form "*a more or less regular series of rhythm-pulses determined by stress and arranged in certain numerical groups....*"[51] Applying his wave theory to passages from *Paradise Lost*, Liddell illustrates his new "wave" model of scansion (Fig. 4). Lanier, as Prins notes, goes even further, "circumvent[ing] nineteenth-century debates about accentual versus quantitative verse by positing musical time as the basis for poetic rhythm."[52] The scansions he includes in his *The Science of English*

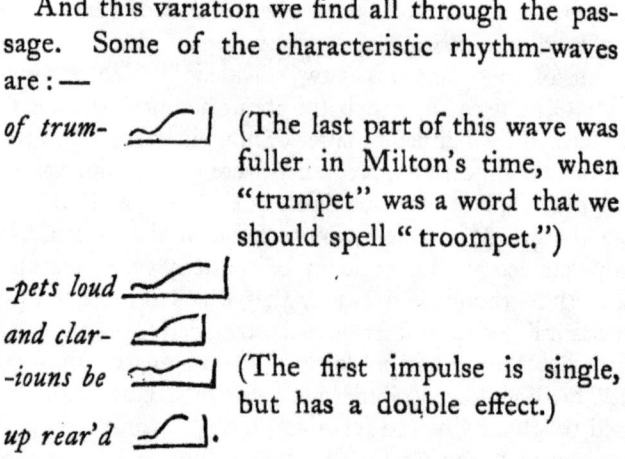

Fig. 4 Example of wave scansion from Mark H. Liddell's *An Introduction to the Scientific Study of English Poetry: Being a Prolegomena to a Science of English Prosody* (London: Doubleday, Page & Company, 1902), 244

INSTRUMENTAL PROSODY 221

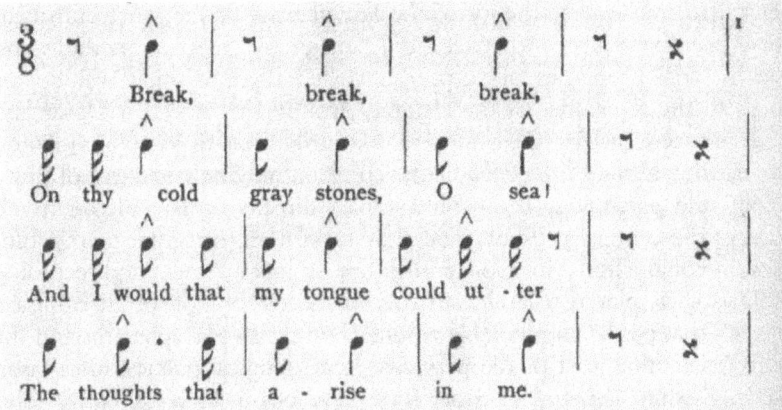

Fig. 5 Musical scansion for Tennyson's "Break, Break, Break," from Sidney Lanier's *The Science of English Verse* (New York: Scribner, 1880), 138

Verse—for example, one for Tennyson's "Break, Break, Break" (Fig. 5)—forsake both the contested longa and ictus for a "diversity of [musical] bars."[53]

By foregrounding meter "as a complex graphic phenomenon"[54] and by beginning to tease out the equally complex relationship between metrical abstraction and concrete sound patterning, Liddell's "rhythm-waves" and Lanier's musical bars gesture toward a more scientific, quantifiable prosody. Nevertheless, both scansions stop short of capturing fully the material properties of what people vocalize and hear when reciting and listening to metrical verse. While they may avoid the contested symbols of classical foot-based notation, they remain what Lanier himself called "signs of sounds," merely alternative ways of signifying and systematizing—as with diacritical marks or simply through a visual emphasis on lineation—"the actual vibratory impact on the tympanum."[55] But what if the actual vibratory impact itself could be measured? A more experimental prosody, one that could get beyond the "signs of sounds" to the sounds themselves, could perhaps resolve the contest of accent and time and settle questions about the duration of proximate feet or intervals.

The representational matrix of scansion is part of the complex interplay between metrical abstraction and embodiment, which can be seen as central to much verse theory of the last decades of the nineteenth century. It is this dialectic—between the "imaginary" metrical modulus and the material properties of corporeal, voiced rhythms—that will be my focus in the remainder of the chapter. Around the time that Dallas and Patmore were making their important contributions to Victorian metrics, developments were underway in the comparatively new sciences of physiology and psychology that would impact directly on late-Victorian and turn-of-the-century prosody. The shift toward experimental methodologies, in conjunction with pioneering work on measurement and recording technologies, played a significant role in the elaboration of an empirical metrics that placed considerable emphasis on the "vocal apparatus and the body"; it is thus part of the pervasive "physiological poetics" that Jason Rudy, Kirstie Blair, and Gregory Tate have begun to historicize.[56] This particular mode of prosodic enquiry developed rapidly in the second half of the nineteenth century—in laboratories of all places. Here, then, where empirical procedures—which I began to examine in "The Automatic Flow of Verse"—were underwriting developments in acoustics, phonetics, and speech physiology, we can witness a significant moment in the conversation not only between idealist and materialist understandings of meter but also between attempts to reconcile poetry as seen on the page, with its diacritical designations, with poetry on the tongue, particularly as rendered visible by the "new languages of recording instruments."[57] This turn toward mechanization enabled a reconceptualizing of not only the discrete properties of metrical verse—including the ongoing contest between accent and time—but also the practice of scansion. As we shall see, the study of meter at the start of the twentieth century was nothing if not *material*—in terms of both signs and sounds—and *mechanized*.

Empirical Measures

In the nineteenth century, as David Cahan observes, "the very character of 'science' changed,"[58] and the rise of a robustly material, mechanized metrics is one corollary of this change. While the natural philosophers of the seventeenth and eighteenth centuries had more or less rejected Aristotelian metaphysics in favor of a more positivist practice that emphasized observation and experiment, it was not until the early decades of the nineteenth century that modernizing scientists "optimistically aimed to establish conceptual foundations and empirical knowledge for a rational, rigorous scientific understanding that [was] accurate, dependable, and universal."[59] This epistemological shift was characterized not only by a transition to a more rigorous and assertively empirical methodology but also by a more specialized and recognizably disciplinary organization of knowledge: "new labels and categories"—such as "biologist" and "physicist"—"reflected the fact that science had both delimited itself more fully from philosophy, theology, and other types of traditional learning and culture and differentiated itself internally into increasingly specialized regions of knowledge."[60] From one such specialized region—physiology—new research methods emerged that prioritized laboratory experiments and exploited up-to-date measurement apparatuses. Moreover, "the dissemination of physiological techniques" shaped thinking beyond the immediate radius of physiology itself.[61] Pioneering work in sensory physiology—specifically acoustics—not only enabled a reframing of "questions lying on the borderland of the physical and the aesthetic enquiry" but also assisted in creating a cadre of expert "metrical scientists," whose ample supplies of data would support—if not always prove—their prosodical postulations.[62]

The move toward a materialist metrics began properly in the 1830s. Particularly in the German-speaking states, where the transition from "speculative, idealistic and Romantic philosophy" (*Naturphilosophie*) to systematic natural science (*Naturwissenschaft*) was caught up in the restructuring of the universities, rising "[s]cientific materialists" such as Johannes Müller were helping to define physiology as an "independent, experimental discipline."[63] In his *Handbuch der Physiologie des Menschen* (1833 and 40),[64] Müller fused various existing bodies of medical and scientific knowledge (e.g., anatomy, neurology, pathology, and vitalism[65]) and asserted the importance of "empirical findings for their own sake."[66] But it was really his successors—notably Hermann von Helmholtz, Emil du Bois-Reymond, Ernst Brüke, and Carl Ludwig—who would set physiology's experimental agenda, reinforcing its allegiances to *Wissenschaftsideologie* and establishing in earnest both its conceptual methodology and its concrete laboratory procedures. Notably different from Müller in their rejection of vitalism in favor of a "rigorous and reductionist" approach that "explain[ed] all living functions in terms of the physics and chemistry of organisms,"[67] this next generation of physiologists nevertheless upheld their predecessor's dedication to empiricism and, if anything, accelerated the pace of physiology's experimental aims. Working in specially designed laboratories—at Heidelberg, Leipzig, Berlin, Vienna, and elsewhere—they focused their attention on questions

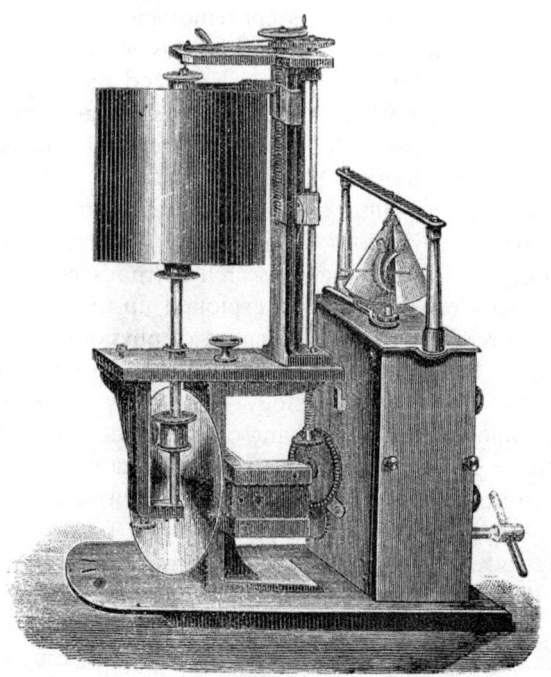

Fig. 6 Drum kymograph according to Ludwig (Trommelkymographion nach Ludwig). Petzold, Wilhelm. Preis-Verzeichniss der Werkstätte für Präcisions-Mechanik von Wilh. Petzold: Abtheilung der Instrumente und Apparate für physiologische Experimente und Vivisectionen. Leipzig, 1891. Reproduced by permission of the Virtual Laboratory, Max Planck Institute for the History of Science, Berlin. http://vlp.mpiwg-berlin.mpg.de/

relating to, among other things, sensory perception. In their attempt "to show that living organisms could be treated like machines,"[68] whose functions were rational and observable rather than the effect of some immaterial (and so immeasurable) "vital" force, the experimental physiologists coming of age in the 1840s used an array of specially designed instruments—many of which, such as Ludwig's Kymograph (Fig. 6), they developed themselves—"to display previously hidden patterns related to physiological functions,"[69] recording and measuring everything from nervous impulses in frogs' legs to color and motion perception in the human eye.

It was specifically in relation to acoustics that physiologists would lay the groundwork for later empirical research into metrical phenomena. At the turn of the nineteenth century, acoustics, like physiology itself, was beginning to establish its disciplinary credentials.[70] As David Pantalony notes, acoustic science moved away from the earlier, mathematically oriented field of harmonics toward a more experimental praxis made possible by machine-assisted measurement procedures, and, significantly, toward the measurement of not only synthetic musical sounds but eventually human voices.[71] Technologies of sound were developing rapidly as the eighteenth century drew to a close, and by the early 1800s, innovations in "inscriptional apparatus"—from Ernst Florens Friedrich Chladni's *Klangfiguren* of the 1780s to the early nineteenth-century tuning fork and piano-wire techniques of Wilhelm Weber and Thomas Young—were subtending "a qualitatively different type of scientific information."[72] This qualitative revolution had a decidedly *quantitative* aspect. Along with a more experimental outlook came a new understanding of how sonic phenomena could be assessed. Where conventional harmonics had "measured" sound largely in terms of abstractions such as ratios and proportions, the new acoustic scientists preferred a more precise "indexical relation" between their calculations and the sound vibrations they studied. As Friedrich Kittler has explained, the advent of an instrument-based experimental acoustics instituted a comprehensive "historical transition ... from a logic to a physics of sound," in which idealized "intervals" were replaced by more empirical "frequencies."[73] Further, accompanying (and in many cases assisting) this transformation was a change in the way measurements themselves were represented. "If one wants to measure and record the quantitative features of sound," note the authors of *Instruments and the Imagination* (1995), then "one must employ a visual image. The ear detects pitch, loudness, and timbre, but not the frequency, amplitude, and shape of sound waves. Recording instruments give us this information by representing the sound visually."[74] By using a new "graphic method" of notation, which I will discuss at length below, acoustical researchers could render "audible vibrations" as "a set of [visible] tracings."[75] Capitalizing on (and often directly contributing to) these new acoustical methods and technologies, experimental physiologists such as Helmholtz began outlining the fundamentals of a physiological acoustics that was equipped to address not only somatic phenomena but also the aesthetics of music and, eventually, poetry.

While the groundwork for a physics of sound, including its propagation in waves and the "laws of vibratory motion," had been established theoretically by the time Helmholtz began to formulate his own contributions to acoustic science, he was nonetheless instrumental in further transforming "the dominating mode of speculative, numerical inquiry" into an experimentally verifiable physiological acoustics.[76] Building on previous theoretical work—Fourier's analysis of harmonics, Ohm's physics of musical sounds, and "Müller's law of specific nerve energies"—Helmholtz innovated acoustical research not only by providing ample "supporting experimental evidence" but also by devising and using in his laboratories a collection of tuning forks and resonators, as well as specially adapted instruments such as the kymograph, to isolate, amplify, and record all manner of "rapid elastic vibrations" (from the sounds of stringed musical instruments to those of real and synthesized voices).[77] Covering the range of acoustic phenomena, from the physical "laws of vibratory motion" and their relation to "processes that take place within the ear itself" to the psychological effects of sound, Helmholtz's acoustics not only advanced according to thoroughly materialist principles, in which the anatomy of the ear played a central role in defining complex sound qualities; further, it established the foundations for a radical transformation in the ways *aesthetic* phenomena were understood and measured, as well as how these measurements could be represented according to the graphic method.[78] Specifically, Helmholtz's attention to the materialities of musical sound—as registered by the ear, but more often by finely tuned laboratory instruments—would transform the study of such musical properties as period and rhythm, and it is here, as we shall see, that the science of sound began to impinge on the study of poetic meter.

As set out in two works, "Über die physiologischen Ursachen der musikalischen Harmonie" (1857) and *Die Lehre von den Tonempfindungen als physiologische Grundlage für die Theorie der Musik* (1863),[79] Helmholtz's physiology of music takes as its starting point the wave character of sound and Fourier's premise "that any complex period vibration may be resolved into a number of simple harmonic vibrations."[80] By supplementing the existing mathematics of musical theory with extensive laboratory data, Helmholtz was able to demonstrate—in measurements that graphic recording rendered precise to hundredths of a second—how and why certain vibrations produced music (while others simply created noise) and how different qualities of tone (e.g., simple, compound, partial, combinational) figure in the creation and perception of musical properties. From here he could analyze nuanced topics, such as the relationship between harmonic overtones. While previous theorists had imagined harmonies in the comparatively abstract terms of intervals and ratios, Helmholtz offered concrete evidence. "What have the ratios of small whole numbers to do with harmony?" he asks in his 1857 lecture. "This is an old riddle, propounded by Pythagoras and hitherto unsolved. Let us see whether the means at the command of modern science will furnish an answer."[81] As Helmholtz would later observe in *Tonempfindungen*, to answer this question "modern science" would need to depart from loosely conceived idealist assertions: "Musicians, as well as philosophers and physicists, have generally contented themselves with saying in effect that human minds were in some unknown manner so constituted as to discover the numerical relations of musical vibrations, and to have a peculiar pleasure in contemplating, simple ratios which are readily comprehensible."[82] In the place of "simple ratios," Helmholtz produces precise measurements supported by graphic records made with a variety of recording apparatus (Figs. 7 and 8). Capable of "teach[ing] more at a glance than the most complicated descriptions," these diagrams give expression to a new, quantifiable language for discussing musical tones and harmonics, a language founded "upon purely scientific, as distinct from esthetic principles."[83] Thus, Helmholtz's studies of music offer radical interventions in longstanding debates—about isochronism, for example[84]—in that they reach beyond the more

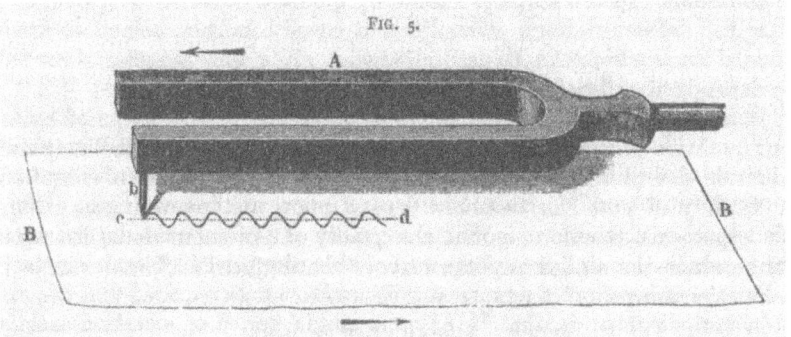

Fig. 7 Illustration of a "Tuning-fork tracing its Curve," from Hermann von Helmholtz's *On the Sensations of Tone as a Physiological Basis for the Theory of Music*, trans. Alexander J. Ellis (London: Longmans, Green, and Co., 1885), 20

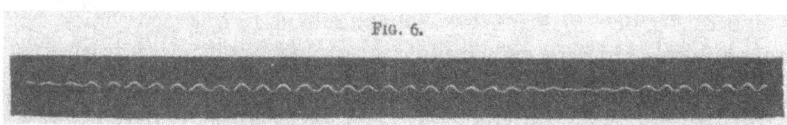

Fig. 8 Example of a "Curve traced in Phonautograph," from Hermann von Helmholtz's *On the Sensations of Tone as a Physiological Basis for the Theory of Music*, trans. Alexander J. Ellis (London: Longmans, Green, and Co., 1885), 20

philosophical language of "proportion," replacing it with a mechanized notation that more accurately expresses fundamental physiological truths: the waveform transmission of sound and the ear's sensitivity to precise and rapid vibrations.[85]

Thus, with the aid of recording and inscription instruments, which were more responsive even than the ear itself, Helmholtz helped to *materialize* the study of music, replacing idealizations of musical phenomena (e.g., Pythagorean integer ratios) with what the French physiologist Étienne-Jules Marey would later describe as the "language of the phenomena themselves."[86] Musical periods could now be expressed graphically as wave-lengths, and loudness could be represented precisely in terms of wave-height. Toward the close of the nineteenth century, this new visible vocabulary for music and the materialist practices on which it was predicated would transform studies of poetry. If "the principles of harmonic proportions" and related matters were "applicable alike to the phenomena of music and of prosody,"[87] as some physiologists (not to mention several musicians and metrists) had already begun to speculate,[88] then perhaps an experimental, "scientific" prosody, one anchored in the physiological acoustics adumbrated by Helmholtz, could be used to accurately define the complex rhythmical character of poetry. While Helmholtz himself may have neglected the sonic features of the verse line (dismissing sounds in poetry as "subordinate auxiliaries of a more musical kind"[89]), his successors were nevertheless willing to extend his vibratory aesthetic to poetic meters. As one of them noted in 1901, "the primary laws of verse, like those of music, [are] laid upon the bedrock of acoustics."[90] Fittingly, Helmholtzian acoustics would go on to underwrite (quite literally) a laboratory prosody in which experimental psychologists, adapting the principles as well as the practices of their physiology forebears, turned their quantifying gaze toward "the measurement of the duration of mental process[es]."[91] By the close of the

1880s, these psychologists-cum-prosodists were exploiting "a collection of special appliances"—many of them borrowed directly from physiology laboratories—to record and measure, with new levels of precision, "the rhythm used in music and poetry."[92] In keeping with Helmholtz's acoustical analyses of music, they centered their researches on the embodied, rather than abstract, elements of versification, preferring the "real," scientific language of pitch and frequency over what previous prosodists had theorized in philological terms borrowed from classical metrics or, as in Patmore's case, the "imaginary" language of musical integers. For a brief moment around the turn of the century, the assertive, quantitative, and thoroughly "modern" language of acoustical prosody positioned itself as a factual alternative to vague theorizing. Science, not philology, would arbitrate in a brave new world of material metrics.

Laboratory Prosody

The *fin-de-siècle* poet Alice Meynell opens the titular essay of her 1892 collection *The Rhythm of Life and Other Essays* with the following memorable declaration: "If life is not always poetical, it is at least metrical." For Meynell rhythm and periodicity are at the heart of all biological, emotional, spiritual, and astronomical processes. "Disease is metrical," she writes, and so too are "sorrow," "[e]cstasy and desolation." The moon has "[h]er metrical phases," and "love itself has tidal times—lapses and ebbs which are due to the metrical rule of the interior heart"; everything, from "a sun's revolutions" to "the rhythmic pangs of maternity," "must wake and rest in its phases." Yet while Meynell insists upon the "metrical" organization of both the physical world and the corporeal and "mental experience of man," she nonetheless resists quantification: "Distances are not gauged, ellipses not measured, velocities not ascertained, times not known."[93] It is not surprising she had trouble assimilating the rhythms of the steam thresher—which perhaps only a sensitive machine could record and accurately quantify—to her conception of meter.

Around the same time, experimental psychologists such as Edward Wheeler Scripture would suggest otherwise: quantification was both possible and desirable. During the first half of the nineteenth century, psychology was still operating within the "philosophy of mind" tradition (part of the Germanic *Geisteswissenschaften*), and as such it was ostensibly more equipped to grapple with Patmore's ideal mental modulus than to pioneer a materialist metrics that measured and graphed the physical vibrations of the verse line. By the second half of the century, however, psychologists in the German states had begun to assert their own experimental agenda. Borrowing extensively from the methods of the physiologists discussed above, they "attempt[ed] to attack," as the English psychical researcher F. W. H. Myers would later note, "the great problems of our being not by metaphysical argument," as their more philosophically inclined predecessors had done, "but by a study, as detailed and exact as any other natural science ...."[94] From the 1870s a new generation of scientists—spearheaded by the "radical empiricist" Wilhelm Maximilian Wundt—began "combining with psychological observation the methods of experimental physiology."[95] In his groundbreaking *Grundzüge der physiologischen Psychologie* (1874), Wundt, who had trained with Müller and Helmholtz in the 1850s, mapped the contours of an inductive psychology that prioritized statistical analysis and "a consolidated 'scientific' outlook, based upon detailed measurement."[96] Five years later, in 1879, he made what was perhaps his most material contribution to the emerging discipline, founding at Leipzig the first *bona fide* laboratory of experimental psychology. Over the next few decades, Wundt's protégés (e.g., James McKeen Cattell, Granville Stanley Hall, Edward Wheeler Scripture, and Edward Bradford Titchener) would go on to work in (and in some instances to establish) similar institutions elsewhere in Europe and in North America. In these state-of-the-art facilities—where discrete workspaces were reserved for, among other things, haptical analysis, "olfactometry," and visual and auditory recognition[97]— psychologists utilizing familiar and modified physiological instruments such as tuning forks (for "recording vibrations and marking time"), kymographs ("to record any process whose course is a function of time elapsed"), chronographs (used for measuring reaction-time in relation to sense impressions), phonautographs (for making graphic recordings and taking measurements of speech), and other apparatuses could accurately "*photograph*," as one psychologist put it, a range of putatively "transient phenomena"[98]—including musical and poetic rhythms.

In the postscript to his book *English Metrists* (1921), T. S. Omond speculated that the "laboratory work" of psychologists "can be of use" in establishing "theoretically and experimentally ... the *real* basis of our verse."[99] Indeed, the materialist methods and technologies—as developed by Helmholtz, Wundt, and their successors—for analyzing frequency, harmony, and related aspects of music and vocal physiology had been making an impact on the subject of metrics for nearly four decades by the time Omond published his prosodical history. As early as the 1880s, for instance, work was underway at Wundt's Leipzig laboratory "to determine the accuracy with which the ear can distinguish musical intervals."[100] If a metronome and a watch can together form "a psychological apparatus of the simplest kind," allowing scientists of music and poetry to measure conscious responses to "the intensity of successive beats,"[101] then one could begin to understand the possibilities afforded by newer, more sensitive chronographic equipment. While Wundt's successors, who had internalized and extended their mentor's methodology, were busy using updated laboratory instruments to "measure at once the rate of change in the brain and of change in consciousness,"[102] they were also actively testing musical perception and phonetic movements in poetry. Drawing not only on Wundt's own researches but also on Helmholtz's musical analyses of the 1850s and 60s, this next generation of psychologists—particularly those working in laboratories housed by American universities such as Cornell, Clark, and Yale—concentrated on the body's interactions with the "rhythms of the poetic text," scrutinizing the functions of tone, pitch, and loudness and working to establish a physical basis for theories of metrical accent and time.[103]

From the 1890s through the 1930s—the period during which experimental prosody can be said to have flourished—psychologists compiled voluminous meter-related "records" in their laboratories in Europe and North America. While some researchers, such as Albert S. Hurst and John McKay, tapped their fingers in time to silent scansions and recorded the results, others preferred a more technologized method that recognized "the advantages of psychological experimentation by the aid of graphic records of the *voice*."[104] This approach was adopted by many turn-of-the-century acoustical prosodists, including Edward Wheeler Scripture and Warner Brown. A staunch adherent of Wundt's empirical method, Scripture rejected as imprecise "experiments on auditory rhythm" based on recorded taps or "sharp clicks" because "investigators did not take any records of the spoken sounds, but only of the rhythmic strokes of the hand."[105] Brown considered tapping unreliable because it functioned as "an objective control like an instrumental accompaniment and the proper voice rhythm is made unduly regular in obedience to this control"—an example of an artificial, external "meter" controlling speech rhythms.[106] In the place of tapping, both Scripture and Brown, along with many of their contemporaries, endorsed a method capable of "eliminating the illusions and errors of observation to which unaided human ears are liable."[107] In his major contribution to metrical science, *Elements of Experimental Phonetics* (1902), Scripture insisted on "the attainment of accuracy and trustworthiness" of measurement and demanded instrumentation capable of producing results "absolutely accurate for all records in thousandths of a second."[108] Like Wundt and Helmholtz before them, Scripture and other experimental psychologists and phoneticians of his generation demanded devices that could take infinitesimally fine measurements from speaking subjects and translate them into decipherable visible impressions. With the help of tuning forks, kymographs, and a range of other laboratory instruments—many of which had served physiologists like Helmholtz well in analyses of sensory perception and sonic vibration—experimental psychologists set out to penetrate metrical mysteries with a new level of accuracy.

The empirical methodology of psychologist-prosodists such as Scripture and Brown enabled them to intervene in some seemingly intractable metrical debates, particularly in relation to questions of accent and time. In *Elements* Scripture devotes discrete chapters to "Accent," "Auditory and Motor Rhythm," and "Speech Rhythm," insisting that, while considerable work had been carried out, a complete, "scientific" explanation of these subjects remained to be articulated. "Great unclearness prevails," he contends, "on account of the confusion among physical, psychological and physiological terms."[109] While to some it may have appeared obvious that "an accented sound is ... one that impresses the hearer more strongly or that requires more mental effort on the part of the speaker," questions about duration and quantity, as well as loudness and pitch, and their "relations" remained unsettled.[110] Further, too many of the available propositions regarding accent had been based on subjective and imprecise sense impressions.[111] What the study of accent required was a range of experimental apparatuses that could detect minute variations in duration and pitch. Experiments made with a "ROUSSELOT voice-key," as outlined by Scripture, indicated that in recitations of trochaic verse "the emphatic syllable [was] usually longer than the unemphatic one."[112] Another experiment, which coupled the voice-key with a "DEPREZ marker" to record "voice vibrations" on a smoked drum, reinforced the link between stress and duration,[113] and some researchers, such as J. P. Dabney in *The Musical Basis of Verse* (1901), went so far as to assert that "accent is *fundamental* in marking off... measures."[114] These and other experiments subtended materially informed theories of accent in poetry, some of which, in fact, served to blur the lines between the material and the imaginary elements of verse. According to Scripture, for instance, "in English at least, increase in duration and rise in pitch are ordinarily associated with increased stress, and that these associations *are essentially mental ones and not interdependent physical or physiological phenomena.*"[115] Here Scripture hypothesizes a possible bridge between the accentual and temporal theories of meter that had been so assiduously debated by earlier generations of prosodists. Duration—what Patmore, in his "Essay," had described as "the time occupied in the delivery of a series of words"[116]—was not the antithesis of accent but a fundamental constituent of it. Scripture's recognition of the "essentially mental" character of stress suggests that Patmore's speculation regarding the abstract, "imaginary" function of meter might have some grounding in experimentally demonstrable fact. What the mind "associates" with the patterning of a given line and the "physical or physiological phenomena" of duration and pitch need not be understood as one and the same thing.

The conclusion that "English verse is [both] ... a pitch-verse and a time-verse"[117] was only one among the many machine-assisted prosodic principles to be confirmed by psychological laboratories. For Scripture and other would-be verse scientists, experiments on accent necessarily intersected with those on rhythm, and here, too, laboratory technicians scrutinized the relationship between the abstraction of meter and "the actual sounds produced in speaking." With instruments "peculiarly adapted to the determination of time intervals," researchers attempted to validate or disprove "prominent views of theorists" such as Patmore regarding the temporal nature of meter.[118] Asking subjects to recite lines of metrical verse, verse scientists used kymographs to record and measure rapid voice vibrations.[119] Some among the many records compiled in this way appeared to vindicate Patmore's theory of isochronous intervals. Drawing on experiments carried out by Ernst Brücke, Ishiro Miyake, and others, Scripture was able to assert, for instance, that "[t]he simplest English poetical line seems to consist of a quantity of speech-sound distributed so as to produce an effect equivalent to that of a certain number of points of emphasis at definite intervals."[120] Similar to what Patmore had called the "ictus" or "beat," "which, like a post in a chain railing, shall mark the end of one space, and the commencement of another,"[121] these "points of emphasis"—what Scripture termed "center[s] of unification, of speech action," or "centroids"—define the boundaries of the foot: "the foot [is] the time between two centroids of speech energy." Further, "[t]he time of a foot," according to Scripture, "is approximately constant";[122] metrical units, he suggests, are more or less equal in time, or "isochronous." Other experiments focused explicitly on what Patmore had called the "perpetual conflict between the law of the verse and the freedom of the language."[123] Laboratory data revealed variations in syllable length, and Scripture would assert that the "actual concrete rhythm of a particular piece of verse is a compromise between the natural [i.e., spoken] lengths [of syllables] and those required by abstract rhythm."[124] Over 30 years later, Wilbur Lang Schramm would suggest a more fundamental disjunction between abstract and material modulations. "There is little physical counterpart," he wrote in 1935, "of the rhythmical regularity we perceive or imagine in verse."[125]

The tension between the abstraction of meter and the material features of spoken verse was always among the central concerns of experimental research, and this tension is particularly evident in debates about the suitability of received prosodic terminology. While Scripture's centroid-spacing may have helped in determining the boundaries of the foot, the foot itself seemed to many experimental prosodists an arbitrary measurement index that had no real basis in experimentally demonstrable fact. Scripture, for one, all but rejected it out of hand. His position was summarized in a 1900 issue of *PMLA* thus: "The unity of English verse is the line, or the phrase. A line of verse cannot be divided into feet ...."[126] Over the next three decades, researchers continued to maintain an empirical distrust of conventional foot prosody, though not all sought to abandon feet entirely. In his 1908 study, Brown produces table after table to demonstrate that the foot—here taken to mean a unit of duration—is little more than an approximation of rhythmic regularity, an "impression" that we may feel but that has no grounding in fact.[127] In one of the last sustained works in the laboratory tradition, *Approaches to a Science of English Verse* (1935), Schramm provides considerable "phonophotographic" evidence to support Brown's assertion. The foot constitutes only an approximate and ultimately imprecise (however convenient) marker of, among other things, accent grouping. Outlining five metrical fallacies, Schramm argues that feet are neither "*equal in total duration*" nor an accurate expression of "the rhythm of the line."[128]

The Graphic Method

In *Elements* Scripture speculated that "it would seem preferable" to express the rhythmic properties of poems in a visual, "centroidal" language—that is, by a scansion that represents graphically the "centers" of speech action. To this end, he proposed a "centroid analysis" and a corresponding notation, which used small and large dots, together with crosses, to designate "primary centroids," "line centroids," and "phrase centroids," respectively.[129] Figure 9 provides an example of Scripture's "centroid" scansion, as applied to lines from Félix Arvers's 1833 "Sonnet d'Arvers." A similar scansion, he suggests, could be used to mark out the rhythmic patterns of English metrical verse. Yet while he concludes his chapter on rhythm with lines from poems by Moore, Bryant, Scott, and Tennyson, he offers no further examples of centroidal notation. Presumably his reluctance to take his centroid analysis further was a consequence of his awareness that laboratory prosody's real contribution to scansion was altogether more instrumental. A more intriguing and authentically graphic way of representing the material properties of verse rhythm resulted from the methods and instruments on which experimental laboratory practice was founded. As Scripture himself points out, centroid analysis provided only a provisional system for imaging the conclusions about accent and rhythm that researchers were capable of deriving from the experimental data generated by tuning forks, registering

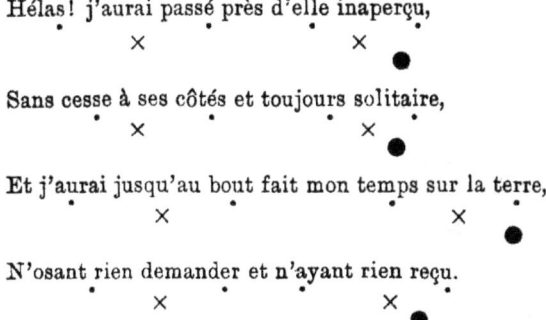

Fig. 9 Example of "centroid" scansion, from Edward Wheeler Scripture's *Elements of Experimental Phonetics* (New York: Charles Scribner's Sons, 1902), 554

drums, and kymographs. Indeed, speaking about the positioning of centroids in the extract from "Sonnet d'Arvers," Scripture explains that he has "indicated them only approximately *without making measurements*."[130] In many respects, Scripture's centroidal notation was no more radical or scientific than the distinctive models suggested around the same time by prosodists such as Liddell and Lanier. Like these diacritical departures, Scripture's dots and crosses were merely "signs" made to stand in for vibratory impulses rather than a true record of the vibratory impulses themselves.

Fittingly, it was the laboratory instruments themselves that would generate a more authentically scientific and visual record of verse rhythm. Laboratory practice, including Scripture's own, was underwritten by what was known among experimental physiologists and psychologists as the "chronographic" or simply "graphic" method, which takes its name from the chronograph ("an instrument for recording time with extreme exactness" [*OED*]). As noted above, the graphic method prioritized "the attainment of accuracy and trustworthiness" of measurement and demanded the most up-to-date instrumentation, which would be able to produce results "absolutely accurate for all records in thousandths of a second." One apparatus—the Hipp chronoscope, for example, a machine for recording measurements in time-reaction experiments—Scripture simply rejected, arguing that it was "not accurate enough."[131] In 1893 *The New York Times* ran a feature on "Yale's Psychological Laboratory and Its Work," including a description of the method "chiefly employed" by researchers at that institution:

> A tuning fork, kept in constant vibration by a current of electricity, is allowed to trace a curve on a revolving drum covered with smoked paper. This gives a representation of a period of time divided according to the rapidity with which the fork vibrates. Using a fork which vibrates 100 times a second, the drum is revolved with such rapidity that the single waves are so long that we make no error in estimating tenths of a vibrations and so reading the results in thousandths of a second.[132]

Pictured alongside this explanation of the graphic process are some of the apparatuses used for taking measurements and producing "waves" that correlate to various vibratory inputs. One is a registering drum, labeled "Made in Laboratory"; another is "Ludwig's Kymograph."[133] With these devices—in particular the kymograph (literally a "wave-writer")—researchers at Yale and elsewhere were capable of "graphing" all manner of sensory impulses, from fluctuations in "muscular energy" to alterations in the rhythmic frequency of metered verse.[134]

In place of "the ordinary routine scansions"[135] prized by a later laboratory prosodist such as Ada Snell (and many other non-experimentalists besides), laboratory instruments were capable of asserting their own unique representations of verse movement, and this is perhaps their most intriguing contribution to a materialist metrics. Because kymographs and other inscriptional devices "are designed," as Brown observed in 1908, "to present in the form of a curve or otherwise the actual sounds produced in speaking," the graphic method provided the logical means of denoting the unsegmented, wave-like movement of sound in voicings of metered poetry. Unlike other systems of scansion, which relied on "signs of sounds," dividing lines into arbitrary notional units (whether feet, bars, or intervals), machine-recorded graphic records enabled psychologists to observe prosodical features that "had not previously been amenable to quantitative study." As Schramm would observe, "connected speech is a continuous flow," irrespective of prevailing conventions for its metrical "[division] into equal or proportionate spaces," and with the aid of instruments such as the kymograph, laboratory metrists could finally render material the fugitive "flow of speech-energy"[136] across a line of verse. By embracing the graphic method, laboratory prosodists such as Scripture, Brown, Snell, and Schramm not only found it possible to scrutinize minute variations in pitch, loudness, period, and other rhythmical qualities; but also they could represent—in the precise, visible language of frequency curves—material characteristics of the metered line that the unaided ear could not perceive. The "specimen records" inscribed by their instruments provided scientists with a unique mechanized "scansion" of the sounds made by a subject intoning a given meter (Figs. 10 and 11). These wave-graphs—whose white peaks and troughs stand out against the smoked black background—allowed experimentally inclined metrists to both *see* and accurately *measure* "the length of time between successive movements" of verse: they could read accent in curve-height and duration in the horizontal spacing of wave-crests (as Helmholtz had done with musical tones).[137]

Ada Snell would adopt the "graphic method" to assess not just isolated metrical sounds and discrete metrical properties but the rhythmical

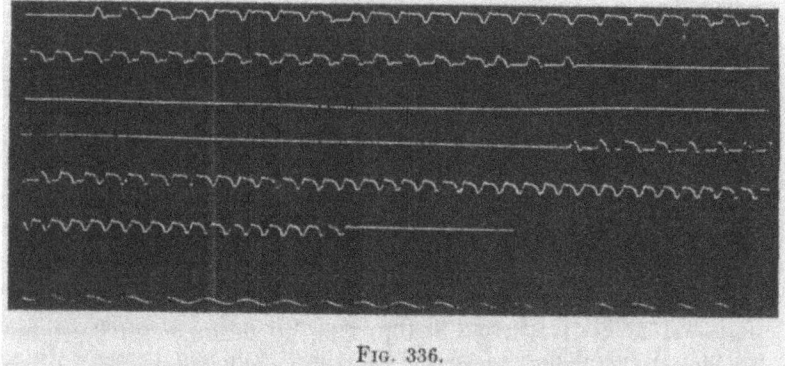

Fig. 10 Example of a "wave-graph" record of a subject "repeat[ing] the sound a continuously in what he felt to be a trochaic rhythm (thus, a' a a' a a' a ...), or an iambic (a a' a a' a a' ...), or dactylic (a' a a a' a a ...), or an amphibraphic one (a a' a a a' a ...)." From Edward Wheeler Scripture's *Elements of Experimental Phonetics* (New York: Charles Scribner's Sons, 1902), 509

movement of whole poems. Hoping "to discover by a scientific method the nature of pause [i.e., caesura] as it occurs in English verse," Snell used a Zimmermann kymograph to capture and analyze the opening lines of Tennyson's "Break, Break, Break," as recited by her colleague.[138] As an appendix to her 1918 study, she includes a fold-out plate of her graphic "record" of the poem (Fig. 12). In the bottom left-hand corner, the opening verses have been transcribed by hand: "Break, break, break, On thy cold grey stones, O sea." Arranged horizontally above these words are what Snell calls "recording pointers," or "lines of reference" for the "arcs" inscribed by the stylus of the recording apparatus, as well as the arcs themselves, which rise and fall irregularly from left to right:

> The arcs and points of starting are indicated on the plate as follows: 1 represents the arc made by the pointer recording the outflow of air through the nose; 2 represents the one made by the pointer recording the air coming in through the mouth; 3 and 4 represent the beginning of the lines made by the pointers recording respectively the nose and mouth tones; 5 is the time line.[139]

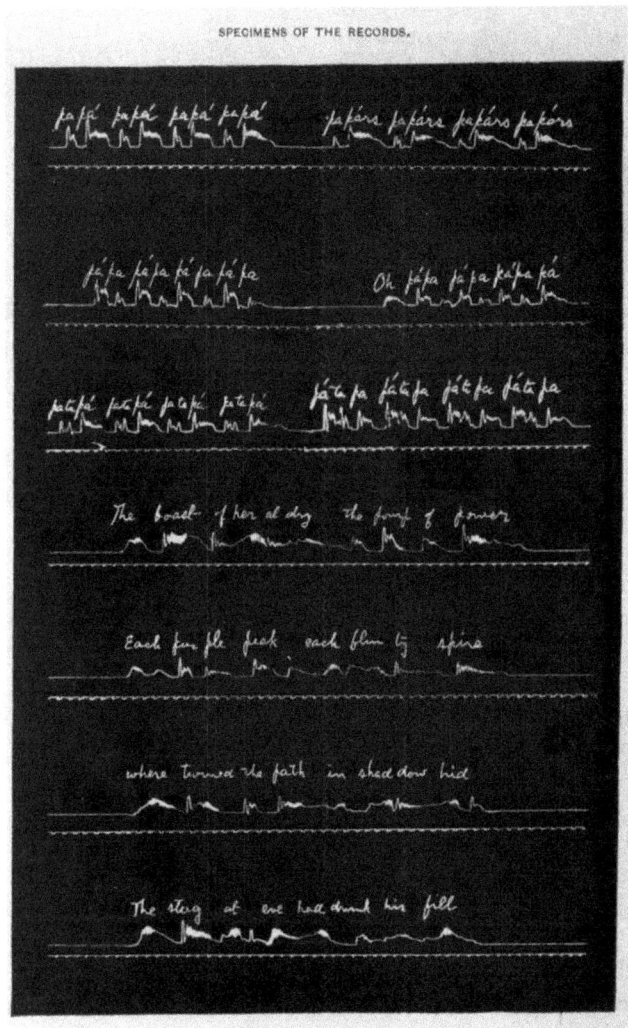

Fig. 11 "Specimens of the Records [of Verses]." From Warner Brown's *Time in English Verse Rhythm: An Empirical Study of Typical Verses by the Graphic Method* (New York: Science Press, 1908)

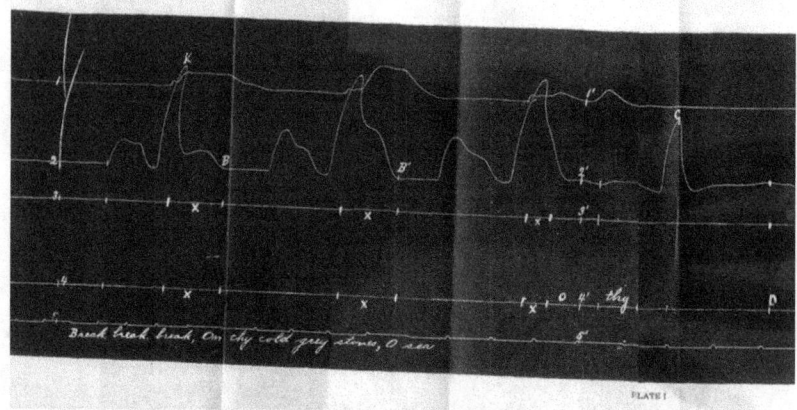

Fig. 12 Plate showing graphic record of Tennyson's "Break, Break, Break," from Ada Snell's *Pause: A Study of Its Nature and Its Rhythmical Function in Verse, Especially Blank Verse* (Ann Arbor: University of Michigan, 1918)

Taken together, the arcs and points that Snell plots constitute a mechanized "scansion" that forsakes the abstract, "imaginary" metrical record in favor of an authentic speech record. Also, unlike both Lanier's musical notation of the same poem and Liddell's "rhythm-waves," which Snell's arcs bring to mind, her "signs of sounds" have an immediate connection with the sounds themselves. Not only could her apparatus actually "*write the sounds* from the nose chamber ... [and] the tones from the mouth"; further, it was capable of "converting the vibrations back again to sound."[140]

As useful as the "graphic method" was for her study, Snell nevertheless understood that it was unlikely to produce the unquestionably accurate and objective rhythmical "record" that Scripture and other turn-of-the-century researchers had confidently anticipated. The sensitivity of the kymograph and the accuracy of its readings notwithstanding, the procedure had "certain limitations," which Snell and other verse scientists were forced to acknowledge. For example, the instruments were incapable of eliminating "variations in results" among readers and acts of delivery.[141] If the human ear had been deemed "unable to distinguish" minute rhythmical and tonal fluctuations "with any accuracy,"[142] then what about the human voice? Could it really be trusted as a delivery medium? Moreover, were these "records" in fact the objective, visual correlative of the "absolute" rhythm of a poem? In one obvious sense they were not. While psychologists' rejection of conventional notation in favor of the graphic method was motivated in part by a recognition of what Eric Griffiths has called "the incapacity of writing unambiguously to transcribe speech,"[143] kymographic scansion highlighted the converse problem: the incapacity of speech—whether that of a psychological subject or the inimitable Tennyson himself—unambiguously to transmit the metrical abstractions latent in the written poem. For all their accuracy, graphic records render visible only one among the "innumerable small departures from [the] *modulus*" of meter; further, they fail to render at all the *modulus* itself—what Yopie Prins has called "an abstract rhythm never quite articulated by human speech."[144] What they do privilege and preserve, by contrast, is a unique rhythmic performance, a graphically singular act of meter.

Just the Facts?

Acoustical prosody reached its apogee in the early decades of the twentieth century, and the "graphic method" underpinned further investigations into the "true" elements of English meter.[145] What emerged from this work, however, was not always a vindication of previous laboratory findings. Snell and other experimentally minded prosodists not only inherited and in some cases extended but just as frequently confounded the "facts" that the psychologists of Scripture's generation had established. Snell, for example, would use kymography to reopen debate about accent and time. In two *PMLA* articles, published in 1918 and 1919, she produced data to qualify Patmore's definition of isochrony, claiming that "units can hardly be said to be even approximately equal in length.[146]" Providing tables showing the relative durations of iambic, anapestic, trochaic, and dactylic meters, she concludes that "it seems more scientific to define verse rhythm not as 'the recurrence of similar phenomena at equal intervals of time,' but as the regular arrangement of stressed and unstressed syllables at intervals of time sufficiently equal to produce a clearly perceptible rhythm." Further, in spite of her articulation of a fully automated notation, she asserts evidence for the material existence of the foot—"The foot is a fact"—and maintains that the only truly "scientific method of scansion ... is one which uses the symbols conventionally used for indicating quantity and which also uses stress marks."[147] Experimental prosody, it would seem, had returned full circle to the unsettled debates of the mid-nineteenth century.

While Scripture, Snell, and other metrists of their ilk had pursued experiments with the hope of establishing beyond all doubt the "facts" of English verse structure, in the end their prosodic "science" did not lead them—or later generations of verse theorists, for that matter—to an indisputable metrical law, verified by machines and agreed by like-minded experts. The materiality of voiced rhythm and the abstraction of the metrical *modulus* refused to find resolution in a unified verse theory, scientific or otherwise. Nevertheless, twentieth-century prosodists continued to work on this and related verse dilemmas; few, however, put their faith in complex measurement apparatus. With the rise of a more pragmatic criticism, mechanized metrics fell into obscurity along with most of its practitioners. Just a decade after the publication of Snell's laboratory research, I. A. Richards, in his landmark *Practical Criticism* (1929), mused wistfully about using a kymograph to resolve the contest between the abstract pattern of meter and what he called the "actual sounds in verse."[148] If he had seriously thought that an instrument would enable an objective intervention in such debates, then one imagines that he would have just produced its graphic "record" and left it at that.

To return to Beerbohm's comic Tennyson—we do not see his meters. But maybe that is fitting enough, if meter truly is an abstraction, something "imaginary" that resists taking material form, resists our efforts to draw its lines and mark its pauses. That said, maybe we can see enough of an imagined metrical recital to trace vibrations against our mind's ear. And maybe we see more than that. In the wavy lines of the illustration's floor covering there is just a hint—fitting, I think—of the graphic undulations of sound that were being recorded around the same time that Beerbohm was asking us to look again at the sounds of Victorian poetry.

Notes

1. [Anon.], "Greek Metres and English Scholarship," *Foreign Quarterly Review*, 23, 46 (1839), 250.
2. Edward Munk, *The Metres of the Greeks and Romans. A Manual for Schools and Private Study*, trans. Charles Beck and C. C. Felton (Boston: James Munroe and Company, 1844), 8, 9.
3. "Greek Metres and English Scholarship," 272.

4. "Greek Metres and English Scholarship," 252, 253, 272, 254.
5. I. A. Richards, *Practical Criticism: A Study of Literary Judgment* (1929; Abingdon: Routledge, 2011), 228–229.
6. See John Hollander, *Vision and Resonance: Two Senses of Poetic Form* (New York: Oxford University Press, 1975).
7. The full saying—"Painting is silent poetry and poetry, speaking painting"—is attributed to the ancient Greek lyric poet Simonides of Ceos (c. 556–468 BC).
8. Gilbert Haven, *The Pilgrim's Wallet: Or, Scraps of Travel Gathered in England, France, and Germany* (New York: Hurd and Houghton, 1869), 215.
9. See R. C. Lehmann, *Memories of Half a Century* (London: Smith Elder, 1908), 132; and Mary Gladstone, *Mary Gladstone (Mrs. Drew): Her Diaries and Letters*, ed. Lucy Masterman (London: Methuen, 1930), 111.
10. Herbert Tucker reminds us that "read[ing] *Maud* straight through" was Tennyson's party piece. See Tucker, *Tennyson and the Doom of Romanticism* (Cambridge, MA: Harvard University Press, 1988), 406.
11. William Michael Rossetti, *Dante Gabriel Rossetti: His Family-Letters*, vol. 1 (London: Ellis and Elvey, 1895), 191.
12. William Allingham, *A Diary*, ed. H. Allingham and D. Kradford (London: Macmillan, 1907), 158.
13. Alfred Tennyson, "The Epic," *Tennyson's Poetry*, ed. Robert W. Hill (New York and London: Norton, 1999), 112–114.
14. Edmund Gosse, qtd. in Paul F. Mattheisen, "Gosse's Candid 'Snapshots,'" *Victorian Studies*, 8, 4 (1965), 341.
15. See F. T. Palgrave, qtd. in Hallam Tennyson, *Alfred Lord Tennyson: A Memoir*, vol. 2 (Cambridge: Cambridge University Press, 2012), 493. Allingham, *A Diary*, 158.
16. See Jed Rasula, "Understanding the Sound of Not Understanding," *Close Listening: Poetry and the Performed Word*, ed. Charles Bernstein (New York: Oxford University Press, 1998), 236.
17. William Russell, *Pulpit Elocution*, 2nd edn (Boston: Draper and Halliday, 1867), 168.
18. Russell, *Pulpit Elocution*, 168.
19. William Russell, *Orthopony; Or, the Cultivation of the Voice in Elocution*, 5th edn (Boston: William D. Ticknor and Company, 1848), 226.
20. Russell, *Orthophony*, 226.
21. Jonathan Barber, *A Grammar of Elocution: Containing the Principles of the Arts of Reading and Speaking; Illustrated by Appropriate Exercises and Examples* (New Haven: A. H. Maltby, 1830), 173. See also J. Weaver, *A System of Practical Elocution and Rhetorical Gesture*

(Philadelphia: Barrett and Jones, 1846), 329. Weaver similarly recommends—in some cases appropriating Barber's phrasing verbatim—repetitive exercises that emphasize the "elements of words" in isolation, before "an attempt be made to sound a short sentence."
22. Russell, *Orthophony*, 227.
23. See F. W. Robertson, *Lectures on the Influence of Poetry and Wordsworth* (London: H. R. Allenson, 1906), 41. Seven years Tennyson's junior, Frederick William Robertson, an Anglican clergyman whose defence of Tennyson's elegy first appeared in 1862, did not view the poem this way, but lamented that others too frequently did. See Robertson, *An Analysis of* In Memoriam (London: Smith, Elder, and Co., 1862).
24. Yopie Prins, "Voice Inverse," in *Victorian Poetry*, 42, 1 (2004), 43–59.
25. Yopie Prins, "Victorian Meters," *The Cambridge Companion to Victorian Poetry*, ed. Joseph Bristow (Cambridge: Cambridge University Press, 2000), 98.
26. That's the sense in which Coventry Patmore uses the term in his influential "Essay on English Metrical Law." Research conducted for this book led to an antedating of this sense of the word in the *OED*, which had previously given 1864 as the earliest recorded usage.
27. Russell, *Orthophony*, 227.
28. Russell, *Orthophony*, 226.
29. Gosse, qtd. in Mattheisen, "Gosse's Candid Snapshots," 341.
30. "Had I not known the poem well beforehand," Gosse notes, "it would have been entirely unintelligible." See Mattheisen, "Gosse's Candid 'Snapshots,'" 341. As it happens, the reading of "Boädicea" that Gosse hears forms part of a discussion of classical verse, and, what is more, the poem had its genesis in "experiments on metre" inspired by the "galliambics of Catullus." See Henry Graham Dakyns, "Tennyson, Clough, and the Classics," *Tennyson and His Friends*, ed. Hallam Tennyson (London: Macmillan and Co., 1911), 197.
31. Lindley Murray, *The English Reader; Or Pieces in Prose and Poetry* (New Haven: Durrie and Peck, 1825), xiv.
32. Noah Webster, *An Improved Grammar of the English Language* (New York: Webster and Clark, 1843), 164.
33. Epes Sargent, *The Standard Fifth Reader* (Boston: John L. Shorey, 1867), 117.
34. Wilkie Collins, *Man and Wife*, vol. 1 (Leipzig: Bernhard Tauchnitz, 1870), 265.
35. David Charles and Alexander Melville Bell, *Bell's Standard Elocutionist* (London: William Mullan and Son, 1878), 139.
36. The scientific impulse that gripped prosody toward the end of the nineteenth century can be understood in the context of the development

of new scientific methodologies. Jonathan Smith discusses the complex interrelation of fact and theory in what he calls the nineteenth-century "science of science." See Smith, *Fact and Feeling: Baconian Science and the Nineteenth-Century Literary Imagination* (Madison: University of Wisconsin Press, 1994), 11–44. Mary Poovey, too, explores the significance of fact-oriented thinking and outlines the creation of "a new social position—the expert," who brought an unflinching numeracy and an abiding belief in empirically demonstrable fact to bear on "abstractions like society, the market, and poverty." See Poovey, *A History of Modern Fact: Problems of Knowledge in the Sciences of Wealth and Society* (Chicago and London: University of Chicago Press, 1998), 15. The figure of the "expert" prosodist, as I go on to show, would fix a similarly quantifying gaze on a variety of aesthetic phenomena. Not all turn-of-the-century prosodists, however, were prepared to take the scientific turn. George Saintsbury, for example, defined his own approach thus: "the subject of our enquiries will be Architecture, not Petrology; Painting, not the enquiry into the chemical constitution of colours; Art, not Science." See *A History of English Prosody from the Twelfth Century to the Present Day*, vol. 1 (London: Macmillan, 1906), 6.
37. Francis B. Gummere, *A Handbook of Poetics for Students of English Verse* (Boston: Ginn, 1885), 4, 133, 167.
38. Mark H. Liddell, *An Introduction to the Scientific Study of English Poetry: Being a Prolegomena to a Science of English Prosody* (London: Doubleday, Page and Company, 1902), 28–29. Liddell hoped to counter the "vague definition of 'poetry'" with a more precise, scientific verse theory; he contended "that Language and Literature presented a field for scientific study much like that of Economics or Ethics, inasmuch as the phenomena which they furnished were neither accidental nor capricious, but the result of the operation of certain fundamental laws as definite and formulable in the one case as in the other provided one took the trouble to investigate the phenomena in a scientific spirit" (vii).
39. Sidney Lanier, *The Science of English Verse* (New York: Scribner, 1880), 24, 23.
40. Edmund Gurney, *The Power of Sound* (1880; New York: Basic Books, 1966), xix. Gurney adopts a musical approach to prosody, similar to that of Lanier. "The fundamental principle of verbal metre," he contends, "is identical with that of the rhythmic factor of melodic forms" (425).
41. Emily Harrington, "The Measure of Time: Rising and Falling in Victorian Meters," *Literature Compass* 4, 1 (2007), 337. See also Dennis Taylor, *Hardy's Metres and Victorian Prosody* (Oxford: Clarendon Press, 1988), 7–48; and Prins, "Victorian Meters," 89–113.

42. Edwin Guest, *A History of English Rhythms*, ed. Walter W. Skeat (London: George Bell and Sons, 1882), 2.
43. Coventry Patmore, *Coventry Patmore's "Essay on English Metrical Law": A Critical Edition with a Commentary*, ed. M. A. Roth (1857; Washington, DC: Catholic University of America Press, 1961), 15.
44. Gummere, *A Handbook of Poetics*, 167.
45. Liddell, *An Introduction to the Scientific Study of Poetry*, 15.
46. Patmore, "Essay on English Metrical Law," 20.
47. Liddell, *An Introduction to the Scientific Study of Poetry*, 15. As T. S. Omond remarks, "Prof. Liddell pushes this [difference between modern English and classical Greek verse] to a denial of quantitative relations in our meter." See T. S. Omond, *English Metrists: Being a Sketch of English Prosodical Criticism from Elizabethan Times to the Present Day* (Oxford: Clarendon Press, 1921), 242.
48. Gummere, *A Handbook of Poetics*, 167. Nonetheless, Gummere's prosody remains more or less indebted to a classical, foot-oriented taxonomy.
49. Patmore, "Essay on English Metrical Law," 15.
50. Yopie Prins, "Historical Poetics, Dysprosody, and *The Science of English Verse*," *PMLA*, 123, 1 (2008), 231.
51. Liddell, *An Introduction to the Scientific Study of English Poetry*, 305, 164, 251 (emphasis original). Liddell refuses to discard out of hand "the whole system of [classical] nomenclature" (305).
52. Prins, "Historical Poetics," 231.
53. Lanier, *The Science of English Verse*, 138. While Lanier may have promulgated a more graphic scansion, he nevertheless remained convinced, like Patmore, that meter is principally a mental phenomenon. Though he argues that "[a] 'bar' in music—or a 'foot' or 'measure' in verse—is exactly one of the 'groups'… only made, not by the imagination, but [*sic*] by an *actual stress clearly calling the ear's attention* to some given tone of each group," he goes on to state in a footnote that "the mind constructs … the rhythm of the piece" (67; emphasis added).
54. Yopie Prins, "Robert Browning, Transported by Meter," *The Traffic in Poems: Nineteenth-Century Poetry and Transatlantic Exchange*, ed. Meredith L. McGill (New Brunswick, NJ, and London: Rutgers University Press, 2008), 206.
55. Lanier, *The Science of English Verse*, 21, 22.
56. See Jason Rudy *Electric Meters: Victorian Physiological Poetics* (Athens, OH: Ohio University Press, 2009); Kirstie Blair, *Victorian Poetry and the Culture of the Heart* (Oxford: Clarendon Press, 2006); and Gregory Tate, *The Poet's Mind: The Psychology of Victorian Poetry, 1830–1870* (Oxford: Oxford University Press, 2012).

57. Thomas L. Hankins and Robert J. Silverman, *Instruments and the Imagination* (Princeton: Princeton University Press, 1995), 9.
58. David Cahan, "Looking at Nineteenth-Century Science: An Introduction," *From Natural Philosophy to the Sciences: Writing the History of Nineteenth-Century Sciences*, ed. David Cahan (Chicago and London: University of Chicago Press, 2003), 8.
59. Mary Jo Nye, "Introduction: The Modern Physical and Mathematical Sciences," *The Cambridge History of Science*, vol. 5, ed. Mary Jo Nye (Cambridge: Cambridge University Press, 2003), 1.
60. Cahan, "Looking at Nineteenth-Century Science," 4. Cahan is thinking not just about science in the universities, where during the middle decades of the nineteenth century various scientific disciplines were becoming "institutionalized," but also about applied science in a number of contemporary industries: one example he cites is the physics of energy conservation (9).
61. Michael Hagner, "Scientific Medicine," *From Natural Philosophy to the Sciences: Writing the History of Nineteenth-Century Sciences*, ed. David Cahan (Chicago and London: University of Chicago Press, 2003), 67.
62. Gurney, *The Power of Sound*, xviii. Poovey, *A History of Modern Fact*, 15.
63. W. F. Bynum, *Science and the Practice of Medicine in the Nineteenth Century* (Cambridge: Cambridge University Press, 1994), 98. Bynum offers a helpful précis of *Naturphilosophie* and *Naturwissenschaft* (95–96). See also Lynn K. Nyhart, *Biology Takes Form: Animal Morphology and the German Universities, 1800–1900* (Chicago and London: University of Chicago Press, 1995), 35–64.
64. William Baly's English translation, entitled *Elements of Physiology*, appeared in two volumes between 1837 and 1842. Most of the German-language texts I will be discussing below were translated into English, often shortly following their original publication. Many of the scientists who would draw on these sources in their later analyses of meter would have been familiar, in any case, with the German editions.
65. See John Galbraith Simmons, *Doctors and Discoveries: Lives that Created Today's Medicine* (Boston, MA: Houghton Mifflin, 2002), 67–70. Vitalism, defined by the *OED* as "[t]he doctrine or theory that the origin and phenomena of life are due to or produced by a vital principle, as distinct from a purely chemical or physical force," was the remnant of a more Romantic, idealist science with which Müller's successors would break.
66. Nyhart, *Biology Takes Form*, 63.
67. W. F. Bynum, "The Rise of Science in Medicine, 1850–1913," *The Western Medical Tradition: 1800–2000*, ed. W. F. Bynum et al. (Cambridge: Cambridge University Press, 2006), 114.

68. Peter J. Bowler and Iwan Rhys Morus, *Making Modern Science: A Historical Survey* (Chicago and London: University of Chicago Press, 2005), 96.
69. David Pantalony, *Altered Sensations: Rudolph Koenig's Acoustical Workshops in Nineteenth-Century Paris* (Dordrecht: Springer, 2009), 41.
70. David Pantalony charts the rise of acoustics within the universities (again, particularly in the German states) and also its growth as a trade (especially in France). See Pantalony, *Altered Sensations*, xxii–xxx.
71. Pantalony, *Altered Sensations*, xxix.
72. Chladni's *Klangfiguren* (or "sound-figures") were patterns formed by dry sand as it moved on a surface set in motion by sound vibrations. Hankins and Silverman, *Instruments and the Imagination*, 130–133.
73. Friedrich A. Kittler, *Gramophone, Film, Typewriter*, trans. Geoffrey Winthrop-Young and Michael Wutz (Stanford: Stanford University Press, 1999), 24.
74. Hankins and Silverman, *Instruments and the Imagination*, 133.
75. Jonathan Sterne, *The Audible Past: Cultural Origins of Sound Reproduction* (Durham, NC: Duke University Press, 2002), 31.
76. Hermann von Helmholtz, *On the Sensations of Tone as a Physiological Basis for the Theory of Music*, trans. Alexander J. Ellis, 2nd edn (London: Longmans and Co., 1885), 3. See Burdette Green and David Butler, "From Acoustics to *Tonpsychologie*," *The Cambridge History of Western Music Theory*, ed. Thomas Christensen (Cambridge: Cambridge University Press, 2002), 246.
77. Green and Butler, "From Acoustics to *Tonpsychologie*," 256, 260.
78. Helmholtz delineated three cognate, though effectively discrete, bodies of knowledge: physical, physiological, and psychological acoustics. Physical acoustics with the ways in which sounds are produced and propagated. Physiological acoustics concentrates not on how sounds are produced but on how they are perceived via "the sensations of hearing." It takes as its object "processes that take place within the ear itself." Combining these two sciences, Helmholtz analyzed both "how the agent [of sound] reaches the nerves to be excited" and "the various modes in which the nerves themselves are excited." Finally, psychological acoustics investigates how sensations processed by the auditory apparatus "result in mental images of determinate external objects"—that is, how our minds conceptualize what we hear. Helmholtz, *On the Sensations of Tone*, 3–4.
79. Both texts were translated by Alexander J. Ellis: the first as "The Physiological Causes of Harmony in Music" (in an 1873 collection of Helmholtz lectures introduced by John Tyndall) and the second as *On*

the Sensations of Tone as a Physiological Basis for the Theory of Music (in 1875).
80. Green and Butler, "From Acoustics to *Tonpsychologie*," 256.
81. Hermann von Helmholtz, "The Physiological Causes of Harmony in Music," *Selected Writings of Hermann von Helmholtz*, ed. Russell Kahl (Middletown, CT: Wesleyan University Press, 1971), 76.
82. Helmholtz, *On the Sensations of Tone*, 2.
83. Helmholtz, *On the Sensations of Tone*, 192, 227.
84. Helmholtz notes that "sound becomes a *musical* tone when such rapid impulses recur with perfect regularity and in precisely equal times." Helmholtz, "The Physiological Causes of Harmony in Music," 76.
85. As Helmholtz's laboratory data reveal, "the human ear is affected by vibrations of the air within certain degrees of rapidity—from about 20 to about 32,000 in a second—and...the sensation of musical tone arises from this effect." See Helmholtz, "The Physiological Causes of Harmony in Music," 81.
86. Étienne-Jules Marey, *La Méthode graphique dans les sciences expérimentales et principalement en physiologie et en medicine* (Paris: G. Masson, 1878), iii; qtd. in Hankins and Silverman, *Instruments and the Imagination*, 139.
87. The quotation is taken from an anonymous review of Thelwall's *King's College Lectures*. See *Monthly Review*, 7, 32 (1828), 545.
88. For music and meter see John Hollander, "The Music of Poetry," *Journal of Aesthetics and Art Criticism*, 15, 2 (1956), 232–244.
89. Helmholtz, *On the Sensations of Tone*, 2.
90. J. P. Dabney, *The Musical Basis of Verse: A Scientific Study of the Principles of Poetic Composition* (New York: Longmans, Green, and Co., 1901), vii.
91. James McKeen Cattell, "The Psychological Laboratory at Leipsic," *Mind*, 13, 49 (1888), 40, 45.
92. E. Bradford Titchener, "A Psychological Laboratory," *Mind*, 7, 27 (1898), 313, 311. Cattell, "The Psychological Laboratory at Leipsic," 38, 50 (emphasis original). Wilbur Lang Schramm would later outline a "phonophotographic study" of English metrics, which involved "photographing the poem" and its "sound waves." See Schramm, *Approaches to a Science of English Verse* (Iowa City: University of Iowa Press, 1935), 68, 15.
93. Alice Meynell, *The Rhythm of Life and Other Essays* (London: John Lane Bodley Head, 1896), 1, 4, 5, 6, 1.
94. F. W. H. Myers, "Human Personality in the Light of Hypnotic Suggestion," *Proceedings for the Society for Psychical Research*, 4 (1886–1887), 1.

95. Alan Kim, "Wilhelm Maximilian Wundt," *The Stanford Encyclopedia of Philosophy (Fall 2008 Edition)*, ed. Edward N. Zalta, http://plato.stanford.edu/archives/fall2008/entries/wilhelm-wundt/. S. Feldman, "Wundt's Psychology," *American Journal of Psychology*, 44, 4 (1932), 617.
96. Wundt's book was translated into English by E. B. Titchener in 1902 as *Principles of Physiological Psychology*. Rick Rylance, *Victorian Psychology and British Culture 1850–1880* (Oxford: Oxford University Press, 2000), 6.
97. See Cattell, "The Psychological Laboratory at Leipsic," 37–51.
98. Cattell, "The Psychological Laboratory at Leipsic," 38, 50.
99. Omond, *English Metrists*, 268 (emphasis added).
100. Cattell, "The Psychological Laboratory at Leipsic," 43.
101. Wilhelm Wundt, *An Introduction to Psychology*, trans. Rudolf Pintner (London: George Allen Unwin, 1912), 3.
102. Cattell, "The Psychological Laboratory at Leipsic," 46.
103. Michael Golston, *Rhythm and Race in Modernist Poetry and Science* (New York: Columbia University Press, 2008), 71. See Audrey B. Davis and Uta C. Merzbach, *Early Auditory Studies: Activities in the Psychological Laboratories of American Universities* (Washington, DC: Smithsonian Institution Press, 1975), 11.
104. See Albert S. Hurst and John McKay, "Experimental Time Relations of Poetic Metres," *University of Toronto Studies, Psychological Series*, 1 (1900), 155–175. Warner Brown, *Time in English Verse Rhythm: An Empirical Study of Typical Verses by the Graphic Method* (New York: Science Press, 1908), 1 (emphasis added).
105. Edward Wheeler Scripture, *The Elements of Experimental Phonetics* (New York: Charles Scribner's Sons, 1902), 538.
106. Brown, *Time in English Verse Rhythm*, 8.
107. Brown, *Time in English Verse Rhythm*, 14.
108. Edward Wheeler Scripture, "Accurate Work in Psychology," *American Journal of Psychology*, 6, 3 (1894), 428–429.
109. Scripture, *Elements of Experimental Phonetics*, 506.
110. Scripture, *Elements of Experimental Phonetics*, 507.
111. Scripture, *Elements of Experimental Phonetics*, 507–508. He remarks: "The various treatments of accent rest upon judgments by the unaided ear. It is unquestionably the fact that here, as in all the senses without exception, attempts to specify anything beyond the general outline ... can result only in a statement of illusions. In a judgment of impressiveness the ear is unable to distinguish with any accuracy, except in extreme cases, the factors of pitch, loudness and length; accents

stated to be due to increased stress may often be due to changes in pitch without the possibility of a detection of the fact by the ear."
112. Scripture, *Elements in Experimental Phonetics*, 508.
113. Scripture, *Elements in Experimental Phonetics*, 509. These are among the many devices recording and graphing devices used by Scripture and his contemporaries. Some are described and even illustrated in *Elements*.
114. Brown, *Time in English Verse Rhythm*, 28 (emphasis added). See also Dabney, *The Musical Basis of Verse*.
115. Scripture, *Elements in Experimental Phonetics*, 513 (emphasis added). Though Scripture insisted that he would "confine" his chapter on accent to "a summary of the disconnected experimental results with no attempt to work them into a theory," he nevertheless went on to offer general conceptual remarks that resonate with existing prosodic theories.
116. Patmore, "Essay on English Metrical Law," 15.
117. Qtd. in Albert S. Cook, "Prosody," rev. of *Studies from the Yale Psychological Laboratory*, ed. by Edward Wheeler Scripture, *Modern Language Notes*, 16, 1 (1901), 56.
118. Brown, *Time in English Verse Rhythm*, 3, 24, 25.
119. Scripture, *Elements of Experimental Phonetics*, 539. See also Ishiro Miyake, "Researches on Rhythmic Action," *Studies from the Yale Psychological Laboratory* (New Haven: Yale University Press, 1902), 1–48.
120. Scripture, *Elements of Experimental Phonetics*, 553.
121. Patmore, "Essay on English Metrical Law," 15.
122. Scripture, *Elements of Experimental Phonetics*, 451–452, 553.
123. Patmore, "Essay on English Metrical Law," 9.
124. Scripture, *Elements of Experimental Phonetics*, 552. See also Patmore, "Essay on English Metrical Law," 9. "The best poet," Patmore stated, "is ... he whose language combines the greatest imaginative accuracy with the most elaborate and sensible metrical organization, and who, in his verse, preserves everywhere the living sense of metre, no so much by unvarying obedience to, as by innumerable small departures from, its *modulus*."
125. Schramm, *Approaches to a Science of English Verse*, 67.
126. [Anon.], "Researches in Experimental Phonetics," by Edward Wheeler Scripture, *PMLA*, 15 (1900), vii.
127. Brown, *Time in English Verse Rhythm*, 77.
128. Schramm, *Approaches to a Science of English Verse*, 69.
129. Scripture, *Elements of Experimental Phonetics*, 553, 555.
130. Scripture, *Elements of Experimental Phonetics*, 555 (emphasis added).
131. Scripture, "Accurate Work in Psychology," 428, 429, 428.

132. [Anon.], "Measurement of Thought: Yale's Psychological Laboratory and Its Work," *New York Times* (Dec. 10, 1893), n. pag.
133. The latter is a variation on the device that was instrumental in the development of experimental physiology from the 1840s, when Carl Ludwig (its inventor), Helmholtz, and others used it to take somatic measurements.
134. Scripture, *Elements of Experimental Phonetics*, 523.
135. Brown, *Time in English Verse Rhythm*, 32.
136. Thus Merriley Borell describes how the kymograph allowed physiologists "to monitor a wide range of physiological events." Undoubtedly, it served a similar function for psychologists intent on "monitoring" metrical "events." See Merriley Borell, "Training the Senses, Training the Mind," *Medicine and the Five Senses*, ed. W. F. Bynum and Roy Porter (Cambridge: Cambridge University Press, 1993), 247. Schramm, *Approaches to a Science of English Verse*, 20. Patmore, "Essay on English Metrical Law," 15. "Researches in Experimental Phonetics," vii.
137. Scripture, *Elements of Experimental Phonetics*, 523.
138. Ada L. F. Snell, *Pause: A Study of Its Nature and Its Rhythmical Function in Verse, Especially Blank Verse*, diss. University of Michigan (Ann Arbor: University of Michigan Press, 1918), 8.
139. Snell, *Pause*, 4–5.
140. Snell, *Pause*, 2 (emphasis added).
141. Snell, *Pause*, 3, 2, 3. Snell attempted "to obtain a somewhat greater variety" by stipulating that "readers [should be] changed at various times." Further, she avoided using "only trained readers," though she did select readers "accustomed to read poetry" (3).
142. Scripture, *Elements of Experimental Phonetics*, 507.
143. Eric Griffiths, *The Printed Voice of Victorian Poetry* (Oxford: Oxford University Press, 1989), 67. Simon Jarvis makes a similar point about scanning being necessarily interpretative: it may purport to be a simple "record" of "the properties of an object," but no single scansion (or "diagram of a performance") is ever simply equal to that performance. See Simon Jarvis, "For a Poetics of Verse," *PMLA*, 125, 4 (2010), 933. Discussing Jarvis's position, David Nowell Smith makes a point apposite to the debate between idealism and materialism that this chapter examines: "Jarvis would refuse the bad choice between two positivisms: an 'idealist' scansion that purports to offer an a priori account of a poem's prosodic structure, untouched by individual performance, and the 'empiricist' scansion which would claim to have described how the poem 'actually sounds." See Smith, "Editor's Introduction: Scansion," in *Thinking Verse*, 3 (2013), 7. www.thinkingverse.com/issue03.html.

144. Patmore, "Essay on English Metrical Law," 9. Prins, "Voice Inverse," 57.
145. See Schramm, *Approaches to a Science of English Verse*, 76–82.
146. Ada L. F. Snell, "An Objective Study of Syllabic Quantity in English Verse," *PMLA* 33, 3 (1918), 408.
147. Ada L. F. Snell, "An Objective Study of Syllabic Quantity in English Verse," *PMLA* 34, 3 (1919), 435, 429, 428.
148. Richards, *Practical Criticism*, 228. Richards imagines using a kymograph "to record (by curves drawn on squared paper)" the rhythms of poetry—"all the physical characters of the sequences of sounds emitted, their strength, pitch, duration, and any other features we choose to examine" (226).

Afterword

My aim in this book has been to examine machines of the nineteenth century and their interface with the period's verse and metrical theorization. The machines it examines are at once material things (the gadgets and gears of industry, science, and idiosyncratic invention), ideas or abstractions (mentally marked beats, theories of proportional spacing, notional groupings of metrical feet), and complex processes and regimes that frequently involved both things and ideas (school curricula, measurement methodologies, and speech technologies). I have argued that a reciprocity existed between the rhythms and meters of poetry and the machine culture that increasingly characterized the century. We can hear the New Prosody's insistence on metrical abstraction and even spacing in the beating of the telegraph, just as we can see in the verse exercises of schoolboys the logic of the factory system. Asserting these connections involved sifting through various historical materials including poems, treatises, textbooks, experimental data, and medical analyses. It was, I felt, a necessary process of uncovering, triangulating, and intertextual weaving that would bring the book's argument closer to conveying the lived experiences of the century's verse technologies.

But how close could I really expect to get? It was a question the significance of which I did not fully appreciate until some way into the process of researching and writing this book. After presenting, to a small group of my Exeter colleagues, work from what is now "Measurement, Temporality, Abstraction," I started to understand how the link between the machines of the past and historical meters had an almost-of-reach material dimension that even careful close reading, involved scansion, and archival plodding could not necessarily recover. Just as the Victorians were preoccupied with their inability to know classical verse as spoken by the ancients themselves, I came to terms, early in the project, with the problem of Victorians' metrical mouthings being, for the most part, beyond my hearing. The paper trail was what I had to follow. But there was also the disconcerting silence of the machines. It would be easy to allow their real materiality to flatten into the two dimensions of the pages on which illustrations of them were printed. In the hundred-plus years between the mechanisms ceasing to move and measure and make noise and me setting out to write about them, it was possible to literally lose touch with them, for them to be legitimately beyond the awareness of my senses. So when my colleague asked me a simple question—*Had I ever heard a steam thresher?*—it not only occurred to me that I had not but also alarmed me that I had not properly considered how far I had advanced in arguments based largely on written accounts and comparatively little first-hand experience of several machines central to the project. Over time, all that is solid melts into air.

Naturally, there remain assertions in the book that it has been impossible, without the aid of time travel, to verify with my own eyes, ears, and hands. But I did what I could, after that wake-up call, to introduce a third, more empirical dimension to my research. I have now heard a steam thresher, which reassured me that my speculations about its beating and buzzing had not been mere fancy. What is more, as the project unfolded I had the great good fortune of handling one of the machines at the heart of it: John Clark's Eureka. My involvement in a parallel project, funded by the Arts and Humanities Research Council, brought me into direct and prolonged contact with this truly amazing apparatus, which I am pleased to say I have not only seen but also participated in transporting, dismantling, conserving, rebuilding, and returning to working order. Very little of it, I should stress, I did on my own: recovering the Eureka's meters was very much a team effort. Our project involved archivists, classicists, computer scientists, conservators, engineering technicians, historians of science and mathematics, and several enthusiastic undergraduates. So many specialized skills came together, working in concert to bring a highly specialized device back from a long period of desuetude. I recall looking on silently as an expert in antique wood conservation painstakingly cleaned the machine's exterior to reveal a poem (reproduced as an epigraph to "Automaton Versifiers") hidden for many years beneath a thick layer of bituminous paint, along with presumably original decorations in what would have been, in the 1830s and 40s, expensive water gilding. Over the shoulder of a metals conservator, I peeked into the machine's interior, while its engine—at first a confusion of wood, wires, and brass—was disarticulated, carefully cleaned, and reassembled. Our project's team learned how part of Clark's mechanism was specially built for the task of manufacturing hexameters, while other parts—such as an ornate brass gear originally belonging to a spit engine (a simple machine for cooking food at the home's hearth)—had been scavenged and adapted. Putting it all back together, we experimented with the Eureka's operation and, with a little coaxing, returned it to state of fairly reliable functionality. Standing next to the real Eureka, a big box inside of which one might well imagine concealing a small person to provide the illusion of considered metrical composition, I was impressed by the uncanny groaning, whirring, and clattering of its moving parts. As its lettered staves moved into position and a line of verse revealed itself in small windows at about eye level, I thought about the strange sounds this mechanical versifier made and the labored slowness of its visible functions: how the drums lurched under an impulse from the engine, producing a palpable *thunk*, and how the letters seemed to creep along their vertical path before coming to rest. I have seen and heard the Eureka compose verses on a few occasions now, and, in spite of my prosodic affiliations, each time it is the mechanics of the machine, rather than of the versifying, that impresses me.

Working up close with the Eureka also taught me an object lesson in interdisciplinarity, something the story told by the book has attempted to corroborate. The process of understanding how Clark's hexameter machine worked was truly collaborative, demanding specialist knowledge from persons whose day-to-day engagement with meter was probably as scant as my understanding of random number generation and cam drives. By pooling our research skills, we gained an insight not just into the workings of the Eureka as a mechanism but into the workings of John Clark's mind. Engaging with meter, as Clark did with his head and his hands, was an undertaking for which book learning was only one among many prerequisites. In one way or another, that is true also of much of the material discussed in this book. The machines of meter did not operate within a hermetically sealed literary orthodoxy. Their apparatus was not limited to the sciences of philology and prosody; rather, it incorporated pedagogy, physiology, psychology, and other branches of learning. Meter had cogs and keys as well as feet, frequencies as well as periods and intervals, flesh and metallic features as well as an ideal silhouette. To take the measure of nineteenth-century verse, as I have attempted to do in this book, is to examine the moving parts of its sundry and intersecting technologies.

BIBLIOGRAPHY

Abbas, Niran B. *Thinking Machines*. Berlin: Lit Verlag, 2006.
"Account of Starting Schools." Joseph Lancaster Papers, J. T. 317, 1, 3. Library of the Religious Society of Friends, London.
Adam, Barbara. *Timewatch: The Social Analysis of Time*. London: Polity, 1995.
Adams, Daniel. *The Monitorial Reader, Designed for the Use of Academies and Schools*. Concord, NH: Roby, Kimball, and Merrill, 1841.
Adams, H. C. *Wykehamica: A History of Winchester College and Commoners, from the Foundation to the Present Day*. Oxford and London: James Parker and Co., 1878.
Allingham, William. *A Diary*. Ed. H. Allingham and D. Kradford. London: Macmillan, 1907.
Altick, Richard D. *The Shows of London*. Cambridge, MA: Belknap Press of Harvard University Press, 1978.
"Answers to the Hitorical and Philosophical Questions." *Universal Magazine* 4 (1805): 422–430.
Anti-Scepticism; Or, an Inquiry into the Nature and Philosophy of Language, as Connected with the Sacred Scriptures. Oxford: n.p., 1821.
Archer, R. L. *Secondary Education in the Nineteenth Century*. London: Cass, 1921.
Armstrong, Isobel. "Meter and Meaning." Hall 26–52.
—. *Victorian Poetry: Poetry, Poetics and Politics*. London and New York: Routledge, 1993.
Armytage, W. H. G. *Four Hundred Years of English Education*. 2nd ed. London: Cambridge University Press, 1970.

Arnold, Matthew. *The Complete Prose Works of Matthew Arnold, Volume 1—On the Classical Tradition*. Ed. R. H. Super. Ann Arbor: University of Michigan Press, 1960.
—. *The Letters of Matthew Arnold*. Vol. 2. Ed. Cecil Y. Lang. Charlottesville and London: University Press of Virginia, 1997.
Attridge, Derek. "Beat." *The Oxford Handbook of Victorian Poetry*. Ed. Matthew Bevis. Oxford: Oxford University Press, 2013. 36–55.
—. *Well-Weighed Syllables: Elizabethan Verse in Classical Metres*. Cambridge: Cambridge University Press, 1974.
Atwood, Sara. *Ruskin's Educational Ideals*. Farnham: Ashgate, 2011.
Austin, Gilbert. *Chironomia; Or, a Treatise on Rhetorical Delivery*. London: n.p., 1806.
Babbage, Charles. *A Letter to Sir Humphry Davy ... on the Application of Machinery to the Purpose of Calculating and Printing Mathematical Tables*. London J. Booth, 1822.
—. *On the Economy of Machinery and Manufactures*. London: Charles Knight, 1833.
Bain, Alexander. *On the Study of Character, Including an Estimate of Phrenology*. London: Parker, Son, and Bourn, 1861.
Barber, Jonathan. *A Grammar of Elocution: Containing the Principles of the Arts of Reading and Speaking; Illustrated by Appropriate Exercises and Examples*. New Haven: A. H. Maltby, 1830.
Barker, Andrew. *Greek Musical Writings: II, Harmonic and Acoustic Theory*. Cambridge: Cambridge University Press, 1989.
Bateman, Frederic. *On Aphasia, Or Loss of Speech and the Localisation of the Faculty of Articulate Language*. London: John Churchill and Sons, 1870.
Bayfield, M. A. *The Measures of the Poets: A New System of English Prosody*. Cambridge: Cambridge University Press, 1919.
Beaumont, Matthew, and Michael Freeman, eds., *The Railway and Modernity: Time, Space, and the Machine Ensemble*. Bern: Peter Lang, 2007.
Bell, Alexander Graham. *The Mechanism of Speech*. 8th ed. New York and London: Funk and Wagnalls, 1916.
Bell, Alexander Melville. *The Elocutionary Manual. The Principles of Articulation and Orthoepy, the Art of Reading and Gesture; Illustrated by Tables, Notations, and Diagrams; with Exercises in Expressive Delivery, and a Copious Selection of Emphasized Extracts, Embodying the Language of the Passions*. 3rd ed. London: Hamilton, Adams, and Co., 1860.
—. *A New Elucidation of the Principles of Speech and Elocution*. Edinburgh: W. P. Kennedy, 1849.
—. *Observations on Speech; the Causes and the Cure of Stammering, Mal-Articulations and Defects; and on the Principles of Elocutionary Instruction; with Numerous Cases Systematically Arranged*. Edinburgh: W. P. Kennedy, 1853.

—. *The Tongue, a Poem, in Two Parts*. London: W. J. Cleaver, 1846.
—. *Visible Speech: The Science of Universal Alphabetics; or Self-Interpreting Physiological Letters, for the Writing of All Languages in One Alphabet*. London: Simpkin, Marshall, and Co., 1867.
Bell, Andrew. *Elements of Tuition, Part III. Ludus Literarius: The Classical and Grammer School; Or, An Exposition of an Experiment in Education, Made at Madras in the Years 1789–1796: With a View to Its Introduction into Schools for the Higher Orders of Children, and with Particular Suggestions for Its Application to a Grammar School*. London: n.p., 1815.
—. *The Madras School, or Elements of Tuition: Comprising an Analysis of an Experiment in Education Made at the Male Asylum, Madras; with Its Facts, Proofs, and Illustrations*. London: n.p., 1808.
—. *Mutual Instruction and Moral Discipline; Or, Manual of Instructions for Conducting Schools through the Agency of the Scholars Themselves*. 7th ed. London: n.p., 1823.
—. *The Wrongs of Children; Or, a Practical Vindication of Children from the Injustice Done Them in Early Nurture and Education; Addressed to Parents, Tutors, Guardians, and Masters: and to Legislators and Governors; Setting forth the Source of Much Human Misery, and Pointing Out the Remedy*. London: n.p., 1819.
Bell, David Charles, and Alexander Melville Bell. *Bell's Standard Elocutionist*. London: William Mullan and Son, 1878.
Bell, J. D. *A Man*. Philadelphia: James Challen and Son, 1860.
Bellon, Richard. "Science at the Crystal Focus of the World." *Science in the Marketplace: Nineteenth-Century Sites and Experience*. Ed. Aileen Fyfe and Bernard Lightman. Chicago and London: University of Chicago Press, 2007. 301–335.
Benson, D. Frank, and Alfredo Ardila. *Aphasia: A Clinical Perspective*. Oxford: Oxford University Press, 1996.
Berg, Maxine. *The Machinery Question and the Making of Political Economy, 1815–1848*. Cambridge: Cambridge University Press, 1980.
Bernard, Thomas. "Extract from an Account of the Schools of Industry at Kendall." *The Reports of the Society for Bettering the Condition and Increasing the Comforts of the Poor*. Vol. 3. London: n.p., 1802. 249–250.
Black, R. Harrison. *The Student's Manual: Being an Etymological and Explanatory Vocabulary of Words Derived from the Greek*. London: Longman, Orme, Brown, Green, and Longmans, 1838.
Blair, Kirstie. *Victorian Poetry and the Culture of the Heart*. Oxford: Clarendon Press, 2006.
Blandford, D. W. "The *Eureka*." *Greece and Rome* 10 (1963): 71–78.
Borrel, Merriley. "Training the Senses, Training the Mind." *Medicine and the Five Senses*. Ed. W. F. Bynum and Roy Porter. Cambridge: Cambridge University Press, 1993. 244–261.

Bowker, Geoffrey C. "Second Nature Once Removed: Time, Space, and Representations." *Time and Society* 4.1 (1995): 47–66.

Bowler, Peter J., and Iwan Rhys Morus. *Making Modern Science: A Historical Survey*. Chicago and London: University of Chicago Press, 2005.

Boyd, H. S. [Letter to the Editor.] *Classical Journal* 37.74 (1828): 327.

Braden, G. "Hexameter." *The Princeton Encyclopedia of Poetry and Poetics*. 4th ed. Ed. Roland Greene et al. Princeton: Princeton University Press, 2012. 627.

Braverman, Harry. *Labor and Monopoly Capital: The Degradation of Work in the Twentieth Century*. New York: Monthly Review Press, 1998.

Bridges, Robert. *Ibant Obscuri: An Experiment in the Classical Hexameter*. Oxford: Clarendon Press, 1916.

Bristow, Joseph, ed. *The Cambridge Companion to Victorian Poetry*. Cambridge: Cambridge University Press, 2000.

—. "Reforming Victorian Poetry: Poetics after 1832." Bristow, *The Cambridge Companion to Victorian Poetry* 1–24.

Broca, Pierre Paul. "Sur le siege de la faculté du langage articulé." *Bulletin de la Société d'Anthropologie* 6 (1865): 377–393.

[Brougham, Henry.] "Progress of the People: The Periodical Press." *Edinburgh Review* 57 (1833): 239–248.

Brown, Warner. *Time in English Verse Rhythm: An Empirical Study of Typical Verses by the Graphic Method*. New York: Science Press, 1908.

Brown, William Haig. *Charterhouse Past and Present*. Godalming: H. Stedman, 1879.

The Brownings' Correspondence. Vol. 1. Ed. Philip Kelley and Ronald Hudson. Winfield, KS: Wedgestone Press, 1984.

Buttler, D. P. *Buttler's System of Physical Training. The Lifting Cure: An Original Scientific Application of the Laws of Motion or Mechanical Action to Physical Culture and the Cure of Disease*. Boston: D. P. Butler, 1868.

Buzard, James, et al. eds. *Victorian Prism: Refractions of the Crystal Palace*. Charlottesville: University of Virginia Press, 2007.

Bynum, W. F. "The Rise of Science in Medicine, 1850–1913." *Western Medical Tradition: 1800–2000*. Ed. W. F. Bynum et al. Cambridge: Cambridge University Press, 2006. 111–239.

—. *Science and the Practice of Medicine in the Nineteenth Century*. Cambridge: Cambridge University Press, 1994.

Cahan, David. "Looking at Nineteenth-Century Science: An Introduction." *From Natural Philosophy to the Sciences: Writing the History of Nineteenth-Century Sciences*. Ed. David Cahan. Chicago and London: University of Chicago Press, 2003. 3–15.

Campbell, Matthew. *Rhythm and Will in Victorian Poetry*. Cambridge: Cambridge University Press, 1999.

Carey, J. *Latin Prosody Made Easy.* London: Longman, Hurst, Rees, and Orme, 1808.
Carlyle, Thomas. *A Carlyle Reader: Selections from the Writings of Thomas Carlyle.* Ed. G. B. Tennyson. Cambridge: Cambridge University Press, 1984.
Carpenter, William B. *Principles of Mental Physiology, with Their Applications to the Training and Discipline of the Mind, and the Study of its Morbid Conditions.* London: Henry S. King and Co., 1875.
Cattell, James McKeen. "The Psychological Laboratory at Leipsic." *Mind* 13.49 (1888): 37–51.
Champneys, Basil. *Memoirs and Correspondence of Coventry Patmore.* Vol. 1. London: George Bell and Sons, 1901.
"A Chapter or Two on Meters." *Friendly Companion and Illustrated Instructor* (March–May 1857): 80+.
Charlesworth, Simon J. *A Phenomenology of Working-Class Experience.* Cambridge: Cambridge University Press, 2000.
Christensen, Lena. *Editing Emily Dickinson: The Production of an Author.* New York: Routledge, 2008.
Clark, John. *The General History and Description of a Machine for Composing Hexameter Latin Verses.* Bridgwater: Frederick Wood, 1848.
—. Letter to his sister, Sarah (Clark) Metford, August 1845. John Clark Papers. Alfred Gillett Trust Archive. Street, Somerset, UK.
Clarke, M. L. *Classical Education in Britain 1500–1900.* Cambridge: Cambridge University Press, 1959.
Clough, Arthur Hugh. *The Poems and Prose Remains of Arthur Hugh Clough.* 2 vols. Ed. Shore Smith. London: Macmillan and Co., 1869.
Collins, Beverley, and Inger M. Mees. *Practical Phonetics and Phonology: A Resource Book for Students.* London: Routledge, 2003.
Collins, Wilkie. *Man and Wife.* Vol. 1. Leipzig: Bernhard Tauchnitz, 1870.
Combe, George. *Education: Its Principles and Practice.* Ed. William Jolly. London: Macmillan and Co., 1879.
—. *Phrenological Development of Robert Burns, from a Cast of His Skull, Moulded at Dumfries, the 31st Day of March 1834.* Edinburgh: W. and A. K. Johnston, 1834.
Connor, Steven. *Dumbstruck: A Cultural History of Ventriloquism.* Oxford and New York: Oxford University Press, 2000.
Cook, Albert S. "Prosody." Rev. of *Studies from the Yale Psychological Laboratory,* ed. Edward Wheeler Scripture. *Modern Language Notes* 16.1 (1901): 54–58.
Copeland, B. J. "A Lecture and Two Radio Broadcasts on Machine Intelligence by Alan Turning." *Machine Intelligence 15: Intelligent Agents.* Ed. K. Furukawa et al. Oxford: Oxford University Press, 1999. 445–476.
Cowie, Evelyn E. "Stephen Hawtrey and a Working-Class Eton." *History of Education* 11.2 (1982): 71–86.

Cowper, William. "*The Task*, Book I." *Eighteenth-Century Poetry: An Annotated Anthology*. 2nd ed. Ed. David Fairer and Christine Gerrard. Malden, MA: Blackwell, 2004. 527–545.

Cox, Edward W. *The Arts of Writing, Reading, and Speaking*. London: G. W. Carleton, 1868.

—. *The Mechanism of Man: An Answer to the Question, What Am I? A Popular Introduction to Mental Physiology and Psychology*. Vol. 2. London: Longman, 1879.

Craig, John. *A New Universal, Technological, Etymological, and Pronouncing Dictionary of the English Language, Embracing All the Terms Used in Art, Science, and Literature*. Vol. 1. London: Henry George Collins, 1848.

Crowley, Tony. *The Politics of Discourse: The Standard Language Question in British Cultural Debates*. Basingstoke and London: Macmillan, 1989.

Cull, Richard. "On the Perception of Metre and Rhythmus, Both in Language and in Music." *Phrenological Journal* 19.86 (1846): 1–10.

Dabney, J. P. *The Musical Basis of Verse: A Scientific Study of the Principles of Poetic Composition*. New York: Longmans, Green, and Co., 1901.

Dakyns, Henry Graham. "Tennyson, Clough, and the Classics." *Tennyson and His Friends*. Ed. Hallam Tennyson. London: Macmillan and Co., 1911. 188–205.

Dalgleish, Walter Scott. *Memorials of the High School of Edinburgh Containing a Historical Sketch with Portraits of the Present Rector and Four of the Classical Masters and Biographical Notices*. Edinburgh: Maclachlan and Stewart, 1857.

Dallas, E. S. *Poetics: An Essay on Poetry*. London: Smith, Elder, and Co., 1852.

Dant, Tim. *Materiality and Society*. Maidenhead: Open University Press, 2005.

Davies, Matt. "Works, Products, and the Division of Labour: Notes for a Cultural and Political Economic Critique." *Cultural Political Economy*. Ed. Jacqueline Best and Matthew Paterson. Abingdon: Routledge, 2010. 48–64.

Davis, Audrey B., and Uta C. Merzbach. *Early Auditory Studies: Activities in the Psychological Laboratories of American Universities*. Washington, DC: Smithsonian Institution Press, 1975.

Davis, Michael. *George Eliot and Nineteenth-Century Psychology: Exploring the Unmapped Country*. Aldershot: Ashgate, 2006.

Dickens, Charles. *Hard Times. For These Times*. London: Bradbury and Evans, 1854.

Dickinson, Emily. *The Poems of Emily Dickinson*. Ed. R. W. Franklin. Cambridge, MA: Harvard University Press, 1998.

Dowling, William C. *Oliver Wendell Holmes in Paris: Medicine, Theology, and The Autocrat of the Breakfast Table*. Lebanon, NH: University of New Hampshire Press, 2006.

Duck, Stephen. "The Thresher's Labour." *Eighteenth-Century Poetry: An Annotated Anthology.* 2nd ed. Ed. David Fairer and Christine Gerrard. Malden, MA: Blackwell, 2004. 261–268.

Ebbatson, J. R. "The Lonely Garden: The Sonnets of Charles Tennyson Turner." *Victorian Poetry* 15.4 (1977): 307–319.

"An Educational Novelty." *Punch* 27 Apr. 1850: 167.

Edwards, T. W. C. *The Eton Latin Grammar, a Plain and Concise Introduction to the Latin Language; Being Lily's Grammar Abridged, for the Use of the Young Gentlemen of Eton College: But with the Addition of Many Useful Notes and Observations, and Also of the Accents and Quantity.* London. n.p., 1826.

Ellingham, C. J. "Apology for the Practice of Latin Verse Composition." *Greece and Rome* 4 (1935): 151–159.

Ellis, Alexander J. *Quantitative Pronunciation of Latin. For the Use of Classical Teachers and Linguists.* London: Macmillan and Co., 1874.

Erikson, Lee. "The Market." *A Companion to Victorian Poetry.* Ed. Richard Cronin et al. Malden, MA: Blackwell, 2002. 345–360.

Esbester, Mike. "Nineteenth-Century Timetables and the History of Reading." *Book History* 12 (2009): 156–185.

Essinger, James. *Jacquard's Web: How a Hand Loom Led to the Birth of the Information Age.* Oxford: Oxford University Press, 2004.

"The Eureka." *Illustrated London News* 19 July 1845: 37.

Examination of the Telegraphic Apparatus and the Processes in Telegraphy. Washington, DC: Government Printing Office, 1869.

Farrar, F. W. *Essays on a Liberal Education.* London: Macmillan and Co., 1867.

—. "Of Greek and Latin Verse-Composition as a General Branch of Education." Farrar, *Essays* 205–240.

Feldman, S. "Wundt's Psychology." *American Journal of Psychology* 44.4 (1932): 615–629.

Finch, Annie. *The Ghost of Meter: Culture and Prosody in American Free Verse.* Ann Arbor: University of Michigan Press, 1993.

Foster, John Bellamy. "New Introduction." Braverman ix–xxiv.

Foucault, Michel. *The Order of Things: An Archaeology of the Human Sciences.* London and New York: Routledge, 1973.

Gagnier, Regenia. *Subjectivities: A History of Self-Representation in Britain, 1832–1920.* New York: Oxford University Press, 1991.

Gargano, Elizabeth. *Reading Victorian Schoolrooms: Childhood and Education in Nineteenth-Century Fiction.* New York: Routledge, 2008.

Gioia, Dana. "Meter-Making Arguments." *Meter in English: A Critical Engagement.* Ed. David Baker. Fayetteville: University of Arkansas Press, 1986. 75–96.

Gladstone, Mary. *Mary Gladstone (Mrs. Drew): Her Diaries and Letters.* Ed. Lucy Masterman. London: Methuen, 1930.

Glaser, Ben. "Scanners, Darkly." Rev. of *Meter Matters: Verse Cultures of the Long Nineteenth Century*, ed. Jason David Hall. *Papers on Language and Literature* 49.3 (2013): 327–333.
Golston, Michael. *Rhythm and Race in Modernist Poetry and Science*. New York: Columbia University Press, 2008.
Gooday, Graeme J. N. *The Morals of Measurement: Accuracy, Irony, and Trust in Late Victorian Electrical Practice*. Cambridge: Cambridge University Press, 2004.
Goodridge, John. *Rural Life in Eighteenth-Century English Poetry*. Cambridge: Cambridge University Press, 1995.
Gordon, Peter, and Denis Lawton. *A History of Western Educational Ideas*. Oxford: Routledge, 2002.
Gosse, Edmund. *Coventry Patmore*. New York: Charles Scribner's Sons, 1905.
Gowers, William. *A Manual of Diseases of the Nervous System*. Vol. 2. London: J. and A. Churchill, 1886.
Gratwick, A. S. "The Latin Hexameter." *Classical Review* 40 (1990): 340–343.
Gray, Herbert Branston. *The Public Schools and the Empire*. London: Williams and Norgate, 1913.
Gray, Robert. *The Factory Question and Industrial England, 1830–1860*. Cambridge: Cambridge University Press, 1996.
"Great Western Difficulties—And the Way Out of Them." *Railway, Record, Mining Register, and Join-Stock Companies' Reporter* 7 Feb. 1857: 85.
"Greek Metres and English Scholarship." *The Foreign Quarterly Review* 23.46 (1839): 242–294.
Green, Burdette, and David Butler. "From Acoustics to *Tonpsychologie*." *The Cambridge History of Western Music Theory*. Ed. Thomas Christensen. Cambridge: Cambridge University Press, 2002. 246–271.
Griffiths, Eric. *The Printed Voice of Victorian Poetry*. Oxford: Oxford University Press, 1989.
Griscom, John. *Monitorial Instruction: An Address, Pronounced at the Opening of the New-York High-School, with Notes and Illustrations*. New York: n.p., 1825.
Groth, Helen, and Natalya Lusty. *Dreams and Modernity: A Cultural History*. Abingdon: Routledge, 2013.
Guest, Edwin. *A History of English Rhythms*. Ed. Walter W. Skeat. London: George Bell and Sons, 1882.
"Guide to Bradshaw." *Punch* 5 Aug. 1865: 44.
Gummere, Francis B. *A Handbook of Poetics for Students of English Verse*. Boston: Ginn, 1885.
Gunderson, Keith. *Mentality and Machines*. 2nd ed. Minneapolis: University of Minnesota Press, 1985.
Gurney, Edmund. *The Power of Sound*. 1880. New York: Basic Books, 1966.

Hagner, Michael. "Scientific Medicine." *From Natural Philosophy to the Sciences: Writing the History of Nineteenth-Century Sciences.* Ed. David Cahan. Chicago and London: University of Chicago Press, 2003. 49–87.
Hale, Edward E. *If, Yes, and Perhaps: Four Possibilities and Six Exaggerations, with Some Bits of Fact.* Boston: Ticknor and Fields, 1868.
Hall, Jason David, ed. *Meter Matters: Verse Cultures of the Long Nineteenth Century.* Athens, OH: Ohio University Press, 2011.
Hankins, Thomas L., and Robert J. Silverman. *Instruments and the Imagination.* Princeton: Princeton University Press, 1995.
Hardy, Thomas. "The Dorsetshire Labourer." *Longman's Magazine* 2.9 (1883): 252–269.
Harrington, Emily. "The Measure of Time: Rising and Falling in Victorian Meters." *Literature Compass* 4.1 (2007): 336–354.
Harrington, J. W., and Barney Warf. *Industrial Location: Principles, Practice, and Policy.* London: Routledge, 1995.
Harrison, Robert Pogue. *The Dominion of the Dead.* Chicago: University of Chicago Press, 2003.
Hart, John S. *A Manual of Composition and Rhetoric: A Text-Book for Schools and Colleges.* Philadelphia: Eldredge and Brother, 1871.
Haugeland, John. *Artificial Intelligence: The Very Idea.* Cambridge, MA: MIT Press, 1985.
Haven, Gilbert. *The Pilgrim's Wallet: Or, Scraps of Travel Gathered in England, France, and Germany.* New York: Hurd and Houghton, 1869.
Hawtrey, S. *A Narrative-Essay on a Liberal Education, Chiefly Embodied in the Account of an Attempt to Give a Liberal Education to Children of the Working Classes.* London: Hamilton, Adams, and Co., 1868.
Hazlitt, William. *Lectures on the English Poets.* London: n.p., 1818.
Helmholtz, Hermann von. *On the Sensations of Tone as a Physiological Basis for the Theory of Music.* 2nd ed. Trans. Alexander J. Ellis. London: Longmans, Green, and Co., 1885.
—. *Selected Writings of Hermann von Helmholtz.* Ed. Russell Kahl. Middletown, CT: Wesleyan University Press, 1971.
Herrick, James B. *A Handbook of Medical Diagnosis for Students.* Philadelphia: Lea Brothers and Co., 1895.
Heyck, Thomas William. "Educational." *A Companion to Victorian Literature and Culture.* Ed. Herbert F. Tucker. Malden, MA: Blackwell, 1999. 194–211.
Hill, Rowland. *Plans for the Government and Liberal Instruction of Boys in Large Numbers; Drawn from Experience.* London: G. and W. B. Whittaker, 1822.
Hollander, John. "The Music of Poetry." *Journal of Aesthetics and Art Criticism* 15.2 (1956): 232–244.
—. *Vision and Resonance: Two Senses of Poetic Form.* New York: Oxford University Press, 1975.

Hollingshead, John. *My Lifetime*. London: Sampson, Low, Marstan and Co., 1895.
Holmes, Oliver Wendell. "The Human Wheel, Its Spokes and Felloes." *Atlantic Monthly* 11.67 (1863): 567–580.
—. *Mechanism in Thought and Morals*. Boston: James R. Osgood and Co., 1871.
—. "The Physiology of Versification: Harmonies of Organic and Animal Life." *Pages from an Old Volume of Life, The Works of Oliver Wendell Holmes*. Vol. 8. Boston: Houghton, Mifflin and Co., 1892. 315–321.
—. "The Physiology of Walking." *Pages from an Old Volume of Life, The Works of Oliver Wendell Holmes*. Vol. 8. Boston: Houghton, Mifflin and Co., 1892. 121–131.
"How To Cure Stammering." *Medical and Surgical Reporter* 29 July 1871: 111.
Howlett, John Henry. *Instructions in Reading the Liturgy of the United Church of England and Ireland*. London: n.p., 1826.
[Hughes, Thomas.] *Tom Brown's School Days*. Cambridge: Macmillan and Co., 1857.
Humez, Alexander, and Nicholas Humez. *On the Dot: The Speck That Changed the World*. Oxford: Oxford University Press, 2008.
Hurst, Albert S., and John McKay. "Experimental Time Relations of Poetic Metres." *University of Toronto Studies, Psychological Series* 1 (1900): 155–175.
Hutchison, Hazel. "Eye Rhyme: Visual Experience and the Poetics of Gerard Manley Hopkins." *Victorian Poetry* 49.2 (2011): 217–233.
Huxley, Thomas Henry. *Methods and Results: Essays*. New York: D. Appleton and Company, 1899.
"Improvisatori." *Arthur's Home Magazine* (Jan. 1855): 9.
Itzkin, Elissa S. "Bentham's Chrestomathia: Utilitarian Legacy to English Education." *Journal of the History of Ideas* 39.2 (1978): 303–316.
Jalland, Pat. *Death in the Victorian Family*. Oxford: Oxford University Press, 1996.
Jamieson, Alexander. *A Dictionary of Mechanical Science, Arts, Manufactures, and Miscellaneous Knowledge*. London: Henry Fisher, Son, and Co., 1829.
Jarvis, Simon. "For a Poetics of Verse." *PMLA* 125.4 (2010): 931–935.
—. *Wordsworth's Philosophic Song*. Cambridge: Cambridge University Press, 2007.
Jones, Robert. *An Address, Delivered at the Opening of the Literary and Scientific Institution, at Staines, on Tuesday, January 12th, 1836*. Staines: J. Smith, 1836.
Ketabgian, Tamara Siroone. *The Lives of Machines: The Industrial Imaginary in Victorian Literature and Culture*. Ann Arbor: University of Michigan Press, 2011.
Kidwell, Peggy Aldrich. "Calculating Machine." *Instruments of Science: An Historical Encyclopedia*. Ed. Robert Bud and Deborah Jean Warner. New York and London: Garland, 1998. 75–77.

Kim, Alan. "Wilhelm Maximilian Wundt." *The Stanford Encyclopedia of Philosophy (Fall 2008 Edition)*. Ed. Edward N. Zalta. http://plato.stanford.edu/archives/fall2008/entries/wilhelm-wundt/.

King, Andrew, and John Plunkett, eds. *Victorian Print Media: A Reader*. New York: Oxford University Press, 2005.

Kingsley, Charles. *Letters and Memories: Novels, Poems, and Letters of Charles Kingsley*. New York: Cooperative Publication Society, 1899.

Kittler, Friedrich. *Discourse Networks 1800/1900*. Trans. Michael Metteer. Stanford: Stanford University Press, 1990.

—. *Gramophone, Film, Typewriter*. Trans. Geoffrey Winthrop-Young and Michael Wutz. Stanford: Stanford University Press, 1999.

[Knight, Charles]. "The Commercial History of a Penny Magazine.—No. III." *Penny Magazine of the Society for the Diffusion of Useful Knowledge* 2 (1833): 465–472.

Kurshan, Ilana. "Mind Reading: Literature in the Discourse of Early Victorian Phrenology and Mesmerism." *Victorian Literary Mesmerism*. Ed. Martin Willis and Catherine Wynne. Amsterdam and New York: Rodopi, 2006. 17–38.

La Mettrie, Julien Offray de. *Man-Machine*. Trans Jonathan Bennett. http://www.earlymoderntexts.com/assets/pdfs/lamettrie1748.pdf. 2010–2015.

Lancaster, Joseph. *The British System of Education: Being a Complete Epitome of the Improvements and Inventions Practised at the Royal Free Schools, Borough-Road, Southwark*. London: n.p., 1810.

—. *Improvements in Education, as It Respects the Industrious Classes of the Community: Containing a Short Account of Its Present State, Hints towards Its Improvement, and a Detail of Some Practical Experiments Conducive to that End*. 2nd ed. London: n.p., 1803.

Landor, Walter Savage. "English Hexameters." *Fraser's Magazine for Town and Country* 42 (1850): 62–63.

Lanier, Sidney. *The Science of English Verse*. New York: Scribner, 1880.

Lardner, Dionysius. *The Electric Telegraph Popularised*. London: Walton and Maberly, 1855.

—. *Railway Economy: A Treatise on the New Art of Transport, Its Management, Prospects, and Relations, Commercial, Financial, and Social*. London: Taylor, Walton, and Maberly, 1850.

"A Latin Hexameter Machine." *Athenæum* 21 June 1845: 621.

"Latin Versification for the Million." *Chambers's Edinburgh Journal* 13 (1850): 205.

Lehmann, R. C. *Memories of Half a Century*. London: Smith Elder, 1908.

Levine, Caroline. "Rhythms, Poetic and Political: The Case of Elizabeth Barrett Browning." *Victorian Poetry* 49.2 (2001): 235–252.

Liddell, Mark H. *An Introduction to the Scientific Study of English Poetry: Being a Prolegomena to a Science of English Prosody*. London: Doubleday, Page and Company, 1902.

Lightman, Bernard. *Victorian Popularizers of Science: Designing Nature for New Audiences*. Chicago and London: University of Chicago Press, 2007.

Lindsay, David. *Madness in the Making: The Triumphant Rise and Untimely Fall of America's Show Inventors*. New York: Kodansha, 1997.

The London Encyclopaedia or Universal Dictionary of Science, Art, Literature, and Practical Mechanics. London: Thomas Egg, 1839.

Long, George. "Observations on the Study of the Latin and Greek Languages." *The Schoolmaster: Essays on Practical Education*. Vol. 2. London: Charles Knight, 1836. 267–305.

Luger, George F. *Artificial Intelligence: Structures and Strategies for Computer Problem Solving*. 5th ed. Harlow: Pearson Education, 2005.

Macdonald, Stuart. "The Progress of the Early Threshing Machine." *Agricultural History Review* 23.1 (1975): 63–77.

Mack, Edward C. *Public Schools and British Opinion, 1780–1860*. London: Methuen, 1938.

Manwaring, Edward. *Stichology, Or the Recovery of the Latin, Greek, and Hebrew Numbers*. London: n.p., 1737.

Marey, Étienne-Jules. *La Méthode graphique dans les sciences expérimentales et principalement en physiologie et en medicine*. Paris: G. Masson, 1878.

Markley, A. A. "Tennyson." *The Oxford History of Classical Reception in English Literature*. Vol. 4. Ed. Norman Vance and Jennifer Wallace. Oxford: Oxford University Press, 2015. 539–557.

Marsh, Joss. "Spectacle." *A Companion to Victorian Literature and Culture*. Ed. Herbert F. Tucker. Oxford: Blackwell, 1999. 276–288.

Martin, Meredith. *The Rise and Fall of Meter: Poetry and English National Culture, 1860–1930*. Princeton: Princeton University Press, 2012.

Marx, Karl. *Capital: A Critique of Political Economy*. Vol. 1. Ed. Frederick Engels and Ernest Untermann. Trans. Samuel Moore and Edwards Aveling. Chicago: Charles H. Kerr and Co., 1906.

—. *Economic and Philosophical Manuscripts of 1844*. Trans. and ed. Martin Milligan. Mineola, NY: Dover, 2007.

Marx, Leo. *The Machine in the Garden: Technology and the Pastoral Ideal in America*. Oxford: Oxford University Press, 1964.

—. "*Technology*: The Emergence of a Hazardous Concept." *Technology and the Rest of Culture*. Ed. Arien Mack. Columbus: Ohio State University Press, 1997. 23–46.

Massey, Gerald. "Thomas Hood, Poet and Punster." *Eclectic Magazine of Foreign Literature, Science, and Art* (June 1855): 169–178.

"Master and Pupil." *All the Year Round* 2–23 Aug. 1890: 117+.

Mattheisen, Paul F. "Gosse's Candid 'Snapshots.'" *Victorian Studies* 8.4 (1965): 329–354.
Matthews, Samantha. "Marketplaces." *The Oxford Handbook of Victorian Poetry*. Ed. Matthew Bevis. Oxford: Oxford University Press, 2013. 655–672.
Maull, Nancy L. "Berkeley on the Limits of Mechanistic Explanation." *Berkeley: Critical and Interpretive Essays*. Ed. Colin Turbayne. Minneapolis: University of Minnesota Press, 1982. 95–107.
May, E. J. *Louis's Schooldays: A Story for Boys*. 2nd ed. Bath: Binns and Goodwin, 1852.
McAllister, David. "'A Use in Measured Language': Poetic Allusion and the Victorian Culture of Death." *Modern Language Studies* 49.3 (2013): 229–243.
McFarland, Thomas. *Romanticism and the Forms of Ruin: Wordsworth, Coleridge, and the Modalities of Fragmentation*. Princeton: Princeton University Press, 1981.
Meadowsong, Zena. "Thomas Hardy and the Machine: The Mechanical Deformation of Narrative Realism in *Tess of the d'Urbervilles*." *Nineteenth-Century Literature* 64.2 (2009): 225–248.
"Measurement of Thought: Yale's Psychological Laboratory and Its Work." *New York Times* 10Dec. 1893: n. pag.
"Memoir of James Pillans, Esq. F.R.S.E., &c. &c., Professor of Humanity in the University of Edinburgh." *Imperial Magazine* 11 (Feb. 1829): n. pag.
Menabrea, L. F. *A Sketch of the Analytical Engine Invented by Charles Babbage*. Trans. Ada Lovelace. *From Gutenberg to the Internet: A Sourcebook on the History of Information Technology*. Ed. Jeremy M. Norman. Novato, CA: historyofscience.com, 2005. 229–280.
Menke, Richard. *Telegraphic Realism: Victorian Fiction and Other Information Systems*. Stanford: Stanford University Press, 2008.
Merz, C. J. "Melody and Rhythm." *New-York Musical Review and Gazette* 13 June 1857: 181.
Meynell, Alice. *The Poems of Alice Meynell*. London: Burns, Oates, and Washbourne, 1923. 119.
—. *The Rhythm of Life and Other Essays*. London: John Lane Bodley Head, 1896.
Midwinter, Eric. *Nineteenth-Century Education*. Harlow: Longman, 1970.
Mill, John Stuart. *Inaugural Address Delivered to the University of St. Andrews, Feb. 1st 1867*. London: Longmans, Green, Reader, and Dyer, 1867.
—. "Thoughts on Poetry and Its Varieties." 1833. *Collected Works of John Stuart Mill, Volume 1—Autobiography and Literary Essays*. Ed. John M. Robson and Jack Stillinger. Toronto: University of Toronto Press, 1981. 341–366.
Miller, Christanne. "Nineteenth-Century U.S. Literary Predecessors." *Dickinson in Context*. Ed. Eliza Richards. Cambridge: Cambridge University Press, 2013. 119–128.

Mitcham, Carl, and Timothy Casey. "Toward and Archeology of the Philosophy of Technology and Relations with Imaginative Literature." *Literature and Technology*. Ed. Mark L. Greenberg and Lance Schachterle. Cranbury, NJ: Associated University Presses, 1992. 31–65.

Miyake, Ishiro. "Researches on Rhythmic Action." *Studies from the Yale Psychological Laboratory*. Ed. Edward Wheeler Scripture. New Haven: Yale University Press, 1902. 1–48.

Müller, Max. *Lectures on the Science of Language: Delivered at the Royal Institution of Great Britain in April, May, and June, 1861*. 2nd rev. ed. 2 vols. London: Longman, Green, Longman, and Roberts, 1862.

Munk, Edward. *The Metres of the Greeks and Romans. A Manual for Schools and Private Study*. Trans. Charles Beck and C. C. Felton. Boston: James Munroe and Company, 1844.

Murray, Brian H. "'Primitive Man' and Media Time in H. M. Stanley's *Through the Dark Continent*." *Victorian Time: Technologies, Standardizations, Catastrophes*. Ed. Trish Ferguson. Basingstoke: Palgrave Macmillan, 2013. 112–131.

Murray, Lindley. *The English Reader; Or Pieces in Prose and Poetry*. New Haven: Durrie and Peck, 1825.

"Musæ Edinenses." *Edinburgh Review* 20.40 (1812): 387–405.

Myers, F. W. H. "Human Personality in the Light of Hypnotic Suggestion." *Proceedings for the Society for Psychical Research* 4 (1886-7): 1–24.

Newman, Francis William. "On the Pronunciation of Greek." *Classical Museum: A Journal of Philology, and of Ancient History and Literature* 3 (1846): 382–404.

Newman, John Henry. *The Idea of a University, Defined and Illustrated*. Ed. I. T. Ker. Oxford: Clarendon Press, 1976.

Nuttall, P. A. "The Eureka." *Littell's Living Age* 7 (1845): 214.

—. "London University." *Gentleman's Magazine* (Dec. 1828): 482.

—. *P. Virgilii Maronis Bucolica; Containing and Ordo and Interlineal Translation Accompanying the Text; a Treatise on Latin Versification and Refrences to a Scanning Table*. London: Simpkin and Marshall, 1826.

Nye, Mary Jo. "Introduction: The Modern Physical and Mathematical Sciences." *The Cambridge History of Science*. Vol. 5. Ed. Mary Jo Nye. Cambridge: Cambridge University Press, 2003. 1–17.

Nyhart, Lynn K. *Biology Takes Form: Animal Morphology and the German Universities, 1800–1900*. Chicago and London: University of Chicago Press, 1995.

O'Brien, R. W. "Telegraph Lines." *Journal of the Telegraph* 2.5 (1869): 57.

O'Connor, Erin. *Raw Material: Producing Pathology in Victorian Culture*. Durham, NC: Duke University Press, 2000.

"Oddities in Music." *Chambers's Journal of Popular Literature, Science, and Arts* 12 (1859): 312–314.

Omond, T. S. *English Metrists: Being a Sketch of English Prosodical Criticism from Elizabethan Times to the Present Day*. Oxford: Clarendon Press, 1921.

On Stammering and Its Treatment. London: John Churchill, 1850.

Otis, Laura. *Networking: Communicating with Bodies and Machines in the Nineteenth Century*. Ann Arbor: University of Michigan Press, 2001.

Pantalony, David. *Altered Sensations: Rudolph Koenig's Acoustical Workshops in Nineteenth-Century Paris*. Dordrecht: Springer, 2009.

Parker, Charles Stuart. "On the History of Classical Education." Farrar, *Essays* 1–80.

Patmore, Coventry. *Coventry Patmore's "Essay on English Metrical Law": A Critical Edition with a Commentary*. Ed. Mary Augustine Roth. Washington, DC: Catholic University of America Press, 1961.

Peltason, Timothy. *Reading* In Memoriam. Princeton: Princeton University Press, 1985.

Peter, John. *Artificial Versifying, Or, The School-Boy's Recreation*. London, 1677.

Phelan, Joseph. *The Music of Verse: Metrical Experiment in Nineteenth-Century Poetry*. Basingstoke: Palgrave Macmillan, 2007.

—. "Radical Metre: The English Hexameter in Clough's *Bothie of Toper-Na-Fuosich*." *Review of English Studies* 50 (1999): 166–187.

"Phrenological Society of Paris—Annual Meeting, Aug. 1834." *Annals of Phrenology*. Vol. 1. Boston: Marsh, Capen, and Lyon, 1834. 402–407.

Pinch, Adela. "Love Thinking." *Victorian Studies* 50.3 (2008): 379–397.

—. *Thinking about Other People in Nineteenth-Century British Writing*. Cambridge: Cambridge University Press, 2010.

Pinkerton, W. "Machine Hexameters." *Notes and Queries* 3 (Jan. 1856): 57–58.

[Poe, Edgar Allan]. "Critical Notices: Drake-Halleck." Review of *The Culprit Fay, and Other Poems* by Joseph Rodman Drake and *Alnwick Castle with Other Poems* by Fitz-Greene Halleck. *Southern Literary Messenger* 2.5 (April 1836): 326–340.

—. "The Rationale of Verse." *The Works of the Late Edgar Allan Poe*. 4 vols. Ed. Rufus Wilmot Griswold. New York: J. S. Redfield, 1950–1956). 2: 215–258.

Poovey, Mary. *A History of the Modern Fact: Problems of Knowledge in the Sciences of Wealth and Society*. Chicago and London: University of Chicago Press, 1998.

Porter, Ebenezer. *The Rhetorical Reader*. New York: Dayton and Newman, 1842.

Porter, Stephen. *The London Charterhouse*. Stroud: Amberley, 2009.

Powell, Walter P. *A Simplified Latin Grammar*. London: John Murray, 1838.

Prescott, George B. *History, Theory, and Practice of the Electric Telegraph*. Boston: Ticknor and Fields, 1860.

Price, Uvedale. *An Essay on the Modern Pronunciation of the Greek and Latin Languages*. n.p., 1827.
The Princeton Encyclopedia of Poetry and Poetics. 4th ed. Ed. Roland Greene et al. Princeton: Princeton University Press, 2012.
Prins, Yopie. "Break, Break, Break into Song." Hall 105–134.
—. "Historical Poetics, Dysprosody, and *The Science of English Verse*." *PMLA* 123.1 (2008): 229–234.
—. "Metrical Translation: Nineteenth-Century Homers and the Hexameter Mania." *Nation, Language, and the Ethics of Translation*. Ed. Sandra Bermann and Michael Wood. Princeton: Princeton University Press, 2005. 229–256.
—. "Robert Browning, Transported by Meter." *The Traffic in Poems: Nineteenth-Century Poetry and Transatlantic Exchange*. Ed. Meredith L. McGill. New Brunswick and London: Rutgers University Press, 2008. 205–230.
—. "Victorian Meters." *The Cambridge Companion to Victorian Poetry*. Ed. Joseph Bristow. Cambridge: Cambridge University Press, 2000. 89–113.
—. *Victorian Sappho*. Princeton: Princeton University Press, 1999.
—. "Voice Inverse." *Victorian Poetry* 42.1 (2004): 43–59.
—. "'What Is Historical Poetics?'" *Modern Language Quarterly* 77.1 (2016): 13–40.
"Public Schoolboys Test Latin Verse Machine." *Clarks Courier* 148 (1963): 7.
"The Public Schools *v.* Belvidere House." *Chambers's Journal of Popular Literature, Science and Arts* 15 (1861): 8–10.
Rabinbach, Anson. *The Human Motor: Energy, Fatigue, and the Origins of Modernity*. Berkeley and Los Angeles: University of California Press, 1992.
Railway Appliances in the Nineteenth Century, or the Rail, Steam, and Electricity, with Illustrative Anecdotes, Engravings, and Diagrams. London: R. Yorke Clarke and Co., 1848.
Ramsay, William. *A Manual of Latin Prosody*. 2nd ed. London and Glasgow: Richard Griffin and Co., 1859.
Rasula, Jed. "Understanding the Sound of Not Understanding." *Close Listening: Poetry and the Performed Word*. Ed. Charles Bernstein. New York: Oxford University Press, 1998. 233–261.
"Remarkable Disorders of Speech." *Otago Witness* 21 Feb. 1889: 31.
Report of Her Majesty's Commissioners Appointed to Inquire into the Revenues and Management of Certain Colleges and Schools, and the Studies Pursued and Instruction Given Therein; with an Appendix of Evidence. Vol. 1. London: n.p., 1864.
"Researches in Experimental Phonetics." *PMLA* 15 (1900): vii.
Review of *King's College Lectures*, by John Thelwall. *Monthly Review* 7.32 (1828): 545.

Review of *Ex Tentaminibus Metricis Puerorum*, by James Pillans. *Quarterly Review* (Dec. 1812): 395–406.
Review of *A Manual of English Prosody*, by Robert Frederick Brewer. *Educational Reporter* 1.3 (1869): 10.
Rice, Stephen P. *Minding the Machine: Languages of Class in Early Industrial America*. Berkeley and Los Angeles: University of California Press, 2004.
Richards, I. A. *Practical Criticism: A Study of Literary Judgment*. 1929. Abingdon: Routledge, 2011.
Richards, Thomas. *The Commodity Culture of Victorian England: Advertising and Spectacle, 1851–1914*. Stanford: Stanford University Press, 1990.
Richardson, John G., and Justin J. W. Powell. *Comparing Special Education: Origins to Contemporary Paradoxes*. Stanford: Stanford University Press, 2011.
Riskin, Jessica. "The Defecating Duck, or, the Ambiguous Origins of Artificial Life." *Critical Inquiry* 29 (2003): 599–633.
Robertson, F. W. *An Analysis of* In Memoriam. London: Smith, Elder, and Co., 1862.
—. *Lectures on the Influence of Poetry and Wordsworth*. London: H. R. Allenson, 1906.
[Robertson, John]. "My Ghosts." *Household Words* 14 Feb. 1857: 165–168.
Robinson, Wendy. *Power to Teach: Learning through Practice*. Oxford: Routledge Falmer, 2004.
Robson, Catherine. *Heart Beats: Everyday Life and the Memorized Poem*. Princeton: Princeton University Press, 2012.
Roncaglio, Alessandro. *The Wealth of Ideas: A History of Economic Thought*. Cambridge: Cambridge University Press, 2005.
Rossetti, William Michael. *Dante Gabriel Rossetti: His Family-Letters*. Vol. 1. London: Ellis and Elvey, 1895.
"Royal Institution." *London Medical Gazette, Being a Weekly Journal of Medicine and the Collateral Sciences* 10 Mar. 1832: 888.
Rudy, Jason R. *Electric Meters: Victorian Physiological Poetics*. Athens, OH: Ohio University Press, 2009.
Ruskin, John. *The Complete Works of Ruskin, Library Edition*. Ed. E. T. Cook and Alexander Wedderburn. 39 vols. London: George Allen, 1903–1912.
—. *Elements of English Prosody for Use in St George's Schools*. Orpington: George Allen, 1880.
—. *Fors Clavigera*. Vol. 2. Orpington: George Allen, 1872.
—. *Fors Clavigera*. Vol. 3. London: George Allen, 1896.
[Russell, John.] *Rudiments of the Greek Language. For the Use of Charterhouse School*. London: n.p., 1826.
—. *Rudiments of the Latin Language. For the Use of Charterhouse School*. London: n.p., 1822.

—. *Rudiments of the Latin Language, with Short Vocabularies. For the Use of Charterhouse School*. London: n.p., 1812.
Russell, William. *Orthophony; Or, the Cultivation of the Voice, in Elocution: A Manual of Elementary Exercises, Adapted to Dr. Rush's "Philosophy of the Human Voice," and the System of Vocal Culture Introduced by Mr. James E. Murdoch*. 5th ed. Boston: William D. Ticknor and Co., 1848.
—. *Pulpit Elocution*. 2nd ed. Boston: Draper and Halliday, 1867.
Rylance, Rick. *Victorian Psychology and British Culture 1850–1880*. Oxford: Oxford University Press, 2000.
Ryle, Gilbert. *The Concept of Mind*. London: Hutchinson's University Library, 1949.
Sabine, Robert. *The History and Progress of the Electric Telegraph with Descriptions of Some of Its Apparatus*. New York: D. Van Nostrand, 1869.
Saintsbury, George. *A History of English Prosody from the Twelfth Century to the Present Day*. Vol. 1. London: Macmillan, 1906.
—. "The Prosody of the Nineteenth Century." *The Cambridge History of English Literature*. Vol. 13. Ed. A. W. Ward and A. R. Waller. New York: Putnam's Sons, 1917. 250–282.
Sapir, Edward. *Language: An Introduction to the Study of Speech*. Mineola, NY: Dover, 2004.
Sargent, Epes. *The Standard Fifth Reader*. Boston: John L. Shorey, 1867.
Schaffer, Simon. "Babbage's Dancer and the Impresarios of Mechanism." *Cultural Babbage: Technology, Time, and Invention*. Ed. Francis Spufford and Jenny Uglow. London: Faber, 1996. 53–80.
Schivelbusch, Wolfgang. *The Railway Journey: The Industrialization of Time and Space in the Nineteenth Century*. Berkeley and Los Angeles: University of California Press, 1986.
Schramm, Wilbur Lang. *Approaches to a Science of English Verse*. Iowa City: University of Iowa Press, 1935.
Scripture, Edward Wheeler. "Accurate Work in Psychology." *American Journal of Psychology* 6.3 (1894): 427–430.
—. *The Elements of Experimental Phonetics*. New York: Charles Scribner's Sons, 1902.
Shaffner, T. P. *The Telegraph Manual: A Complete History and Description of the Semaphoric, Electric, and Magnetic Telegraphs of Europe, Asia, Africa, and America, Ancient and Modern*. New York: Pudney and Russell, 1859.
Shaw, George M. "The Telephone and How It Works." *Popular Science Monthly* (Mar. 1878): 559–569.
Simmons, John Galbraith. *Doctors and Discoveries: Lives that Created Today's Medicine*. Boston, MA: Houghton Mifflin, 2002.
Smith, David Nowell. "Editor's Introduction: Scansion." *Thinking Verse* 3 (2013): 1–14.

Smith, Jonathan. *Fact and Feeling: Baconian Science and the Nineteenth-Century Literary Imagination*. Madison: University of Wisconsin Press, 1994.
Southey, Charles Cuthbert. *The Life of the Rev. Andrew Bell*. Vol. 3. London: John Murray, 1844.
Snell, Ada L. F. "An Objective Study of Syllabic Quantity in English Verse." *PMLA* 33.3 (1918): 396–408.
—. "An Objective Study of Syllabic Quantity in English Verse." *PMLA* 34.3 (1919): 416–435.
—. *Pause: A Study of Its Nature and Its Rhythmical Function in Verse, Especially Blank Verse*. Diss. University of Michigan. Ann Arbor: University of Michigan Press, 1918.
Spurzheim, J. G. *Phrenology, Or the Doctrine of Mental Phenomena*. Vol. 1. Boston: Marsh, Capen, and Lyon, 1833.
Staunton, Howard. *The Great Schools of England: An Account of the Foundation, Endowments, and Discipline of the Chief Seminaries of Learning in England*. London: Sampson, Low, Son, and Marston, 1865.
Steege, Benjamin. *Helmholtz and the Modern Listener*. Cambridge: Cambridge University Press, 2012.
Steele, Timothy. *Missing Measures: Modern Poetry and the Revolt against Meter*. Fayetteville: University of Arkansas Press, 1990.
"The Step from Versification to True Poetry." *Lloyd's Magazine* 7.2 (1879): 124–125.
Stephens, Henry. *The Book of the Farm*. Vol. 2. Edinburgh and London: William Blackwood and Sons, 1844.
Sterne, Jonathan. *The Audible Past: Cultural Origins of Sound Reproduction*. Durham, NC: Duke University Press, 2003.
Stiles, Anne. *Popular Fiction and Brain Science in the Late Nineteenth Century*. Cambridge: Cambridge University Press, 2012.
Stowe, David. *The Training System of Education, for the Moral and Intellectual Elevation of Youth, Especially in Large Towns and Manufacturing Villages*. 7th ed. Glasgow: Blackie and Son, 1846.
[Stowe, Harriet Beecher]. *Little Foxes*. Boston: Ticknor and Fields, 1866.
Strachan, John, and Richard Terry. *Poetry*. Edinburgh: Edinburgh University Press, 2000.
Stray, Christopher. *Classics Transformed: Schools, Universities, and Society in England, 1830–1960*. Oxford: Clarendon Press, 1998.
Sturken, Marita. "Mobilities of Time and Space: Technologies of the Modern and Postmodern." *Technological Visions: The Hopes and Fears that Shape New Technologies*. Ed. Marita Sturken et al. Philadelphia: Temple University Press, 2004. 71–91.
Sussman, Herbert L. *Victorian Technology: Invention, Innovation, and the Rise of the Machine*. Santa Barbara: Praeger, 2009.

Swade, Doron D. "Calculating Engines: Machines, Mathematics, and Misconceptions." *Mathematics in Victorian Britain*. Ed. Raymond Flood et al. Oxford: Oxford University Press, 2011. 239–260.

—. "Calculation and Tabulation in the Nineteenth Century." Diss. London: University of London, 2003.

Swift, Jonathan. *Gulliver's Travels*. Ed. Paul Turner. Oxford and New York: Oxford University Press, 1971.

Swinburne, Algernon Charles. *The Swinburne Letters*. Ed. Cecil Y. Lang. 6 vols. New Haven: Yale University Press, 1959.

"Table Talk." *Once a Week* 28 Jan. 1871: 118.

"Talking Machines." *All the Year Round* 24 Sept. 1870: 393–396.

Tate, Gregory. *The Poet's Mind: The Psychology of Victorian Poetry 1830–1870*. Oxford: Oxford University Press, 2012.

Taylor, Dennis. *Hardy's Metres and Victorian Prosody*. Oxford: Clarendon Press, 1988.

"Telegraphic Symbols." *The American Merchant* 1.6 (1858): 370.

"Telegraph Posts Indicators of Time and Speed." *The London Anecdotes Reader: The Electric Telegraph*. London: David Bogue, 1848. 60.

Tennyson, Alfred. *The Poems of Tennyson in Three Volumes, Second Edition, Incorporating the Trinity College Manuscripts*. Ed. Christopher Ricks. Berkeley and Los Angeles: University of California Press, 1987.

—. *Tennyson: A Selected Edition*. Rev. ed. Ed. Christopher Ricks. Harlow: Longman, 2007.

—. *Tennyson's Poetry*. Ed. Robert W. Hill. New York and London: Norton, 1999.

Tennyson, Hallam. *Alfred Lord Tennyson: A Memoir*. Vol. 2. Cambridge: Cambridge University Press, 2012.

[Thackeray, William Makepeace]. "The Eureka." *Punch* 9 (1845): 20.

Thelwall, John. *The Vestibule of Eloquence*. London: n.p., 1810.

Thompson, E. P. "Time, Work-Discipline, and Industrial Capitalism." *Past & Present* 38 (Dec. 1967): 56–97.

Titchener, E. Bradford. "A Psychological Laboratory." *Mind* 7.27 (1898): 311–331.

"To the Editor of *The Monthly Magazine*." *Monthly Magazine* 3.16 (1797): 258.

Topham, Jonathan. "The *Mirror of Literature, Amusement and Instruction* and Cheap Miscellanies in Early Nineteenth-Century Britain." *Science in the Nineteenth-Century Periodical* Ed. Geoffrey Cantor et al. Cambridge: Cambridge University Press, 2004. 37–66.

Tucker, Herbert F. "Of Moments and Monuments: Spacetime in Nineteenth-Century Poetry." *Modern Language Quarterly* 58.3 (1997): 269–297.

—. *Tennyson and the Doom of Romanticism*. Cambridge, MA: Harvard University Press, 1988.

Tupper, Martin. *My Life as an Author*. London: Sampson, Low, Marston, Searle, and Rivington, 1886.
Turner, Charles [Tennyson]. "The Steam Threshing Machine." *Small Tableaux*. London: Macmillan and Co., 1868. 62–63.
Turner, Mark. "Periodical Time in the Nineteenth Century." *Media History* 8.2 (2002): 183–196.
Ure, Andrew. *The Philosophy of Manufactures: Or, an Exposition of the Scientific, Moral, and Commercial Economy of the Factory System of Great Britain*. London: Charles Knight, 1835.
Ure's Dictionary of Arts, Manufactures, and Mines. 6th ed. Ed. Robert Hunt. 3 vols. London: Longman, Green, and Co., 1867.
Vendler, Helen. "Introduction: Dickinson the Writer." *Dickinson: Selected Poems and Commentaries*. Ed. Helen Vendler. Cambridge, MA: Harvard University Press, 2010. 1–26.
"View of a Classical School." *Chambers's Edinburgh Journal* 9 (1840): 207.
Vincent, David. *Literacy and Popular Culture: England 1750–1914*. Cambridge: Cambridge University Press, 1989.
"The Voice, the Ear, and Music." *Dwight's Journal of Music* 28.22 (1869): 377–378.
Voskuhl, Adelheid. *Androids in the Enlightenment: Mechanics, Artisans, and Cultures of the Self*. Chicago: University of Chicago Press, 2013.
Walker, John. *A Key to the Classical Pronunciation*. 9th ed. London: n.p., 1830.
Waquet, Françoise. *Latin, Or, the Empire of the Sign*. Trans. John Howe. London: Verso, 2001.
Wardle, David. *English Popular Education, 1780–1975*. Cambridge: Cambridge University Press, 1976.
Warren, S. Edward. *Elements of Machine Construction and Drawing*. New York: John Wiley and Son, 1872.
Watson, Hewett C. *Statistics of Phrenology: Being a Sketch of the Progress and Present State of That Science in the British Islands*. London: Longman, Rees, Orme, Brown, Green, and Longman, 1836.
Weaver, J. *A System of Practical Elocution and Rhetorical Gesture*. Philadelphia: Barrett and Jones, 1846.
Webster, Noah. *An Improved Grammar of the English Language*. New York: Webster and Clark, 1843.
Whitbread, Nanette. *The Evolution of Nursery-Infant School: A History of Infant and Nursery Education in Britain, 1800–1970*. London: Routledge and Kegan Paul, 1972.
White, Dorrance S. "Humanizing the Teaching of Latin: A Study in Textbook Construction." *Classical Journal* 25 (1930): 507–20.
White, Fred D. *Approaching Emily Dickinson: Critical Currents and Cross Currents since 1960*. New York: Camden House, 2008.

Williams, James. "The Jokes in the Machine: Comic Verse." *The Oxford Handbook of Victorian Poetry.* Ed. Matthew Bevis. Oxford: Oxford University Press, 2013. 817–833.

Williams, Raymond. "Literature and Rural Society." *The Raymond Williams Reader.* Ed. John Higgins. Malden, MA: Blackwell, 2001. 109–118.

[Willis, Robert.] *An Attempt to Analyse the Automaton Chess Player, of Mr. De Kempelen.* London: n.p., 1821.

Wilson, Elizabeth. *Affect and Artificial Intelligence* Seattle: University of Washington Press, 2010.

—. "Imaginable Computers: Affects and Intelligence in Alan Turing." *Prefiguring Cyberculture: An Intellectual History.* Ed. Darren Tofts et al. Cambridge, MA: MIT Press, 2004. 38–51.

Wimsatt, W. K. and Monroe C. Beardsley. "The Concept of Meter: An Exercise in Abstraction." *PMLA* 74.5 (1959): 585–598.

Winston, Brian. *Media, Technology, and Society—A History: From the Telegraph to the Internet.* London: Routledge, 1998.

Woolbert, Charles Henry, and Severina Elaine Nelson. *The Art of Interpretative Speech: Principles and Practices of Effective Reading.* New York: F. S. Crofts, 1927.

Worcester, Joseph. *A Universal Critical and Pronouncing Dictionary of the English Language.* London: Henry G. Bohn, 1863.

Wordsworth, William. *The Poetical Works of William Wordsworth.* Vol. 5. Ed. Edward Dowden. London: George Bell and Sons, 1893.

Wundt, Wilhelm. *An Introduction to Psychology.* Trans. Rudolf Pintner. London: George Allen Unwin, 1912.

Wyhe, John van. *Phrenology and the Origins of Victorian Scientific Naturalism.* Aldershot: Ashgate, 2004.

Yearsley, James. "Stammering, Its Causes, Varieties, and Treatment." *Lancet* 2 Dec. 1843: 244–248.

Young, Robert M. *Mind, Brain, and Adaptation in the Nineteenth Century.* Oxford: Oxford University Press, 1970.

INDEX

A

Abbas, Niran, 121
Abstraction, metrical, 7, 11, 22, 27, 47, 221, 241
Accent, 3, 5, 15, 16, 45, 78, 79, 88, 126, 172, 214, 219, 231, 232, 234, 235, 241
Acoustics, 40, 88, 222, 223, 225, 226, 228
Adam, Barbara, 25, 134
Adams, Daniel, 68
Adams, H.C., 85
Agriculture, 36
Ainsworth, William Harrison, 15
Aler, Paul, 83, 191
Allingham, William, 212, 214
Alphabet, 30, 31, 44, 66, 113
Altick, Richard, 129
Analytical Engine, 119, 121
Archer, R.L., 85
Armstrong, Isobel, 28, 179
Armytage, W.H.G., 103
Arnold, Matthew, 123, 139
Arnold, Thomas, 86
Articulation, 16, 19, 45, 68, 178, 184, 186, 196, 241
Attridge, Derek, 104, 105
Atwood, Sara, 110
Austin, Gilbert, 68
Automatism, cerebral, 175

B

Babbage, Charles, 9, 111, 117–119
Bailey, Nathan, 131
Bain, Alexander, 172, 188, 193
Baly, William, 247
Barber, Jonathan, 243
Barrett, Edward, 79–81
Barrett, Elizabeth, 2, 3, 77, 79
Bateman, Frederic, 10, 194
Bateman, Henry, 24
Bayfield, M.A., 28
Beats, 5, 7, 17, 23, 25, 27, 29–35, 40, 231
Beauchamp, Ken, 56
Beaumont, Matthew, 12
Beerbohm, Max, 210, 211, 242
Beethoven, Ludwig van, 171
Bell, Alexander Graham, 43, 59, 159
Bell, Alexander Melville, 2, 88, 178, 197, 216

Bell, Andrew, 8, 65, 66, 132
Bell, J.D., 36
Bellon, Richard, 159, 160
Bentham, Jeremy, 89
Berg, Maxine, 12
Bernard, Thomas, 65
Bevis, Matthew, 12, 156, 201
Blackie, John Stuart, 138
Black, R. Harrison, 17
Blair, Kirstie, 204, 222, 246
Blandford, D.W., 144, 158
Bois-Reymond, Emil du, 223
Borell, Merriley, 252
Bowker, Geoffrey C., 50
Bowler, Peter J., 248
Boyd, Hugh Stuart, 79
Bradshaw's General Railway, 24
Brain, 10, 33, 85, 151, 171, 174, 175, 177, 184, 187, 191, 193–196, 231
Brewer, Robert Frederick, 166
Bridges, Robert, 156
Bright, Charles and Edward, 27
Bristow, Joseph, 143
Brougham, Henry, 160
Brown, Warner, 231
Browning, Elizabeth Barrett. *See* Barrett, Elizabeth
Browning, Robert, 211
Brüke, Ernst, 223
Burns, Robert, 169
Butler, David, 248
Butler, D.P., 165
Bynum, W.F., 247, 252

C
Caesura, 39.. *See also* Pause
Cahan, David, 222
Campbell, Matthew, 177
Carey, John, 83
Carlyle, Thomas, 1, 18
Casey, Timothy, 16, 49

Cattell, James McKeen, 230
Champneys, Basil, 168
Charlesworth, Simon J., 58
Charterhouse School, 124
Chladni, Ernst Florens Friedrich, 225
Clarendon Commission, 63, 84, 89, 143
Clarke, M. L, 108
Clark, John, 6, 9, 11, 113, 115, 116, 121, 123, 149
Classical poetry and prosody, 31, 62, 182
Clough, Arthur Hugh, 1, 123, 126, 139
Collins, Beverly, 43
Collins, Wilkie, 216
Combe, George, 169, 173
Computers, 118, 121, 131, 138, 147, 148, 150–152
Connor, Steven, 159
Cook, Albert S., 231, 250
Copeland, B.J., 163
Counterpoint, 11, 21, 46, 47
Cowie, Evelyn E., 110
Cowper, William, 35
Crystal Palace, 48, 159
Cull, Richard, 199

D
Dabney, J.P., 232, 249, 251
Dactyl, 78, 81, 122, 124, 125, 128, 134, 151, 219
Dakyns, Henry Graham, 244
Dallas, E.S., 16, 32, 33, 171, 183, 222
Dant, Tim, 95
Davies, Matt, 157
Davis, Audrey B., 250
Davy, Humphrey, 93, 150
de Colmar, Charles-Xavier Thomas, 118
Descartes, René, 175, 177
Diaeresis, 129

Dickens, Charles, 82, 83, 182
Difference Engine, 118, 119, 122, 131, 138, 147, 150
Division of labor, 66, 74, 117, 118
Dobell, Sydney, 33, 181
Duck, Stephen, 34, 35, 38
Duffell, Martin J., 155

E
Ebbatson, J.R., 41
Education Act, Forster, 96
Edwards, T.W.C., 105
Egyptian Hall, 9, 111, 113, 123, 130, 135, 137, 140, 141, 143, 151
Ellingham, C.J., 127, 146
Ellis, Alexander J., 87
Elocution, 3, 68, 73, 174, 177, 179, 181, 216, 218
Empiricism, 176, 223
Enjambment, 126
Erickson, Lee, 12
Esbester, Mike, 24, 52
Essinger, James, 154
Eton College, 70, 74, 84, 87, 93, 105, 147, 166
Eureka Latin Verse Machine, 9, 111, 113–163, 176
Everson, Richard, 157

F
Faber, Professor, 112, 113, 149, 150
Factory Acts, 65, 92
Factory system, 1, 8, 17, 47, 63, 75, 92, 117, 177
Farrar, Frederic William, 90–93, 140
Feldman, S., 250
Flow, rhythmical, 5, 43–48, 111–113, 165–206
Foot prosody, 5, 219, 234
Foucault, Michel, 138
Fourier, Jean-Baptiste Joseph, 226

Fowler, O.S., 170, 174
Freeman, Michael, 12
Frequency, 40, 41, 225, 229, 230, 237

G
Gagnier, Regenia, 84, 108
Gall, Franz Joseph, 170, 192
Gargano, Elizabeth, 96
Gladstone, Mary, 243
Glaser, Ben, 12
Golston, Michael, 250
Gooday, Graeme, 17, 50
Goodridge, John, 34, 56
Gordon, Peter, 95
Gosse, Edmund, 212, 213
Gradus ad Parnassum, 8, 24, 64, 83, 86, 127, 143, 174
Grammar, 3, 24, 62, 66, 69–71, 73–75, 83, 90, 215
Graphic method, 225, 226, 236, 237, 241
Gratwick, A.S., 141, 158
Gray, Robert, 12
Green, Burdette, 248
Griffiths, Eric, 241, 252
Griscom, John, 99
Guest, Edwin, 16, 219
Guild of St George, 98
Gummere, Francis, 218, 219
Gurney, Edmund, 88, 219

H
Hagner, Michael, 247
Hale, Edward Everett, 30
Hall, Granville Stanley, 230
Hankins, Thomas L., 152
Hardy, Thomas, 41, 42, 117
Harrington, Emily, 219
Harrington, J.W., 56
Harrison, William, 15
Hart, John Seely, 124

Haugeland, John, 154
Haven, Gilbert, 211, 215
Hawtrey, Stephen, 93, 166
Hazelwood School, 72, 73
Helmholtz, Hermann von, 10, 21, 40, 43, 87, 176, 223, 226–229, 231, 232, 237
Herschel, John, 49
Hexameters, 6, 8, 9, 11, 38, 81, 88, 113, 114, 116, 122, 123, 125, 126, 128–131, 137, 139, 142, 145, 150, 195
Heyck, Thomas William, 99
Hill, Rowland, 72, 73
Historical prosody, 3, 4
Hollander, John, 210, 243, 249
Hollingshead, John, 152
Holmes, Oliver Wendell, 2, 10, 43, 44, 177, 185, 188, 189, 212
Homogeneity, 19
Hopkins, Gerard Manley, 21
Howlett, John Henry, 76, 105
Hughes, Thomas, 86
Humez, Alexander and Nicholas, 55
Hurst, Albert S., 231
Hutchison, Hazel, 21

I

Iambic, 15, 35, 124, 189, 241
Ictus, 16, 18–20, 27, 32, 33, 35, 41, 172, 221, 233
Imagination, 25, 34, 94, 115, 151, 170, 171, 192, 225
Intelligence, artificial/machine, 9, 121, 122, 138, 151, 152
Isochronous intervals, 7, 16, 32, 172, 219, 233
Isochrony, 16, 23, 25, 31, 241
Isotropy, 23, 25

J

Jacquard loom, 72, 119
Jaquet-Droz, Pierre, 115, 116, 119
Jarvis, Simon, 179

K

Kay-Shuttleworth, James, 81–83
Kempelen, Wolfgang von, 9, 44, 111, 115, 149
Kennedy, Benjamin Hall, 90
Ketabgian, Tamara Siroone, 94
Key, T.H., 92
Kidwell, Peggy Aldrich, 153
Kim, Alan, 250
King, Andrew, 146
Kingsley, Charles, 123, 126
Kittler, Friedrich, 5, 18, 225
Knight, Charles, 146

L

Laboratory, 2, 4, 11, 176, 193, 223, 226, 228, 230, 231, 233–237, 241, 242
La Mettrie, Julien Offray de, 176, 177
Lancaster, Joseph, 8, 65–68, 70, 71, 93, 132, 182
Landor, Walter Savage, 123, 155
Lanier, Sidney, 180, 218–221, 236, 240
Lardner, Dionysius, 20, 32
Latin poetry, 5, 78, 208
Lawton, Denis, 95
Le Fanu, Sheridan, 157
Lehmann, R.C., 243
Levine, Caroline, 3
Liddell, Mark H., 218–221, 240
Lightman, Bernard, 141
Lindsay, David, 152

Lineation, 190, 221
Logaœdic verses, 125
Longfellow, Henry Wadsworth, 123, 125, 126
Long, George, 91
Lovelace, Ada, 119
Ludwig, Carl, 223, 224, 236
Luger, George F., 154

M
Macdonald, Stuart, 58
Mack, Edward C., 73, 74
Maillardet brothers, 115, 116
Manwaring, Edward, 132, 143
Marey, Étienne-Jules, 228
Marryat, Frederick, 156
Marsh, Joss, 141
Martin, Meredith, 4, 11, 81
Marx, Karl, 42, 117
Marx, Leo, 18
Mathematics, 144, 145, 226
Matthews, Samantha, 12
Maull, Nancy L., 175
Maxwell, James Clerk, 21
May, E.J., 85
McKay, John, 231
McKendrick, John Gray, 43
McLuhan, Marshall, 55
Meadowsong, Zena, 58
Mees, Inger M., 43
Menabrea, Luigi Federico, 119
Menke, Richard, 19, 46
Merzbach, Uta C., 250
Merz, C.J., 35
Meynell, Alice, 2, 38, 40, 229
Midwinter, Eric, 65
Mill, John Stuart, 89
Mitcham, Carl, 16, 49
Mixed measures, 9, 64, 124, 126, 128
Miyake, Ishiro, 233
Modulation, 5, 6, 42, 43, 45, 46, 183, 188, 209, 214, 216, 234

Monitorial education, 64–81, 83
Monotone, 41, 64–81, 83, 212–214, 216
Morse code, 27, 30, 31
Morse, Samuel F. B., 27
Morus, Iwan Rhys, 248
Müller, Johannes, 176, 223
Müller, Max, 138
Munk, Edward, 207, 208
Murray, Brian, 44
Murray, Lindley, 215
Music, 4, 10, 32, 35, 115, 172, 182, 208, 225, 228, 229
Myers, F.W.H., 230, 250

N
Newcomen, Thomas, 62
Newman, Francis W., 88, 123, 139
Newman, John Henry, 146
New Prosody, 7, 8, 11, 18, 19, 21, 25, 28, 34, 38, 45, 46, 171
Noad, Henry Minchin, 49
Norman, Jeremy M., 154, 203
Nöth, Winifred, 56
Novels, 19, 157
Nuttall, P.A., 142, 143
Nye, Mary Jo, 247
Nyhart, Lynn K., 247

O
O'Brien, R. W., 19, 51
O'Connor, Erin, 94
Ohm, Georg Simon, 226
Oman, Charles, 86
Omond, T.S., 18, 32, 230
Oratory, 170, 213
Orortund reading, 213
Otis, Laura, 18, 175
Oxenford, John, 139

P

Pacey, Arnold, 40
Palgrave, Francis Turner, 212
Pantalony, David, 225, 248
Parker, Charles Stuart, 90, 91
Patmore, Coventry, 2, 7, 10, 16, 20, 23, 28, 32, 33, 46, 139, 171, 173, 210, 219, 222, 233, 241
Pause, 215.. *See also* Caesura
  end-of-line, 215
  medial, 215
Pedagogy, 9, 25, 114, 143
Periodicals, 4, 15, 139–141, 178
Periodicity, 3, 229
Peter, John, 131, 132, 143
Phelan, Joseph, 4, 123, 139
Philology, 138, 139, 229
Phonograph, 44
Phrenology, 169, 170, 172–175, 193
Physics, 176, 219, 222, 223, 225, 226
Physiology, 2, 4, 10, 40, 43, 171, 175–178, 185, 188, 193, 209, 222, 223, 226, 229, 230
Pillans, James, 70–72
Pitch, 4, 40, 46, 89, 214, 216, 219, 229, 231–233, 237
Plunkett, John, 146
Poe, Edgar Allan, 45, 169, 182
Polyrhythmia, 26, 28
Poovey, Mary, 157, 245, 247
Positivism, 252
Powell, Justin J.W., 96
Powell, Walter P., 104
Prescott, George B., 31
Price, Uvedale, 77, 78
Princeton Prosody Archive, 11
Prins, Yopie, 3, 19, 20, 123, 124, 180, 214, 241
Printing, 2, 67, 146
Prose, 19, 71, 73, 75, 77, 86, 126, 172, 173, 179, 196, 217
Psychology, 10, 173–175, 177, 187, 188, 193, 196, 197, 209, 222, 229, 230
Pythagoras, 227

Q

Quantitative meter, 75–77, 79, 80, 82, 88, 129, 139, 225, 229, 237

R

Railways, 2, 5, 15, 17, 19, 21, 23, 25, 27, 34, 41, 46, 83
Ramsay, William, 124
Randomness, 122, 130, 136, 150–152
Rasula, Jed, 212, 243
Respiration, 178, 180–183, 188–190, 208
Rhythm, 3, 11, 15, 16, 23, 28, 33, 36, 39, 42, 46, 73, 167, 180, 183, 189, 195, 207, 208, 218, 220, 229, 230, 232, 235, 240–242
Rice, Stephen P., 121
Richards, I.A., 6, 207, 242
Richardson, John G., 96
Richards, Thomas, 48
Riskin, Jessica, 153
Robertson, Frederick William, 244
Robinson, Wendy, 81
Roncaglio, Alessandro, 154
Rossetti, D.G., 211
Rossetti, W.M., 212
Rudy, Jason R., 10, 22, 27, 33, 181, 222
Rugby School, 86
Ruskin, John, 26, 91
Russell, John, 73–75, 77–79, 81, 84, 124
Russell, William, 213
Rylance, Rick, 250

S

Sabine, Robert, 30
Saintsbury, George, 155, 245
Sanitor, E.H., 61, 62
Sapir, Edward, 29
Sargent, Epes, 216, 244
Scansion, 4, 5, 10, 11, 30, 45, 46, 63, 70, 76, 84, 87, 88, 137, 183, 216, 221, 235, 237, 241
Schaffer, Simon, 115
Schivelbusch, Wolfgang, 19
Scholastic prosody, 8, 11, 112, 113, 122, 127, 128, 141, 196
Schramm, Wilbur Lang, 234, 237
Scott, Edouard Léon, 10
Scripture, Edward Wheeler, 2, 229, 231–233, 242
Shadwell, Lancelot, 123
Shaffner, Taliaferro Preston, 27
Shaw, George M., 59
Silverman, Robert J., 152
Simmons, John Galbraith, 247
Smith, Adam, 117
Smith, Alexander, 33
Smith, David Nowell, 252
Smith, Jonathan, 245
Snell, Ada, 237, 240, 241
Southey, Charles Cuthbert, 102, 103
Spasmodic poetry, 33, 181, 182, 190
Spectacle, 113, 115, 116, 137, 140, 148
Speech, 4, 6, 10, 20, 23, 34, 42–44, 46, 47, 87, 129, 175, 178, 179, 181, 182, 189, 194, 195, 209, 222, 237, 240, 241
Spondee, 81, 122, 124, 125, 128, 151
Spurzheim, Johann Gaspar, 172
Stammering, 46, 47, 181, 182, 189, 195, 197
Standardization, 17, 18
Stanley, Henry Morton, 45, 46
Staunton, Howard, 102
Steam Navigation Guide, 24
Steege, Benjamin, 59
Steele, Timothy, 160
Stephens, Henry, 57
Sterne, Jonathan, 200, 248
St Mark's School, Windsor, 93, 94
Stow, David, 69
Stowe, Harriet Beecher, 166
Strachan, John, 157
Stray, Christopher, 102, 108, 110
Sturken, Marita, 18
Substitutions, metrical, 2–4, 35, 115, 124–126, 137, 150
Sussman, Herbert, 25
Swade, Doron David, 154
Swift, Jonathan, 157, 203
Swinburne, Algernon Charles, 123, 147
Swing Riots, 36
Syllabification, 45, 46, 69, 88, 195
Syncopation, 7, 26, 28

T

Tables, of logarithms; versifying, 83, 118, 119, 131, 132, 137, 142, 143, 149, 209, 241
Tate, Gregory, 187, 222
Taylor, Dennis, 84, 182
Taylorism, 118
Telegraph, 2, 5, 18–20, 23, 26, 27, 29, 30, 32, 33, 40, 46, 93
Telephone, 43, 44, 178
Temporality, 15, 23, 26, 41, 45
Tennyson, Alfred, works of
  "Break, Break, Break," 11, 28, 179–182, 184, 217, 221, 238
  "Epic," 212
  In Memoriam, 184, 187, 189, 210, 213, 216
  Maud, 180, 182
Terry, Richard, 157

Thackeray, William Makepeace, 62, 81, 149
Thelwall, John, 179
Threshing machine, 34, 36, 38–40, 42, 43
Titchener, Edward Bradford, 230
Topham, Jonathan, 160
Tucker, Herbert F, 3, 4, 11
Tupper, Martin, 81, 84
Turing, Alan, 151
Turner, Charles Tennyson, 36, 37, 39
Turner, Mark, 53

U
Ure, Andrew, 116, 165

V
Van Noorden, P. Ezekiel, 115
Vaucanson, Jacques, 9, 115, 177
Vibration, 40, 41, 43, 44, 213, 225–227, 230, 232, 236, 242
Vincent, David, 97
Virgil (Publius Vergilius Maro), 61, 88, 125, 142
Vitalism, 223
Voice, 5, 11, 21, 26, 34, 41–45, 47, 83, 111, 178, 182, 183, 187, 209, 212, 214–216, 218, 231, 240
Vowels, 31, 43, 44, 75–77, 79–81, 112, 212–214

W
Waquet, Françoise, 144
Wardle, David, 96
Warf, Barney, 56
Warren, S. Edward, 13
Watt, James, 62
Weaver, J., 243
Weber, Wilhelm, 225
Webster, Noah, 215
Wheatstone, Charles, 44, 111
Whitbread, Nanette, 96
White, Dorrance S., 145
Will, 4, 17, 41, 65, 89, 119, 130, 142, 166, 176, 177, 182, 184, 187, 189, 196, 211, 222, 227
Williams, James, 126
Williams, Raymond, 58
Willis, Robert, 115, 116
Wilson, Elizabeth, 151
Wimsatt, W.K., and Monroe C. Beardsley, 13
Winchester College, 85, 86, 89
Wood, Nicholas, 20, 21
Woolbert, Charles Henry, and Severina Elaine Nelson, 60
Worcester, Joseph, 50
Wundt, Wilhelm Maximilian, 230

Y
Yearsley, James, 2, 181–183, 195
Yonge, C.D., 84
Young, Robert M., 173, 193
Young, Thomas, 225

Printed in the USA
CPSIA information can be obtained
at www.ICGtesting.com
LVHW011223240923
759164LV00009B/1162